GUIDING MODERN GIRLS

Girlhood, Empire, and Internationalism in the 1920s and 1930s

Kristine Alexander

UBCPress·Vancouver·Toronto

26 25 24 23 22 21 20 19 18 17   5 4 3 2 1

Printed in Canada on FSC-certified ancient-forest-free paper
(100% post-consumer recycled) that is processed chlorine- and acid-free.

Library and Archives Canada Cataloguing in Publication

Alexander, Kristine, author
Guiding modern girls: girlhood, empire, and internationalism in the 1920s and 1930s /
Kristine Alexander.

Includes bibliographical references and index.
Issued in print and electronic formats.
ISBN 978-0-7748-3587-9 (hardcover). – ISBN 978-0-7748-3588-6 (pbk.)
ISBN 978-0-7748-3589-3 (PDF). – ISBN 978-0-7748-3590-9 (EPUB).
ISBN 978-0-7748-3591-6 (Kindle)

1. Girl Guides – England – History – 20th century. 2. Girl Guides – Canada – History
– 20th century. 3. Girl Guides – India – History – 20th century. 4. Girls – England –
History – 20th century. 5. Girls – Canada – History – 20th century. 6. Girls – India –
History – 20th century. I. Title.

HS3353.A44 2017   369.46309'042   C2017-905496-1
                                             C2017-905497-X

Canadä

UBC Press gratefully acknowledges the financial support for our publishing
program of the Government of Canada (through the Canada Book Fund),
the Canada Council for the Arts, and the British Columbia Arts Council.

This book has been published with the help of a grant from the
Canadian Federation for the Humanities and Social Sciences, through the
Awards to Scholarly Publications Program, using funds provided by
the Social Sciences and Humanities Research Council of Canada.

UBC Press
The University of British Columbia
2029 West Mall
Vancouver, BC V6T 1Z2
www.ubcpress.ca

CONTENTS

ILLUSTRATIONS

ACKNOWLEDGMENTS

THIS BOOK HAS BEEN a long time in the making, and it's a real pleasure to be able to thank all the individuals and institutions that made it possible. It began more than a decade ago at York University, where I was fortunate enough to benefit from the engagement and guidance of Bettina Bradbury, Stephen Brooke, and Douglas Peers. I am particularly grateful for Bettina's wisdom and friendship, which continue to inspire and sustain me. Molly Ladd-Taylor, Celia Haig-Brown, and Dominique Marshall provided valuable advice and feedback on an early version of this manuscript, as did the members of the York University British History Writing Group and Bettina Bradbury's monthly reading group. I also owe special thanks to Robert J. Young and Tamara Myers, whose teaching and mentorship at the University of Winnipeg inspired me to become a historian.

For allowing access to their collections and for forcing me to think critically about archives, I would like to acknowledge the Archive Committee at Ontario Guide House, the Archives of the National Council of the Girl Guides of Canada – Guides du Canada, the Girl Guiding UK Archives, the Archives of the Manitoba Council of the Girl Guides of Canada – Guides du Canada, the Archives of the New Brunswick Council of the Girl Guides of Canada – Guides du Canada, the British Scout Association Archives, and the Girl Scout National Historic Preservation Center. I am particularly thankful to Lynn Austen, Margaret Courtney, Yevgenya Gribov, Marlene Miller, Catherine Mort, Paul Moynihan, Pat Styles, and Karen Stapley. This project has also benefited from the assistance of librarians, archivists, and other employees at the Bharat Scouts and Guides; the British Library; the Cambridge University Centre for South Asian Studies; the Glenbow Museum and Archives; the Margaret Cousins Memorial Library; the Nehru Memorial Library; the Provincial Archives of Manitoba; the World Association of Girl Guides and Girl Scouts; and the Yale University Divinity School Library and Archives.

I would not have been able to complete this book without the support, financial and otherwise, of a number of individuals, institutions, and funding bodies. Jonathan Vance and Christopher Kent, were – and still are – generous and encouraging mentors whose support has meant a lot to me. In 2013, I started a tenure-track job at the University of Lethbridge and am beyond thankful for the support and inspiration of my colleagues and students in the Department of History and the Institute for Child and Youth Studies. For all manner of administrative help at the U of L, thanks especially to Bev Garnett and Jenny Oseen. I am also grateful for the financial support I have received from the Social Sciences and Humanities Research Foundation of Canada and the Canada Research Chairs program.

I have presented parts of this book at conferences and workshops too numerous to list here, and I am thankful for the feedback I received at all of them. Corrie Decker's comments about colonial girlhood and colonial girls at the 2014 North American Conference on British Studies were particularly helpful as I revised the manuscript. I have been lucky enough to discuss my project with a number of scholars whose work I admire, and I especially appreciate the support and advice I have received from Antoinette Burton, Cynthia Comacchio, Harald Fischer-Tiné, Geraldine Forbes, Miriam Forman-Brunell, Mona Gleason, Malavika Kasturi, Linda Mahood, Charlotte MacDonald, Mary Clare Martin, Francine McKenzie, Susan Miller, Sarah Mills, Hugh Morrison, Tamara Myers, Jane Nicholas, Fiona Paisley, Leslie Paris, Timothy Parsons, Adele Perry, David Pomfret, Tammy Proctor, Veronica Strong-Boag, Sharon Wall, Carey Watt, and Sophie Wittemans. Mischa Honeck, Cecilia Morgan, and Tait Keller read the entire manuscript and provided valuable feedback, for which I can't thank them enough. I also received detailed and thoughtful comments from two anonymous reviewers and would like to thank them and my editor at UBC Press, Darcy Cullen.

I am fortunate to have found friends and academic co-conspirators in different parts of Canada and the world, all of whom continue to make me want to be a better scholar and teacher. Thanks especially to Jennifer Alexander, Jenna Bailey, Lou Barrett, Tarah Brookfield, Susan Cahill, Stephanie Carvin, Val Deacon, Sarah Duff, Cindy Ermus, Elizabeth Galway, Sarah Glassford, Christine Grandy, Jarett Henderson, Greg Kennedy, Lynn Kennedy, Sean

Kheraj, Heather Ladd, Fiona MacDonald, Heidi MacDonald, Kim Mair, Sheila McManus, Kristine Moruzi, Alison Norman, Jan Newberry, Janay Nugent, Stephanie Olsen, Serge Pellis, Bill Ramp, Amy Shaw, Michelle Smith, Simon Sleight, Erin Spring, Jamie Trepanier, Karen Vallgårda, Amy von Heyking, and the much-missed Toronto Area Canadian Women's History Group.

This work would also not have been possible without my family, many of whom put up with me when I was a rebellious Brownie in Winnipeg in the 1980s. I started this project with enthusiastic and generous support from my grandparents, Margaret and Donald Fiddler and Sigrun Kissack, as well as my great-aunt Bernice Ashton. The long process of research and writing was punctuated by their deaths, and I wish they could have lived to see me finish my first book. J.P. Marchant reminds me daily that there are all kinds of things to laugh about, as do my parents, Bruce and Linda Alexander.

Guiding Modern Girls

INTRODUCTION

As LEADER OF THE "Swallow Patrol" of the 8th (Battersea) Girl Guide Company in south London during the 1920s, Eileen Knapman kept a diary describing her group's activities.[1] In October 1928, she wrote:

> Miss Chalk, who is now our District Commissioner, came to one of our meetings. We had games, tests, Patrol work, and ι.. INSPECTION!!! We survived, however, and Miss Chalk thought we were smart! The only things which did not come up to scratch, were our ties, which each member of the Company seems to wear at a different length! We have now abandoned knots for signalling, and we do our best to poke one another's eyes out, in the process of "flag-wagging." Half of us can't signal properly, and the other half don't know the alphabet, so we shall have to buck up! Catherine Skelton "flew up" from Brownies into our Patrol.[2]

Across the Atlantic, Winnifred Thompson, head of the "Nightingale Patrol" of the 21st Guide Company in the Canadian city of Winnipeg, similarly recorded her Guide company's pursuits – though with far fewer exclamation marks – in a handwritten logbook. At a meeting on 22 October 1928, for instance, she noted that some members of her company practised their "ambulance" skills for an upcoming public display, "while the other Guides present played volleyball." Thompson recorded that girls from the 21st Guides had recently qualified for badges in Morse flag signalling, bed making, fire making, and "health rules"; she also wrote that the group, which met weekly at St.

Alban's Anglican Church, "reviewed the drill for the display and Mrs. Foster came down and taught us some Brownie songs to sing at the Brownie Flying Up Ceremony to be held November 10."[3]

Three months later, in January 1929, a mixed group of white and Indian girls and women attended the All-India Guide Camp on the grounds of Belvedere, the viceroy's winter residence in Calcutta (now the National Library of India). A scrapbook commemorating the camp, now in the Girl Guiding UK Archives in London, includes a series of black-and-white photographs in which girls and women in saris and British-style Guide uniforms are shown cooking, eating, and playing together in the outdoors.[4] Like their contemporaries in Battersea and Winnipeg, these Guides were divided into small groups named after birds; the scrapbook includes photographs labelled "Sparrow Patrol" and "Pigeon Patrol." Many of these photographs are accompanied by handwritten comments and images, including sketches of tents and a drawing of two girls dancing to music from a gramophone.

These records, proof of Guiding's global reach during the early twentieth century, also illustrate a number of the movement's defining characteristics: wearing uniforms, playing games, and singing songs; earning badges for skills related to health, domesticity, and first aid; engaging in physical activities like hiking and volleyball; practising marching and signalling for public performances; and camping out, tying knots, and practising woodcraft. Created with youthful and adult readers in mind, these diaries and scrapbooks demonstrate individual responses to Guiding's activities while hinting at several aspects of the consumer-minded early twentieth-century modern girlhood that Guide leaders sought to train and contain.

The Girl Guide movement was officially established in England in 1909 by Boy Scout founder and imperial war hero Robert Baden-Powell, in the wake of a wave of popular concern about white racial degeneration, appropriate gender roles, and the future of the British Empire. With its uniforms, badges, and promises of camping and adventure, Guiding offered a combination of freedom and control that appealed to girls and women in a range of contexts, with the result that Guiding spread rapidly across the British Empire and, indeed, the world. During the 1920s and 1930s, over a million girls in more than forty colonies and countries (including British settler societies like Canada and South Africa, colonies like India and Jamaica, as well as a range of countries beyond the British Empire, including the United States, France, Hungary, and Poland) joined the Guides, a single-sex, age-graded organization whose leaders hoped to train girls to successfully navigate the dangers, temptations, and opportunities of modern life.

The fact that Guiding could take root in such different soils was a point of pride for many of the movement's supporters. This was especially so during the 1920s and 1930s, a period marked by the emergence of the figure of the flapper or Modern Girl, attempts to rearticulate the British Empire as a friendly interracial "family," the creation of the League of Nations, rising anticolonial nationalisms, economic contractions, the dawn of European fascism, and the development of a modern consumer-based youth culture. Baden-Powell, for instance, boasted in the British Guide Association's 1934 annual report that the "international aspect" of Guide work held "a wonderful promise of possibilities for the future. In all our British Overseas Dominions, Colonies, and Protectorates," he wrote, "the oncoming generation already shows a considerable leaven of boys and girls linked in this personal tie with their Brother Scouts and Sister Guides in the Old Country. This is not confined to white youth, but includes Indians and the natives of all our African States."[5]

Baden-Powell's words point to a number of themes that I address in this study: they conflate the "imperial" with the "international," for instance, and stress the importance of creating personal ties between young people from different racial categories across national and colonial boundaries. They also, like the Guide and Scout movements more broadly, link children and youth with futurity and hope while describing huge swathes of the earth as Britain's possessions. At the same time, this passage also points towards two of my main research questions: How did the British-based Guide organization deal with both "white" and "Native" girls and young women during the 1920s and 1930s? And how did girls and young women understand and respond to the movement's attempts to guide them towards a service-oriented, "useful" future?

Guiding Modern Girls answers these questions by analyzing the Guide movement's ideals and programs in three places: in England, the heart of a vast empire whose urban and industrial problems had inspired a number of social reform efforts; in Canada, a rapidly urbanizing white settler society whose federal government was committed (through a variety of initiatives, including the Scouts and Guides) to the destruction and assimilation of Indigenous cultures; and in India, a British colony with an enormous, varied, and increasingly nationalistic population.

Youth in general, and girls and young women in particular, have often been singled out as "problems" in urban, industrialized societies. By the late nineteenth century, young women's enthusiastic engagement with new leisure, employment, and educational possibilities had begun to lead social commentators to lament the fact that many of them seemed to prefer pleasure and autonomy to domesticity and deference.[6] Adult fears about young women, social norms, and cultural change were at the heart of a number of late nineteenth- and early twentieth-century debates about modernity.[7] These concerns about young women's aesthetic and leisure choices – and their potential political and demo-graphic consequences – intensified during the 1920s and 1930s. This was in large part a response to the global emergence of the Modern Girl, a figure whose cropped hair, short skirts, and active, consumer-oriented lifestyle symbolized all that was exciting, new, and sometimes threatening about life after the First World War.[8] Worries about modern girlhood were also central to the Guide movement's ideals and programs, which variously emphasized domesticity, citizenship, engagement with nature, physical culture, and im-perial and international friendship – in ways that often supported class- and race-based hierarchies.

While framing the interwar Guide movement as a response to the possibilities and threats embodied by the imagined figure of the Modern Girl, this book is also concerned with a broader range of youthful feminine subjects: female children and adolescents from a variety of circumstances, subject positions, and settings who came of age in a time generally acknowledged as "modern." The concept of modernity has been wielded by scholars in ways that often, as Frederick Cooper reminds us, "contribute more to confusion than to clarity." Historians interested in clarity, Cooper suggests, should listen to their sources: "If modernity is what they hear, they should ask how it is being used and why."[9] The word "modern" recurs throughout many of the sources on which this book is based, a number of which also explicitly situate the First World War as a turning point in the lives of girls and women. Throughout the 1920s and 1930s, Guide leaders in England, Canada, and India regularly described girls as "modern" in ways that often combined hope and anxiety. Their writings also stressed the importance of using modern pedagogy and lauded the op-portunities created by modern travel and communication technology.

These modern increases in mobility and global interconnectedness, which were also implicated in the construction and maintenance of hierarchies of gender, class, race, and age, took on a new intensity after 1918 as individuals, organizations, and nation-states turned to internationalism and youth to ar-ticulate their hopes for a peaceful future. In his study of the relationship be-tween British imperialism and the emergence of international society during the early twentieth century, Daniel Gorman writes, for example, that "inter-nationalism came of age in the 1920s."[10] References to youth, growing up, and adult hopes for future generations appear regularly in the literature on the history of internationalism – as they did in the words of contemporaries – but the place of actual young people in early twentieth-century internationalism has been less well studied. This is especially true of girls, and this book makes a girl-focused contribution to what is presently a small group of studies of young people and internationalist thought and organizing.[11] It is also an addition and a response to the historical and literary scholarship on girls and British imperialism as well as the historiography of women's internationalism during the 1920s and 1930s.[12]

Internationalism is also, as Manu Goswami has recently written, about imagining potential futures.[13] In the immediate aftermath of the First World War, the leaders of the global Guide movement promoted a conservative politics of futurity that both privileged and looked beyond the British Empire. Like its masculine counterpart, the Boy Scouts, the postwar Guide organization sought to create a peaceful future shaped by a strong and familial British Empire, stable and often hierarchical social structures, and League of Nations-style international relations. With its emphasis on teaching girls the skills they would need as future mothers, Guiding was also an exercise in what queer theorist Lee Edelman calls reproductive futurism, in which modern girls themselves were often seen as less important than the future children they were expected to bear.[14]

Fiona Paisley rightly notes that historians have shown relatively little interest in the entwined histories of girlhood and imperial/international Guiding, despite the fact that "the rapid growth of Guides and Brownies around the world points to a fascinating history."[15] While Allen Warren and Tammy Proctor comment on the "imperial and international" nature of the early twentieth-century Scouts and Guides, they do so by using mostly British sources to touch briefly on aspects of both movements in a number of different colonial and national settings.[16] In this book, which is based on archival research in Canada, India, and England, I aim to provide a more detailed and nuanced account of race, gender, class, and imperial/international Girl Guiding in these three specific contexts. I also add a multi-sited dimension to the scholarly literature on the history of youth movements, much of which continues to focus on single regional and national contexts.[17]

Guiding Modern Girls uncovers the ideas, activities, and responses of girls like Winnifred Thompson, Eileen Knapman, and the All-India campers in combination with those of the movement's British founders, the elite group of mostly white women who created Guide policy at the national and international levels, and the women who led local Brownie, Guide, and Ranger companies in England, Canada, and India during the years between the two world wars.[18]

Juxtaposing the experiences and voices of these different groups of girls and women reveals that, while the Guide movement's official program was a product of adult anxieties and aspirations, it also reflected ongoing and often unacknowledged negotiations between adults, adolescents, and children as well as between local, national, imperial, and global contexts. Working across different imperial sites in this way also reveals how Guiding's upper-level leaders, like the white women in charge of other imperial and international organizations during the years between the world wars, sought both to encourage global sisterhood and to monitor and control the growth of the movement in different colonial and national contexts.

I use organizational records, periodicals, fiction, press coverage, social surveys, photo albums, prescriptive literature, and individual Guides' diaries and scrapbooks to analyze the ideals and practices of the Girl Guide movement in England, Canada, and India during the 1920s and 1930s. These three locations, while distant and different in many respects, were nonetheless connected in some significant ways by Guiding's imperial and transnational networks. These networks facilitated the circulation of ideas, texts, and goods, gave some women and girls the chance to travel internationally, and offered similar experiences and ideals to members around the world. While emphasizing the universalizing nature of its programs, international and imperial Guiding during these years was also based on notions of status and difference. This tension between the movement's acknowledgment of similarity and its continued dependence on class- and race-based notions of difference is especially evident when one considers the comparative workings of the movement in the metropole, the dependent empire, and a settler colony. This approach, still a relative rarity in imperial history and the history of childhood, highlights points of difference and a surprising number of similarities between sites that have seldom been studied together.

How did so-called "white," "Indian," and "Native" girls and women (to use Baden-Powell's race-based parlance) in different parts of the British Empire understand and engage with the Guide movement's ideals and practices? How did Guiding's expansion into new locations with differently diverse populations affect its ideology and programs? *Guiding Modern Girls* answers these questions by juxtaposing the development and reception of the movement in England, Canada, and India during the interwar years. It explores how ideas about girlhood travelled across borders, and asks how they were complicated and changed by factors like race, class, and religion by tracing the circulation and reshaping of the Guide movement's texts, consumer goods, and ideals across three distant and different parts of the British Empire.

The Guide movement was a response to early twentieth-century struggles over the meanings of girlhood, empire, and internationalism. *Guiding Modern Girls* sheds new light on Guide leaders' attempts, during the interwar years, to create a conservatively modern ideal of imperial and international girlhood. Focusing primarily though not exclusively on England, Canada, and India, I argue that Guide literature and programs both reflected and contributed to this conservative modernity, most notably by combining an older emphasis on maternalism and domesticity with an emphasis on bravery, independence, and female masculinity, and by promoting a friendly familial version of international and imperial relations that was nonetheless still influenced by older ideas about race- and class-based hierarchies and the British "civilizing mission." My second major argument is that, despite its limitations, the Guide movement's structure still allowed some girls and young women in various local contexts to adapt and use it for their own, sometimes subversive, ends. Twentieth-century girls were more than merely disputed symbols and potential problems to be re-formed, and their responses to Guide character training reveal that the movement was both contested and flexible.

The 1920s and 1930s were a time when hierarchies of gender, race, class, and age were constructed, undermined, and rebuilt in locations across the world. For this reason, they have been characterized by a number of scholars as a period of conservative modernity. The British historian Alison Light, for example, uses the term to characterize the interwar years as a time marked by tension "between old and new, between past and present, between conserving and moving on."[19] Katie Pickles and Jane Nicholas similarly highlight the confluence of conservatism and change in interwar Canada, while Jon Lawrence uses the concept of conservative modernity to argue that "entrenched ideas about supposedly natural social hierarchies" continued to exert a powerful influence in British culture and politics until at least the 1950s.[20]

Lawrence's argument, which ignores age and gender, applies equally to the powerful desire, visible in social institutions like the Guides, to contain newly assertive modern girls and to shore up established patterns of age- and gender-based hierarchy. To this end, *Guiding Modern Girls* adds an imperial and international dimension to Tammy Proctor's important claim that Guiding and Scouting in interwar Britain were effectively "a mix of modern activities and nineteenth-century values."[21] The Girl Guides' version of conservative modernity promoted a universal ideal of girlhood. It was also a colonial modernity, in which mostly white women used ideas of progress, mobility, and "modern" pedagogical methods in ways that often reified racial hierarchies and promoted unequal power relations between Britain and its dominions and colonies. The

history of Guiding, then, needs to be understood both as a promise of emancipation and change, and as an attempt to hold onto older conventions and
maintain hierarchies based on age, gender, race, and class.[22]

How did the tensions between Guiding's conservative and progressive elements play out in different imperial locations? This question first occurred to
me when I began to read the periodicals published by Canadian Guide headquarters in the 1920s and 1930s for what I had initially imagined would be a
project centred on Canada. I was struck by the regularity with which these
publications mentioned the British Empire, internationalism, and the League
of Nations, while making links and pointing out similarities between people
and places that are usually studied separately. In addition to providing information about uniforms, badges, and goings-on in different parts of Canada,
monthly magazines like the *Canadian Guider* featured articles about Guiding
across the British Empire and the world, and a number of them singled out
Guiding in South Asia for special attention. The articles I encountered in these
sources provided proof of the existence of Guide companies in India, and their
appearance in English-Canadian magazines was clearly an example of Western
imperial and international feminism's long-standing interest in "eastern" women.
At the same time, however, I also wondered what had motivated South Asian
women and girls to join a British-based organization whose metropolitan
leaders promoted both imperialism and internationalism.

My decision to follow this archival trail from Canada to India and England
was inspired by several areas of scholarship. These included the new imperial
history, many practitioners of which examine the British Empire as a series of
networks or webs in which relationships between so-called "peripheral" locations are just as important as those between metropole and colony.[23] In deciding
to analyze England, Canada, and India in the same frame, I was also inspired
by the transnational turn in historical research – an approach that, in the words
of Ann Curthoys and Marilyn Lake, "highlight[s] historical processes and relationships that transcend nation states and that connect apparently separate
worlds."[24] This type of scholarship also, as the late C.A. Bayly pointed out,
"raise[s] critical issues about transnational flows, but do[es] not claim to embrace
the whole world."[25]

While this book contributes to the fields of imperial and transnational history by asking how, through the Guides, thousands of girls and women in three
particular locations participated and were represented in activities and discourses that transcended national and imperial boundaries, it is not a conventional comparative study of places with similar demographic and political
features. Instead, it examines the circulation and alteration of ideas and practices

across and within multiple *different* locations. This aspect of my work draws on the methods of multi-sited ethnography, an approach that, like imperial and transnational history, aims to understand "social phenomena that cannot be accounted for by focusing on a single site " by following and juxtaposing people, relationships, and associations across space.[26] The shape and content of *Guiding Modern Girls*, then, is the result of my decision to follow frequent mentions of three particular different places in the interwar Guide movement's organizational literature and publications. Instead of isolating each location in separate sections, *Guiding Modern Girls* juxtaposes and analyzes archival findings from England, Canada, and India in thematically organized chapters.

One of the threads running through these thematic chapters is a commitment, inspired by girlhood studies and children's history, to take girls' experiences seriously and to give them equal weight to those of adults. This was a challenging undertaking, not least because the voices of the diverse groups of Indian, Canadian, and English girls and young women who donned the Guide movement's uniforms during the 1920s and 1930s are difficult to find among the copious documentary traces the movement has left behind. This is largely because archives reflect the hierarchies and assumptions of the societies that produce them – and evidence created by girls has seldom been seen as important enough to preserve.[27]

Mary Jo Maynes writes that studying girls reveals "the inadequacy of prevailing notions of historical agency" especially clearly.[28] It also reveals the inadequacy of existing methods of archival collection and categorization, as girls' actions and choices are generally far less visible in conventional textual sources than are those of boys, women, and men. Some girls' voices are present in archival scraps and fragments – in marginalia, diaries, logbooks, and other texts that are often not seen as important enough to mention in collection descriptions, catalogues, and finding aids. And just as their experiences were fragmented along the lines of geography, class, race, and politics, so have these factors affected which sources and whose ideas have been seen as important and as worth preserving.

Like a number of other twentieth-century voluntary organizations, the Girl Guides has largely held on to its own records, in collections that often consist of both carefully selected documents and uncatalogued pieces more haphazardly acquired. Many sources related to the history of Guiding in Britain and across its former empire are kept at the Girl Guiding UK Archives, located on one of the upper floors of the movement's central London headquarters – an imposing building on Buckingham Palace Road that testifies to the movement's ability to acquire valuable property and align itself with elites. During most of the time I conducted my research, the British Guide archives were looked after by a single employee whose duties included managing the archival collections, regulating access to documents, and working with volunteers (former Guides and Guide leaders, now mostly in their seventies and eighties) who run smaller local Guide archives, sometimes out of their own homes. This reliance on voluntary labour, a necessity for non-profit organizations with limited funds, means that vast quantities of Guide records face an uncertain future as the movement's elderly unpaid archive workers literally die off.[29]

Concerned with race, gender, class, and young people's responses to Guiding's ideals and practices, I was less interested in photographs of the movement's adult founders or members of the British royal family than I was in scrapbooks and photograph albums created by so-called "unimportant" girls and women. These albums were some of the richest sources I encountered, and I was saddened to learn that a number of similar albums, donated by former Guides from Britain and around the world, had been disposed of simply because the girls and women featured in the photographs could not be identified.

The Girl Guiding UK Archives, like the British suffrage archives that have been studied by Laura E. Nym Mayhall, had clearly been put together and catalogued with the goal of privileging one narrative and "trajectory of experience while devaluing and obliterating any others."[30] This official narrative of Guide history is a story of female emancipation, interracial cooperation, and cheerful heterosexuality. Yet I also found myself unable to ignore the exclusions and silences that characterized this collection, having witnessed first-hand the destruction of documents whose contents were seen as unimportant or threatening to the organization's reputation. This repository, home to a rich collection of textual and visual evidence about the history of girlhood throughout the twentieth century, has now been closed for several years.[31] Its future is uncertain, and I regret that I have been unable to secure permission to publish any parts of its photographic collection, which includes images of Girl Guides from England and across the world.

By contrast, the National Council of the Girl Guides of Canada – Guides du Canada employs a full-time archivist and is open to researchers. As in the UK, this national repository is supplemented by a series of volunteer-run provincial Guide archives. In these archives, as in the Girl Guiding UK collection, the voices of middle-class, urban, and suburban white Protestant girls are easiest to locate – especially in logbooks or diaries describing what took place at various Guide groups' weekly meetings. These documents provide information about individual responses and specific local contexts, which makes them a valuable counterweight to the mountains of prescriptive literature produced by Guide headquarters. In Canada, I also sought information about Indigenous Girl Guides in the diaries and logbooks of Anglican missionaries, and in the annual reports of the Department of Indian Affairs, which supported Scout and Guide companies in Indigenous residential schools.

Because of the political and organizational changes that affected South Asia and its voluntary organizations in the decades after Independence, Indian Guides from the 1920s and 1930s were more difficult to trace than were their Canadian and British counterparts. In Delhi, I was received warmly at the headquarters of the Bharat Scouts and Guides (a co-educational organization since 1951) but soon learned that they had virtually no documents dating earlier than the 1980s. I had better luck at the Margaret Cousins Memorial Library in Sarojini Naidu House, the headquarters of the All-India Women's Conference (AIWC), a voluntary organization established in 1927 to promote female education and social reform. The leaders of this organization described Guiding as a way to modernize Indian girlhood through physical culture and character training, and its annual reports and conference programs include references to Guides as honour guards and volunteer workers at AIWC events and conferences.

In India during the 1920s and 1930s, most Guide companies were attached to schools, such as the Brahmo Girls' School in Calcutta (which was attended by middle-class Indian girls sponsored by a Hindu social reform group called the Brahmo Somaj) and the Lawrence Royal Military School (an institution for the mostly working-class children of British soldiers).[32] The public and private archives I visited in London and Delhi did not contain any texts created by the girls (Hindu, Muslim, Parsi, British, or Anglo-Indian) who had been Guides in late colonial India. While female literacy was far lower there than in Canada and England, the fact that most Guide companies were based in schools means that this lack of sources is not because the women and girls who belonged to the movement could not read or write. Instead, I suspect that written records of individual groups' activities were simply not preserved for a variety of practical and political reasons, including the changes wrought by Independence and Partition and the amalgamation of the Indian Scouts and Guides into a single co-educational body in 1951 – an organization that, I suspect, was not especially interested in locating and preserving documents produced mainly by white women during the early twentieth century – a period characterized by what Indian Guide leader Lakshmi Mazumdar, writing in the 1960s, called "a bitter struggle" for "national liberation."[33]

The production and preservation of evidence about girls' responses to Guiding's prescriptions and practices reflects a number of past and present power imbalances: between English and "other" languages, "white" and "non-white" racial categories, the printed word and non-textual forms of knowledge, and the imperial and organizational centre and peripheries.[34] Age and gender are important here, too, as ideas about what counts as evidence and what is worth preserving continue to reflect gendered power relationships between children, adolescents, and adults. My understanding of how girls made their own meanings and cultural practices out of Guiding is also shaped by the knowledge that many photographs, letters, and other sources have not survived, whether because of decolonization, organizational priorities, or the desire to suppress aspects of the organization's past that may be seen as embarrassing or unsavoury. Silences and gaps are an important part of the history of girlhood and the Guide organization, and I occasionally interrupt and punctuate my analysis of archival evidence with reminders of the unanswerable questions this research has raised.

Writing a book based on geographically disparate and often incomplete sets of primary sources was a daunting task, for political as well as for practical reasons. Some scholars expressed concern that I, a white woman trained primarily in Canadian and British history, would presume to speak for girls and women of colour, and reminded me that many groups are uncomfortable with outsiders making claims about and basing careers on the history of their communities. However, in a settler society that is clearly not "post" colonial, even historians whose projects remain within the borders of the Canadian nation-state must grapple with these issues. With this in mind, I have sought to produce a self-conscious work of scholarship that draws attention to inequalities while being careful not to silence or speak for its subjects. I take seriously Alison Light's insistence that "feminist work must deal with the conservative as well as the radical imagination," and I have tried to proceed with what Ruth Roach Pierson calls "methodological caution" and "epistemic humility."[35]

The book begins with a descriptive chapter about the movement's Victorian origins and early twentieth-century growth. Chapter 1 begins in 1857, the year of Baden-Powell's birth and of the Indian "Mutiny," an event that hardened British racial thinking and influenced the imperial imagination well into the twentieth century. The first part of this chapter uses Baden-Powell's education, colonial military career, and late marriage to the much younger Olave St. Clair Soames to outline the metropolitan concerns about gender, race, class, empire, and nation that led to the founding of the Scouts and Guides in the years before the First World War. The second part of the chapter describes Guiding's organizational structure and traces its growth in England, Canada, and India to 1939.[36]

The rest of the book concentrates on the 1920s and 1930s. It is structured thematically, though I have tried to remain attentive to events and shifts that occurred within this period. Chapter 2, entitled "Guiding Girls toward the Private Sphere: Training for Homekeeping, Mothercraft, and Matrimony," deals with the Guide movement's attempts to train modern girls for their expected future roles as domestic managers, mothers, and wives. I argue that the movement's emphasis on these more conventionally feminine pursuits remained relatively constant during the interwar years and that the movement's single-sex organizational structure also – ironically – created spaces for some girls and especially women who rejected those roles. This gendered aspect of Guide training was tied to ideas of race, nation, and empire, and I also ask how the movement's emphases on motherhood and domesticity were used in different national and colonial contexts.

Chapter 3, "'We Must Give the Modern Girl a Training in Citizenship': Preparing Girls for Political and Social Service," analyzes the Guide movement's attempts to create a generation of "good" responsible citizens by training girls and young women in politics, health and cheerfulness, voluntary service, and emergency preparedness. I argue that, while it promoted new opportunities for women and girls and emphasized international tolerance, Guiding's citizenship training program was also a conservative undertaking, characterized by telling silences about the groups it excluded. I also highlight several conflicts between metropolitan leaders' official and implicitly white vision of imperial/international citizenship and the different (and sometimes subversive) loyalties and identities that were promoted in Guide groups across the British Empire.

Chapter 4 places Girl Guide camps within the broader history and historiography of summer camping and outdoor tourism, while also emphasizing the movement's more specific ties to militarism and colonialism. As Scouting and Guiding spread around the world during the early twentieth century, so did their emphasis on woodcraft, nature study, and camping. By the interwar years, the frontier and woodcraft skills that were so central to Baden-Powell's original vision were being taught to girls and boys from a wide variety of backgrounds, including young people from some of the same cultures whose "primitive" values and behaviour Guides and Scouts were encouraged to emulate through woodcraft and camping. This chapter examines the complexities and contradictions of Guiding's camping and woodcraft programs in Canada, India, and England by focusing on questions of religion, gender, national identity, and race.

Chapter 5 analyzes Guide rallies, the large public performances that were regularly staged by the movement's leaders in England, Canada, and India throughout the interwar years. By looking closely at historical pageantry, mass exercise, and military drill, I shed new light on Guiding's attempts to mass-produce strong and uniform young female bodies. I also examine the raced and gendered meanings of these public spectacles and comment on the relationship between Guide rallies and the public events staged by fascist youth groups in the 1930s.

Chapter 6 focuses on the Guide movement's attempts to foster friendliness, cooperation, and sisterly goodwill among girls across national and colonial boundaries. I discuss how the movement promoted the idea of a "Guide sisterhood" in the 1920s and 1930s, the bureaucratic and organizational changes that occurred in these years (including the formation of the World Association of Girl Guides and Girl Scouts in 1928), international and imperial Guide camps and conferences and the stable of properties in which they were held, as well as the movement's use of periodicals, radio, and the cinema to reach the hundreds of thousands of girls and young women who would never have the chance to attend an international gathering. I conclude this chapter with a discussion of how these efforts were hampered by material constraints and the persistence of hierarchical racial thinking. The conclusion of *Guiding Modern Girls* summarizes my findings and traces how Guiding changed in England, Canada, and India during and after the Second World War.

Together, these chapters show how ideas and activities developed in Britain were adopted and adapted in different parts of the world, sometimes by groups of girls and women for whom they had not originally been intended. They highlight the uneven archival landscapes that confront historians of girlhood, imperialism, and voluntary organizations, while tracing the place of age, gender, race, and class in the interwar Guide movement's often contradictory pronouncements about modernity, conservatism, and change. In England, Canada, and India, Guiding was an adult-led attempt to shape girls' lives in ways that would benefit future husbands and children as well as occasionally conflicting national and imperial communities. Yet modern girls and young women in these three different imperial sites responded to and sometimes rejected the movement's program and ideals in a variety of ways.

Chapter 1

GUIDING'S BEGINNINGS
Victorian Antecedents and
Early Twentieth-Century Growth

THE EXPERIENCES OF EARLY twentieth-century Girl Guides in Calcutta, Winnipeg, Battersea, and beyond were, in many ways, legacies of developments in Britain and its empire from the mid-nineteenth century on. In this chapter, beginning in 1857 (the year of Baden-Powell's birth and a pivotal year in British racial and imperial thinking), I describe the significant Victorian and Edwardian social and cultural developments that preceded the establishment of the Scouts and Guides in 1908 and 1909, respectively. I then describe the founding of both organizations and outline Guiding's goals and organizational structure before tracing the movement's growth in England, Canada, and India to 1939. I place Guiding within a longer history of the British Empire and introduce several characters and themes that recur throughout the book.

Victorian Antecedents

Like a number of his biographers, Robert Baden-Powell often described himself as a man who had lived "two lives": (1) a Victorian life, characterized by militarism, violence, and expansionist imperialism, and (2) a twentieth-century life in which, as the aging patriarch of the Scout and Guide movements, he promoted peace and familial tolerance among young people across the British Empire and the world.[1] Whereas Baden-Powell and his biographers insisted that his militaristic "first life" had ended when he founded the Scouts in 1907–08, I show that some aspects of his earlier persona and beliefs continued to influence the Guides and Scouts at least until his death in 1941.

Robert Stephenson Smyth Baden-Powell was born in London to Henrietta Grace and the Reverend Baden Powell (Savilian professor of geometry at Oxford, d. 1860) in 1857 – the year of the Indian "Mutiny" and a turning point in British thinking about race and empire that caused the British in India and throughout the Empire to intensify their attempts to impose and maintain what Partha Chatterjee calls "the rule of colonial difference."[2] The effects of this newly hardened racial thinking were felt across the globe and were accompanied by changes in imperial administration. In India, British administrators (vastly outnumbered by the non-white populations they sought to rule) attempted to isolate themselves physically and socially as debates about the future of the Raj focused on the gendered and racialized discourses of sexual violence that had been generated during the Mutiny and its aftermath. During the next several decades, race-based discourses and policies also assumed greater importance in settler colonies. In mid- to late nineteenth-century Canada, for instance, colonial, provincial, and national governments used immigration schemes, the regulation of mixed-race marriages, and the creation of an oft-amended Indian Act in an attempt to consolidate white power and create an orderly settler society.[3]

These ideological and material shifts began while the young Baden-Powell was a student at Charterhouse, one of the nine original English public schools identified in the Public Schools Act, 1868. His tuition was paid by a Gownboy Foundationer Scholarship, a sign of the high status but relative lack of capital that was to characterize most of his adult life. Significantly, Baden-Powell's time at Charterhouse coincided with the rise of the public school story, the genre of popular boys' fiction best represented by Thomas Hughes's novel *Tom Brown's Schooldays* (first published in 1857). Many aspects of the future Chief Scout's experience at Charterhouse conformed to the Victorian public school ideal described by Hughes and his contemporaries – a worldview that emphasized masculine athleticism, "character," chivalry, honour, group loyalty, "playing the game," and training boys for imperial leadership and war.

While Baden-Powell was away at school, his sister Agnes (b.1858), who would later become the first president of the Girl Guides, was living a very different though no less representative Victorian life in London. Like many other British daughters of educated men, Agnes Baden-Powell was denied formal schooling. Living at home with her mother and sisters (their father had died when she was two years old), Agnes watched as her brothers enjoyed and sometimes squandered the educational and cultural opportunities afforded them by their gender. Because contemporaries and historians alike seem to have believed that Agnes was a less important figure than her brother, relatively little is known about her upbringing. It is, however, possible to speculate that her early life was at least partly shaped by the ideals of Victorian girlhood identified by Carol Dyhouse: economic and intellectual dependency, deference towards fathers and brothers, service and self-sacrifice, and the sexual division of labour.[4] The very different childhood experiences of the male and female Baden-Powell siblings are a reflection of the gendered model of separate spheres that was embraced by the mid-nineteenth-century British middle classes. This ideal, which saw marriage and motherhood (or, failing that, caring for elderly parents) as the most suitable careers for elite and middle-class women, clearly shaped the possibilities and material conditions of Agnes Baden-Powell's life.

It is also possible (indeed, tempting) to speculate about Agnes Baden-Powell's childhood reading habits; like many of her contemporaries, she may have enjoyed reading the boys' adventure books and periodicals that were popular during her youth.[5] Biographer Tim Jeal notes with regret that her brother, an indifferent though popular student at Charterhouse, seldom referred to the books he read as a boy.[6] His later writings, however, suggest a familiarity with the adventure fiction made popular during his youth by men like Charles Kingsley and R.M. Ballantyne. As literacy increased in the wake of the 1870 Education Act, more and more young British people bought and shared these books – texts whose emphasis had shifted by the late nineteenth century from the evangelical imperialism of Ballantyne to the more aggressively expansionist writing of men like G.A. Henty. These adventure novels, echoes of which appear in Scout and Guide texts published during the early twentieth century, functioned as what Martin Green calls "the energising myth of English imperialism" – a myth that encouraged British children to view their nation's empire as "a source of riches, opportunities, and adventure."[7]

The material and mythical opportunities of empire clearly appealed to Robert Baden-Powell. Having failed his Oxford entrance examinations after leaving Charterhouse, he left his sister and their formidable widowed mother and, in a classic Victorian flight from maternal influence and the domestic sphere, joined the British army.[8] At the age of nineteen, he was gazetted as a sub-lieutenant in the 13th Hussars, who were then stationed in the northern Indian city of Lucknow. Baden-Powell sailed for India in late 1876, the year in which the Indian Act was passed in Canada and Disraeli proclaimed Queen Victoria Empress of India.

He spent most of the next twenty-five years occupying various military posts in India, Afghanistan, and Africa. He fought against Native troops in the Second Anglo-Afghan War (1878) as well as in Zululand (1888), Ashantiland (1895), and Matabeleland (1896). Like Garnet Wolseley, who fought the Ashanti

in Africa and the Métis in Canada, Baden-Powell's military career and reputation were based on the violent suppression of Native resistance in different
parts of the British Empire – a strategy of domination that was directly related
to the hardening racial thinking of his childhood. Many aspects of his life in
the army were similar to those he had known at Charterhouse and included
sports, the formation of intense same-sex friendships, and amateur theatrical
productions that sometimes featured female impersonation. To supplement his
meagre income, Baden-Powell began his publishing career during this time
by writing articles about his military exploits for various periodicals. He also
wrote and illustrated several books, including *Reconaissance and Scouting* (1884)
and *Pig-sticking or Hog-hunting* (1889).

Baden-Powell sailed for England after the Matabeleland campaign, but he
soon returned to South Africa. It was during the Second Boer War, or South
African War, that he further honed his ideas about scouting and attained
empire- and even worldwide celebrity status. While many contemporaries
described this conflict as a war between different groups of white men, Baden-
Powell's actions there clearly crossed racial lines: while he used the siege of
the town of Mafeking to create a cadet corps of young British boys (a precursor
of sorts to the Scouts), Baden-Powell also ordered starving black Africans
to be executed by firing squad for stealing food, had over a hundred others
flogged, and gave the remaining black inhabitants of the garrison "the choice
of starving to death in the town or running the gauntlet of the Boers."[9]

The telling and retelling of the story of the siege and relief of Mafeking in
the British and colonial press transformed Baden-Powell into a heroic figure
of national and imperial importance. As war correspondent Lady Sarah Wilson
wrote in the *Daily Mail* in March 1900, "It is strange to reflect how a man
whose very name six months ago was almost unknown to the British public
has now secured the confidence of the whole Empire, so that it firmly believes
that no situation, however desperate, will prove too much for his resourcefulness and courage."[10] Baden-Powell was not the first British military hero to
have been celebrated in this way; his experience is a perfect example of the
mid- to late nineteenth-century masculine ideal that, as Graham Dawson notes,
linked imperialist patriotism, manly virtues, and war. This model of masculinity was constructed relationally, and Dawson notes that it "was complemented
by a vision of domestic femininity, at home with the children and requiring
protection. The nation itself came to be conceived as a gendered entity, analysis
of which is necessarily bound up with the theorizing of dominant, hegemonic
versions of masculinity, femininity and sexual difference."[11] These ideas about
Britishness and the idealized and largely separate realms of public martial

masculinity and domestic maternal femininity lasted far longer than the Mafeking celebrations, and they influenced how Baden-Powell (and many others) came to understand his identity and the respective roles of the Scouts and Guides. A representative quote from the Boy Scout handbook (first published in 1908), for example, insists that "manliness can only be taught by men, and not by those who are half men, half old women."[12]

Edwardian Anxieties and Cultural Influences

The Edwardian social anxieties that emerged from the Boer War combined with new ideas about childhood and adolescence in ways that had a significant influence on Baden-Powell's thinking about youth. For despite the unprecedented patriotic outpouring that had followed the relief of Mafeking, the British victory in South Africa was hard-won – even Pyrrhic. It had taken 450,000 British troops three years to defeat only 40,000 Boers, and when Baden-Powell returned to England in 1903 to take up the post of inspector-general of cavalry, he found many of his contemporaries there in a state of panic about class relations, gender roles, and the future of the British "race" and empire. The hierarchies that had defined his early life and military career suddenly seemed far less certain, not least because so many British men (three of every five volunteers, by contemporary estimates) had been unable to meet the minimum physical requirements for military service in Africa. Confidence in Britain's race and empire and its prescribed gender roles was further undermined by the 1904 publication of *Report of Britain's Interdepartmental Committee on Physical Deterioration*, a government initiative that had been prompted by the ill health and poor physical condition of so many Boer War volunteers. The Interdepartmental Committee Report, which was widely read and cited as proof of Britain's precarious position atop the racial ladder, linked the poor health of British children to living conditions in industrial cities.[13]

The year 1904 also saw the publication of another enormously influential text, G. Stanley Hall's *Adolescence*. Hall, an American psychologist and leader of the child-study movement, theorized about the links between young people, "primitiveness," and "savagery" in ways that influenced many early twentieth-century educators and youth leaders. Concerned mainly with white boys, he characterized non-white peoples as "adolescent races" and argued that the psychological and emotional development of women, as Dyhouse notes, was similarly "arrested in the adolescent phase."[14]

The Anglo-American ideas about gender, age, civilization, and racial fitness exemplified by Hall's work and British studies of "degeneration" were embraced by social reformers across the English-speaking world. In the Canadian context, middle-class Anglo-Celtic educators, doctors, church and voluntary leaders, and social workers often linked their concerns about civilization and national-racial decline with worries about the moral and physical "unfitness" of non-British immigrants.[15] These worries were not unrelated to the spread of Scouting and Guiding, and they lend support to John Springhall's argument that "fear and self-interest had as much to do with the setting up of the early youth movements as altruism."[16]

On the one hand, then, these early twentieth-century concerns about urban life and degeneration were fears about men and boys, as represented most clearly by the oft-cited stereotype of sunken-chested, slack-jawed working-class loafers smoking cigarettes on urban street corners. On the other hand, however, popular worries about efficiency, fitness, and degeneration were also about girls and women: concerns about the "softening" effects of urban life on men were also fears about effeminacy, and anxieties about waning national strength and virility were often accompanied by a conviction that women were becoming aggressive. In some respects this concern applied especially to middle-class women, whose public visibility (in the suffrage movement, for example) contributed to men's fears that they were becoming too strong.

Working-class women and girls aroused a different kind of anxiety as middle-class social commentators, politicians, doctors, and government officials expressed fears about the effects of physically inferior, "lazy," and untrained mothers on future generations of military personnel and industrial workers. As Anna Davin shows, these experts consistently overlooked the environmental causes of infant morbidity and mortality, while linking these problems to the "ignorance" of working-class mothers.[17] The report of the British Inter-departmental Committee on Physical Deterioration, for example, singled out poor urban women for their supposed "ignorance of household affairs, hygiene and nutrition; their diminished sense of maternal obligation and their wrong-headed notions of infant care."[18] Prominent among the committee's recommendations was the creation of a scheme of gendered social and domestic education that would prepare girls for their future roles as wives, mothers, and household managers.

It must be noted that these gendered concerns about social purity, physical deterioration, and national efficiency were also discourses about whiteness, in which women and girls of Anglo-Saxon and Anglo-Celtic descent were made responsible for the future of the British "race" and empire. This link between British girlhood and racial health was complicated in different parts of the British Empire, where many Indigenous and settler girls simply did not fit into this specific raced and gendered ideal. On the one hand, as Paisley shows, those British and dominion experts who were so concerned about white girls' health and domestic skills could often only conceive of Indigenous youngsters as dysgenic subjects. "While knowledge of racial and social hygiene was to protect the future of the white race," she writes, "precocious sexual development, juvenile delinquency, and criminality were coded as dark and primitive."[19] But Paisley's work, alongside that of historians like Carol Devens, also reveals a parallel Anglo-American belief in the value and possibility of white settlers' attempts to assimilate Indigenous girls.[20] Teaching these girls domestic skills was seen as a way to spread "civilized" lifeways and to ensure that non-British women and girls – from immigrant and Indigenous communities alike – would bear and rear a new generation of useful citizens and workers.

Some early twentieth-century white feminists challenged the gender bias and misogynist consequences of the evolutionary theories that made women responsible for race degeneration, but they generally did so in ways that failed to challenge the hierarchical racial thinking on which these theories were based. Mariana Valverde notes in particular that white Canadian women missionaries imagined Third World women as "downtrodden victims of cultural practices more sexist than anything existing in Christian countries."[21] This was especially true of India, as the figure of the degraded Indian woman was central to nineteenth- and twentieth-century Western attempts to colonize and "modernize" the East.[22] What most missionaries and other colonizers missed, however, was the fact that social reform movements existed in India at this time as well. Initiated by men in the mid-nineteenth century, Indian social reform had by the early twentieth century expanded to include middle-class women's groups like the All-India Women's Conference and the Women's Indian Association, whose members concerned themselves with issues like female education and widow remarriage.[23]

Young people were central to these various social reform movements, as experts, politicians, and voluntary leaders across the world drew on and added to an international body of theories about childhood and youth. In the early years of what many hoped would be "the century of the child," children in a range of contexts started to be seen as national and imperial assets whose well-being was too important to be left solely to their parents. While educators, legislators, and social commentators had begun to mark out childhood and adolescence as distinct stages of life, Baden-Powell was also thinking about youth, as shown by an article on "Scouting and Smoking" he wrote for the June 1904 issue of the *Brigadier*. In this piece, he described visiting a Boys' Brigade group in Glasgow and set out an initial framework for what would eventually become boy scouting. While warning against the moral and physical dangers of cigarette smoking, he also speculated about devising "some form of Scout-training" that would "not only sharpen the wits of the boy but would also make him quick to read character and feelings, and thus to be a better sympathizer with his fellow-men."[24]

These early ideas about "Scout-training," which partly reflected Baden-Powell's experience with his young cadet corps in Mafeking, were also clearly influenced by contemporary psychological and educational theories. Stanley Hall and the Italian physician and educator Maria Montessori, both of whom divided young people into age-based categories and stressed the importance of play, had especially significant effects on Baden-Powell's thinking. Several quotes from his early writings illustrate this debt. Scouting, he wrote, "is in line with the most modern educational thought, and it works on the most primitive human instincts."[25] In 1916, he explained his decision to divide boys into Wolf Cubs (ages eight to twelve), Boy Scouts (eleven to eighteen), and Old Scouts (later known as Rovers, aged eighteen and up) by claiming that "the principle is in accord with that of the most up to date educationalists. It continues the education of the kindergarten and Montessori's method in due sequence."[26] Baden-Powell was less forthcoming, however, about his debt to Ernest Thompson Seton, the English-born and Canadian-raised writer, artist, and naturalist. Seton had been running "Indian" camps for white boys in the United States since 1900, and in 1906 he had published a handbook entitled *The Birch Bark Roll of the Woodcraft Indians*, a text that outlined his ideas about boy training and nature lore. Baden-Powell and Seton met in London that year, and Seton was named Chief Scout of America in 1910. However, Baden-Powell's reluctance to acknowledge Seton as a "co-founder" of Scouting combined with Seton's dislike of the movement's nationalist and imperialist aims led to a rift between the two men, and Seton's position was not renewed after 1914.[27]

Baden-Powell's early twentieth-century ideas about the importance of "boy training" were also, in many ways, a reflection of the cultural importance of childhood in the Edwardian period — an anxious age in which many writers used child characters to try to counteract the over-civilized nature of modern, urban life. J.M. Barrie's *Peter Pan*, with its boy protagonist who refuses to grow up, made a particular impression on Baden-Powell. He saw the play in February 1905, less than two months after its debut in London, and was so taken with the story that he returned (for the first of many times) the very next night.[28] Rudyard Kipling, the British author and poet whose writings variously celebrated "savage" childhood and the colonizing potential of British youth, similarly influenced Baden-Powell. The two men first met in Lahore in 1882 and saw each other again in Cape Town in 1901, by which time both of them were well-known figures in Britain and across the Empire. They kept up a correspondence, and Kipling was an honoured guest at the Scout Jamboree that was held at the 1924 Imperial Exhibition at Wembley. The connection between the two men also went beyond the personal as Baden-Powell drew heavily on Kipling's *Kim* and *The Jungle Book* to create Scouting's programs and handbooks.[29]

Brownsea Island and Scouting for Boys: The Scout Movement Begins

Baden-Powell combined his educational and cultural ideas for the first time in the summer of 1907, when he organized an outdoor camp for several dozen working-class and public-school boys on Brownsea Island in Dorset. Over a period of ten days, this single-sex, cross-class group of youngsters played games, learned frontier skills, swam, and slept under the stars. Their experiences, while reflective of their leader's Edwardian enthusiasms and concerns, were also coloured by his Victorian military exploits in Africa and across the British Empire: Baden-Powell woke the boys each morning with a Kdbele kudu horn (one that he had allegedly captured from an African warrior while fighting in the Matabele campaign), taught them his interpretation of Zulu chants, and, every night, told them camp fire "yarns" about his imperial adventures.[30] The Brownsea Island camp, which juxtaposed imperialism and militarism with child-centred activities and the spirit of social tolerance, would later be explained by Baden-Powell and his biographers as a key moment of transition between his "two lives" and the different worldviews they represented.

Baden-Powell, of course, was far from an unknown figure in 1907. Many across Britain and the Empire remembered him as the hero of Mafeking, and he continued to attract publicity and material support throughout the early twentieth century, most notably by securing financial backing for his nascent youth training scheme from C. Arthur Pearson, the owner and publisher of the *Daily Express*. Pearson, who loved the idea of the Brownsea Island camp, sent Baden-Powell on a British speaking tour and published *Scouting for Boys: A Handbook for Good Citizenship* in six fortnightly parts, starting on 15 January 1908. Complete, cloth-bound copies were available on 1 May 1908 for two shillings. *Scouting for Boys*, the foundational text of Scouting and (later) Guiding, was an affordable three-hundred-page volume, written in an informal and conversational style that mixed Edwardian concerns about gender, race, class, and empire with what Elleke Boehmer calls the conjunction "of colonial disorder and play, so characteristic of late-Victorian children's literature."[31] It is divided into six parts: Scoutcraft, Tracking and Woodcraft, Camping and Campaigning, Endurance and Chivalry, Saving Life and Patriotism, and Notes for Instructors and Games. The book sold well immediately, and has never been out of print. Until the Second World War its sales were second only to that of the Bible in the English-speaking world, and it has been translated into more than eighty-five languages.[32]

Baden-Powell's masculine character training scheme was based on the hope that implicitly white/British youngsters could undo some of the damage that had been done to their "race" by modern, mass culture. Ironically, however, the ideal of mass production was clearly central to the ideals and practices of Scouting and Guiding. By emphasizing uniforms, age-defined ranks, and tests for decorations and awards, the movements (dubbed "character factories" by Michael Rosenthal) sought to create a generation of standardized, efficient, and properly gendered young people.[33]

As more and more British boys joined Scouting's "character factory," the movement's leaders decided to celebrate its growth by organizing a mass rally at the Crystal Palace in south London. It was at this first public demonstration of Scout work, held in September 1909 and attended by some 11,000 boys, that the question of girls' involvement in Scouting first came to Baden-Powell's attention. A group of girls appeared at the rally dressed in a variety of make-shift uniforms and demanded to be included in the proceedings.[34] Numerous girls and women across Britain, in fact, had embraced Baden-Powell's scout-ing scheme in 1908 and 1909. In Camberwell (London), for example, Sybil Canadine and several other girls established their own Scout troop at St. Mark's Church with the help of a local Boy Scout leader. Other groups of female scouts registered their companies with Scout headquarters by using male aliases or their first initials.[35] Baden-Powell was initially unenthusiastic about the notion of "girl scouts," having originally conceived of Scouting – at least in part – as a masculine antidote to the feminizing influences of home and family.

The Start of the Girl Guides

Before too long, however, Baden-Powell agreed to sponsor a separate uni-formed youth organization for girls. His "Scheme for the 'Girl Guides'" was published in the Boy Scout *Headquarters Gazette* in November 1909 and was reprinted in two instructional pamphlets (known as Pamphlet A and Pamphlet B) several months later. Concerned that boys would resent girls' use of the

"Scout" name, he insisted that the new movement be called the Girl Guides – a name that, like much of the Guide movement itself, was rooted in colonialism, militarism, and domesticity. The name "Guide," first of all, was taken from a group of Indian soldiers who had served under Baden-Powell's command on India's Northwest Frontier during the 1870s. He claimed to have chosen the name in recognition of these men's "general handiness and resourcefulness under difficulties, and [of] their keenness and courage" – words of praise that were perhaps tempered somewhat by his decision to lend their name to a group of female children.[36] Baden-Powell, it is clear, was also motivated by the term's more traditionally feminine meanings. Of the need for feminine character training (and likely with his own female relatives in mind), he wrote that "girls must be partners and comrades, rather than dolls. Their influence in after-life on the actions and quality of the men is very great; they become their 'Guides.'"[37] While early twentieth-century girls could therefore be the "partners and comrades" of their male counterparts, Baden-Powell's decision to assign boys a far more active verb shows that he still believed in the importance of maintaining some version of a gender hierarchy.[38]

Being made into Guides was a disappointing shift for many of the British girls who had belonged to early Scout troops. They had been attracted to Scouting because it gave them access to freedoms and experiences that were generally unavailable to them because of their gender. In early twentieth-century Britain, as Sally Mitchell shows, being or acting like a boy often seemed to be the only way that girls could experience "active games, a serious education ... adult rights and responsibilities ... physical and geographical freedom ... [and] safe passage through public spaces." She writes that, for many English girls, "the only way to envision and practice becoming a competent and complete adult" seemed to lie in boyhood and masculinity.[39]

Having enjoyed the freedoms and responsibilities of *Scouting for Boys*, some British girls reacted with anger and dismay to the new Girl Guiding scheme, which separated them from boys and promised to impart a range of "feminine" skills and virtues. The Scout patrol names they had chosen for themselves (Wolves and Wildcats, for instance) were quickly replaced by the more conventionally feminine names of flowers and birds. One girl later recalled that she could "still remember the feeling of anti-climax, of being let-down, almost insulted. Who wanted to be womanly at our age? Girls wanted adventure, not 'home training.'"[40] Children's author and British Guide commissioner Kitty Barne expressed a similar belief in her 1946 book *Here Come the Girl Guides*, writing: "undeniably it was a come-down to find yourself no longer a Scout, no longer a Wildcat or a Nighthawk, but a Violet or a Lily of the Valley in a patrol of Girl Guides."[41] Still, despite its continuing emphasis on maternal and domestic training, Guiding remained in some ways a space in which girls could take on independent and sometimes masculine roles and identities. And despite adult avowals to the contrary, it was also a flexible and contested organization as the girls it was meant to train embraced, altered, ignored, and sometimes laughed at various aspects of its character training program.

Baden-Powell, uninterested in leading this new feminine youth movement, gave the position of president to his younger sister Agnes, who in 1909 was fifty-one years old and still living with her elderly mother in central London. In official and academic histories of Guiding, Agnes Baden-Powell is known and often mocked for her gender conservatism and repeated assertions that the Guides would not turn girls into tomboys.[42] The movement's first two prescriptive texts (Pamphlet A, by Robert Baden-Powell, and Pamphlet B, co-authored by Agnes and Robert), described the basic contours of the movement while boasting that it would train girls "in womanliness as well as usefulness."[43] Pamphlet B alluded to the disappointment felt by some girls who had been Scouts by including two "actual letters which passed between a [British] mother in India and her daughter at school in England on the subject of Girls' Scouting." This undoubtedly fictional epistolary section, in which the disapproving mother agrees to let her daughter become a Guide if she promises not to become a tomboy, lists many of the gender fears that girls' scouting had aroused. While insisting on the importance of remaining "womanly," the Guide's mother wrote that girls should not lose their modesty, take too much exercise, whistle (because it might produce "a man's mouth ... with big strong lips, and perhaps a moustache"), use vulgar slang, or have dirty hands.[44]

There were also, however, less conventionally feminine aspects to Pamphlets A and B, both of which stated that the three primary aims of Guiding were to teach girls "to make themselves of practical use in case of invasion," "to prepare themselves for a Colonial life in case their destiny should lead them to such," and "to make themselves generally more useful to others and to themselves by learning useful occupations and handiwork, and yet retaining their womanliness."[45] This combination of "womanliness" with practical skills related to military defence, the British Empire, and the outdoors also characterized *The Handbook for Girl Guides or How Girls Can Help Build the Empire*, published in 1912. Again jointly written by the Baden-Powell siblings, it was similar in form and content to *Scouting for Boys* but insisted that Guiding would teach girls "how to be women – self-helpful, happy, prosperous, and capable of keeping good homes and of bringing up good children."[46] This volume was divided into seven main sections: Girl Guides' Pursuits, Finding the Injured (divided between "Woodcraft" and "Open-Air Pursuits and Tracking"), Tending the Injured ("Saving Life" and "Hospital Duties"), Frontier Life, Home Life, Patriotism, and Hints to Instructors.

Even at this early stage, then, Guiding was only partly about home and domesticity; the movement's early texts also promoted the idea that girls could play more public and assertive roles of national and imperial importance. "Perhaps you don't see how a mere girl can be of use to the great British Empire," the 1912 handbook claimed, "but by becoming a Guide and carrying out the laws every girl can be of use."[47] Bravery and acting in conventionally masculine ways are recommended at several points in *How Girls Can Help Build the Empire*, in sections encouraging girls and young women to act courageously and decisively in dangerous situations.[48] One chapter, for example, includes a section on Japanese self-defence that describes "how to secure a burglar with eight inches of cord."[49] The book also contains other bracing tales of youthful feminine bravery, several of which feature white heroines using firearms to kill or subdue exotic animals and "dangerous" Indigenous peoples. "Camp-Fire Yarn No. 21 (Self-Defence)," a story about a British girl who shoots a tiger from the balcony of her family's bungalow in India, insisted that "girls can even be brave enough to shoot tigers, if they can keep cool."[50] The story of Madeleine de Verchères, subtitled "A Brave Canadian Girl," is also included in *How Girls Can Help Build the Empire* – one of many early twentieth-century retellings of this narrative that demonized the Indigenous inhabitants of New France while celebrating young Madeleine's ability to fire guns and hold her family's fort against invasion.[51] Agnes Baden-Powell explained this story by telling readers that "the Red Indians, who lived in the wilder parts, were continually fighting the white settlers, and were very cunning in watching for opportunities to attack the colonists."[52] The rule of colonial difference, established more than half a century before, still clearly influenced the Baden-Powells' thinking about white and Indigenous peoples. Yet it is also worth noting that, in gendered terms, these stories presented roles for British girls that would have been inconceivable during Agnes's metropolitan Victorian childhood.

Part regulatory project and part liberating adventure, the Girl Guides offered a combination of freedom and control that, despite the disappointment felt by some of its earliest members, attracted the attention of women and girls around the world within months of its establishment in England in 1909. English-Canadian women and girls started forming companies in 1910, and many aspects of the early Guide ideology were epitomized by an evening entertainment given by Canadian Girl Guides and members of the St. John Ambulance Brigade at Massey Hall in Toronto on 3 December 1912. The evening began with a film about the relief of Lucknow during the Indian "Mutiny" of 1857, and a play in which St. John Ambulance Society volunteers acted out the setting up of a field hospital after a battle in the Balkans. The film and the play, and especially the Guide performances that followed them, received a wide range of press coverage – much of which was preserved in a scrapbook kept by a Toronto Guide named Grace Blood. One journalist called the evening's entertainment a "remarkable display" in which the Guides had "proudly and efficiently perform[ed] tasks that make girls better housekeepers, more capable in the arts of cooking, washing, sick-nursing, training and caring for children." The same article described the Guides' imperial pageant and camp display, as well as a first aid demonstration in which "the guides showed how they could treat a child with a scalp wound, how to reduce a dislocated limb, resuscitating a drowned girl, attending a child with convulsions, and hospital bed making."[53]

It was also in 1912, on a ship bound for the West Indies, that the fifty-four-year-old Robert Baden-Powell met the woman who would become his wife. Olave St. Clair Soames, who, like Agnes Baden-Powell, had received an informal and often disjointed home-based education, was travelling with her brewery-owner father. Olave was twenty-three (more than thirty years younger than Baden-Powell), and it was her athletic and boyish gait, as opposed to other more conventionally feminine attributes, that initially caught his eye. Her diary entry for 3 January 1912 describes meeting "Lieut-General Sir Robert Baden-Powell 'The Boy Scout' who is so nice. He talks so nicely about Mafeking and all his interesting experiences and is so modest and sweet."[54] Olave Soames's relationship with "the Boy Scout" and imperial war hero seems to have turned romantic quite quickly: they were married in October 1912, and among their wedding gifts was a car (the first of several) that was purchased with donations made by Boy Scouts from across England.

The couple honeymooned in North Africa, and Olave's diary contains a press clipping about their voyage that captures the ideals of sensible womanhood, outdoor life, and domesticity that would become so important to the Girl Guides. Printed in the conservative tabloid the *Daily Sketch*, the article was entitled "Honeymooning in the Desert: How Baden-Powells Managed with One Saucepan." Quoting the Chief Scout, the article stated that the newlyweds had spent their entire holiday camping out in the wild and praised Olave for her practical and rustic domestic skills.[55]

The First World War

The Baden-Powells had been married for less than two years when the First World War began in the summer of 1914. The war, a global conflict that raised new questions about gender and citizenship, changed the shape of the British Empire and provided opportunities for Guides and Scouts in different countries to demonstrate their usefulness. It was also seen by many Guide leaders as a decisive turning point – an event that had somehow made the world more "modern."[56]

On one level, the war gave credence to the citizenship claims that British military nurses had been making since the late nineteenth century in that it offered thousands of women from Britain and the dominions the hope of travel, better pay, adventure, and an escape from conventional feminine ideals. The wartime visibility of the Voluntary Aid Detachments and other uniformed groups also intensified existing concerns about women's roles, especially since many of these organizations' members used the masculine language of military heroism to explain their wartime experiences.[57] These uniformed women received hostile treatment from some journalists and members of the British public, in ways that resembled prewar concerns about Girl Scouts "aping" boys and soldiers.

Wartime fears about gender roles and relationships also affected non-uniformed women and girls, as some observers thought that all female civilians were taking too much pleasure in their new war-related freedoms. Politicians and social commentators worried that young women in particular would choose to neglect their maternal and domestic duties – a decision that could have dire consequences for established gender and racial hierarchies. Guiding itself was promoted as a way to stop "khaki fever" – the colloquial term for those British girls and young women who dared to smoke, use cosmetics, occupy public space, and fraternize with soldiers on leave.[58] Young female munitions workers were seen as especially vulnerable to the excitement and temptations of wartime, and Guide companies were started in many factories to provide surveillance and what contemporaries called "a higher idea of discipline and self-control."[59]

The Guide movement responded to the war with a characteristic mix of gender conservatism and practical action. The April 1915 issue of the *Girl Guides' Gazette*, for instance, featured an article in which Robert Baden-Powell discussed "How Girl Guides Can Help to Repair the Losses of the War." Echoing the gender, race, and class fears that had motivated eugenicists and other "experts" since the Boer War enlistment crisis, Baden-Powell asserted that "one of the greatest evils of war is that it kills off a large proportion of the best of our men – the bravest and strongest are those who suffer most, while the skulkers and weaklings are left to survive." "It is the duty of everyone who has the future of the country at heart," he wrote, "to look forward and see what he or she can do to remedy this damage to our race." In language reminiscent of the 1904 *Report of the Interdepartmental Committee on Physical Deterioration*, he lamented the existence of "an immense amount of preventable disease among our rising generation," a demographic time bomb that he claimed would require "special steps to get every child developed morally and physically, in body and mind, to become a useful citizen of the State, instead of being, as so many are, wasters or invalids." Total war gave new urgency to the Edwardian ideology of imperial motherhood, as Baden-Powell insisted that, "if the Guides knew enough about preventing these ailments, and about cooking and health-giving exercises, they might do much to remedy matters among the rising generation among them."[60]

While Girl Guides in Britain and across the Empire were given new war-related reasons to think of themselves as future mothers, they were also encouraged to contribute to the war effort in other, more concrete, ways. Tens of thousands of girls across the British Empire made and collected goods to be sent overseas, both to war-affected Belgian children and Allied troops. Often in cooperation with the Boy Scouts, they also raised money and volunteered for a range of war-related charities and purchased and equipped two recreation huts and an ambulance for Allied soldiers in France. Press coverage of Guides' charitable endeavours sometimes stressed the movement's pan-imperial nature as well, as when the *Toronto Daily Star* reported on 8 March 1918 that Guides in India had raised 2,243 rupees for Allied prisoners of war in Germany.[61] British Girl Guides also acted as messengers and clerical helpers in British censorship offices and at the London headquarters of MI5, the intelligence and counter-security agency.[62]

The end of the Great War, which brought changes to suffrage laws and an increased desire to return to prewar social norms, also had far-reaching effects on the British Empire. While British propaganda had favoured the image of an imperial family of nations fighting together for the sake of democracy, the experiences of non-white colonial soldiers were often marked by segregation and racism. After the war, these men's experiences combined with Woodrow Wilson's discourse of national self-determination to give a new impetus to anticolonial nationalist movements around the world.[63] Yet the war and its aftermath, which were also characterized by demonstrations of imperial loyalty by diverse groups of people, demonstrated as well the complexity of identities and allegiances that the British Empire continued to produce throughout the early twentieth century.

Structure and Aims of the Postwar Guide Movement

It was also during the First World War that Olave Baden-Powell decided to take a more active role in the Girl Guides. Through speeches, handbooks, articles, and committee work, she sought to mould the movement and to rise through its ranks by defining herself as young and modern, often in direct opposition to her sister-in-law, Agnes. Relations between the two women had always been tense, and, as early as March 1913, Olave was confiding to her diary that she found Agnes "rather trying."[64] With her husband's approval, Olave replaced Agnes as president of the Girl Guides in 1917 and was named Chief Guide in 1918. Agnes reluctantly accepted the position of honorary vice-president in 1920, but her continuing desire to be involved in the organization she had helped to establish remained a source of conflict. In 1928, for example, the Chief Scout and Chief Guide informed her that she would not be welcome at the Imperial Camp for Overseas Guiders that was being held that summer in the New Forest. Hurt and determined to take part despite her sister-in-law's wishes, the sixty-six-year-old Agnes came to the camp and attempted to watch the proceedings from a hiding place in the shrubbery.[65] Olave's diaries from the 1920s contain several other references to Agnes "going about making trouble," but she is far less visible in all official records from the 1930s.[66]

Olave's first instructional handbook, *Training Girls as Guides: Hints for Commissioners and All Who Are Interested in the Welfare and Training of Girls*, was published in 1917. On the one hand, this text was an attempt to strike out in a new direction by celebrating the emancipatory effects of the Great War on British women and girls. Because of their newly demonstrated aptitudes, Olave wrote, "women in the future will be called upon to take the place of men in very many different spheres of activity." On the other hand, however, *Training Girls as Guides* also contains a number of statements about gender roles and social order that resemble the conservative ideas expressed by the author's much older husband and sister-in-law. Echoing popular wartime concerns about "khaki fever," the book rails against cosmetics and "brazen flappers" and insists that, "because she may be a future mother, and because we need the very best brand of womanhood for maternity, we must guard our girls."[67] *Training Girls as Guides* also laments the apparent growth of "class hatred and rebellious discontent," and promises to teach modern young women "that [it] is necessary to submit to authority."[68]

Once Agnes had been deposed as head of the Girl Guides, her handbook *How Girls Can Help Build the Empire* was replaced in 1918 by Robert Baden-Powell's solely authored *Girl Guiding: A Handbook for Brownies, Guides, Rangers, and Guiders.* Like *Training Girls as Guides, Girl Guiding* explained the Great War as a watershed that had created new social conditions and increased the need for girls' character training. This text, which is similar in form and content to *Scouting for Boys,* was reprinted dozens of times during the 1920s and 1930s. According to Baden-Powell, the aim of the Girl Guide movement was "character development through happy citizenship through natural rather than artificial means."[69] The movement sought to create a self-regulating body of young female citizens, as shown by Baden-Powell's assertion that "the imposition of formal exercises and discipline from without is exactly the reverse of our principle of encouraging energy and self-discipline from within."[70]

The object of Girl Guide training, he wrote, was "to give our girls, whatever may be their circumstances, a series of healthy and jolly activities which, while delighting them, will afford a course of education outside the school."[71] The movement's didactic aims (and the fact that Baden-Powell believed parents and schools to be unable to provide the "right" sort of training for girls and young women) are also shown in his description of the four main components of Guiding. The movement, he wrote, would provide girls with invaluable training in:

1. CHARACTER AND INTELLIGENCE, through games, practices and activities, and honours and tests for promotion;
2. SKILL AND HANDICRAFT, encouraged through badges for proficiency;
3. PHYSICAL HEALTH AND HYGIENE, through development up to standard by games and exercises designed for the purpose;
4. SERVICE FOR OTHERS AND FELLOWSHIP, through daily good turns, organized public service, etc.

In *Girl Guiding* and *Training Girls as Guides,* husband and wife explained the need for Guiding with reference to several Victorian and Edwardian social anxieties. Racial degeneration, infant mortality, urbanization, the supposed physical and moral weakness of the working classes, and the fate of the British Empire are all discussed as motivating forces behind different aspects of the Guide program. Robert Baden-Powell, for example, stated simply that one of the movement's main goals was "to attract, and thus raise the slum girl from the gutter."[72] His wife's training manual for leaders also revealed a class-based anxiety about young female inhabitants of the "slums," and explained the need for Guiding: "In our bigger cities one can walk for mile upon mile through sordid and dingy streets. One wonders how in the world any human beings can exist here, much less lead clean and wholesome lives."[73] Through Guiding, she wrote, "we can alter the character of the inhabitants so that they will be able to rise out of the squalor and the misery of such homes and so that they may all aspire to live and work in healthier, happier surroundings."[74] In language reminiscent of missionary conversion narratives and the melodramatic "before-and-after" publicity photographs of poor children used by Barnardo's homes, the Chief Guide sought – with obvious disregard for the wishes of working-class parents and their children – to emphasize the power of her youth movement to create industrious and efficient citizens of good character.

The formation (and, as necessary, alteration) of "character" was a primary aim of Guiding and Scouting. An oft-used term during the late nineteenth and early twentieth centuries, "character" referred both to the Victorian public school ideal and to a set of traits that occupied a central place in contemporary educational and psychological theories. A concept that was widely seen as being responsible for the success or failure of both individuals and nations, it was based on self-control, self-reliance, duty, and industry – qualities that, of course, the empire-building British often ascribed to themselves. Anxieties about the standard of British "character" in an age of increased international competition are obvious in Baden-Powell's claim, made in *Girl Guiding*: "that nation comes to the fore which has the most character in its citizens." Their assumed status as future mothers made girls' character training especially significant since, as Baden-Powell also insisted, a "mother's influence gives ... the first impetus to character [and a] ... mother cannot give that which she does not possess herself."[75]

Class, race, and age were also central to the concept of character as promoted in interwar Guide literature. The continuing influence of Samuel Smiles's emphasis on thrift and self-help, which linked poverty to flaws in character, is evident in Olave Baden-Powell's insistence that urban crime and juvenile delinquency "would be unnecessary were the character of our nation developed along the right lines and at a pliable age."[76]

The discussions of character in these Guide texts are also similar to Stanley Hall's recapitulation theory: non-British boys and girls, who "naturally" possessed fewer of these important characteristics, could nonetheless, through the mental, moral, and physical training provided by the Baden-Powells' youth movements, improve their own characters by progressing through a set of evolutionary stages. The American-influenced and consumer-based youth culture that was developing during the 1920s and 1930s further heightened Guiding's concern with character, as adults worried about the individual and collective effects of young women's apparent disregard for the important ideals of modesty, duty, and self-control.

By the end of the First World War, the Guides' gendered program of training in character, handicrafts, health, and service had been divided into several age-based categories: Brownies (the youngest group, known as Bluebirds in India), Girl Guides (for girls between eleven and sixteen), and Rangers (for girls aged sixteen and up). Brownies and Bluebirds wore brown uniforms, saluted by holding up two fingers on the right hand, and had to promise to do their "duty to God and the King [and] to help other people every day, especially those at home."[77] Guides had to make a similar promise, wore dark blue uniforms, saluted with three fingers, and had to obey a ten-part Guide Law that included such tenets as following orders, helping others, being thrifty, and, importantly, remaining "pure in word, thought, and deed."[78] Guides over the age of sixteen became Rangers, a pursuit that Baden-Powell claimed would give them the chance of "doing service for others and also of picking out a career for [themselves], and at the same time of having a healthy happy time in good comradeship with others of [their] age."[79]

The Guide "game," which included swearing to do one's duty to God and the King of England, also required girls to promise to be trustworthy, loyal, obedient, thrifty, "pure," and "a sister to every other Guide, no matter to what creed, country, or class the other belongs."[80] Uniforms, which made members of the movement instantly recognizable and purported to lessen superficial divisions between girls, could also highlight differences of class and ability. Across the British Empire, these uniforms were also instruments of colonial discipline that could be – and often were – modified and reinterpreted by Indigenous youngsters.[81] Girl Guides in all contexts were expected to earn badges to reflect their achievements in a variety of areas, from domestic service and child nursing to hiking and carpentry. Like their contemporaries in the Scouts, Guide leaders used their positions to express popular concerns, and the Guides were one of a number of early twentieth-century youth organizations whose leaders stressed the moral, spiritual, and physical benefits of camping and nature study for modern young people.

This outdoor aspect of the Guide program held multiple and sometimes contradictory meanings; Baden-Powell stressed the physical and disciplinary benefits of Guide camps while many of the girls themselves enjoyed a previously unknown degree of gender freedom during their company camps and hikes. At the same time, the movement sought to reach disabled girls through its Extension Branch (which created modified badge tests, games, and exercises), and it established a postal service-based program called Lone Guides for girls who lived in isolated places. Interwar Guiding also emphasized self-sacrifice and voluntarism, and encouraged all of its members to be thrifty – a directive that conflicted somewhat with the movement's other role as a retail provider of uniforms, accessories, camping goods, and reading material.[82] Guide companies in different countries all participated in rallies – spectacular public demonstrations of Guide work that frequently attracted thousands of spectators. Finally, the girls and young women who donned the movement's uniforms in various locations between the two world wars were encouraged, by their local leaders and by the movement's official structure and prescriptive texts, to "look wide" and learn about the cultures and lives of girls in other parts of the British Empire and the world.

The Interwar Years:
Imperial and International Expansion and Growth

This imperial and international aspect of the movement became especially prominent after the First World War, as membership numbers increased across the globe.[83] Crucially, imperial and international Guiding also allowed the Baden-Powells to distance themselves from Victorian militarism (and later from European fascism) by connecting their youth movements and the British Empire with the League of Nations, familial internationalism, and peace. The Guide movement's global growth, like its official emphasis on imperial and international cooperation, was also linked to a number of other developments that affected the lives of girls and women during the years between the two world wars. These included the increased accessibility of international travel and the advent of cinema and radio, the latter of which contributed to the construction of mass cultural communities that had the potential to unite people across the boundaries of age, race, geography, and class. Cinema and radio, like the modern fashions and pastimes they depicted, were embraced by girls and young women around the world, as evidenced by the post-First World War figure of the Modern Girl and the concerns about gender, leisure, sexuality, and age that she provoked.

Of course, the degree to which these developments affected girls and young women was not the same. Levels of material and linguistic access to modern communication technologies and the ideas they transmitted varied greatly: the experience of a European immigrant to Canada, for instance, differed on many levels from that of a young factory worker in Lancashire, whose experience of modernity, in turn, would have borne little resemblance to that of a student from a mission school in Calcutta. But girls from these very different places contributed to the Guides' exponential membership expansion during the 1920s and 1930s. Through the Guides, girls with vastly different life experiences and identities came into contact with each other and with an international youth culture whose members both reacted to and influenced the various political, social, and cultural developments that shaped the world after 1918.

Guiding developed differently in Britain, Canada, and India, in ways that reflected the unique and often messy complexities of local contexts and the broader geopolitical shifts that both preceded and followed the First World War. Unsurprisingly, the movement's largest membership figures were achieved in Great Britain. By 1928, for example, there were 430,000 British Guides, Brownies, and Rangers – outnumbering the Scouts by more than 90,000.[84] Although Guiding was initially a middle-class phenomenon in the United Kingdom, both Scouting and Guiding claimed a cross-class membership there by the 1920s.[85] British Guide groups were most successful in towns and cities, and frequently met at neighbourhood schools. Some companies were organized along religious lines and were based in churches or synagogues. As during the First World War, there remained a number of factory-based Guide and Ranger groups – reflections of a continuing middle-class desire to train and contain the young working-class women who were seen as especially vulnerable to the temptations of modern consumer and youth culture.

It is important, however, to note that not all Britons embraced the training offered by the Scouts and Guides. Like numerous other early twentieth-century social reformers, many Guide and Scout leaders (especially those at the highest levels) aimed to establish a non-antagonistic capitalist social structure and did not want to erase class differences. While some working-class youth saw these movements as opportunities for education and social mobility, other left-leaning Britons were troubled by the movements' support of capitalism and class hierarchies. Some working-class parents, for example, worried about the anti-trade union rhetoric that Baden-Powell sometimes expressed in popular daily newspapers such as the *Daily Mail* and the *Telegraph*.[86] Many working people were also alarmed by the use of Boy Scouts as strikebreakers in the United States and Britain and, still reeling from the devastation of the Great War, suspected that the movement was training soldiers instead of peace-loving future citizens.[87] Some Guides (though far fewer than Scouts) were harassed in the streets; girls in Liverpool, for instance, reported being pelted with rotten eggs and chased by "hordes of jeering boys."[88] Other young people rejected the Scouts and

Guides by joining different types of youth groups, including those organized by political parties and the socialist Woodcraft Folk and Co-operative Comrades' Circles.[89]

The Canadian Girl Guides also faced competition from other youth groups during the interwar years, most notably the Anglican Church-based Canadian Girls in Training (CGIT), left-leaning and socialist youth groups, and, for older adolescents in Quebec, L'Action catholique.[90] Despite these organizational rivalries, however, Guiding remained the biggest girls' organization in Canada from its inception in Ontario in 1910. The development of Guiding in Canada reflected that country's unique demographic and geographical characteristics, a fact that was not lost on either Canadian or British leaders. An article by "A Canadian Guider" printed in a *Collins' Girl Guides Annual* boasted that Canadian Brownies "seem to have inherited from the Indian a natural sense of companionship with the birds and the beasts." This same article also sought to establish the popularity of Guiding among non-British immigrants by noting that "in one company, we may have many nationalities represented – a Swedish leader may have a Finn for her second; a Silesian works for her badge side by side with a Dane."[91] Guiding was most popular in Canadian cities and towns, but the movement sought to accommodate girls and young women in isolated rural settings through the Lone Guides, a system of newsletters that sought to create "virtual" Guide companies connected by the postal system. Canada's French Catholic population was less eager to embrace Guiding's Anglo-centric national-imperial vision. Numerous French Catholic Guide companies were established throughout Canada during the interwar years, but they remained separate from English-Canadian Guiding and British imperial headquarters until 1939.[92]

As in England, many Canadian Guide groups met at local schools, neighbourhood halls, and houses of worship.[93] Because of the established cultural and demographic ties that linked early twentieth-century English Canada with Great Britain, Anglican Church-based companies were especially prevalent there. Guide leaders also often cooperated with the Imperial Order Daughters of the Empire, another "forgotten colonizer" whose mostly middle-class, Anglo-Canadian members used flag presentations, scholarship programs, and essay contests to promote their vision of a "better, British Canada."[94]

Ornamentalism and status-consciousness also defined some aspects of Guiding in Canada, as governors general and lieutenant-governors, business leaders, and their wives occupied key honorary and practical positions within the organization.[95] The movement's links to the country's English-speaking elites were especially evident during the Baden-Powells' 1923 trip to Canada, during which they stayed with Lord and Lady Byng at Government House in Ottawa and visited McGill University and the University of Toronto, both of which awarded Robert Baden-Powell honorary doctorates. While in Toronto, Baden-Powell also gave an invited speech at the 1923 Imperial Education Conference, at which he proudly claimed that the Guides and Scouts had been "found particularly useful in the schools for Red Indian children, just as [they] had also proved useful in a like manner on the West Coast of Africa and in Baghdad."[96]

The formal connection between Guiding and Scouting and Canada's Department of Indian Affairs, which got stronger as the twentieth century progressed, was especially evident in the formation of mandatory companies and troops at numerous residential and industrial schools.[97] Guiding also touched Indigenous children in Canada through its links to Protestant missions, as demonstrated especially clearly by an article published in the international Guiding magazine the *Council Fire* in April 1938. Entitled "The Most Northerly Company in the World," the article described Guides and Brownies from an Anglican mission school in Aklavik on the Mackenzie River. The layers of colonial authority under which Guiding operated in settings such as this were made especially evident in the accompanying photograph, which showed the uniformed girls forming "a Guard of Honour to welcome the Bishop of the Arctic, Bishop Fleming, who visited them by aeroplane this summer." On that day, the article stated, "twenty-four Eskimo and Indian girls of the Mission were enrolled in the presence of the Principal and other members of the school, and representatives of the Hudson Bay Company [sic] and the Royal Canadian Mounted Police."[98]

Mission school companies also prospered in South Asia during the 1920s and 1930s, but their development − like that of the Indian Guide movement more generally − followed a somewhat different path. The first Boy Scout groups in India, established in 1908, were restricted to white boys. Before long, however, Indian men and boys had started to establish their own, unofficial troops − a development that, as Carey Watt shows, caused British state and military officials to worry that "Indian scout troops would abuse the physical training and martial elements in the boy scouts and then degenerate into centres of seditious and revolutionary activity."[99] While failing to arouse similar concerns (likely because of British officials' inability to believe that girls could pose any sort of threat to imperial stability), Guiding was also initially restricted to girls of British descent.[100] The first of these racially exclusive Guide companies in India, a demonstration of ongoing British anxieties about racial boundaries, was established at a British girls' school in Jabalpur in 1911.

However, it was the near simultaneous establishment of rival organizations for Indian girls (the Seva Samiti Guides, whose leaders were affiliated with north Indian social service networks; Annie Besant's Sister Guides; and the Girl Messenger Service at the American Mission School in Lucknow) that ultimately forced British Guide headquarters to reconsider its racially exclusive membership policy.[101] The first all-Indian Girl Guide company was established at the Panch Howd Mission School in Pune in 1916.[102] Mrs. Maurice Bear, the British woman who was Chief Guide Commissioner in India during this early period, described the situation as follows:

> The question of native guides is a very pressing one and an attempt has been made to affiliate with the Girl Messenger Service of Lucknow, which is on Girl Guides' Lines, and has been doing successful work. At present, this attempt is in abeyance, until the opinion of the founder of the Messengers who is at present in America can be obtained, she having opposed affiliation at a former date chiefly on the ground that the Guiders teach loyalty to the British Empire while the Messengers are taught loyalty to their own country, India. As the loyal bonding together of all daughters of the Empire, whether English, Canadian, South African, Australian or Indian, etc., is a great asset and makes a great bond, this part of our service could not be abandoned without rendering on the whole no use and indeed harmful [sic] ... and shows the need of a Girl Guide movement among Indian girls all the more.[103]

Guide membership in late colonial India was significantly smaller than in Canada and the United Kingdom, with 18,970 members in 1929, and 38,129 in 1935.[104] While questions of "loyalty" continued to complicate matters, membership in the movement nonetheless soon came to reflect much of India's diversity. As reported in the *Council Fire*, by the late 1920s there were "Girl Guides in Hindu, Mahomedan, Indian Christian, Parsee, Jewish, Theosophical, Brahmo-Somaj and Buddhist schools ... in British India and in Indian states ... in criminal tribes settlements, and [in] purdah."[105]

Aside from anecdotal descriptions of the "infinite variety" of Indian Guides, however, I have had trouble finding more details about the caste and religious composition of the movement. I have determined, however, that most interwar Guide companies were attached to schools. This focus on school-based companies meant that only a small minority of Indian girls joined the movement during the decades before Independence; one survey, conducted between 1927 and 1937, found that only 14 percent of Indian girls who enrolled in school (themselves already a minority) continued their formal education until the fourth grade.[106] Indian Guiding also had strong links to the Young Women's Christian Association (YWCA), and the annual All-India Training Camp for Guiders was often held at the YWCA compound at Ootacamund, a hill station in the Nilgiri Hills.

As Satadru Sen writes, "exclusion and inclusion, 'colonization' and 'liberation' become almost hopelessly entangled when the colonial institution is also the instrument for producing national children and modern adults."[107] This statement is especially true of early Indian Guiding, as some groups were run by British and American teachers and missionaries, while others were headed by middle-class Indian women. By the early 1920s, the movement had attracted the support of many educated Indian women, who saw it as a way to "modernize" their nation's girls and young women. In 1920, for example, Lady Abala Bose (wife of the well-known scientist Sir J.C. Bose and the founder-secretary of the Brahmo Girls' School) was appointed Guide Commissioner for Bengal.[108] At the 1928 All-India Women's Conference on Educational Reform in Delhi, a group of sari-clad Guides met delegates' trains, served as an honour guard for the conference president the Maharani Saheb of Baroda, and carried messages during meetings.[109] In February 1930, the movement was described in the *Indian Ladies' Magazine* (a periodical published by and for educated elite women) as "a great crusade for the teaching of citizenship to the girls of this country, a crusade in which Indians and Europeans co-operate in constructive work."[110] Significantly, these examples complicate Carey Watt's argument that Guiding was irrelevant and largely ignored in late colonial India because "girls and young women [there] generally were not intended to be active public citizens."[111]

The adoption and adaptation of Guide ideas and practices by elite Indian women coincided with a number of other developments, including the rise of Gandhian nationalism; the passage of the Government of India Act in 1935; and the involvement during the 1930s of more women in anti-colonial terrorism. It also took place against the backdrop of the global controversy that had erupted in 1927 after the publication of Katherine Mayo's virulent anti-nationalist polemic *Mother India*, a text that sought to justify the British presence in India with reference to "degraded" Hindu sexual and social practices. The text also, as Mrinalini Sinha shows, caused upper-caste and middle-class women's organizations in India to articulate a collective identity of the "Indian woman citizen."[112]

Much had changed, in other words, as the Baden-Powells only partially realized when they travelled to India early in 1937. Olave Baden-Powell wrote a detailed account of their trip in her diary, describing their time at the viceroy's palace in Lutyens' newly rebuilt Delhi, a visit to the Taj Mahal, and a series of meetings with Guide leaders from British India and the Princely States, including Sherene Rustomjee, American missionaries, the Yuvarani of Mysore, and the Rani of Sangli. After a train trip to Madras, she described meeting "250 Guides & Bluebirds on the platform. Shake hands & smile & they garland me & sing. The same thing happens, with small lots of Guides waiting to greet me at about 4 other stations down the line. I get out & shake hands with dozens of hot brown paws, and we beam upon each other."[113] At the end of their Indian journey, the Chief Guide reflected on her experiences by casting Guiding as a happy sisterhood that would liberate Indian women and girls from their apparently "degraded" positions. Echoing Mayo's *Mother India* and nineteenth-century missionary discourse, she wrote: "I have grown terribly interested by all I have seen of India this time, and it is all such a queer mixture – a land of contradictions, and I do feel that Guiding has a great deal to bring of happiness to these backward people & this tour has been most worthwhile."[114]

The Baden-Powells returned contentedly to England in March 1937, but there were problems to come – foreshadowed perhaps by Olave's belief in Indian "backwardness" and her description of South Asian Guides' hands as "hot brown paws." During the first week of May 1937, not long after his return from the subcontinent, Robert Baden-Powell spoke to a group of British journalists about the problems and possibilities of Scouting in India. His words were disseminated globally by Reuters wire service on 8 May 1937 and caused an immediate outcry. "India at present suffers," he is reported to have said, "from three main handicaps as a Nation – Lack of Character, Lack of Health and Lack of Unity. Scout training, however, aims at producing these qualities which India now lacked."[115] This unflattering description, published in numerous Indian newspapers, inspired widespread anger and prompted many Indian Scout leaders to consider leaving the movement. As Indian Guide leader Lakshmi Mazumdar explained in the 1960s, in 1937 India "was engaged in a fight for national liberation, and in the midst of a bitter struggle with the ruling power, an apparently unwise statement from a member of the ruling nation, however great and illustrious he might have been, was enough to add fuel to the smouldering fire."[116]

Baden-Powell sought to dampen the flames by claiming to have been misunderstood and writing letters of apology. To the Nawab of Chhattari (Chief Scout Commissioner for India), for example, he wrote:

> To me it was unbelievable that my remarks could be understood in this light when I have been working for over twenty years in trying to give young India

the joy and good comradeship of Scouting, independent of all political, religious or military aims, for no other object than their own good. I am extremely sorry that this should have given any anxiety to those good men, the Scouts, who have worked so hard successfully, in building a strong and sensible citizenhood for India.[117]

In a letter published in the *Sunday Statesman* (Calcutta), on 13 June 1937, Baden-Powell further sought to make amends by claiming:

Scouting has been taken up and encouraged by the educationists all over the world as teaching character, health, and co-operation in service – qualities which are needed just as much in England and in all countries, as in India. Indian Scouts have not only developed these qualities among themselves but have extended, through personal expeditions, that sense of brotherhood with other nations about the world. And this is a great step towards international goodwill and peace.[118]

These apologies and attestations of goodwill were deemed insufficient, and a number of Indian Scout leaders severed their links with Britain and established a new group, the Hindustan Scout Association, in 1938.[119] Significantly, however, the Indian Guide movement chose to maintain its links with Britain and the World Association of Girl Guides and Girl Scouts.[120]

Conclusion

The shape of global Guiding was further changed by several other developments that took place in the late 1930s. Despite the many similarities between Scouts and Guides and European fascist youth groups, the start of the Second World War caused the World Association of Girl Guides and Girl Scouts and most of its member nations to neglect empire and internationalism while articulating their opposition to the totalitarian regimes of Germany and Italy. On a material level, the war also changed Guide activities and leaders' explanations of them. As in the First World War, doing practical, unpaid, and often gendered types of war work became a focus for Guides across the world between 1939 and 1945. At the same time, the movement also lost several of the individuals whose ideals had influenced its direction. Katharine Furse, who as president of the World Bureau had steered the World Association of Girl Guides and Girl Scouts since its inception in 1928, stepped down from her post in 1939. That same year, the Baden-Powells left Britain and retired to a small cottage in Nyeri, Kenya.[121] Speaking at the Tenth World Conference in Switzerland in 1938, the Chief Guide explained this move as a marker of the third and final phase in her husband's life: "The Chief [Scout] had one life before he met me, as a man of war; he then had a second one, in our life together, as a man of peace; and now we are starting our third life, with him as a man of leisure."[122] Baden-Powell's African life of leisure did not last long; he died on 8 January 1941 at the age of eighty-three and was buried in Kenya. However, the Chief Scout's ideals — appropriated and altered by groups of women and girls across the world — exerted a defining influence on the shape of Guiding during the 1920s and 1930s.

Chapter 2

GUIDING GIRLS
TOWARD THE PRIVATE SPHERE
Training for Homekeeping, Mothercraft,
and Matrimony

THE JANUARY 1928 ISSUE of the *Council Fire*, Guiding's explicitly internation-alist quarterly magazine, included a statement from Robert Baden-Powell – a positive assessment, from the Chief Scout's point of view, of the movement's impact on its members. Girls and women across the British Empire and the world, he claimed, "are really the better citizens, more sound in character, more successful in home-keeping, mothercraft and matrimony than they would have been if they had not had our training."[1]

While encouraging modern girls and young women to be hardy and re-sourceful citizens, interwar Guide texts and activities were also clearly based on the assumption that girls' futures were going to include housekeeping, mar-riage, and the bearing and rearing of efficient and moral children. This under-standing of femininity, which had obvious ties to the nineteenth-century Anglo-American ideology of separate spheres, shifted and broadened during the early twentieth century as different communities across the globe sought to harness motherhood, domesticity, and marriage in support of various im-perialist, nationalist, and racial causes.[2]

Domestic, maternal, and marital education schemes, while intended to im-part practical skills and feelings of loyalty and allegiance to sometimes con-flicting communities, were also attempts to create gendered identities. Some feminist scholars have criticized early twentieth-century domestic training programs for "wasting girls' time" and reinforcing a gendered division of labour that often channelled women into domestic service work and other low-paying or unpaid employment.[3] Other historians have linked the persistence of maternal and domestic training during the 1920s and 1930s to adult worries about developing youth cultures and a desire to restore the hierarchies of gender, class, and generation that been had disrupted by the First World War.[4] But as Mary Hancock, Birgitte Søland, and other scholars show, these schemes could also be used to forge national and generational identities in ways that were not completely oppressive.[5]

This chapter engages with these broader issues by making several inter-related arguments. First, I argue that interwar Guiding's attempts to train girls to be good mothers, efficient household managers, and companionate wives in Canada, India, and England – which combined an emphasis on scientific methods with references to girls' "natural" domestic and maternal instincts – must be understood as an example of the movement's modern gender con-servatism. The meanings and experiences of this conservatism were not uni-form, however, and this first section also traces the ways in which questions of empire, race, class, and nation influenced Guiding's ideologies and practices in these different contexts. The final part of the chapter argues that, while promoting such conventionally feminine identities and pursuits, Guiding also created space for women and girls who rejected these gendered ideals.

A report summarizing the subjects discussed at the tenth World Conference for Guiders in Adelboden, Switzerland, published in the *Council Fire* in 1938, illustrates this point especially clearly. When training girls "for their future lives as wives, home-makers, [and] bringers-up of children," the report insisted that Guide leaders should "adhere closely and return constantly to the original sources of our Movement, as given by Baden-Powell," while also "moderniz[ing] our ideas and our outlook."[6] Guide publications and activities from Canada, India, and England during the 1920s and 1930s show similar attempts to bal-ance "modern" ideas and practices with the older ideas about girls' duties and futures that were expressed most vocally by Baden-Powell. On the one hand, interwar Guide leaders' insistence on the importance of training girls to be good homekeepers, mothers, and wives had much in common with Victorian and Edwardian ideas about race, class, empire, and gender. On the other hand, however, the movement's training in these areas also reflected realities and concerns specific to the 1920s and 1930s: the desire, especially in Canada and England, to return to prewar gender roles, a new emphasis on science and the professionalization of housework and motherhood, and the use of maternal and domestic training for imperialist and nationalist purposes. But interwar Guiding's conservatively modern emphases on homekeeping, motherhood, and matrimony were also complicated and sometimes contradicted by the movement's status as a global single-sex community.

Training for Motherhood

Training for motherhood, a central part of Guide ideology and practice since Agnes Baden-Powell's early writings about "womanliness," continued to play a significant role in the movement throughout the 1920s and 1930s. Reflecting the social trauma of the Great War, imperialist and nationalist aspirations, and the influence of new scientific and psychological theories, Guide leaders in Canada, England, India, and beyond used a range of texts and activities to stress girls' reproductive and maternal duties. In *Girl Guiding*, first published in 1918 and reprinted nearly every year during the 1920s and 1930s, Robert Baden-Powell hinted broadly at the domestic and imperial troubles that could be caused by a generation of "girls who have never taken the trouble to learn what they ought to do with children."[7] Linking maternal training to national service, the Chief Scout asserted: "there is no way in which a girl can help her country better than by fitting herself to undertake the care of children."[8]

Infant mortality, an issue that, since the late nineteenth century, had often been linked to racial degeneration and neglectful mothering, continued to be discussed in this way in Guide texts published during the interwar years. Olave Baden-Powell's *Training Girls as Guides*, written in 1917 and reprinted several times after the First World War, referred vaguely to a "serious increase in infant mortality," and explained it as the result of large numbers of implicitly working class, white/British women who were raising children without having educated themselves in health and hygiene.[9] Despite the fact that infant mortality rates in Britain, Western Europe, the dominions, and the United States had actually been falling steadily since the late nineteenth century, Guide texts produced during and after the war continued to claim that infant deaths were increasing and that this increase was occurring because mothers had not bothered to learn how to care for them.[10] Rhona Mason, the author of several articles in Guide periodicals about the value of maternal training, similarly argued in the August 1922 issue of the *Girl Guides' Gazette* that

> every year, thousands of healthy babies die and others are left mutilated for life, through the ignorance of those who should be caring for them. If Guiders would give just a very little of their precious time and energy to try to grasp and absorb the reality of these facts ... they would find their time was not wasted from their Guides' or their country's point of view.[11]

As in the Edwardian period, these claims obscured the broader social and environmental causes of infant mortality and ill health by blaming "inferior" and "ignorant" working-class mothers for having neglected their national and imperial duties. They were also, though often not explicitly, reflections of anxieties about *white* infant deaths in Britain and settler societies. As Philippa Mein Smith writes, most early twentieth-century efforts to improve maternal knowledge and infant health were "not for indigenous mothers and babies."[12] While true in the sense that many white settlers thought of Indigenous peoples as a "dying race" whose members were therefore beyond help, Mein Smith's argument neglects assimilatory educational institutions, sites in which a number of Indigenous girls and young women in the dominions (through domestic science classes and the Girl Guides) received "modern" maternal and domestic training. Mary Ellen Kelm demonstrates that continuously high infant mortality rates among Canada's Indigenous populations between 1900 and 1950, a period in which white infant mortality dropped precipitously, were often explained as a logical consequence of Indigenous women's allegedly "primitive" and "unhealthy" maternal practices. Throughout the first half of the twentieth century, she writes, residential schools were seen by the state, missionaries, and voluntary organizations as a way to "save a 'race' dying from maternal neglect." These institutions, at some of which Guiding and Scouting were used to reinforce educators' messages about "correct" gendered behaviour, were often discussed as a way to lead "the First Nations to health, both by removing children from the clutches of supposedly negligent and ignorant parents, and by teaching them Euro-Canadian standards of cleanliness and care."[13] Earning Guide badges in child care and cooking was seen by white educators and the federal Department of Indian Affairs as a way to make Indigenous girls conform to these Euro-Canadian standards. However, Guiding's efforts to train Indigenous girls in motherhood and domesticity sometimes confounded dominant white conceptions of Indigenous abilities and racial hierarchy.

Discussions of infant and child mortality in late colonial India, meanwhile, included climate-based anxieties about the survival of white children and the idea that Indian women were especially prone to infanticide.[14] White colonial authorities seem not to have been as worried about Native infant mortality rates in South Asia, but as Samita Sen indicates, some late nineteenth- and early twentieth-century social reformers sought to combat infant mortality by focusing on the failings of individual mothers and the need to rectify them."[15] While infant mortality did not feature in any of the discussions I found of Guiding and maternal training in South Asia, it is possible that the movement's claims about educating girls to reduce infant deaths might have appealed to adults in India for this reason.

The secondary literature on imperial attempts to reform non-white and colonized mothers, like the scholarship on empire and domesticity, often stresses the ways in which these projects reinforced racial hierarchies and notions of difference. Simply put, the leaders of maternal and domestic reform projects often discussed their goals in Manichean terms, with clearly defined ideals and examples of people and behaviours that did not measure up. This binary thinking also extended to discourses about the broader significance of domestic and maternal training, as the proponents of these schemes often justified their interventions with references to civilization and savagery, modern science and backwardness, industry and indolence, and order and chaos. Yet what is striking about the Guide texts I have examined, many of which include descriptions of Guide groups from around the world alongside advice pieces about baby care and cleaning, is the relative absence of these comparative discussions about maternal practices and "civilization." I understand this silence to mean two things: (1) that the authors of these official texts were primarily (though perhaps not consciously) concerned with whiteness and (2) that they saw maternal and domestic training as a way to unite girls and young women from different backgrounds in a shared, gender-based project about feminine "usefulness" that did little to challenge existing hierarchies of class and race.

These silences also characterize interwar Guide leaders' oft-expressed concerns about the quality of children that modern Brownies, Guides, and Rangers would (it was assumed) eventually produce. Rhona Mason, whose August 1922 article in the *Girl Guides' Gazette* had linked infant mortality to maternal ignorance, also insisted that modern girls were responsible for both the moral character and the physical health of "future generations."[16] Unsurprisingly, Robert Baden-Powell made similar claims about the ways in which Guide training would improve the children he assumed most Girl Guides would eventually bear. Emphasizing discipline, self-reliance, cheerfulness, and duty, he wrote that Guiding would remedy the sad fact that many "girls, some of the future mothers of our race, have had little character training as a direct part of their education."[17] Baden-Powell's claims, which espoused reproductive futurism while foregrounding the importance of white "racial" responsibility, also likely reflected the concern that modern young women's love of commercial amusements, cosmetics, and new types of employment would lead them to neglect or mismanage their maternal duties.

On the one hand, then, these discourses, which implied that learning relevant Guide skills would make girls' future children into healthy citizens of good character, had changed relatively little since the Edwardian era. But in official texts published during the 1920s and 1930s, older concerns about race, class, gender, infant mortality, and health often existed alongside references to psychological ideas and an insistence on the importance of "modern" methods of child-rearing. In periodical articles and at conferences throughout the interwar years, Guide leaders spoke confidently about girls' "natural" maternal instincts while simultaneously expressing concern that these instincts were being undermined or blunted by modern life. In "Some Thoughts on the Psychology of Girl Guiding," published in the January 1922 issue of the *Girl Guides' Gazette*, Catherine R. Newby, vice-principal of St. Christopher's College in Blackheath, south London, advised Guide leaders to "examine ... the natural instincts, desires and modes of thinking and acting of the normal girl ... [and to discover] in what ways a useful structure can by nurture rise upon this foundation of nature." "Deep rooted in every girl," she wrote, "is the great maternal urge dominating her interests at every stage – an unconscious process it may be, but yet there."[18] It was up to Guide leaders, Newby implied, to find and encourage this "great maternal urge" in all of their Brownies, Guides, and Rangers. The same issue of the *Gazette* also featured an article entitled "Mothercraft and Our Older Girls," in which Rhona Mason wrote: "In these times of ultra-civilization mother instinct is so hampered that children die from sheer want of knowledge, not want of life ... Some women profess to dislike children, but nevertheless mother love is natural to every small girl, yet it may be killed in later years." She urged Guiders to "nurse and foster this spirit and give it a larger meaning and they can teach their girls to look after the babies that will assuredly come into their lives."[19]

Mason's confidence that modern girls would "assuredly" follow their "instincts" and eventually become biological mothers – and her belief that they nonetheless needed strong encouragement and training to do so – was echoed in other Guide texts published during the 1920s and 1930s. In her 1935 book *An A.B.C. of Guiding*, for example, British Guide author A.M. Maynard claimed that Guiding appealed to girls' "primary psychological instinct" to "mother, protect, [and] care for" others. Guide training, she contended, was important for modern girls because it "develops *unselfishness*, appealing as it does to the mother instinct."[20] On one level, Maynard's explanation of Guide training resembles the many Victorian girls' novels whose mostly British authors had stressed feminine self-sacrifice in place of self-sufficiency.[21] At the same time, however, it also reveals a more modern worry: that growing numbers of girls and young women, as white birthrates fell across the industrialized West, preferred to spend their leisure time thinking of themselves rather than of their future children.

Discussions of the complicated relationship between maternal instincts and modern life also took place at international Guide events. At the 1938 World Conference in Switzerland, for instance, Guide leaders from countries including Belgium, Britain, Canada, China, India, and Poland listened to a speech entitled "The Psychological Structure of Woman" delivered by Dr. E. Aeppli, a psychologist and former girls' school teacher from Zurich. In previous centuries, Aeppli claimed,

> it was assumed that the girl would marry young, bear children in rapid succession, and lead the life of a housemistress and mother. Girls who did not do this went into convents, dedicated themselves to some special social work, or simply withered away. To-day marriage, though the primary, is not the only career for a girl; she goes through school, training courses, special studies; she aims at acquiring some definite position, as a secretary, a nurse, a teacher, a laboratory-worker, a doctor, a lawyer ... The modern young woman can no longer depend merely on the maternal instinct of her sex or on the instruction given her by her mother.[22]

While describing the many doors that had opened for modern women and girls, Aeppli also insisted that more traditional gender roles had not disappeared entirely: "The girl in the future is destined to care for others ... She will have to look after those weaker than herself, therefore she develops qualities of gentleness and sympathy."[23]

Dr. Aeppli, like Guide leaders from other national contexts, clearly worried that girls' "natural" instincts, even if properly nurtured, were insufficient for the challenges of the modern age. Guide magazines, while emphasizing the importance of "character" and "instincts," therefore also urged leaders to "teach your girls the most modern theories."[24] Guiding's "modern" and "scientific" approach to child care was epitomized by the Child Nurse badge, a badge that was mandatory for all Guides and that was the subject of many detailed discussions in the movement's books and magazines. To qualify for the badge, girls were required to demonstrate elementary cleaning and sewing skills, and to explain in detail how a child between two and five years old should be clothed, fed, "kept clean in person and clothing," "kept in healthy surroundings," "given rest and exercise," and "kept happy and good, through self-control and occupation."[25] It is unsurprising, but nonetheless worth noting, that there was no similar badge related to fatherhood or child care for Boy Scouts during these years.

Guide leaders and authors based many of their ideas about teaching the Child Nurse badge on the international discourse of "scientific motherhood"

– a group of theories espoused by medical and psychological experts that stressed the importance of regimentation and schedules. In this respect, Guiding was part of what Veronica Strong-Boag calls the post-First World War "behaviouralist crusade" through which experts, educators, voluntary organizations, and the state publicized the importance of establishing regular habits in infancy in order to improve children's health and to create a generation of disciplined and self-regulating young citizens and workers.[26] Rhona Mason, for example, urged readers of the *Girl Guides' Gazette* to familiarize themselves with the work of Dr. Truby King, the New Zealand health reformer whose ideas about the importance of regular feeding, sleeping, and bowel movements were influential throughout the English-speaking world.[27] King's reform agenda, which led to significant decreases in infant mortality, was also motivated by a eugenic belief in the importance of motherhood for white racial health. Like Baden-Powell, King linked motherhood with national and imperial service; his motto was "Perfect motherhood is perfect patriotism." Like the Edwardian British reformers discussed by Anna Davin, he also emphatically denied the role of poverty and environment on infant health, declaring that lack of training for motherhood was "NOT a class question but a universal failing of civilized communities."[28]

The idea of "civilization," though not often discussed by advocates of scientific motherhood (who were more likely to refer to modernity and measurements), was nonetheless central to their prescriptions about parenting. Reflecting the ideals of factory production and military precision, Guide leaders across the world urged girls to learn the importance of regimentation for the sake of their future children.[29] Keeping infants on a strict schedule was often discussed as a matter of grave importance for individual lives as well as national and imperial communities, and one of Truby King's well-publicized beliefs was the notion that "lack of regularity in babyhood was ... responsible, not only for hysteria, epilepsy and imbecility, but also for other forms of degeneracy or conduct disorder in adults."[30]

Notions of time, promptness, and the importance of sticking to a schedule, of course, were not just applied to children in this period; they were also central to European colonizers' efforts to civilize and modernize non-white peoples of all ages. Although not discussed as such in any of the primary documents I consulted, training colonized children to follow Euro-Canadian concepts of time was a central goal of Canadian schooling for Indigenous children in the early twentieth century. Promptness and following schedules were seen by white educators and administrators as important tools in the assimilation project and were regarded as skills (reinforced through Guiding and Scouting) that would stand Indigenous girls and boys in good stead in their assumed future roles as domestic servants and manual labourers.[31]

These rigid concepts of disciplinary time were also, as Sumit Sarkar notes, imposed "particularly abrupt[ly]" in colonial South Asia.[32] Dipesh Chakrabarty's work on late nineteenth- and early twentieth-century Bengal argues that some nationalist reformers, most of whom were men, called on Indian women to "schedule and regulate all aspects of their children's lives." In this insistence on the importance of "proper" management of time by housewives and mothers, Chakrabarty writes, it is possible to find "the voice of the colonial modern looking to orient domesticity to the requirements of the civil-political."[33] In Indian Guiding, however, this stress on punctuality seems to have been emphasized most strongly by leaders whose groups comprised marginalized – as opposed to middle-class – girls. The February 1939 issue of the *Guider*, for example, featured an anonymous account of the activities of a Ranger group in Bombay Presidency whose members belonged to a caste and ethnic group identified as "criminal" by the Criminal Tribes Acts of the late nineteenth and early twentieth centuries.[34] The author of the article, who appears to have been the group's leader, wrote that she had begun their first meeting with a discussion of time, telling her girls: "Rangers are supposed to be responsible people who, if they say they will come at 6.30 will come at 6.30, instead of half an hour or three quarters of an hour late, like you are doing. Let's see if you can turn up punctually." As proof of the movement's power to create punctual and community-minded citizens, the author claimed that, at their next meeting, the girls all arrived on time and said that they wanted to buy oranges to take to patients at the Municipal Hospital. "Our experiences here with criminal tribes' girls," the article stated proudly, "proves that Guiding has a great deal to give for any girl, and is helping to turn these people from half-savage wanderers to respectable citizens, ready to take their part in the making of the New India."[35]

Guide publications often stressed the importance of scheduling and time management at meetings, camps, and in the home. Guides and Scouts across the globe were also encouraged to manage their bodies according to a strict schedule; Baden-Powell in particular often stressed the importance of using diet and exercise to ensure that young people's digestive systems functioned regularly.[36] The Chief Scout's belief in the importance of regimented elimination routines was supported during the interwar years by Guide leaders and by "scientific" health reformers. An article published in the *Guide* magazine (the movement's periodical aimed at girls) in November 1938, for example, stressed the importance of keeping young children's digestive systems running "like clockwork." Framed as advice for girls intent on earning the Child Nurse badge, the article began by stating that every child should be made to do some vigorous exercise before eating breakfast. "Five minutes after he has finished breakfast," the article continued,

> he should be sent to the bathroom. That rule ought be as infallible as the one which makes him brush his teeth *before* breakfast. Even if the visit seems to be a wasted one the routine should be kept up. In due course the visit will *not* be wasted: the habit will become as regular as clockwork, and there will be no difficulties or impediments later on in the day when he is at school. If a second visit can be arranged after lunch, too, then let that habit become as regular as the morning one.[37]

Strong-Boag analyzes this adult desire to establish clockwork-like "elimination routines" in modern infants, and she notes that bowel movements were "a potential battleground between mother and child."[38] Many of the Australian mothers studied by Mein Smith were quick to admit defeat in this particular battle, writing, for example: "my baby had no time for Truby King whatsoever."[39] At this point, I think it is worth remembering that, despite the efforts of the movement's adult leaders, it is impossible to know (though tempting to speculate about) how much or how little time most individual Girl Guides had for the Child Nurse badge or for Truby King and the regimented style of child care he represented.

In India, the Child Nurse test and other related badges were complicated by child marriage. This practice, which, along with female infanticide and sati, had a long history of use by the British as "proof" of India's lack of civilization, became the subject of a global controversy after the 1927 publication of *Mother India*, the sensational anti-nationalist text in which American writer Katherine Mayo uses child marriage and child-motherhood to argue against India's fitness for self-government.[40] The furor caused by Mayo's text was intense and multifaceted. On the one hand, it was used by Indian feminists to make claims against both the imperial state and the nationalist movement while arguing for legislation increasing the age at which girls could be married. But, as Antoinette Burton's work on barrister and social reformer Cornelia Sorabji shows, some Indian women remained loyal to Britain and "openly shared" Mayo's beliefs about child marriage as an indicator of Indian "degradation."[41] Sorabji's sister Susie Sorabji also opposed Gandhian nationalism and remained loyal to Britain; she cultivated links with the Canadian Imperial Order Daughters of the Empire and ran a co-educational and integrated school in Pune, where she was active in the Girl Guides and Junior Red Cross.[42]

The desire to raise the legal age of marriage for girls united groups of Indian women from a range of religious and ideological positions, and was characterized by a coordinated campaign undertaken by several organizations, including the All-India Women's Conference, the Women's Indian Association, and the National Council of Women in India. Largely as a result of their efforts, the Child Marriage Restraint Act (also known as the Sarda Act) was passed on 28 September 1929 by the British Indian Government. The act raised the age of marriage for girls to fourteen years, but the colonial government did little to enforce it, and very few men were prosecuted.[43]

The complicated and complicating factor of child marriage is, perhaps predictably, discussed in relatively few Western-produced Guide texts. When mentioned, it was generally as a reason to enrol girls in Guiding and as a justification for testing Indian Guides for certain badges at an earlier age. The section on Kashmir in the movement's 1927 Annual Report, for example, noted: "unhappily, the early marriage of girls in Kashmir makes it impossible to keep the older girls in the company; they all leave us between the ages of 12 and 13, and a great many marry even earlier than that."[44] The report on India prepared for the 8th World Guide Conference by a Muslim Guide leader named Iqbalunnisa Hussain, which was published in the *Council Fire* in October 1934, also contained similar statements about child marriage and Guiding. Writing some six years after the passage of the symbolic but largely ineffectual Sarda Act, Hussain commented:

> Bluebird work is only the beginning, and we hope many of the children will pass on to be Guides. But in India, due to early marriage and connected other customs, all will never have that privilege, so while we can let us train the Indian child (who will so soon have the responsibility of wifehood and motherhood thrust upon her) in character and intelligence, skill and handicraft, physical health and development, and service for others.

Some Second Class Guides, she noted, took the Child Nurse test instead of the Morse Code test – a substitution that she insisted was "most important, as the legal marriage age [was] still only fourteen, and infant mortality terribly high. The fact that girls who bec[a]me Guides [were] taught to look after a child appeal[ed] very much to the mothers."[45]

Interwar Guide periodicals also featured numerous other articles describing how to teach girls the maternal skills they would need to pass the Child Nurse test and to be effective mothers later in life. English Guide leader Elsie Meredith, captain of the 3rd Bideford Company in Devon, wrote to the *Girl Guides' Gazette* in November 1926 that her company used a doll named Mary to prepare for the test by teaching girls about the care and feeding of infants. "Her food is inexpensive," she wrote, "pictures of jellies, spongecakes, oranges, custards are easily cut from advertisements; butter, loaves and fruit can be modeled in clay, and most of us can draw and paint some part of her diet ... Meals have been planned and laid, with a clean cloth, on a chair; while an assortment of eatables makes a fine trayful for Kim's game."[46] Meredith's reference to "Kim's game," a memory game based on Rudyard Kipling's 1901 novel of the same name, also demonstrates the continued influence of the imperial mythology of Victorian and Edwardian fiction.[47] At the same time, her account of using "Mary" to teach child nursing skills raises a number of important but likely unanswerable questions. How often did the 3rd Bideford Guides dress and "feed" their doll? Did training for motherhood play a major or a marginal role in their weekly Guide meetings? What did the girls themselves think about this part of the movement?

Guide publications regularly recommended the use of games and contests to train girls in the "science" of child-rearing. In October 1923, for instance, the *Girl Guides' Gazette* encouraged leaders to take advantage of Brownies' "strong maternal instinct[s]" by playing a baby-carrying game at weekly meetings. The author suggested that each Brownie should bring a baby doll, wrap it in a coat, and "walk along a chalked line, carrying the baby on the left arm in the usual way, and then ... sit down on a chair and transfer the baby to the lap without jerking it." The accompanying explanation of the game also shows that baby-carrying, like many other aspects of Guiding's maternal training scheme, was meant to teach girls appropriate feminine behaviour as well as practical skills: "for practice in quietness and self-control such a game could hardly be bettered, though doubtless it could not be played for very long."[48]

Guide leaders and authors also sought to make the movement's maternal training activities accessible to disabled girls by altering and adapting related tests and practice exercises. Margaret Russell's *The Mauve Games Book for Cripple, Hospital, Blind, Deaf and Post Guide Companies* (published in London by the British Guide Association), for example, suggested a "child nurse game" that, unlike the aforementioned Brownie baby-carrying game, did not require participants to walk, balance, or carry small objects. This adapted game did not, however, alter or lessen its emphasis on rigid scheduling and clear right and wrong answers. The game, Russell wrote, should be acted out like a play:

> One Patrol acts a day in the life of a baby (say 3 years old), taking the parts of nurse, mother, baby, aunt, brother, sister, etc., and dressing up if possible. They announce what time it is when baby gets up, has its meals, rest (chalking the face of a clock on a blackboard if this can be arranged), and what they give it to eat. The rest of the Company criticize and make a list of any mistakes that are made.[49]

Criticizing and listing mistakes, while obviously seen as important pedagogical tools, were not the only method Guiding used to teach modern girls about child care. Local and national Guide councils and other businesses and community groups also tried to encourage the development of girls' maternal "instincts" and skills through organized competitions. In 1938, for example, the *Winnipeg Tribune* sponsored a baby clothes-making competition for local Ranger companies.[50] Guide companies from across Canada also regularly participated in "home nursing" competitions – contests that combined maternal and domestic skills with first aid and nursing with the aim of training girls to be useful as mothers, wives, citizens, and paid workers. These competitions were open to groups based in churches and synagogues, neighbourhood halls, as well as public schools and Indigenous residential schools, and their results sometimes worked to undermine dominant ideas about racial hierarchies and "advancement." The "Overseas Dominions" section of the 1928 British Guide Association annual report, for instance, stated that a "North American Indian" company from the Blood Reserve in southern Alberta won that year's province-wide home nursing championship.[51] This victory is especially significant when considered alongside Kristin Burnett's work on the importance of Indigenous women's healing work in Native-newcomer relations on the Blood Reserve and other communities in western Canada.[52]

The pride and excitement that such an achievement could elicit are also evident in a report from the early 1920s in which Sidney Rogers, principal of the Mohawk Institute Residential School in Brantford, Ontario, described the activities of that institution's Guide company. In January 1924, he wrote, a group of Guides from the Institute

> went in sleighs to the Armouries to practice for the Brantford Parade at which they were inspected by the Lieutenant Governor. This parade was on the 26th January and our troop was splendid ... our girls secured the First Prize for their

display of needle-work and second prize for first aid work. The drill display by our troop was second to none.[53]

The military nature of education at the Mohawk Institute (which included regular drill practice for all male and female students) meant that these girls would have been familiar with marching in formation before even joining the Guides. As Alison Norman points out, girls at the institute also made uniforms for the school's pupils and practised embroidery with the principal's wife and other non-Indigenous teachers. Sewing and embroidery were important skills in Mohawk culture as well, and girls from the institute had been winning prizes for their sewing, embroidery, and crochet work at the local Six Nations Agricultural Fair since the late nineteenth century.[54]

It is difficult to discern what groups of girls in different contexts thought of the movement's attempts to equip them with domestic and maternal skills. Some glimpses, however, of girls' ambivalent responses to maternal training exist in published discussions of child care competitions. Starting in 1918, Britain's National Baby Week Council cooperated with the Girl Guides to sponsor an annual essay contest for Guides, Rangers, and Guide Leaders.[55] Norah March, BSc., secretary of Britain's National Baby Week Council, explained the purpose of these contests in a 1923 issue of the *Girl Guides' Gazette*: "We must bear in mind that untold harm may often result to a baby through wrong management. Many grown-up people suffering from weakness of body and of mind, are experiencing the results of want of knowledge on the part of their mothers."[56] Explanations of the contest's rules and purpose often used scientific (and sometimes Darwinian) language, and topics included: "How I would train a child to become a good and healthy citizen," "How Nature Takes Care of Young Things," "The Care of Young Life," "Dangers which may Assail a Little Baby and How I Will Guard Against Them," "How a Parent (Plant or Animal) Takes Care of Its Young," and "'The Survival of the Fittest in Nature,' as shown by a study of plants or animals, and what thoughts this gives on human life."[57]

Regrettably, though perhaps not surprisingly, no copies of contestants' responses to these ideologically loaded essay topics seem to have been preserved in public or private archival collections. But the winners of the National Baby Week Guide essay contests were announced annually in the *Girl Guides' Gazette*, and these announcements show not only that most girls and young women chose not to enter these competitions, but also that many of those who did join wrote answers that did not satisfy the contest's adult judges. The judges of the 1922 contest seem to have been particularly disappointed in the quantity and quality of that year's responses. They noted in the *Gazette* that there had "not [been] many entries" that year and that, of the essays by Rangers and Cadets on nature study and child nursing, "very few ... showed a good or wise grasp of the principle." "Only in the case of the winning essay," the judges lamented, "was a good standard of work reached: in the remainder of the essays the standard was not very high."[58] Writing "scientific" papers about heredity and child health, an exercise that was meant to bolster and demonstrate girls' maternal skills, appears not to have appealed to many members of the movement.

It is, of course, frustratingly difficult to find much evidence regarding what the movement's young members actually thought about this part of Guide training. Did interwar Girl Guides, like their Edwardian predecessors, prefer more "adventurous" activities to "home training"? Many girls and young women seemed to especially enjoy escaping conventionally feminine identities and roles at camp. British Guide Eileen Knapman's description of her company's maternal training activities indicates that many girls were more ambivalent than enthusiastic about babysitting and infant care training programs.[59] Knapman, who chronicled the activities of her south London Guide group between 1928 and 1930, described being tested for the Child Nurse badge in a way that clearly reveals her understanding and humorous critique of the measurements and strictures of "scientific" child care. On 23 January 1928, she wrote:

> Two Swallows trotted down to Tennyson Street, in the pouring rain, with drooping hat brims, and hearts in their boots, to enter for the "Child Nurse" Badge. There were heated arguments on the way, as to whether one puts a baby into a bath head or feet first, and whether a boy of one year, five months should be allowed to use a carving knife or a garden fork to eat his dinner.

The girls' "arguments were quite unnecessary," Knapman reported, "as the exam was a written one, and (presumably) easy, as both of them passed!"[60]

Training for Domesticity

While assuring modern girls of their importance as future mothers, Guide leaders in interwar Canada, India, and England consistently promoted domesticity as a non-negotiable part of girls' character training. The movement's emphasis on "home-keeping," like its training for motherhood, combined older concerns and ideals with a newer insistence on the importance of modern and scientific techniques.

Unlike much nineteenth- and early twentieth-century prescriptive literature, Guide texts from the interwar years make relatively few comparisons between "civilized" and "primitive" homes and domestic practices in different parts of the world. Instead, most official writing on the subject from the 1920s and 1930s represents "home-keeping" as a common duty of girls and women across the globe – a way to make connections and emphasize similarities based on the performance of useful gendered labour. An essay entitled "The Homemakers" published in *The Guiding Book*, a British edited collection "sold for the benefit of the Girl Guides Association and for the Extension of the Movement Throughout the World," provides especially clear proof of this official desire to emphasize similarity instead of difference. "The essential features of home-making," the author claimed, "are the same in Australia as in Canada, in South Africa as in Newfoundland. The Dominions and the Colonies differ from the Motherland in methods but not in interpretation of 'Home, Sweet Home.'"[61]

While placing Guiding's domestic training program within an explicitly imperial frame (a small frame, however, that did not include much room for cultural variation), the essay also describes its importance with a combination of references to twentieth-century life and Victorian ideals. After cataloguing a range of "modern" advancements, including electricity, airplanes, steamships, motor-cars, moving pictures, and gramophones, the essay notes that "girlhood's horizon is far more wide than in earlier days." And yet, like many other interwar Guide leaders, the author still insisted that "women will ever be the homemakers of the world."[62] The essay concludes with a quotation from *Sesame and Lillies*, English author and art critic John Ruskin's 1865 treatise on the contrasting natures and duties of men and women: "the man's work for his own home is to secure its maintenance, progress, and defence; the woman's to secure its order, comfort, and loveliness."[63]

This use of Ruskin's nineteenth-century ideas about gender difference, separate spheres, and the importance of feminine domesticity provides further proof of the conservative nature of interwar Guiding's "modern" ideals, and similar references to the importance of domestic duties appear in other Guide texts published during and after the First World War. Olave Baden-Powell's *Training Girls as Guides*, for example, explained Guiding as a way to re-establish "traditional" links between girls and the private sphere. "Times have changed," she wrote, "and nature with it, and the Guide clubroom with its wholesome activities is the one means which will bring the girls back to their rightful sphere."[64] By teaching modern girls and young women "how to help themselves and others, especially in the matter of cooking and cleaning, sewing etc," Olave claimed (in tones not dissimilar to the ones used by her older sister-in-law

Agnes) that the movement would bring them "back into" their homes – an increasingly difficult task in a world being changed by mass media, expanding educational opportunities, and youth culture.[65]

While not all official texts placed such heavy-handed stress on the movement's reputed ability to return girls to the private sphere, interwar Guide leaders and authors in a range of contexts did express the assumption that "home-keeping" was a naturally feminine pursuit for which modern girls needed to be trained. In February 1921, for instance, Canadian Guide Captain Winifred V. Head told the *Toronto Star Weekly* that "one of the most beautiful things about guide work is that it gives the halo of romance to every-day tasks, laundering of a blouse, cooking a meal, making a fire, romance for which the soul of the child craves."[66] In the official Guide handbook, Baden-Powell wrote that "every Guide is as much a 'hussif' as she is a girl. She is sure to have to 'keep house' some day, and whatever house she finds herself in, it is certain that that place is the better for her being there."[67]

"Usefulness" was a key concept in all aspects of Guide training, as leaders explained the movement as an antidote to the rise of frivolous consumer culture and apparently selfish modern girls. In British Guide texts from the early 1920s, it was also represented as a way to reform white working-class wives, mothers, and daughters. These texts represented skilled domestic management as a feminine duty and argued that its neglect would result in a range of social ills. It is not difficult to discern the influence of Samuel Smiles's Victorian tracts on this type of Guide writing, for, as Dyhouse notes, his globally influential writings on self-help were "replete with clichés and anecdotes about labouring men driven to the pub by wives who couldn't cook or have the evening meal ready by a welcoming fire when their husbands returned from work."[68]

Training Girls as Guides includes one such anecdote: a story about a labourer who, following his daily visit to the pub, lurched drunkenly into the street and was hit by a truck. Miraculously, the man survived his injuries (though the text neglects to mention whether or not it was a Girl Guide who rescued him), and when his wife arrived at the hospital, she explained the situation by saying: "I didn't cook his dinner right. He complained that the house was dirty. But what could I do? I married when I was only eighteen, and I didn't know how to cook or manage the house. And then he began taking leave of an evening, and used to go round to the public-house and take too much."[69] Economic instability, the lure of male companionship, and the trauma of the Great War were of course not mentioned as possible reasons for this particular working-class husband's descent into drink; it was his wife's lack of domestic training that was to blame

– a situation that could easily have been avoided, the text implied, with the help of the Girl Guides.

A similar narrative about the importance of domestic training for working-class British girls was published in the *Girl Guides' Gazette* in January 1921. In this piece, a Guide leader named Mrs. Fryer described her experience running a factory company for female munitions workers in the Midlands during the First World War. "I always took the Home badges with the Company," she wrote, "as the girls were hopelessly ignorant on anything to do with the home." Fryer supported this point by describing a young munitions worker who had explained her apparent inability to light a fire by saying:

> "As soon as I left school I went into a soap factory, and Mother said it was less trouble to do the jobs herself than to teach me." I asked her what sort of home she was going to have when she married one of her boys (she probably had seven or eight in different parts of the country). "Oh!" she said, "I suppose I'll pick it up somehow." Surely we must step in and start Guides for these girls, they are willing to learn if only we will teach them in the right way and not let them think that we are "trying to make them good."[70]

This last sentence, further proof of the movement's emphasis on "right" and "wrong" approaches to leisure and homekeeping, also hints at the class and generational conflicts that Guiding's domestic training scheme must sometimes have caused but that were seldom in mentioned in official sources.

British Guiding in particular must be understood as a response to working-class women's perceived flight from domestic service work during and after the Great War.[71] While domestic service actually remained the largest employer of women in England until the 1940s, the interwar "servant problem" (like the not unrelated contemporary moral panic about white infant mortality) was also a reflection of anxieties about gender, class, and generation. Many older middle-class and elite women – including Olave Baden-Powell, whose diaries contain a number of prejudiced and frustrated references to her household's rotating cast of servants – believed that domestic service work was the best job for young working-class women because of the moral and physical surveillance it provided, its emphasis on class- and gender-based deference, and its presumed relevance to girls' future roles as wives, mothers, and managers of their own homes.[72] Olave Baden-Powell discussed Guiding as a beneficial activity for future domestic servants in *Training Girls as Guides*. "It is surely as fine a thing," she wrote, "to be a good servant as it is to be a good master, and in order that one may serve one must be fitted for such service in knowledge and capabilities."[73] This sentence, which I suspect would not have appealed to the adolescent members of Mrs. Fryer's Midlands factory company, also illustrates Guiding's support of the class-based hierarchies that continued to divide British society.

But as promoted across the world, Guide domestic training was about more than class and domestic service. Unlike the movement's maternal training, which sought to prepare girls for a feminine duty it was assumed they would fulfill at some point in the future, homekeeping could be practised right away, even by the movement's youngest members. The name and organization of the Brownies makes this especially clear. Simply put, "Brownies" are figures from English folklore – good fairies who appear at night and clean domestic spaces while human beings are asleep. Baden-Powell explained the link between these figures and his ideal of girlhood in the Guide handbook, telling readers in a section on Brownies:

> You are a strong and active little girl. You could sweep the floor; you are clever enough to lay a fire and light it; you could fill the kettle and put it on to a boil; you could tidy up the room and lay the breakfast things; you could make your bed and clean your boots and fold up your clothes. You could do all these things before any one else was up, so that when father and mother came down they would think that the fairies had been at work in the house.[74]

This passage provides a clear explanation of the gendered meanings of this kind of unpaid work: girls in particular had a duty to perform household labour and to do so in a quiet and unobtrusive way without asking for recognition.

This gendered labour was also affective work, important because it would ensure the happiness of future husbands and children. As the Chief Scout wrote in 1933, "the technical knowledge of homekeeping and mothercraft ... [is] invaluable not only for the bringing up of healthy children, but also for keeping the menkind strong and contented."[75] The ways in which this emphasis on cheerful domesticity reinforced Victorian and Edwardian conceptions of self-less femininity becomes yet more apparent when one considers the name that Baden-Powell chose for the equivalent junior wing of the Boy Scouts: Cubs, a noun that, instead of modest home-based toil, suggests images of young animals playing roughly together, without duties or responsibility.

A.M. Maynard's 1935 book, *An A.B.C. of Guiding*, which asserted the importance of appealing to girls' maternal instincts, also explained the movement's domestic training with references to instinctual behaviour. Like Stanley

Hall and other contemporary educators, medical experts, and youth workers, Maynard believed that domesticity was central to girls' psychological development. Calling "the urge for possession and home-making" one of the "strongest instincts in girlhood," Maynard argued (in a section entitled "B for Bed-Making") that Guide training would seize and nurture girls' "natural" home-making inclinations. Guide training in domesticity, she believed, made each girl *useful*. In her desire to pass her tests she asks to be allowed to make beds, lay and light the fires, cook milk puddings, etc. Her home is full of new interests."[76]

Domestic training for Brownies, Guides, and Rangers also emphasized the importance of science and "modern methods." Influenced by the new science of home economics, interwar Guide texts represented housekeeping as a "skilled profession" for which all girls needed to be trained. On top of the practical training offered by badge work and group activities, girls and young women were also encouraged to educate themselves by reading expert advice about domestic work. Guide periodicals often featured lists of recommended reading and generally placed suggested books about motherhood and domesticity together. Books recommended by the *Girl Guides' Gazette* included *The Care and Nursing of Babies and Children* by L. Haden Guest; *Lessons on the Care of Infants*; *The Hygiene of Food and Drink* issued by the Board of Education; and *Home Nursing* by Isobel Macdonald.[77]

Badges and other formal requirements were also used to promote the movement's "modern" skilled domestic ideal. Brownies, for instance, had to promise to "help other people every day, especially those at home."[78] They were also required to prove that they had done good turns at home, to be able to tie the tie on their uniform and plait their own hair, and to show that they knew how to "wash up the tea things."[79] Becoming "Second Class" Brownies required further demonstrations of domestic labour, including "mak[ing] something useful, showing the hemming stitch"; "darn[ing] an article or do[ing] the darning stitch"; and "lay[ing] a table for two for dinner."[80] To achieve this rank girls also had to throw a ball, keep their fingernails and teeth clean, observe nature, tie knots, and name the parts of the Union Jack. For "First Class" status, Brownies had to "clean forks and spoons"; "knit a child's scarf or jumper, or some other garment"; "lay and light a fire; make tea and a milk pudding"; "fold clothes neatly ... and clean [a pair of] shoes."[81] The domestic imperative was also promoted in Guiding, with the only three mandatory badges for all members being Child Nurse, Needlewoman, and Cook. Other related and apparently popular badges included Laundress and Domestic Service.[82]

Guide officials took steps to adapt relevant tests and activities so that all girls, regardless of location or (dis)ability, could benefit from the movement's training in domesticity. The second revised edition of Vera Cleeve and Joan Fryer's *Extension Book* (published by the British Girl Guides Association in 1936) suggests several different ways to ensure that "hospital" and "crippled" Brownies could learn the "correct" way to "wash up the tea things."

> If the Brownie is unable to handle full-sized cups and plates, dolls tea things can be used. When washing up is not possible, i.e. in a hospital, a mop for washing up can be made instead; the mop can be made of "cotton" thread (used for knitting swabs) made like a woolly ball and fastened to the top of a stick (a bamboo is the best as the string can go up the centre to fix the mop at the top.)[83]

A different official text, the *Mauve Games Book for Cripple, Hospital, Blind, Deaf and Post Guide Companies*, suggested the following method for teaching Cook's badge skills to Post Guides living in isolated communities: "Each Leader is sent the same list of stores. She then decides on the Menu and gives a dish or part of a dish to each Guide. They describe fully how they would cook the dish given them. The Captain marks the Menu and cooking, and criticizes the dinner in the next lecture."[84] Did any Post or Extension Guides follow these detailed published instructions? While it is worth stopping to imagine how individual girls and young women in Canada, India, and England may or may not have planned menus through the post or washed a set of doll's dishes, it is also important to note that the fact that many disabled girls living in institutions would likely never actually have to perform these tasks was not seen to matter.

While badges such as Cook and Laundress received less attention in Guide texts than did the Child Nurse badge, Guide magazines and books from the interwar years still included a number of articles on cooking and entertaining. The 1923 *Collins' Girl Guides Annual,* for example, included an essay entitled "Notes on Table Laying" by Mary MacKirdy, a prolific cookbook author and instructor at the Glasgow School of Domestic Science. Set alongside chapters on "Lifesaving Drills" and "Route-Finding among Mountain Tops," MacKirdy's piece gave detailed instructions about how to arrange decorations, linens, cutlery, and dishes for morning tea, a breakfast table, lunch, tea tables, a four-course dinner, a party buffet table, tea tables, and supper or high tea.[85] These instructions, like so much of Guiding's domestic training program, were quite culturally and class-specific, with no space for caste-based food strictures, meals eaten without cutlery, or working-class families' experiences of hunger during the economic contractions of the 1920s and 1930s.

In an age of mass-produced clothing and household goods and global economic uncertainty, these texts also encouraged girls and young women to learn the conventionally feminine domestic skills of sewing, knitting, and embroidery. In February 1939, for instance, the *Guide* magazine featured an article entitled "Only Two Stitches" that promised readers "an Easy-To-Work Design [they] will be able to use in all sorts of ways." Featuring an embroidery pattern depicting intertwined flowers and leaves, the article suggested that Guides use the pattern to "improve" their "tablecloths, tray-cloths, serviettes ... cushions, aprons, tea-cosies, work-bags, [and] table-mats."[86] Embroidering this pattern on a range of household goods, the article further suggested, would also provide valuable practice time for Guides who hoped to earn the Needlework badge. The article also implied that this was feminine work, a wholesome and home-based activity that could (and ideally would) encourage thrift and replace commercialized leisure in the lives of many girls and young women. Official Guide needlework patterns and requirements, like the movement's pronouncements on entertaining and table settings, were also quite culturally specific: the ways in which Gandhi had reinterpreted traditional domestic activities as acts of anti-colonial resistance, for example, were never discussed (or likely even thought of) in the movement's mostly metropolitan prescriptive literature.[87]

This cultural specificity also defines the many domestic skill-building games that were recommended in Guide literature. A 1923 book entitled *Team Games for Girl Guides*, for example, includes instructions for a "Domestic Service Game," in which Guides had to race to match dirty household surfaces with their appropriate cleaning products.[88] "Homekeeping" games are also featured in Vivien Rhys Davids's popular book *Brownie Games* (first published in 1925, it was revised in 1926 and had been reprinted five times by 1931). Examples included "The Dinner Bell," a game about the proper placement of cutlery, and "Prettiest Table for Party," an activity in which groups of girls competed to produce the most attractive table setting.[89]

Once again, I can only speculate about how (or if) these games and activities were used by Guide groups in different settings. Did many (any?) groups actually play them? And how did the movement's young members respond? Some domestic training activities are discussed and represented in the logbooks and photograph albums of Guides and Guide leaders. Winnipeg Guide Winnifred Thompson's logbook from the late 1920s, for example, describes girls being tested for and receiving their Laundress and Domestic Service badges, but it spends much more time describing things like food, outdoor games, and hikes.[90] London Guide Eileen Knapman's logbook from the same

time period describes doing laundress and cook demonstrations at a joint
Scout-Guide display in December 1929. At this public entertainment, she wrote,
the Brownies and Guides demonstrated life in camp, sang, did Scandinavian
dances, and competed against some Boy Scouts in team games. The display
also featured demonstrations of the "useful" skills the girls had learned in
pursuit of their Child Nurse, Laundress, and Cook badges:

> For Child Nurse, Cath and Vera bathed a doll (purloined from Cathie's small
> sister!) & put it to bed. (P.L. & the Brownies helped, by taking it for walks!)
> (Will P.L. NEVER grow up?!!!!) For Laundress, our clothes-line was fastened
> to two chairs, & it kept collapsing, so we had to employ two Brownies, to sit on
> the chairs. It amused the audience, even if it did rather try our patience. In
> Cook's Titch and Nick astounded the audience by producing a plum pudding
> in the lightning space of 3 minutes. (It was only Vera's football covered with
> inky paper, & a piece of holly! But it looked most realistic). Nick broke a basin.
> (She would!)[91]

The diary kept by Monica Storrs, a British Anglican missionary who started
Guide and Scout groups in northern British Columbia in the late 1920s, also
describes her attempts to teach domestic skills to girls whose "racial" backgrounds she described as including Danish, "Italian (Roman Catholic),"
American, French-Canadian, "halfbreed," English, German-Italian, "three-
quarters Indian," and "real Scotch."[92] One evening in March 1930, Storrs
commented that her Guides

> practiced bed-making; and Mrs. Millar's spare bed where I sleep every Saturday
> night was stripped and made up nearly a dozen times and I am sure more care-
> fully than ever before. We had a few serious differences of opinion, the two
> principal ones being:
>
> 1. Whether the pillows should go outside or underneath the counterpane.
>   They all held to the former as more pretty. But I got my way in the end
>   — at least, in theory.
> 2. How often you should strip. The general opinion was, that to do it every
>   day, as sometimes in England, is morbid if not hysterical. Here we arrived
>   at a compromise of *at least* twice a week![93]

Storrs's emphasis on teaching "proper" bed-making skills, when considered
alongside her attempts to categorize the ethnically heterogeneous group of

children who joined Scouting and Guiding, may be read as an attempt to use domestic and cleaning rituals to promote "superior" British lifeways in a settler society inhabited by Indigenous, mixed-race, and non-British peoples.[94] Her Guides' insistence that such time-consuming labour was "morbid if not hysterical," meanwhile, provides evidence that these metropolitan ideals were contested and sometimes, in fact, rejected.

I have been unable to find similar written accounts of Guide domestic training in late colonial India. I have, however, found photographs of Guides and Rangers cooking, sewing, and performing other types of domestic labour. A number of these images are pasted on the pages of an album depicting Guide companies in Bangalore between 1932 and 1934, presented to British Division Commissioner Miss Watson and kept in the Girl Guiding UK Archives in London. In a photograph with the caption "Domestic Service," members of the No. 7 Church of England Zenana Mission Company shows eight Indian Guides sitting on the grass, washing pots, pans, and dishes. Other photographs show sari-clad Guides and Bluebirds from the 9th and Goodwill Girls' High School doing "Cooks' Badge Work" with various sizes of pots; still others show Guides working on their "Needlewoman's & Knitter's Badges" in the outdoors.[95]

Guiding Husbands, or Training for Matrimony

Guiding's emphasis on preparing all girls and young women to be good homekeepers and mothers rested on one final assumption: that its members would ultimately end up in companionate, consensual, monogamous heterosexual marriages. This type of union, based on Christian doctrine and English common law, was often held up during the nineteenth and early twentieth centuries as proof of white, Anglo-Saxon racial and cultural superiority. There is an extensive body of scholarship on the imperial, national, and racial dimensions of the history of marriage, in which scholars demonstrate the centrality of the institution to empire- and nation-building projects and to efforts to create and maintain boundaries between "races."[96] Guide discussions of girls' assumed future marriages, like its training for motherhood and domesticity, reflected little of this concern with boundaries and difference. Rather, they simply assumed that all members of the movement aspired to the same ideal: a combination of Victorian notions of domestic piety with more "modern" discussions of marriage as a "career" and a companionate partnership. The very different social, cultural, and religious contexts in which many of the movement's million-and-a-half members lived their lives are, once again, conspicuously absent from most of the movement's published pronouncements on the subject.

Officially, then, Guiding attempted to train girls and young women for marriage while encouraging them to follow the parallel but often conflicting tracks of domestic maternity and career-oriented citizenship. At the Ninth World Conference in Stockholm (held in 1936), delegates listened to a speech by Miss Margrethe Parm, a Norwegian Guider who was active in both the World YWCA and World Association of Girl Guides and Girl Scouts, entitled "What Ideals of Womanhood Shall We Give Our Girls?" Life remained simple for modern men, Parm claimed, in whose career-focused lives marriage was only "an incident." In educating modern girls, however, Guide leaders faced the difficult task of "mak[ing] them run along two tracks." Young women in the twentieth century, Parm argued,

> have to compete with men in the struggle for existence; they must have the same vocational training, they must fight their way, as a man does, so as to be self-supporting. They must be trained as men are trained, but at the same time they must be trained as women, because they may marry, and we want them to be the best mothers and wives and comrades to their husbands. This was the only life for women a hundred years ago, but to-day they have to be prepared for both these possible lives.[97]

Due at least partly to the growing influence of psychological and sexological experts, companionate marriage was widely discussed during the interwar years as the only acceptable life path for modern women. As Cynthia Comacchio argues in the Canadian context, female sexuality after the First World War "was still carefully regulated within heterosexual relations sanctified by marriage; it was still grounded in residual Victorian notions about superior feminine self-control, hence feminine virtue and deportment. Above all, it was still oriented towards motherhood."[98] Penny Tinkler's work on girls' magazines in England between 1920 and 1950 similarly demonstrates that "a heterosexual identity expressed through monogamous marriage remained central to perceptions of mature womanhood; adjustment to heterosexuality was widely seen as essential to the formation of an adult woman's identity and the successful fulfillment of her 'natural' roles as wife and mother."[99] As Judith Walsh notes, some male social reformers promoted companionate marriage in late nineteenth-century India; this ideal was also espoused in the interwar years by many of the middle-class members of the All-India Women's Conference.[100] The January–February 1935 issue of the *Indian Ladies' Magazine*, for example, promoted companionate relations between the sexes by recommending Winifred Holtby's 1934 study of the British women's movement

Woman and a Changing Civilization as a text that "exposes many of the pretenses, which block the progress of women, who should always be *equal partner* with man in everything."[101]

Unlike the maternal and domestic aspects of Guide training, matrimony was not the subject of detailed discussions, activities, or badge tests during the interwar years. The relative absence of detailed discussions of the skills required for success in marriage also likely reflected a belief that all aspects of Guiding's training program would work together to create the ideal modern wife – a good racial mother, an efficient homekeeper, and an informed and responsible global, imperial, and national citizen.

Marriage was sometimes discussed in very general terms, however, by the Baden-Powells and other Guide leaders. Training girls for their assumed futures as useful, helpful, and companionate wives remained central to Baden-Powell's idea of the movement from its inception until his death in 1941. Morality, domesticity, unselfishness, and feminine "guiding" or influence, qualities that had been encouraged in mothers, sisters, and wives since at least the mid-nineteenth century, were lauded by the Chief Scout in 1919 at a post–Great War victory rally for children held at the Albert Hall in London. After noting the growth of Guiding in "all parts of our Empire and in most of the civilized countries of the world," he sought to explain the importance of the movement with a statement that would not have been out of place in his sister Agnes's Victorian girlhood. "A Brownie in her own home, doing her little daily good turn," he claimed, "is setting an example which may convert many a selfish grown-up man."[102]

Many of Baden-Powell's published writings also contain passages that emphasize the importance of training girls for their moral duties as wives. A wife, the Chief Scout contended in *Girl Guiding*, "can be the making or the marring of the man. She can be his true GUIDE." He further claimed that "if a man is well-married, that is if he has a clean bright home, with a cheery understanding wife (especially if she's a good cook) and jolly healthy children it means ruin – to the club and public-house." "But to be such a comrade," Baden-Powell insisted, "a girl must have known work herself. She must have gone through the struggle against failure and have enjoyed the triumphs of success to be able fully to sympathize with her partner in his troubles and to be of use in helping him through them."[103] Professional success, he asserted,

is neither the end and aim nor the greatest joy of the girl's life. She has still before her her reward, all the sweeter when it has been won by hard work, the glorious reward of having a home of her own, the shrine of her life, a man after her own heart to share it as her pal and protector (for however independent and self-reliant she may have felt in her time there comes a joy in snuggling down under the care of a strong loving arm).[104]

The Chief Scout struck a similar note in a report on the future of Guiding published in the British Guide Association's 1933 Annual Report:

> The technical knowledge of homekeeping and mothercraft will, for instance, continue to be of paramount importance in a woman's life, the practice of economy, skill in cooking and nursing, all are invaluable not only for the bringing up of healthy children, but also for keeping the menkind strong and contented. This is all a direct contribution to the welfare of the country.[105]

Olave Baden-Powell clearly felt that she had found an ideal companionate "pal and protector" in the Chief Scout. In *Training Girls as Guides*, published when the Baden-Powells had been married for less than a decade, she expressed a series of beliefs about feminine influence and marriage that were remarkably similar to the views held by her husband. "The little girl at home," she wrote, "influences her brothers and sisters, and to a certain extent her father also." The broader social importance of this gendered moral influence only increased with time, as each young woman was sure to influence "for good or for evil the young man who crosse[d] her path."[106] Like many of her contemporaries, Olave Baden-Powell represented companionate heterosexual marriage as the ideal to which all Guides should aspire: "The young wife, as she rules her home, influences her man and can make or mar his career, his work and his whole life."[107]

The Baden-Powells' marriage, as Proctor shows, was held up as a gendered ideal for Scouts and Guides to emulate in their own adult lives.[108] Olave Baden-Powell's diary also provides ample proof of the relish with which she played her wifely role. "Making" her husband's career while promoting her own seems to have been her primary concern during the interwar years as she travelled with him, nursed him through illnesses, and made afternoon and evening visits with him to the cinema. Motherhood, on the other hand, appears to have played a far smaller role in the Chief Guide's sense of self: she disliked breastfeeding, was ambivalent about their three children (especially her son Peter, who had rickets and was often discussed as a "disappointment"), and spent months every year travelling with her husband.

Pronouncements about the importance of wifely influence were also expressed in the Canadian context during the 1920s and 1930s. As with the movement's promotion of motherhood and domesticity, this discourse valorized an

Anglo-Protestant ideal without discussing immigrant, French Catholic, or Indigenous marriages. Delegates at the 1925 annual meeting of the Canadian Council of the Girl Guides Association in Toronto, for example, listened to a keynote speech in which Dr. Bruce MacDonald, principal of St. Andrew's College (a private boys' school north of Toronto), praised the movement for its role in creating morally influential though largely passive future wives. Lauding the "tremendous influence" of women and girls "on the thoughts and actions of the mere male," MacDonald proclaimed that "womanly counsel, womanly chiding, womanly encouragement, womanly guidance provide much more frequently than we imagine that subtle atmosphere of the man's life, which has so much to do with the character of his performances and of his attitude towards responsibility." Building on the ideals of active masculinity and passive femininity that had influenced Baden-Powell's naming of his boys' and girls' youth organizations, MacDonald told his audience that "men may scout, but women guide. Long may the organization prosper in its efforts to prepare the girls of the world for their place in the life of the body politic."[109] While the interwar Guide movement in some ways prepared girls to play a more active role in "the body politic," the fact that the Canadian Guide Council invited MacDonald to speak and published his address in its annual report shows that these older, more conservative ideas about femininity and the uses of girl training still had a place in the movement after the First World War.

Guiding was also explained as training for future wives in India, where British colonizers and some Indian nationalists and social reformers also valorized the ideal of companionate marriage between consenting adults as a sign of civilizational progress.[110] While some sources emphasized the importance of Guide training for potential child brides, other texts (during the debates about *Mother India* and the Sarda Act) supported the ideal of companionate marriage more explicitly. In 1935, the *Indian Ladies Magazine*, the periodical whose educated Indian editors published numerous articles in support of the Girl Guides, featured an article insisting that "home training is not surely enough for women!" "What woman really needs, I think, is a happy marriage in which she can, together with her man, have 'a more spacious and more worthy life than now,' and not be trammelled and held by chains and fetters, though such may be of gold and jewels."[111]

Despite these many references to the importance of happy and relatively egalitarian marriages, interwar Guide texts had little to say about sexuality. A fairly explicit warning against masturbation and keeping company with girls "who tell you nasty stories" in 1912's *How Girls Can Help Build the Empire* was not reprinted in later Guide handbooks.[112] The closest interwar Guiding came to making such prohibitions appeared in a vaguely worded section of the Guide Law requiring girls and young women to remain "pure in word, thought, and deed."[113] In this respect, Guiding was part of a broader culture of taboo and feminine respectability that shaped and often hindered girls' pursuit of sexual knowledge during the 1920s and 1930s.[114] The relative rise in public discussions of female sexual pleasure during this period (always contained within heterosexual marriage, as outlined in publications by Marie Stopes and Margaret Sanger) was clearly aimed at adult women and *not* girls, and the authors of Guide texts, like most of their contemporaries, sought to protect girls and young women with euphemisms and silences.

It is therefore not surprising that official publications have next to nothing to say about courtship during 1920s and 1930s – a period when commercial amusements and automobiles had started to shift the activities of unsupervised heterosexual couples in many parts of the Western world "from the front porch to the back seat."[115] When such matters were discussed, it was usually in references to the sexual morality of young working-class women – the member of Mrs. Fryer's factory company, for example, who was said to have "seven or eight boyfriends" in different parts of the country. Although British Guides and Rangers did start to organize more co-educational activities with their Scout counterparts during the interwar years, some girls remained dissatisfied.[116] May Rainer, a young British woman whose frustration with Guiding's extreme reticence about sexuality and mixed-sex socializing ultimately led her to leave the movement, explained her decision by saying that, "having had so many restrictions at home, the thought of constantly being told you must not talk to the young men in the Scout Hut by a prejudiced old maid" made her quit.[117]

Significantly, these generational clashes also occurred during a time when heterosexuality was normalized and romantic and sexual relationships between women were increasingly pathologized. Official Guide discussions of marriage, which left much unsaid, were clear about one thing: monogamous *heterosexual* unions were the ideal to which all girls and young women should aspire. In the interwar years, this was at least partly due to the promotion, by psychological, sexological, and medical experts, of the idea that marriage and heterosexuality were necessary for "normal" women's health and happiness.[118] This shift affected various cultural products aimed at girls; schoolgirl stories, for example, ceased to include casual references to romantic friendships and physical intimacy between girls during the interwar years, and this concern about "abnormal" relationships between girls and young women was also expressed in some Guide publications.[119] An article in the January 1937 issue of the *Canadian Guider* by

University of Toronto psychology professor J.D. Ketchum, for example, sought to advise leaders about how to deal with girls who developed "crushes" on fellow Guides or Guide leaders. Entitled "Some Emotional Problems," the piece stated that intense attachment to peers and senior Guides was a normal phase (presumably on the way to a psychologically "mature" ideal of hetero-sexual womanhood) but emphasized the importance of "help[ing] the young-ster gradually to grow out of her 'attack,' without having been made to feel ridiculous ... or important."[120]

A Global Single-Sex Community

Ironically, while the movement may not have posed any radical or overt chal-lenges to the continued association of femininity with motherhood, marriage, and the home, its programs and structures also made space for girls and (es-pecially) women whose lives and identities did not conform to these ideals. Guiding – while normalizing heterosexuality and pathologizing "crushes" – was also a global single-sex community in which it was possible to lead a full life that was not centred on marriage, motherhood, or domesticity. This side of the movement, which defined the lives of a visible minority of upper-level leaders, complicates Martha Vicinus's claim that communities of single middle-class women "had become ideologically and conceptually obsolete" by the interwar years.[121]

During the 1920s and 1930s, many prominent Guiders were single women; some were never married, while others were widowed or divorced. At one 1926 imperial camp for Guide leaders, for example, over 80 percent of the almost three hundred women present were unmarried.[122] Katharine Furse, who ran the World Association of Girl Guides and Girl Scouts from 1928 until 1938, was widowed in 1904 after only four years of marriage, while Alice Behrens, the first Guider-in-Charge at Foxlease (the British Guide house in the New Forest), was active in the movement for several decades before her marriage late in her thirties to Boy Scout Leader Arthur Gaddum. Ida von Herren-schwand, who ran the international Guide training centre "Our Chalet" in Switzerland between 1932 and 1952, was also single, as was her eventual re-placement, Penelope "Pen" Wood-Hill.[123]

Margrethe Parm, the Norwegian Guider whose speech at the Ninth World Conference in 1936 advocated training girls for careers while also training them "to be the best mothers and wives and comrades to their husbands," also never married. She wrote a celebratory biography of an unmarried female physician named Louise Isachsen and has been discussed as part of an early twentieth-century Norwegian "community of spinsters" whose members celebrated feminine self-sufficiency and rebutted sexologists' accusations of deviance.[124]

British Columbia Guide leader and Anglican missionary Monica Storrs was another single woman, and her diary includes several discussions of her unease with conventionally feminine domestic tasks. When May Birley, a woman with whom she sometimes lodged, took to her bed with a headache, the daily tasks of housekeeping fell – unusually – to Storrs. "All I could do," she wrote, "was to turn entirely domestic, and try to become a general farm-hand. It's rather pathetic how slow and stupid I am at it all." Despite her readiness to lecture Canadian Guides about bed-making and cleaning techniques, Storrs readily admitted her "undomestic" nature to her diary, writing of her housekeeping experience that "the sad part was that it took me nearly all day (except three hours away for the Scouts) without any cooking except poached eggs for supper – whereas Miss Birley does it all, and cooks all our meals and often goes out and nurses somebody as well!"[125] Storrs also had a long-term relationship with a British woman named Adeline Harmer, who joined her in the Peace River region in 1931.[126]

Despite the movement's constant emphasis on heterosexual marriage, discomfort with the "problem" of crushes, and a former Girl Guiding UK archivist's reluctance to preserve evidence of loving relationships between adult women, long-term same-sex partnerships were part of the Guide movement during the 1920s and 1930s. Fiona Paisley and Leila Rupp both write about the part played by these relationships in late nineteenth- and early twentieth-century women's internationalism, and Guiding needs to be seen in this broader context.[127] Like other international women's organizations, Guiding allowed a minority of women to develop alternative families and communities at the same time as it promoted a conservative ideal of "modern" femininity. Proctor's history of the Guide and Girl Scout movement in the twentieth century states, for example, that Lady Helen Whitaker and Ann Kindersley (an author and editor of several British Guide books published during the 1920s and 1930s) were "constant companions" and that both held important roles in the Guide executive, while Mrs. Walter [Fflorens] Roch and Miss Clementina "Kit" Anstruther-Thomson also "developed a close and long-lasting relationship."[128] Proctor also notes that Marguerite de Beaumont, who claimed to have been among the "Girl Scouts" at the 1909 Crystal Palace Rally and later wrote a biography of Baden-Powell, "bought a home and horse farm in 1934 with Doris Mason, a fellow Guider and Boy Scout volunteer. The two women gave copious amounts of time and energy to the Girl Guide and Boy Scout movements while running their equine business and developing a network of close female friendships over their Guiding years."[129]

Conclusion

Why did Guide leaders in interwar England, India, and Canada, some of whom rejected these ideals in their own lives, continue to stress homekeeping, motherhood, and matrimony throughout the 1920s and 1930s? These conventionally feminine attributes sat uneasily beside Guiding's promotion of outdoor life and international citizenship – a juxtaposition that led (and continues to lead) some members of the movement to claim that its emphasis on conventionally feminine identities and pursuits was merely a strategic move: a ploy to trick men and conservative members of the public into supporting what was really an emancipatory scheme of girl-training. Writing in 1946, for example, British Guide author Kitty Barne claimed that the first Guide prescriptive texts "cleverly camouflaged" their discussions of camping under the heading "Finding the Injured" – a trick that, she argued, threw "dust in the eyes of anxious mothers haunted by the spectre of the dreaded tomboy their daughters might become."[130]

As with the movement's suggested "Domestic Service" and "Baby-Carrying" games, one can only speculate about whether Guiding's continued emphasis on stereotypically feminine roles was a subversive strategy or a sincere expression of gender conservatism. In this respect, the movement had much in common with the first British women's colleges – institutions whose Victorian founders asserted that they would make their students into "good wives and mothers" while simultaneously enunciating the very different goals of autonomy, public service, and self-actualization. To a certain extent this was a strategic choice that allowed these women to pursue their feminist agenda from a position of ideological strength and to legitimate aspects of their program that, as Ellen Jordan comments, "seemed to contradict conventional definitions of femininity."[131]

But this persistent championing of motherhood, homekeeping, and matrimony also had several unintended consequences, as it trapped the movement's defenders within the scripts of conventional gender ideology. Like these Victorian educators, interwar Guide leaders seldom overtly questioned dominant definitions of femininity; indeed, they promoted them as a universal ideal – a way to emphasize similarity without acknowledging differences. Their attempts to improve girls' maternal and domestic skills combined assumptions about "natural" instincts with a desire for modern, scientific guidance. Teaching girls to be feminine and useful in the present and the future was presented in Guide texts as something that could rival commercialized leisure pursuits and benefit all girls equally. Yet a number of leaders also explained domestic badges and activities as particularly important for the characters and careers of working-class girls and young women. While it is difficult to find evidence of how most Guides in interwar England, Canada, and India understood and responded to the movement's emphasis on domestic, maternal, and marital education, sources like Eileen Knapman's logbook and periodical articles lamenting British Guides' poor showing in National Baby Week essay contests provide some evidence of how the movement's ideals and practices were used, and sometimes rejected, by different groups of women and girls.

Chapter 3

"WE MUST GIVE THE MODERN GIRL A TRAINING IN CITIZENSHIP"
Preparing Girls for Political and Social Service

THE 1925 ANNUAL REPORT of the British Guide Association, which featured information and membership numbers from around the world, also included an essay entitled "Why I Believe in the Girl Guides" by C. Grant Robinson, a historian from the University of Birmingham. Acknowledging both the recent extension of the British franchise to most women over the age of thirty and the likelihood that it would soon be extended still further, Robinson claimed that these changes had put the average British girl "on terms of equality with a boy" – a shift that he, like many of his contemporaries, saw as nothing short of "a revolution."[1] Similar "revolutionary" electoral changes had in fact been taking place in a piecemeal and incomplete way around the world since the late nineteenth century; Canadian women (with some significant racialized exceptions) received the federal vote in 1918, and the Government of India Act of 1935 would soon enfranchise some women there (again, with exceptions) on the same terms as men. Throughout the 1920s and 1930s, Guide leaders across the British Empire sought to position themselves and their growing youth movement at the centre of these exciting political developments. On the one hand, they wanted to claim and celebrate the range of new possibilities that was opening up for young women; on the other hand, many also believed that Guiding was needed to train and contain these newly enfranchised and, it was feared, socially irresponsible flappers and modern girls.

While continuing to insist on the importance of motherhood, domesticity, and marriage, Baden-Powell – like many of his contemporaries – saw 1918 as a turning point for female citizens. Referring to British women's voluntary and paid war work, their recent partial enfranchisement, and the traumatic legacy of the Great War, he wrote in 1919 that the next generation of young women and girls would require "a very high standard of patriotic citizenhood to meet the tremendous responsibilities which will rest upon its shoulders."[2] Chief Guide Olave Baden-Powell echoed her husband's sentiments that same year in a speech to the Women's Canadian Club at the University of Toronto, claiming that the Great War had shown that girls and women could be "efficient, capable citizen[s]."[3]

The Baden-Powells' emphasis on the importance of training responsible, efficient, and capable young female citizens was echoed throughout the next two decades by Guide leaders around the world. A 1934 article published in the *Canadian Guider* magazine, for instance, referred proudly to the fact that the country's Guides, "the future women of Canada, [would] meet their responsibilities and privileges of citizenship with a spirit that will be a real influence for good, in the life of our Dominion."[4] The elite group of educated, middle-class Indian women who supported Girl Guiding and other types of social and educational reform in South Asia also explained the benefits of the movement in terms of citizenship. The *Indian Ladies' Magazine* claimed in 1927, for instance, that Guiding would teach girls both domestic virtues and "the wider duties of good citizens, whereby they will grow up to be loyal and useful members of the body politic."[5]

Guide leaders presented the movement's citizenship training program as an exercise in cooperation and tolerance that would encourage girls to look beyond national and racial boundaries. A February 1930 article also published in the *Indian Ladies' Magazine* argued that the "movement is a great crusade for the teaching of citizenship to the girls of this country, a crusade in which Indians and Europeans co-operate in constructive work."[6] This emphasis on cooperation among different nationalities and races was similarly promoted by the World Association of Girl Guides and Girl Scouts (WAGGGS), whose 1938 biennial report emphasized the movement's "power of uniting its members, regardless of race or creed" – a power that, according to WAGGGS director Katharine Furse, would enable Guiding to "educat[e] the coming generation in world citizenship."[7]

Citizenship was an issue of global concern during the years between the two World Wars. This was especially true of the British Empire, as the partial extension of the franchise and the rise of anticolonial nationalisms raised a host of questions about loyalty, identity, community, and political obligations and rights. In settings as varied as Canada, India, and England, politicians, social commentators, and activists all insisted on the importance of moulding young people into "good citizens." This chapter asks how citizenship was defined and taught by the Girl Guides in England, Canada, and India during the 1920s and 1930s. It analyzes the movement's multiple attempts to create a generation of useful and responsible citizens by training girls and young women in politics, health and happiness, voluntary service, and emergency preparedness. While it promoted new opportunities for women and girls and emphasized international tolerance, Guiding's citizenship training program was also a conservative undertaking, characterized by several telling silences. This analysis of the movement's conservatively modern vision of citizenship also highlights several conflicts between metropolitan leaders' official and implicitly white vision of imperial/international citizenship and the different (and sometimes subversive) loyalties and identities that were promoted in Guide groups across the Empire.

Citizenship is a complicated concept, weighed down by a long history and a web of complex and sometimes contradictory meanings. It is, to begin with, a legal term, denoting the duties and rights that accompany full membership in a nation-state or society. (Throughout history, of course, this definition has also worked to deny these things to various groups of people.) As Keith McClelland and Sonya Rose note, by the early twentieth century the political or legal definition was frequently paralleled by a discourse that stressed "good citizenship" and the various obligations that underpinned it.[8] This concern with responsibility and good citizenship was not a unidirectional force that spread outward from the imperial centre; as Carey Watt has shown, India also experienced an explosion of voluntary citizen-training initiatives during the early twentieth century. Looking globally to countries like Japan and the United States, South Asian associations and initiatives sought to create "patriotic citizens who would serve India as opposed to 'King and Empire.'"[9] This focus on duties, service, and loyalty – to sometimes conflicting communities and identities – is different from the rights-based concept of social citizenship linked to the rise of the British welfare state that emerged in the post-Second World War writings of T.H. Marshall.[10] Whereas much of the scholarship that engages with and critiques Marshall's ideas examines citizenship as status, the global Guide movement – and therefore this chapter – focuses instead on citizenship as a set of practices.[11]

The Guide movement's attempts to teach the responsibilities of good citizenship to the very different members of its interracial "empire family" were critically inflected by gender. In most societies, the rights and obligations of citizenship had historically been masculine and were often determined by factors like property ownership and military service. But this centuries-old link between citizenship and masculinity had been largely severed by the interwar years, as the franchise was extended to women in dozens of contexts around the world.[12] This new understanding of women as citizens (and of girls as young or future citizens) was an enormous shift, but it is worth remembering that these claims to citizenship were generally made first by white women, and often by speaking for "degraded" colonized women or by demanding the same rights as men of colour.[13] However, recent scholarship indicates that the language of citizenship could also be used by excluded and racialized groups to contest colonialism and demand equal rights.[14]

Citizenship, a concept that since the late eighteenth century had been especially associated with republicanism and revolutions, was especially hard to define in the British imperial context. There were officially no citizens in the interwar empire; instead, the men, women, and children who inhabited the metropole, dependencies, and dominions were all subjects of the British sovereign. However, as Daniel Gorman rightly notes, the "unofficial, rhetorical, and localized nature of citizenship [in the British imperial context] gave rise to great discrepancies among imperial subjects in rights, benefits and duties."[15] These discrepancies diminished somewhat with the late nineteenth- and early twentieth-century extension of the franchise, but – as this chapter will demonstrate – they did not disappear entirely.

Politics

Politics occupied a central place in interwar Guiding's efforts to train the next generation in citizenship, as leaders encouraged girls and young women to educate themselves about local and national political systems and imperial and world affairs. During the 1920s and 1930s, Guides, Rangers, and their leaders discussed the responsibilities of women's newly granted political citizenship in publications and at meetings and conferences across the world. At one such conference, held in England in 1925, a Ranger named Miss Matheson claimed that "a good citizen must not only know how we are governed, but she should also know something about the industrial laws."[16] Four years later, the *Guider* published an article on political citizenship by Dame Helen Gwynne-Vaughan, the prominent British botanist and former Chief Controller (Overseas) of the Women's Auxiliary Army Corps who was also an active member of the World Association of Girl Guides and Girl Scouts. According to her, Guide citizenship training would encourage young women to fulfill their electoral duties while thinking critically about "what our votes in combination can effect."[17]

Margaret Warren of the 23rd Toronto Rangers wrote in the *Canadian Girl Guide* in 1930 that young female citizens had a responsibility to educate themselves about political parties and their parliamentary representatives. Women who chose not to vote, she insisted, were "poor citizen[s]" who were lacking in respect for their forebears who had "fought for the franchise."[18] This concern that modern young women were taking the efforts of older, more serious-minded feminists for granted is evident in a number of published Guide discussions of citizenship from the interwar years. Like Sylvia Pankhurst and Eleanor Rathbone, many Guide leaders appear to have seen the issue in generational terms and worried that "amongst crowds of young women, the emancipation of today displays itself mainly in cigarettes and shorts."[19] Articles published in Guide magazines throughout the 1920s and 1930s sought to counteract young women's apparent frivolity by suggesting that they equip themselves for their future roles as citizens by learning about subjects like taxation, the secret ballot, the Imperial Conference, and juvenile courts – topics that, until recently, had been the exclusive province of men. In its coverage of the 1930 All-India Women's Educational Conference at Trivandrum, the *Indian Ladies' Magazine* reported on conference president Hester Smith's similar insistence that "we must give the modern girl a training in citizenship, which will involve a study of the present Government and social institutions of her country, together with some knowledge of its past history."[20]

The leaders of the Guide movement agreed that reading and self-education were especially important pursuits for future citizens. Every month the *Girl Guides' Gazette* and its later incarnation the *Guider* featured a list of books and pamphlets leaders were encouraged to use at meetings and to tell their girls to read. The January 1923 issue, for instance, urged leaders to order a series of pamphlets describing the Exchequer and the control of expenditure, dominion home rule (it explained self-government as natural for white settler societies but was conspicuously silent on the question of India), the reasons for price increases and decreases, manufacturing and production, and the executive, legislative, and judicial arms of the state. Other recommended books included *The Teaching of Modern Civics* by G.M. White, C. Kent Wright's *The Parish Pump and How It Works* (a study of local government in Britain), and *English Citizenship* by Frederic Swann, the latter of which was said to be particularly useful because it "explains clearly and simply how our country is governed, and will help the busy Guider to face the budding Socialist or the eager citizen with sound facts and arguments."[21] Most of these recommended readings dealt solely with British political systems – a reflection, perhaps, of this internationalist organization's continuing metropolitan focus.

Winnifred Kidd, MA, a Guide leader who had represented Canada at the First World Disarmament Conference in Geneva in March 1932, wrote a series of articles for the *Canadian Guider* advising leaders how to teach girls and young women about international cooperation and the League of Nations. "Every Guide in our great sisterhood can do something to help," Kidd wrote, "and having sister Guides in so many sections of the world should make us see how important it is to build up tolerance and understanding between countries of the world." Kidd said that she planned to give several "Camp Fire talks" to her own company about the results of the Treaty of Versailles, and she urged Guiders to facilitate similar discussions and to explain such terms as "'Equality of Status,' 'The Security Thesis,' and 'Qualitative Disarmament' so that Guides will understand what these terms mean when used in newspapers."

The organizational aspect of Guiding was also often explained as practical training for the next generation of female citizens. In October 1922, Captain V. Daly of the 9th Leamington Guide Company described the Court of Honour (a monthly executive meeting of each Company's Captains and Patrol Leaders) as a "governing body" that should be run "like a little parliament with the Captain as Prime Minister."[22] While imagining themselves as members and prime ministers of "little parliaments" across the world, good Guide citizens were also meant to acquire a variety of leadership and organizational skills that would help them should they decide to enter formal politics. A February 1924 article from the *Girl Guides' Gazette*, for example, told readers "How to Arrange a Public Meeting" with reference to planning, publicity, and the importance of rules of order.[23] Guides and Rangers were also encouraged to practise public speaking, described in the March 1925 *Girl Guides' Gazette* as "an accomplishment within the reach of all who will only take the trouble to master it."[24] Groups often organized events at which members could practise these skills, as on 4 May 1934, when English Rangers from the London suburbs of Crofton Park and Forest Hill staged a debate entitled "Should Married Women Work."[25]

These texts and activities, while reflecting new public possibilities for girls and women, nonetheless maintained what Patricia Grimshaw calls "a solid wall of silence" about the continued political exclusion of many groups of women across the world.[26] Whether intentionally or not, Guiding's definition of citizenship as a series of responsibilities and privileges (as opposed to a series of rights) obscured the fact that many women around the world were still emphatically not citizens in this most basic political/electoral sense – a reality that Guide training was not enough to overcome. As in the English elementary school texts studied by Stephen Heathorn, the Guide movement's approach to citizenship stressed duties and obligations in ways that often "elided discussions of political rights" and conflicts.[27] Guiding's emphasis on obedience and loyalty also revealed the movement's support of an organic social ideal built on the acceptance of hierarchies and deference – an understanding that did not necessarily include the idea that all citizens were deserving of full political rights. These Guide leaders, like a number of their contemporaries, appear to have believed instead that a citizen was first and foremost "an individual who accepted his or her role as a productive member of the social order, a person who was a threat neither to the state nor to established social relations."[28]

The conservatism of the official Guide movement's stance on citizenship and rights becomes even more apparent when it is contrasted with those of several other interwar organizations and initiatives. The British Commonwealth League (BCL), for instance, was a voluntary organization run mainly by women from Britain and the dominions whose members sought to create a trans-imperial platform from which to address questions of women's citizenship and rights. Through conferences on subjects like "The Citizen Rights of Women within the British Empire" (1925) and "The Social and Industrial Position of Women Other Than British Race, Governed Under the British Flag" (1927) the BCL, while still assuming that white women were especially qualified to lead and speak for "others," did discuss and attempt to challenge the political exclusion of Indigenous and other groups of women across the Empire.[29] The modern idea of children's rights, represented most forcefully during this period by Eglantyne Jebb's Save the Children Fund and the 1924 League of Nations adoption of the Geneva Declaration of the Rights of the Child, is also conspicuous in its absence from most Guide texts published during the 1920s and 1930s.[30] Jebb's work and the Geneva Declaration were discussed in several of the periodicals aimed at Guiding's adult leaders, but they seem not to have been deemed important or appropriate enough to warrant inclusion in Guide publications for young people.

During the interwar years, then, Guiding sought to teach its over 1 million young members about governance, taxation, and electoral systems, while encouraging them to believe in the ideal of a familial and tolerant British-dominated global empire. These facts rest somewhat uneasily alongside the insistence, voiced often by leaders in various national contexts, that "both Scouting and Guiding are fundamentally non-political."[31] Based on a narrow definition of politics, this assertion made the world order envisioned by Guide policy makers – an ideal based on self-discipline, obedience, loyalty to the British monarchy, and respect for the British Empire – appear to be natural and "apolitical." The movement's attempt to uphold the imperial status quo was not entirely new; as Jessica Harland-Jacobs shows, late eighteenth- and early nineteenth-century British Freemasons defined the term "political" in a similar way, "equating it with challenges to the state and excluding from its meaning any act designed to uphold the state (which allowed them to continue to claim they did not discuss political matters)."[32]

Guide groups who challenged the movement's official view of the world, as in India and French Canada, were often labelled by metropolitan leaders as "political," troublesome, and disobedient. This tendency is especially evident in Olave Baden-Powell's diary and private correspondence about Guiding in India, which feature frequent complaints about the political nature of Indian nationalism and the Seva Samiti Guides, a separate unaffiliated Guide group linked to the Seva Samiti of Allahabad, a nationalist organization whose members provided social service at melas (festivals) and during famines, epidemics, and floods.[33] While in Nagpur with her husband in February 1937, for example, the Chief Guide wrote in her diary about "loaf[ing] about & talk[ing] with Esme Eastley etc & do[ing] plotting with Lady Haig & Mrs. Kharepat (U.P.) as to how to tackle the imitation Seva Semiti Guides run by 'Congress.'" Not quite two weeks later, while staying at the governor's mansion in Lucknow, she recorded her "struggle to get a memo done quickly against time about the Seva Samiti Scout situation & spend precious hours on it – instead of being able to revel in this charming garden! This Government House is a very nice one – very big and they keep about 100 servants and 4 cooks!"[34]

The Chief Guide's exasperation with this rival group continued into 1938 and was likely intensified by the furor that had followed her husband's hastily retracted statements about the Indian nation's lack of "character" and "health" in mid-1937. In a letter dated 18 March 1938 to an unknown but presumably British Guide leader in India, she wrote:

> Freda [the woman who would soon be taking charge of the Indian Guides] will not have an EASY job solving this problem of the S.S. [Seva Samiti] Guides, and there are plenty of difficulties ahead! BUT, as you say, they are there to be overcome, and Freda has got some fine good people to support and advise and work for her, and in the end one can but hope that Indian people WILL see reason and stop this starting up of separatist things, so obviously tinged by politics.[35]

The political nature of Indian nationalism and its occasionally deleterious effects on British-based Guiding were also lamented in the fourth Biennial

Report of the World Association of Girl Guides and Girl Scouts (1936–38), which noted:

> Whilst every endeavour is made to keep Guiding apart from politics, the changes taking place in Government have created unrest outside the Movement. This has consequently suffered by the loss of grants and in some places by the loss of personnel. In Western India the municipalities closed down the companies in their schools and we consequently suffered a loss of 3,000; in other places, however, expansion has been marked, so that we have a loss of only 500 or so on our total number.[36]

The Chief Guide's 1935 report on Canadian Guiding portrayed Quebec's French Catholic Guide movement as similarly disobedient, "separatist," and "political." According to the Chief Guide, the only trouble with Quebec provincial commissioner Mrs. Phillip Mackenzie "is that she is definitely English and Protestant, and is not very tolerant with the queer odd difficult backward and trying French Canadian element." Displaying a similar lack of tolerance herself, the Chief Guide noted that "Quebec is therefore rather torn in twain – the rich, busy go ahead vigorous English business centre of Montreal and the completely cow-like villages of the country and the burstingly French Canadian R.C. Quebec City." She anxiously mentioned the existence of "renegade" companies of French Catholic Guides, who were suspected "of working sub rosa, in touch we THINK with the Guides de France."[37] While francophone Guides did use various French-language texts produced by the Catholic Guides de France, they also had a close relationship to the Catholic Church in Canada – a fact that worried both the Chief Guide and Sarah Warren, the Toronto-based Chief Commissioner of the Canadian Girl Guides. Correspondence between Warren, Olave Baden-Powell, and the Archbishop of Quebec about the possibility of creating a separate organization for Catholic French-Canadian Guides contains several unsurprising instances of Anglo-Protestant anti-Catholic thinking. But Warren and Baden-Powell's decision on the matter (that a separate organization would not be satisfactory) was also explained in gendered terms: as a rejection of the Church's apparent desire "that men should conduct, or at any rate oversee, Guide activities."[38] Finally, the Chief Guide stated: "it would be a really serious precedent if your Canadian Roman Catholics formed an altogether seperate [sic] Movement" – a precedent that, she feared, could defeat Guiding's "great aims of unity and true friendship."[39] This last statement, however, neglects to mention that a similar precedent had in fact already been set in South Africa, where Guide and Scout groups were strictly segregated by race.[40]

Health and Cheerfulness

Aside from being simultaneously politically informed and appropriately "non-political," the duties of Guide citizens also included maintaining their own health and happiness, engaging in voluntary social service, and being prepared and willing to endanger their own lives in the event of an emergency. Guide leaders often reminded girls that citizenship was "not merely reading books"; good citizens, the movement insisted, also had a duty to successfully manage their bodies and emotions.[41] The equation of the physical health of individuals with the fitness of the body politic was not new in the early twentieth century, and indeed some aspects of Guide training during these years continued to reflect the idea that healthy female bodies were important primarily because of the male children they might bear. But the "discovery" of adolescence in the early twentieth century also ushered in the idea, promoted by a variety of social scientific and medical experts, that young people should be trained to embody an ideal of citizenship that was characterized by self-control and physical robustness. This emphasis on bodily management, through which Girl Guides in widely different settings learned to do physical exercises, hike in the outdoors, and consider the nutritional content of their food, had obvious links to other contemporary developments, including the increasing popularity of physical culture and European fascism.

Interwar Guide texts frequently referred to the importance of health and fitness. The 1931 edition of the Guide handbook, for instance, proclaimed that the movement would train girls in "physical health and hygiene, through development up to standard by games and exercise designed for the purpose."[42] The handbook described physical culture as a responsibility of citizenship, urging each reader to "make yourself strong so that you can be helpful to other people."[43] The movement also used texts, badges, and activities to teach girls and young women about its "Six Rules of Health" – "Fresh Air, Cleanliness (Personal and Surroundings), Exercise, Food, Clothing, [and] Rest."[44] In this respect Guiding was part of a broader international child health movement through which educators, medical professionals, and voluntary organizations sought to make young people knowledgeable about and responsible for their own physical well-being.

Monica Storrs, the Anglican missionary who ran Guide and Scout groups in the Peace River country in northern British Columbia, discussed her not entirely successful attempts to teach Guiding's health rules to an outspoken group of Guides in her diary. In her entry for the week of 22 February 1930, Storrs wrote:

Thursday was Guides as usual ... I took the Rules of Health with the six Seniors, and had the funniest discussion because they were so ingenious in explaining to me how in Canada it is impossible to keep any of them! The climax arose over teeth. I gave them a very impressive little account of germs in the mouth, and what they do, not only destroying the teeth but poisoning the system, etc. At the end, there was a little pause and then the Senior Patrol Leader remarked: "That's funny because my father has perfect teeth and excellent health, and he has never cleaned his teeth in his life, but always laughs at us for doing it![45]

According to Storrs, three weeks later they again "revised the six Rules of Health, and tried to sift all the reasons why none of them could *possibly* be kept out here."[46]

Guides were also encouraged to use and therefore strengthen their bodies in a variety of ways: by practising drill, by hiking in the outdoors, and by participating in games and sports. Guide citizens' physical activities were explained variously as healthy modern pastimes, as an imperial and national duty, and as Darwinian-sounding lessons in "healthy competition." Glimpses of what specific groups of girls actually did can be found in annual reports, scrapbooks, diaries, and photograph albums. Guides from Pune, India, played basketball in their saris in the early 1920s, while English companies from Battersea played netball on Wandsworth Common.[47] Canadian Guides in Winnipeg participated in annual track and field days, while the 7th Bangalore Guides practised Swedish gymnastics in the outdoors.[48] Finally, the logbook kept by members of the Nightingale Patrol of the 21st (St. Alban's) Winnipeg Guide Company records that the girls began one January meeting by running laps around the church hall – not to keep fit, but to keep warm.[49]

These efforts to mould and maintain fit and healthy feminine bodies could be understood as a way to "serve" a variety of communities – and not always the ones intended by the Guide movement's British headquarters. As Watt shows, early twentieth-century Indian and Western populations shared a set of common assumptions about "the connections between the citizen's physical health and the likelihood that he would constructively serve society."[50] East and West diverged, however, about the definition of the society that young people were meant to serve. In India, where the movement included British, Eurasian, Hindu, and Muslim girls (in segregated as well as in integrated groups), British leaders (and some loyalist South Asian women) explained Guiding as service to the Empire, while other educated middle-class Indian women saw the movement as a way to encourage girls to serve a reinvigorated and independent India.

Girls in India had relatively fewer opportunities for physical activity than did their "Guide sisters" in Canada and Britain, and, indeed, the secondary literature on physical culture, citizenship, and nationalism in India focuses almost exclusively on men and boys.[51] But there was also a movement for physical culture for South Asian girls in the 1920s and 1930s, and the Indian Guides, with their basketball games and gymnastics practices, were part of it. In February 1928, the *Indian Ladies' Magazine* addressed the question of girls and physical culture: "Seeing that we are taught almost from our childhood that all forms of sport are unsuited to girls, and that we must not grow up like boys, is it surprising that the average Indian girl is pale, and far from being as strong as she might and should be?" The article clearly linked physical fitness and service to India, stating that, "besides affording such excellent and regular exercise and fresh air, sports teach us how to pull together – *i.e.* the true team spirit which is so essential to the welfare and happiness of any nation." Encouraging Indian girls "to take part in every form of sport as heartily as do the girls in the West," the author insisted, would help to "build up a stronger and healthier nation than we have [had] in the past."[52] An August 1928 article from the same magazine approved of a resolution passed at the All-India Women's Educational Conference in Delhi, which held that "a complete course of physical training should be made compulsory in all boys' and girls' schools, and should include as much cheerful recreation out of doors as possible, also eurythmics and Girl Guiding on Indian lines." Cheerful recreation, exercise, and Girl Guiding, it was argued, would help educated young Indian women to "stand by their men-brethren and help their activities towards the uplift of the land, and raising the Indian nation in the estimation of the other nations of the world."[53]

The Guide vision of healthy citizenship, whichever community it was meant to benefit, was about more than just bodies; good Guide citizens were also expected to manage their emotions and appear cheerful in all aspects of their lives. As Christine Kotchemidova shows, the early twentieth century saw the rise of a hegemonic culture of cheerfulness that emphasized self-control and "linked physical health to emotional stamina."[54] By the early 1930s, this expectation of efficient cheerfulness and emotional restraint exerted a powerful influence on norms of self-presentation and interpersonal relations in schools, homes, and the workplace. The international Guide movement clearly supported this performative emotional ideal, which was enshrined in the Guide Law: "a Guide smiles and sings under all circumstances."[55]

Performing cheerfulness "even in the worst circumstances" was often explained to Guides as a patriotic duty. In 1927, for instance, an English Ranger Commissioner named R. Tyacke wrote: "by adding to the common stock of happiness, you are really doing something for your country; you will be able to feel that your citizenship is more than a vague word somehow mixed up with senior Guiding."[56] Baden-Powell's writings often referred to "happifying" – that is, to the duty of Boy Scouts and Girl Guides to make themselves and others cheerful. In a July 1929 article in the *Council Fire*, for example, he wrote that every Girl Guide should smile because it "happifies or brightens up numbers of her passers by, among the depressing hundreds of glum faces that they otherwise meet."[57] The same article, which presented cheerfulness as a way of coping with modernity, urbanization, and mass society, also claimed that getting each Guide to happify herself and others would "make her the 'happy, helpful citizen' whom we need, and this, after all, is the real aim of our endeavour in Guiding."[58]

Happiness and helpfulness were more than public duties for Guide citizens: they were also private and particularly feminine responsibilities, since the domestic duties of women and girls were assumed to include the maintenance of a happy and harmonious home. An article on "Citizenship" in the October 1922 issue of the *Girl Guides' Gazette* made this connection especially clear. "In private life," the author stated, "we can make those round us easy or uneasy, happy or unhappy, by our conduct, our manner, our fashion of speech, our attitude towards our daily duties. A scowling, ungracious daughter, a scolding wife, an impatient mother, a forgetful and careless help, an unwilling worker, brings discredit on all those offices."[59]

Happifying, of course, was a culturally specific phenomenon – an expectation that was based squarely on middle-class Protestant Anglo-American ideals.[60] It was also part of interwar Guiding's civilizing mission – a perfect example of Sara Ahmed's observation that "colonialism is justified not only to increase human happiness but to teach the natives to be happy."[61] In fact, official Guide publications often depicted non-white girls (particularly those from so-called "Eastern" cultures) as unhappy or as not cheerful enough – which, by extension, meant that they were flawed or incomplete citizens in desperate need of Guide training. The Chief Guide expressed this idea most explicitly in 1934, when she wrote that Guiding would promote the twin "Missions of Happifying and bringing real Hope for Peace in the world."[62] Her use of the term "mission" is telling, not least because of its obvious similarities to the writings of British missionaries, who used a global comparative framework to contrast the privileges of Christian women with the sufferings of their "heathen" sisters.

Three years after her initial reference to the Guides' imperial and global happifying mission (on the eve of the controversy caused by her husband's assertion that South Asian populations were lacking in character and health), the Chief Guide wrote once again about cheerfulness as a sign of good citizenship and civilization. Repeating many of the negative assumptions found in Katherine Mayo's virulent 1927 polemic *Mother India*, Olave Baden-Powell asserted: "Nowadays the young girl in her Purdah School can be claimed for marriage in her early teens, [and] she is thrust 'behind the screens' for the remainder of her life ... [which] brings more unhappiness and misery than one cares to think about to many young women of the twentieth century." Guiding, she claimed, could "bring a great HAPPINESS" to these young women's sadly restricted lives.[63]

While obviously related to ideas about maintaining morale in times of war and to the early twentieth-century emphasis on physical and emotional robustness, Guiding's insistence that young people were responsible for their own well-being in these areas also had some more insidious effects. Echoing the Victorian ideas about thrift and self-help that had been popularized by Samuel Smiles, the movement's emphasis on health and happifying gave young women the message that ill health and emotions like anger and fear were their own fault – and that these problems were damaging the body politic as well as their own selves.[64] Like the late Victorian and Edwardian discourse of imperial motherhood studied by Anna Davin, Guiding's citizenship training program implicitly blamed individuals for failing to be cheerful and healthy, while obscuring the numerous environmental factors that could (and did) impede the development of young citizens' physical health and emotional well-being.

The Guide movement's stress on physical and emotional self-management, and its related lack of discussion of environmental factors, supported a number of conservative regimes, including colonialism and a laissez-faire approach to poverty. As Davin writes, no amount of youthful initiative, cheerfulness, or pluck "could remove the basic handicaps of overcrowding, of damp, ill-drained, airless, bathless, tapless lodgings, of shared and filthy ash closets and middens." No amount of Guide training or collection of health badges "would ensure a supply of fresh uncontaminated milk, or provide food when there was no money."[65] The notion that happifying and the cultivation of physical robustness were primary duties of all citizens was thus impossible to reconcile with the experiences of poor children (whose numbers grew as global economic troubles increased during the 1920s and 1930s), and of the members of Guide companies who resided in colonizing institutions. Healthy bodies and cheerful countenances must have been especially hard to conjure up for Guides in state-sponsored Indigenous schools, which often weakened rather than strengthened Indigenous youngsters by exposing them to disease, hunger, and abuse.

Social Service

In addition to political knowledge, health, and cheerfulness, the Girl Guides' vision of good citizenship also emphasized voluntarism and social service. This aspect of the movement's program was part of a post-First World War internationalist vision that sought to explain the British Empire as a community of citizens united through social service.[66] But the movement's emphasis on good turns and volunteer work (which were often explained in the language of duty and self-sacrifice) was also used to create social bonds on the local and national levels. Social service was a priority for many early twentieth-century educators and social reformers, and the Guides' efforts in this vein were paralleled by those of other groups around the world, including the English National Council of Social Service, the Salvation Army, the YWCA, and the All-India Women's Conference. Lord Meath, the British founder of Empire Day and the Duty and Discipline Movement, urged readers of the *Girl Guides' Gazette* to remember the importance of "Responsibility, Duty, Sympathy, and Self-Sacrifice." In 1923, he wrote in that publication: "I trust to you to show that you are worthy of the Citizenship which is now yours by law as well as by Right."[67] Meath's vision was similar to that espoused by the Canadian Girl Guides Association, whose 1935–36 annual report stated that "community service, the real spirit of citizenship for which our Guides are striving, now plays a large part in the company programme as well as the individual 'Good Turn.'"[68] That same year, some members of the movement in India attended a "Social Service Conference" at the YWCA compound in Ootacamund, a hill station where many Guide training events were also held. The more than forty women who attended this conference (Hindus, Parsis, and Christians from four Indian provinces, two princely states, Britain, Europe, and the United States) came together "in one happy family" to "study how to become more useful to their motherland through social service."[69]

The first chapter of the Girl Guide handbook explained the movement as a system of training in "service for others and fellowship, through daily good turns, organized public service, etc."[70] Service expectations increased with age, with Brownies being expected to help their mothers and sisters in the domestic sphere through activities like setting tables and doing dishes. Expectations for Guides were slightly broader; *Steps to Girl Guiding*, an abridged edition of the official handbook produced for girls in India, explained that Guide training would do the important work of making girls "fit for service" since a Guide's "first duty is to be helpful to other people, both in small everyday matters and also under the worst of circumstances."[71] Rangers, meanwhile, were meant to undertake a wider variety of public and private voluntary tasks to serve their communities and nations as well as the British Empire and the world.

The Guide movement's emphasis on social service was noted in England by social investigators from the London School of Economics, who reported in the 1935 *New Survey of London Life and Labour* that London Rangers frequently volunteered at hospitals, infant welfare centres, institutes for the blind and deaf, and first-aid associations.[72] This type of service resembled older voluntary forms of female charity at a time when social work was being professionalized; it also reinforced links between femininity and domestic and child care work. Volunteering with babies and children at hospitals and infant clinics gave young women opportunities to practise "scientific" child care and the performance of cheerfulness under trying conditions – skills that, as Baden-Powell and other leaders often reminded them, would equip them well for their assumed futures as homekeepers, mothers, and wives. It also raises important though, again, ultimately unanswerable questions about infants' tendency to reject rigid schedules and the ability of Guiding to strengthen modern girls' maternal "instincts."

While teaching maternal skills and encouraging girls and young women to make "appropriate" use of their leisure time, volunteer work also often excluded many young working-class women who did not have time to spare, while implying that the most important social roles for female citizens were maternal and voluntary. At the same time, however, doing unpaid work in traditionally feminine roles could sometimes lead to paid employment – another responsibility of good Guide citizens who were meant to support themselves and practise thrift to avoid burdening their families and the state.

Guide leaders in Canada also explicitly linked citizenship and social service through unpaid labour. This connection was especially visible in "Canadian Girl Guide Week," a publicity blitz that took place in late October 1936, designated 22 and 23 October as "Citizenship and Service Days." (Other "days" included Homecraft and Handcraft Day, International Day, Extension Day, and Out-of-Door and Health Day). Canadian Chief Commissioner Sarah Warren encouraged leaders to use this opportunity to publicly

> introduce or emphasize a community service project in which all the companies may work for the winter's service programme. Guides might also, as citizens, undertake some special service for their town or city on these days. Stress cooperation with the Boy Scouts through Scout-Guide Toy Shop activities. This might be started or advertised at this time. Publicity through press, radio or at meetings should emphasize citizenship training through Guiding.[73]

Descriptions of Canadian Guides' volunteer activities in publications and organizational records reflected both the economic hardships of the 1930s and the ethnic and racial divisions caused by mass immigration and the state's attempts to assimilate Indigenous peoples. One Canadian voluntary undertaking that received a great deal of coverage in Guide periodicals and the local press was the annual Scout and Guide Christmas toy shop, at which boys and girls "collect[ed] and restore[d] broken and discarded toys and dolls, sending them out to children who would otherwise face the tragedy of an empty stocking."[74] This was similar to the British Guides' Christmas Stocking Trail, through which Guides "ma[de] and collect[ed] toys and small presents" before distributing them to needy children.[75] As was often the case with combined Girl Guide/Boy Scout activities, the Canadian Guides performed the typically feminine work of "run[ning] the doll section, laundering clothes, dressing the dolls, and also repairing the soft toys."[76] In 1928, over 50,000 toys were redistributed from eighty-five shops across Canada. In Winnipeg, the toys were "sent to the children of British settlers who arrived in 1928, to the Peguis Indian Reserve, the Elkhorn Indian School and to children in the Winnipeg Immigration Halls, as well as other needy children in the city."[77]

In interwar Canada, voluntary social service was widely seen as a way to promote comradeship and social stability – qualities that were deemed especially important as European immigration increased, economic troubles worsened, and the political and social threats embodied by the Russian Revolution and the labour unrest of 1919 remained fresh in people's minds. Like the Imperial Order Daughters of the Empire, an organization to which many of them also belonged, Anglo-Canadian Guide leaders often explained their mission as one of "Canadianization."[78] Joyce Wolton, a Guider from England who visited Winnipeg in 1928 to conduct training courses, also embraced this idea. As a local newspaper pointed out, her speeches emphasized "the part played by the Girl Guide movement in instilling in the younger generation the ideals of British citizenship" and claimed that, "owing to the constant flux of foreign civilizations into this country[,] ... the Girl Guides were needed even more in Canada than in England."[79] In 1928, for example, the Captain of a company from the town of Morden was commended by the Manitoba Council for "trying to turn fourteen little German girls into good Canadians."[80] At the same time, however, it is important not to see "ethnic" Guide companies as simply the recipients or victims of a top-down Canadianization scheme. As John Herd Thompson indicates, many groups of Eastern European immigrants actively embraced the symbols of British imperialism in Canada during the 1920s and 1930s – a sign that he interprets as proof of their understanding of the British

Publicity shot in Calgary from the 1920s showing a Canadian Boy Scout and Girl Guide with repaired Christmas toys for needy children. *Glenbow Archives, NA-4487–5*

Empire as a diverse community whose members could hold multiple identities and loyalties.[81]

Needy children and adults, whether fully "Canadianized" or not, were the objects of many Canadian Guide service activities during the interwar years. In 1935, for example, the Canadian Guide Association reported:

The stress of unemployment conditions has brought many new opportunities for service and Guides have redoubled their efforts this year to co-operate with local welfare and relief organizations. Among the many "Good Turns" are contributions of food, money, books, toys, fuel and clothing. Many needlewoman badges have been won in making baby layettes, children's clothes and quilting. Knitting sweaters, caps and mittens has earned knitters badges for many Guides and Rangers. One Division supplied 166 families with food and clothing at Christmas and quantities of books, toys and candy were sent to Out-Post Red Cross Hospitals for Children.[82]

Canadian Guides also made and donated clothes to impoverished families, raised money for food and fuel, and organized Christmas dinners for unemployed men.[83]

Feeding unemployed men and providing material aid to poor families also destabilized the ideology that linked masculinity – and indeed citizenship – with breadwinning and economic independence. Guide groups in Britain as well as Canada engaged in this type of activity throughout the 1930s, and one example, discussed in the January 1933 issue of the *Council Fire*, provides especially clear proof of the ways in which Guide service during periods of high unemployment could further undermine the already endangered male breadwinner ideal. Entitled "Adoption of an Unemployed Man," the article describes the efforts of a Guide company from Denbighshire, Wales, to provide material aid to a needy and deserving miner. Using language that in some respects echoed the discourse of scientific motherhood, the article's author described the Denbighshire Guides' decision "to adopt an unemployed man and start him in a business of his own." The Guides contributed money themselves and solicited donations from members of other companies. Ultimately, they chose to help "a married man of [the coal mining town of] Penycae, near Wrexham" who "felt that his best chance of employment was to start a business as a carrier." The article states that "within twenty-four hours ... a two-ton Morris lorry was bought, licensed and insured for him by the Guides" and that the man soon obtained a contract to carry milk to Liverpool.[84]

The Brownies, Guides, and Rangers who repaired toys, donated food, raised funds, and "adopted" this unemployed man were clearly "good citizens" who sought to serve others and help their communities. But what of the men, women, and children who were the objects of their charity? On the one hand, the material aid these people received marked them as worthy members of local, national, and imperial communities. On the other hand, however, it also implied that they were outsiders, individuals whose incomplete economic citizenship (lack of means or earning power) made them into passive recipients of Guiding's generally middle-class, white/British social service work.[85]

In India, Guiding's social service activities joined a broad spectrum of other philanthropic initiatives that combined older South Asian "living traditions" with new notions of active citizenship and foreign ideas about service and charity. As the *Indian Ladies' Magazine* explained to its educated middle-class readers in 1927, Indian Guides performed "an invaluable service to the young people in this country by ... encouraging not only a spirit of cheerful comradeship in work and at play, but [also] of active social service."[86] The complexities of these nationalist but not completely anti-Western ideas about community service and uplift were lost on many British Guide leaders, who often described the importance of the training they hoped to provide in ill-informed and reductionist terms. The Chief Guide, for example, told readers in the United Kingdom that "if *purdah* is breaking down and Indian women are gradually taking a more active interest in the welfare of their country, they need to be specially fitted [through Guiding, it was implied] for playing their part as citizens."[87]

As in other settings (and despite these stereotypical descriptions), Indian Rangers often served their communities by doing volunteer work with women and children. In 1934, for example, an Indian Guide official named Iqbalunnisa Hussain reported in the *Council Fire* that Rangers in India had "proved themselves good citizens" during the past year by: "helping regularly with Guides, Bluebirds, or Wolfcubs in schools for blind, deaf, or otherwise defective children, and in a reformatory for boys"; "visiting regularly and teaching games, handicrafts, etc., in a children's remand home, and helping in a nursery school in a mill area"; "collecting and repairing old toys for the Red Cross Society"; and "teaching and demonstrating village hygiene and sanitation and helping with adult education in villages."[88]

While Guide citizens' social service pursuits and the meanings ascribed to them varied across these three national and colonial contexts, the Guide movement's emphasis on duty and voluntarism was also clearly a reflection of widespread early twentieth-century concerns about leisure, paid work, and young women's use of public space. Throughout the late nineteenth and early twentieth centuries, medical and psychological experts, the state, and voluntary organizations all sought to tell girls and young women that managing their leisure time efficiently was part of their duties as citizens.[89] This "obsession with working girls' time off," prompted by the rise of commercial amusements and increasing numbers of single working women in cities, appears in Guide texts published throughout the interwar period.[90] Olave Baden-Powell's condemnation of cosmetics and "brazen flappers" in *Training Girls as Guides*, for example, insisted that Guiding's maternal and citizenship training would be enough to tempt young women away from commercialized leisure.[91]

But Guide sources and contemporary social surveys also show that many older adolescent members of the movement were likely to neglect their social service duties in order to dress up and "idle" in public spaces like cinemas and dance halls. Claire Langhamer demonstrates that young wage-earning women in interwar England saw the years between leaving school and marrying "as a time of freedom and independence; a period with no major responsibilities and no developed sense of duty to others."[92] Being unmarried and working for pay gave young women the belief that they had a right to determine how to spend their time and money. Numerous Guides and Rangers (especially in the United Kingdom) were also wage-earners, and many seem to have similarly rejected their duties as Guide citizens. The 1st Foots Cray Guide Company from Southeast London, for instance, included several shop assistants and a dressmaking apprentice, the latter of whom quit in 1927 at the age of sixteen because of a "loss of interest."[93]

Many other modern young women seem also to have lost interest in Guiding during the 1920s and 1930s – an era whose other attractions included reading, dancing, rambling, and watching films. Langhamer notes that modern commercialized and mixed-sex forms of leisure fit older adolescent interests more closely than did so-called "old-fashioned" youth groups.[94] Guiding's homosocial aspect was sometimes derided as especially old-fashioned and restrictive; as Jill Julius Matthews argues, by the 1920s in England, "women-only groups were falling into disfavour against the mixed-sex companionate form."[95] May Rainer, the young British woman who had described her former Guide leader as "a prejudiced old maid," was clearly not alone in her rejection of the movement's emphasis on single-sex socializing.[96]

In her 1937 study of the leisure pursuits of fourteen- to nineteen-year-old wage-earning girls from Manchester, Joan Harley found that groups like the Guides and Rangers tended to lose members once girls reached late adolescence. Many of the older teenagers she interviewed felt that they had outgrown Guiding's "discipline and activities and fe[lt] silly and self-conscious in their uniforms."[97] These young women – British citizens who would soon be able to vote – tended especially to abandon Guiding at the age of sixteen or seventeen, "due to their interest in boys and their desire to meet them."[98] Ranger numbers across the globe were consistently lower than were those of the Guides and Brownies, and the movement often had difficulty holding on to adult leaders as well. In 1931, for instance, the Winnipeg Division Guiding

Executive Committee lamented the fact that "fifty percent of the company and pack leaders had found it necessary to resign."[99]

Accidents, Heroism, and Chivalry

Even when young female citizens neglected their social service duties or abandoned the movement entirely, leaders hoped that their Guide training – however brief – would have left them prepared and willing to act in case of accidents and emergencies. While obviously related to female military nursing and the rise of voluntary ambulance and first aid societies, Guiding during the interwar years also encouraged girls and young women to see themselves as chivalrous risk-takers, able to cope – as well as, or perhaps better than, men and boys – with the hazards and traumas of modern life. The Guide movement encouraged girls to fulfill this particular duty of citizenship by being prepared for emergencies, practising first aid, saving lives in a variety of accidents, and imagining themselves in traditionally masculine roles.

Good Guide citizens, the movement's program and publications insisted, were well-versed in first aid and would think nothing of risking injury or death to help others in accidents and emergencies. This part of Guide training started with Brownies, who were required to demonstrate, among other things, how to "bind up a cut finger or a grazed knee [and to] know what to do if clothing catches fire."[100] As girls moved through the program's age-defined ranks, they were expected to spend more and more time imagining themselves as first aid experts and potential life-savers. The "service" requirements for First Class Guides included knowing how to deal with "shock, asphyxiation (artificial respiration), fire accident or ice accident, unconsciousness from accidents, fits, or fainting," while the additional responsibilities of Rangers included demonstrating the "ability to deal with three emergencies (household and out-of-doors) and know[ing] how to arrest bleeding."[101] While these practical skills were undoubtedly seen as important for girls as future mothers, they also presented opportunities for public action and a degree of gender freedom.

Voluntary life-saving societies and public concern with accidents in Europe and the United Kingdom were the products of nineteenth-century wars and middle-class concerns about urban life. Roger Cooter shows that accidents, especially if they involved automobiles or trains, symbolized the uncertainties and dangers of modern urban life, and he argues that voluntary organizations' efforts to manage them constituted an attempt to contain, militarize, and discipline disorderly urban spaces.[102] Much of his analysis of voluntary life-saving in late-Victorian Britain could apply equally to the interwar Girl Guides: "In stark contrast to the accident as a symbol of the socially arbitrary, transgressive, unbounded, unstable and perilous," Cooter writes, "were the hierarchically organized and ordered, uniformed and 'de-individualized' but 'vitalized' volunteers encouraged to fight in the war against 'accidental injury.'"[103] Worrying about and planning for accidents were also gendered pursuits; as Ann Summers notes, British women used first aid training and war nursing to make some initial claims to public citizenship during the late nineteenth and early twentieth centuries.[104]

Burns, choking, poison, fainting, broken bones, electric shock, factory accidents, and automobile and railway collisions are some of the many emergency situations in which Guide citizens were urged to imagine themselves. Baden-Powell, for example, encouraged girls to picture "a sudden accident near [them], and think out what [they] should do in similar circumstances."[105] Although less insistently than he did in Guide texts published before and during the First World War, he still occasionally peppered his published discussions of accidents with references to military preparedness. "When you see an accident in the street or people injured in an air raid," he wrote in the 1931 Guide handbook, "the sight of torn limbs, the blood, the broken bones, and the sound of the groans and sobbing all make you feel sick and horrified and anxious to get away from it – if you're not a Girl Guide. But that is cowardice: your business as a Guide is to steel yourself to face it and to help the poor victim."[106] Members of the movement were also encouraged to practise their ambulance and first aid skills by acting out a variety of modern and occasionally militaristic emergency scenarios. For the sake of authenticity and to minimize "feminine" squeamishness, Baden-Powell recommended that girl citizens splatter their "victims" with sheep's blood to ensure the right amount of gore.[107]

Guides everywhere participated regularly in these staged scenes of disaster and disorder, though sheep's blood seems never to have been employed. The logbook kept in 1928–29 by Winnifred Thompson, leader of the Nightingale Patrol of the 21st (St. Alban's) Guide Company in Winnipeg, for instance, describes girls working towards and receiving first aid badges (22 October and 10 December 1928) and doing "ambulance work" at a public display (3 October 1928).[108] Eileen Knapman, leader of the Swallow Patrol of the 8th Battersea Guide Company in London, also wrote – in greater detail and with her trademark sense of humour – about her company's adventures in accident training. On 4 June 1928, for example, twelve members of her

Company went in for [the] Ambulance Badge, including two Swallows. We spent the evening first aiding imaginary broken limbs, cuts, bruises, and grit in the eye; we surpassed ourselves in artificial respiration (secretly breathless, wondering if the patient would grunt); we answered questions on every emergency possible (and impossible!), from an ice accident, to the baby swallowing the new Austin 7, and the result was that we all passed![109]

Monica Storrs's northern British Columbia Guides seem also to have found humour in accident training; her diary entry for the week of 8 February 1930 notes that the Senior Guides "had a crowded hour of great joy and giggling restoring each other rather drastically from choking, fainting and nasal haemorrhage."[110]

Similar types of "accident play" also took place at international Guide events, where they could sometimes contribute to feelings of confusion and misunderstanding among girl citizens of different nationalities. Dame Katharine Furse, head of the World Association of Girl Guides and Girl Scouts, described several such instances at Our Chalet, the international Guide house in Switzerland. On one occasion during the 1930s, she wrote, "there were several amusing stunts devised. The Chalet 'caught fire.' Whistle was blown and the patrol leads had to get every member of their patrol safely outside. Then Briggsie was detailed to jump out of a first floor window onto four blankets held as a jumping sheet." Accidents were also "devised" on another occasion, according to Furse,

with much resulting panic and incorrect treatment. One "patient" was walking back from the swimming bath and had been "taken bad" so the patrol were told. No sign of a fall or violence but she was treated for a broken leg and a broken arm! Much of the panic seemed to have been caused by everyone speaking different languages. It did seem to show some of the difficulties of internationalism![111]

Guides in India also spent much of their time practising ambulance and first aid work. A Guider training camp at the American Presbyterian Mission compound at the Panhala hill station (attended by "one Parsee, one Mohamedan, eight Jains, ten Christians, and ... five Hindus") included a "First Class Ambulance demonstration of how to deal with those wounded in an automobile accident."[112] A logbook depicting Guide activities in Bangalore during the early 1920s features photographs of girls covering each others' limbs in splints and bandages, while a 1933 newspaper report of an Empire Day rally in Madras stated:

The Y.W.C.A. Rangers (Capt. Miss Wildegose) rendered first-aid to a fainting girl; St. Joseph's Convent Guides (Capt. Miss Innes) rescued drowning girls and gave efficient respiration treatment ... But the best thing in an interesting programme was the demonstration given by Stanes Guides (Capt. Miss Berlies) who showed how to rescue children from a burning house (most graphically depicted!) and, having rescued them, to render first aid and carry the injured away on stretchers.[113]

These examples of the Guide movement's global reach also complicate Watt's assertion that "Indian-controlled girl guide movements received little attention in the Indian press because girls and young women generally were not intended to be active public citizens."[114] Watt's work, which focuses on men and boys, even uses Indian Guides' first aid and nursing training to make this argument – a stance that becomes increasingly untenable when considered beside the ideals espoused by the Guides and the All-India Women's Conference.

Some girls and young women actually used their skills to save lives in a number of dramatic rescues and were celebrated as courageous heroines in the movement's annual reports, periodicals, and handbooks. During the 1920s and 1930s, these texts frequently featured detailed descriptions of daring life-saving Guides from around the world, whose actions were explained as demonstrations of "the practical results of Guide training in resource, observance, un-selfishness and devotion to duty."[115] This aspect of Guide citizenship training was part of a broader late nineteenth- and early twentieth-century impulse to promote life-saving and to recognize acts of "everyday heroism" by presenting individual lives and acts as models to be emulated. Crossing national and imperial boundaries, the results of this movement included the presentation by state and voluntary organizations of medals for bravery, the veneration of girl heroines like Madeleine de Verchères and Grace Darling, and the Watts Memorial to Heroic Self-Sacrifice in London, a garden featuring tablets commemorating sixty-one "everyday British heroes" who had perished while saving the lives of others.[116] Recent scholarship by Shobna Nijhawan and Nandini Chandra similarly shows that, in early twentieth-century India, nationalist Hindi children's magazines also printed stories of Indian girls' heroic deeds and encouraged readers to submit their own stories of feminine bravery.[117]

The international Guide movement expressed pride in its members' life-saving abilities and sought to recognize the brave citizens within its ranks with three awards for gallantry: the Bronze Cross, the Silver Cross, and the Badge of Merit. Published examples of actions that that had warranted these awards included "plucky behaviour in stopping runaway horses," the "rescue of a girl caught by the hair in a revolving shaft of machinery," "first aid rendered in railway accident although personally injured," as well as saving other children from fires, drowning, and motor vehicle accidents.[118] In 1922 in Ceylon, a Tamil patrol leader from the 2nd Jaffna Company rescued one of her schoolmates from a well, while a Silver Cross was awarded in 1924 to an English Guide "who pluckily saved a small child from being run over by a motor lorry. She dashed into the middle of a crowded street, and was able to throw the child clear of danger, though she herself was knocked down by the lorry and her arm broken."[119]

Mary Cadogan and Patricia Craig, in their foundational study of nineteenth- and twentieth-century girls' fiction, make light of Guiding's obsession with accidents and lifesaving. In a chapter devoted to Girl Guide novels, they deride the "banal adventures" depicted in "successive Guide stories, with heroines endlessly receiving medals for spectacular bravery." The characters in Guide fiction, they write, were usually most "in danger of drowning in the vacuity of their own pseudo-heroics."[120] However, situating these narratives within a broader historical analysis of girlhood, gender, and citizenship suggests that Guiding amounted to considerably more than banal and vacuous exercises in self-congratulation.

Especially significant in gendered terms were the movement's numerous published descriptions of young female citizens saving the lives of men and boys. The heroic narratives celebrated in these various publications are remarkable in their difference from the dependent and docile ideal of Victorian girlhood studied by Carol Dyhouse.[121] In 1920, for example, an English Guide was recognized for rescuing "a man whose hand was caught in the rollers of a steam-driven machine."[122] In 1933, "Wilhelmina Bekker, a Brownie in the 1st Ugie Pack [Ugie Industrial School], Cape Province, South Africa," received a Silver Cross for saving the life of a fifteen-year-old boy who had been burned by a fire in the school's engine room. English Guide Gwen Whittack of the 1st Cheltenham Company also received a Silver Cross that year, for "div[ing] into the river Severn, fully clothed, and [swimming] to the help of a young man who, by the time she reached him, had sunk twice. The river at this point [was] tidal, and about fifty yards wide, and twenty feet deep in places, and Gwen was the only person to go to the rescue." The citation continued: "there is little doubt that, but for Gwen's courage and prompt action, the man would have lost his life. Gwen is aged sixteen, and is a good swimmer."[123]

These examples of youthful female heroism, which celebrated the performance of qualities traditionally associated with masculinity, implied that all modern girls had the potential to be equal, engaged, and critically useful public citizens. At the same time, however, some members of the movement still explained Guiding as part of a mission to rescue South Asian girls from the "backward" trappings of caste and purdah. An article published in the *Guide* magazine in 1939, for example, insisted that, "in India, caste rules still affect girls very strongly." The article celebrates the heroic actions of Meiku, "an Indian Ranger [who] put her [Guide] promise before caste, when a man in a factory where she was working, fainted and fell, hurting himself badly by the fall. All the other workers ran away, and no other girl in the factory would break her caste by touching the man. Meiku, however, had learned first aid as part of her Ranger Service," so she sent someone for help and stopped the man's bleeding.[124] Imperialist assumptions aside, this example (like the descriptions of brave and adventurous girls published in Hindu children's magazines during the same period) also complicates Watt's claim that girls and women were not thought of as public citizens in late colonial India.

The movement's published rescue narratives, like several other interwar Guide texts, often described Guide citizens' courageous actions (and the movement more generally) by using the traditionally masculine language of knighthood and chivalry. This was a significant shift from late-Victorian and Edwardian narratives of chivalry, which generally focused on active men rescuing passive women and children.[125] The second (1930–32) Biennial Report of the World Association of Girl Guides and Girl Scouts, for example, called Guiding "a modern knighthood of women," while the 1939 edition of *Hints on Girl Guide Tests* told readers that "Guide Laws have come down to us from the days of chivalry. As the knights of old, so we to-day strive to live up to the spirit which underlies them."[126] This "spirit of chivalry" was quite conservative in some ways, based as it was on a strict code of behaviour, oaths of loyalty, and the acceptance of inherited privilege. Yet it also, as some Guide novels show, encouraged girls to imagine themselves in typically masculine roles. The young protagonist in *Joan of Glen Garland*, a 1934 Guide novel set in Toronto, for example, reads Tennyson's stories about King Arthur's knights and thinks to herself that "she would have liked to have lived in those days and reported each morning, with other worthy knights; at Camelot, in readiness for any hazardous undertaking which her King thought fit to assign. 'That would be something like life,' she thought, 'mounting a snorting charger and galloping off to save a beautiful princess in distress.'"[127]

These texts may be understood, on the one hand, as celebrations of the many new social and political possibilities that had opened up for women and girls in the years since 1918; on the other hand, they may be also read as attempts to make Guiding and its ideals of service and discipline appeal to the many modern young women who preferred mixed-sex socializing and commercial amusements. In 1928, for example, the *Guide* magazine stated that joining the Rangers would make young female wage-earners "feel worth while ... [by] lift[ing] them from a drab-coloured toil into the romance of adventurous service."[128] Throughout 1928, the *Guide* stressed the movement's links to chivalry, adventure, and service through a series of articles entitled the "Ranger Round Table." These articles combined an emphasis on English heritage (describing King Arthur's Hall at Tintagel, for example) with more broadly applicable calls for responsible imperial citizenship:

> There is now a modern Fellowship of the Knights of the Round Table, open to men and women, boys and girls, seeking as we are to revive the Old Order and all it stood for ... And in questing it does not matter whether the deeds are great or small, or whether they are done at home or outside, it is the spirit of service, the love that is in them, that gives them their value.[129]

The Round Table, of course, was also the name of an early twentieth-century political movement promoting closer union between Britain and its self-governing colonies.[130] A conservative successor to the nineteenth-century imperial federation movement, its invocation in interwar Guide magazines is further proof of the movement's support of an imperial ideal that, like its vision of citizenship more generally, promoted a vision of internationalism that privileged both the British Empire and the United States.

Conclusion

Citizenship, then, was defined and taught by Guide leaders in interwar England, Canada, and India as a series of related responsibilities. Good citizens, according to the movement's conservatively modern pronouncements on the subject, were politically aware future voters who had educated themselves about local, national, imperial, and global issues – and who did not support socialism and "political" anti-colonial movements or worry too much about "rights." They were also: physically healthy, determinedly cheerful, and self-disciplined young women; selfless volunteers, happy to forego the temptations of commercial amusements to help both their female relatives at home and a range of "needy" people within their own communities; and trained life-savers, ready and chivalrously willing to rescue women and girls, men and boys, from all kinds of emergency situations. Girls around the world were encouraged to pursue this definition of good citizenship in a variety of ways: through reading and badge tests; attending and organizing meetings, conferences, and plays; participating in physical exercises; learning to manage their emotions; volunteering; practising imaginary accidents; and playing accident games.

From 1918 until the late 1930s (when fascism and the threat of a second world war changed the tone and content of Guide explanations of citizenship training), these activities and the discursive backdrop against which they took place did go some way towards creating the movement's stated ideal of an imperial, international, and interracial body of tolerant and cooperative citizens. Citing the movement's official indifference to "differences of class, creed, colour or country," the 1934 Girl Guides annual report proclaimed that Scouting and Guiding "were widen[ing] the outlook of our future citizens, so that they may see beyond such narrow-mindedness and aim for the good of the country and their fellow-man rather than for one mere section of a community."[131]

And yet, in some respects Guide citizenship training was nothing if not narrow-minded. Emphasizing duty, obligations, and loyalty to the bonds of Empire, Guide citizenship training embodied what Ken Osborne calls "a double mission of control and emancipation, of socialization and education, sometimes emphasizing the one and sometimes the other." Osborne notes that critics of citizenship education (like some critics of Guiding and Scouting) have claimed that it "pays rhetorical lip-service to the one, speaking glowingly of autonomy, liberation, participation, and the like, while, in fact, devoting all its efforts to enforcing conformity, subordination, and acquiescence."[132]

Seen in this light, many aspects of the Guide movement's duty-based citizenship training program appear remarkably conservative: political training reflected fears about new electorates and modern leisure as well as a desire to maintain the social and political status quo; emphasizing health and cheerfulness worked to support colonialism and to make individuals and not the state responsible for their own well-being; volunteer work emphasized class and race-based differences between citizens and the recipients of charity, further supported a limited state role in social welfare, and continued to link women to unpaid labour.

At the same time, though, other parts of Guide citizenship training did open some new doors for girls and young women in England, Canada, India, and beyond. As modern female citizens, interwar Guides – unlike many of their mothers and grandmothers – were told they could vote, speak in public, enjoy strenuous physical exercise, and take decisive action in dangerous situations. They were encouraged to read widely and think carefully about their places in the British Empire and the world, and some of them rejected and occasionally mocked the movement's more stringent requirements. And if these modern girl citizens were as engaged with the world as Guiding intended them to be, it is also possible that they noticed and perhaps questioned some of the assumptions and silences in its official texts.

Chapter 4

MOULDING BODIES
AND IDENTITIES IN THE OUTDOORS
Religion, Gender, and Racial-National
Narratives at Girl Guide Camps

DURING THE EARLY TWENTIETH century, as Guiding and Scouting spread throughout the world, their official publications repeatedly emphasized the supposedly universal appeal of outdoor pursuits, and Guide magazines often featured articles about camping in different national and colonial settings. Articles published in the *Guider* and the *Council Fire*, for instance, included "Hints for Camping in the Tropics," "English and American Camping," "Happy Camping in Canada," and "A Hike in Hyderabad, India."[1] As with their treatment of domesticity and citizenship, these Guide texts used camping and woodcraft to stress similarities among the movement's far-flung members, but in ways that often emphasized class- and race-based categories of difference.

Camping and woodcraft, which occupied a central place in the mythology of Guiding and Scouting, were the products of a particular set of circumstances in late nineteenth- and early twentieth-century North America and western Europe as middle-class adults, concerned about the physical and moral effects of urban life, sought beauty, authenticity, and a restorative escape through antimodernism and wilderness tourism.[2] By the interwar years, these concerns – and their resulting emphases on the physical, mental, and spiritual benefits of rural retreats – had become an accepted part of Western industrialized mass culture. The decline of child labour, the rise of compulsory education, and the advice of a new class of experts on family relationships and the nature of childhood worked together to popularize the idea that children in particular would benefit from studying nature and learning how to live in the "wilderness."

Before setting off on a hike or spending their first night out under the stars, Guides would likely have heard and read about Baden-Powell's adventures in colonial military encampments and his first Scout camp on Brownsea Island, and they would have discussed woodcraft and camping at their company meetings. And, despite the movement's oft-repeated suggestion that Baden-Powell had invented camping, Guides around the world would also have experienced their companies' outdoor activities as part of a broader cultural phenomenon that included school gardens, open-air education, and the visibility of camping supplies in department store catalogues and displays.

Strangely, since, in other contexts, Guide leaders often worried about branding and competition from rival youth groups, the movement's organizational records from the interwar years demonstrate very little concern about competition from other camping organizations or from the less structured and heterosocial outdoor pursuits offered, for example, by the British rambling movement. Instead, most early twentieth-century Guide and Scout texts insist that camping had been virtually unknown before Baden-Powell held his experimental cross-class camp for boys in 1907. Camping, however, was far from a new pursuit in the early twentieth century; it had, in fact, existed for centuries in military terms as armies in combat and on the march also slept, cooked, and exercised in the outdoors.

In his early twentieth-century camps for young people, Baden-Powell clearly sought to reproduce some of the discipline and sense of adventure he had experienced in British army encampments in Afghanistan, India, and Africa. His army career, like the numerous contemporary descriptions of Guide and Scout camps as "militarily precise," shows that living "under canvas" had a longer and more violent imperial history than is suggested by studies that analyze these pursuits solely within the contexts of the child study and social reform movements. During the 1920s, Guide camping's connection to the military was also apparent on a purely material level, as many companies (especially in Britain) camped in surplus army tents that were sold at bargain prices after the end of the First World War.

Because of their links to Baden-Powell's vision, and – more important – because of their reliance on centrally produced ideals and training materials, Guide camps in England, Canada, and India were run on similar lines. Accommodations, of course, varied: some groups in Canada and Britain acquired permanent campsites during the 1920s and 1930s, while groups in all three places also continued to camp in tents on borrowed or rented land. Guide campers across the world participated in many of the same activities, including cooking, cleaning, swimming, and telling stories around a camp fire. Like the

Snapshot of the First Jasper Park Girl Guide Company, October 1929.
*Archives of the National Council of the Girl Guides of Canada – Guides
du Canada, APH #1911*

rest of the movement, Guide camping was structured according to age:
Brownies and Bluebirds were generally considered too young for overnight
excursions, Guides camped out under adult supervision, and Rangers were
allowed considerably more freedom – some went on trips without adult supervision, and others spent weekends travelling by boat and automobile. The
freedom offered by these outings, however, was never meant to be complete,
since adult leaders often explained overnight camping as a physically and morally preferable leisure choice for consumer-minded (and, especially, working-
class) young female citizens. In 1928, for instance, the *Guider* magazine
insisted:

> [Rangering] is of the greatest value in catering for the physical needs of the
> industrial girl, particularly when her work is sedentary. The outdoor interests,
> especially camping, hiking and simple open-air pleasures, are the best possible
> antidote to the indoor life led by the majority of industrial girls. These girls tend
> to become too dependent upon outside and wage-draining agencies (e.g. cinemas,
> charabanc trips) for their recreation.[3]

Early twentieth-century Guide camps, like numerous other aspects of the movement, were characterized by a curious combination of freedom and regimentation. As David Macleod writes about the Boy Scouts, many Guide leaders planned their camps around the twin tenets of "careful scheduling and incessant busyness" — concepts that also defined much of the movement's approach to "scientific" child care.[4] The scrapbook kept by one Toronto Guide in the 1920s includes a newspaper article praising the "military precision" of a Guide camp held on the shores of Rice Lake in Ontario. The Guides' tightly organized days, "the essence of camp success," included activities like flag-raising, tent inspection, and swimming, all of which were scheduled in fifteen and thirty minute increments.[5] British Columbia missionary and Guide leader Monica Storrs also believed in the importance of rigid camp schedules; of an overnight Guide excursion near Fort St. John in July 1930, for instance, she commented: "It's boiling, blazing hot now, and the children don't want to do anything but bathe. I have to ration them strictly to three times a day, and keep an iron control of their manoeuvres."[6]

But leaders' careful preparations and attempts to control young people's daytime activities were sometimes followed by fairly wild nights. A Canadian journalist confirmed this dichotomy in the 1920s, reporting that, on the first night of a Manitoba Guide camp, all forty-five girls had wanted to "talk all night; and at 3 am some of them decided to get up and dress. At this unearthly hour a grand pillow fight started and hostilities were carried on in lively fashion for awhile."[7] Newspaper articles describing similar hijinks away from parental supervision occupy pride of place in a number of Guide scrapbooks; a clipping pasted in the logbook of the 2nd Forest Hill Company (London, England), for example, refers cryptically to a series of "nocturnal feats" at a 1930 summer camp, through which some girls had their supplies of sweets "mysteriously replaced by tennis-balls."[8]

Campcraft for Girl Guides, an instructional book published by the British Guide Association in 1933, insisted that camping and woodcraft were healthy and practical ways to satisfy every girl's "longing for adventure."[9] *How Guides Camp*, a British instructional pamphlet published in 1935, suggested that a typical carefully scheduled day should include "'Hoisting of the Colours' and prayers – generally before breakfast – orderly work, possibly a Bathing Parade, a 'Rest Hour' after dinner, and organized games, woodcraft, and other activities, the day ending very often with a 'Camp Fire.'"[10] This pamphlet also reminded leaders that every Guider in charge of a camp had to hold a Camper's Licence, the acquisition of which required her to "pass tests in such things as arrangement of a camp site, with regard to suitable soil, water supply, etc. She must have a knowledge of all matters pertaining to camp and personal hygiene. She must be a proficient cook, and know how to provide well balanced, economical meals suitable for all weathers."[11]

On another level, then, Guide camping was also about bureaucracy and the filling out of forms. As the movement and its administrative structure expanded during the interwar years, so did concerns about liability and costs. These worries were far from unreasonable, as camping trips involved a number of risks that even Guide first aid training could not entirely eradicate. In August 1930, for instance, three English Guides from Norfolk died after eating poison mushrooms on a hike, while two years later a twelve-year-old London girl named Daisy Tomkins died after falling from a train returning from a Guide camp at Minehead in Somerset.[12] These tragic accidents were covered in the national press and were surely related to the movement's eventual decision to establish an insurance scheme in cooperation with the National Council of Girls' Clubs in Britain.[13]

Most Brownies, Guides, and Rangers managed to avoid such disasters, however, and thousands of them hiked and camped in places like farmers' fields and the grounds of estates throughout the 1920s and 1930s. In Canada and Britain, this practice of camping in tents on borrowed or rented land was eventually supplemented (and in some cases supplanted) by the establishment of permanent Guide campsites. These new permanent camping grounds often featured modern cooking facilities, cabins with beds, and central recreation buildings whose features might include soft chairs, a gramophone, or a lending library. These developments were a source of concern to some Guide leaders, who wondered whether providing girls with the comforts of home would undo the toughening effects of camping itself. The international Guide movement's acquisition of permanent campsites also highlights a central aspect of the Guide movement's influence and longevity: its knack for eliciting the support of local elites and translating that support into material gain. British annual reports and periodicals published during the 1920s and 1930s frequently described the processes through which wealthy patrons donated houses and acres of rural property for camping to the Girl Guides. In England, these gifts included Waddow Hall in Lancashire (178 acres and a seventeenth-century manor house, acquired in 1927) and the Beaudesert County Camp Site in Staffordshire (a 123-acre gift from the Marquess of Anglesey). Canadian Guide camping also depended on the patronage of local elites, though on a somewhat smaller scale. In 1928, for example, the Guides' Winnipeg Division bought a permanent summer camp at Ponemah on Lake Winnipeg, a purchase that was made possible through gifts of five hundred dollars from the Elks Society and one thousand dollars from prominent local businessman James Richardson.

While the Guides in late colonial India did have some wealthy patrons (most often British governors and the rulers of princely states), they did not receive any donations of property or financial gifts big enough to afford a permanent camping site. They did, however, often receive material aid from the British Indian Army, along with missionary groups and the aforementioned colonial officials and Indian nobility. In 1931, for instance, the organizers of a Guide camp held on the grounds of Government House in Pune (attended by a mixed group of over sixty girls, including Indian Christians, Parsis, Jews, Muslims, and Anglo-Indians) borrowed "tents from the Indian Army with Sepoys to help pitch them, and got lorries from the Tank Corps."[14] Similar types of material support – which must have done little to help campers achieve the Guide ideal of self-reliance – were also given to the movement's All-India Camps, intercultural and interdenominational outdoor events that were held annually in cooperation with the YWCA. In March 1932, for example, the *Guider* reported that the All-India Camp had recently "been held in the beautiful hill fort of Panhala, which has been well described as 'a jewel in the crown of His Highness the Maharajah of Kolhapur State.'" At Panhala, the magazine reported, the All-India campers slept not in tents but in bungalows lent by the American Presbyterian Mission and Colonel L.E. Lang, the Resident of Kohlapur State. Lang also "arranged for engineers to erect latrines, set out washing stones near the well, put up our two flagstaffs, and prepare the site generally for our occupation. The State generously provided free lorry transportation for all the Guiders to and from Kolhapur, about fourteen miles each way."[15]

Overnight camping, whether in bungalows or bell tents, was an integral part of Guide ideology and programs. At the same time, however, it was also a curiously separate activity that was only ever experienced by a minority of the movement's members. Economic limits to participation were especially widespread during the interwar years. As S.D. Sleigh, the captain of the 1st Smethwick Company (a "factory company" for young female employees of the Chance Brothers Glass and Lighthouse Works, near Birmingham), reported in 1922, unemployment and economic uncertainty frequently made "camping impossible, as there [was] neither time nor money to spare."[16] Despite this harsh reality, Guide books and periodicals throughout the 1920s and 1930s continued to describe camp as a place where "adventure depends neither on circumstances nor money."[17] The fact that access to the adventures of camp actually depended on both money *and* circumstances, however, was emphasized by the multiple pages of advertisements for camp equipment that were published in every Guide periodical.

Nonetheless, Guiding also made a variety of efforts to bring the benefits of its outdoor pursuits to the hundreds of thousands of girls and young women who never made it to camp. Girls were encouraged, for instance, to educate themselves about local plants and wildlife, and to earn badges for nature study and outdoor skills. Afternoon hikes and day-long rural excursions also allowed urban, working-class girls and women to experience, if only for a few hours, the joys of camp life. Young women from the Smethwick works company, while unable to afford an overnight camp, did spend "several very happy half days in the country on Saturdays." Two especially memorable outings, their captain wrote in 1922, "were enjoyed when two of the directors treated the girls to a long motor ride to the country, when a delightful time and hearty tea were much enjoyed."[18] Guides and their leaders hiked and trekked in South Asia as well; photographs from the 1925 All-India Guiders' Training Camp show a group of Indian and British women walking along a path through tall grass and dipping their feet in a stream – learning, it was implied, about the kinds of outdoor activities they could pursue with their own Guides.[19]

Many leaders and authors of Guide texts were especially concerned with what Guide author H.B. Davidson called "practical woodcraft for town companies."[20] Davidson, like a number of her contemporaries, hoped that urban companies would make some effort to learn about nature, and she was especially concerned that as many as possible should experience the romantic and "primitive" magic of a Guide camp fire. While acknowledging that "indoor Pow Wows" lacked "the hypnotic effect of the leaping flames of the bonfire," a 1932 article in the *Canadian Guider* advised urban Guide leaders to create a "very realistic illusion of the out-of-doors" by filling a pie plate with sawdust and bits of tallow candle, then lighting it on fire.[21] Similar "illusions of the out-of-doors" were also attempted in India during these years; in December 1923, for example, two Bluebird flocks and two Guide companies at a mission school in Ajmer held a fundraising recital that featured an indoor campfire made from "a strong electric bulb covered with red tissue paper."[22]

Natural Spirituality or Imperial Christianity?

Campfires, shared rituals, and an understanding of the wilderness as sacred space led many Guide leaders and authors to explain camping and nature study as activities that would foster a sense of spirituality and reverence in modern girls and young women. The supposedly obvious connections between God and nature, which had been discussed in novels, sermons, and prescriptive literature across the English-speaking world since the late nineteenth century, were emphasized in many of Guiding's outdoor activities. The formal discussion of woodcraft at the Sixth World Guide Conference, held in England in July 1930, focused explicitly on these links. The session was opened by a British Ranger Commissioner named Phyllis M. Bond, who claimed that, "when the Founder unfolded his plan of Scouting and Guiding, he gave to the youth of the world an outdoor game in which, as he says, they might find health of mind, body and soul through the wonders and beauties of nature and the tonic of God's open air."[23]

While not explicitly part of many Guide activities, adult concerns about secularization and the spiritual effects of modern consumer culture did underlie much of the movement's ideology and programs, as demonstrated most clearly by the non-negotiable place of "God" in the Guide promise.[24] (Despite Guiding's many unofficial ties to British Protestantism, the movement was officially open to young people from all religions, provided they were willing to swear to "do their duty to God," the British monarch, and their nation of origin.) This religious or spiritual side of Guiding, which was sometimes complicated by Imperial Headquarters' denunciations of Catholics and "other" religious groups, surfaced especially often in interwar discussions of camping as leaders hoped that modern girls would come to see the natural world as the work of a benevolent deity. However, looking for God in the "outdoor game" of Guiding could also reveal contradictions between the movement's insistence on natural spirituality and its links to formal Christian observances and Protestant missions.

Baden-Powell's writings, which were often cited orally and in print by interwar Guide leaders, referred glowingly to the spiritual and religious benefits of camping and woodcraft. One article entitled "Nature Study in the Guide Movement and What Underlies It," published in the *Girl Guides' Gazette* in 1921, outlined his beliefs on the subject particularly clearly. Referring to the recent carnage of the Great War, the Chief Scout expressed disappointment that, "in these days of so-called intelligent education and organized religion, war conducted with all the savagery of primitive heathens should still be possible between peoples who profess and call themselves Christians." While praising the "civilized" and mostly European internationalism and peace efforts of the League of Nations, Baden-Powell decried "the falling off in the attendance at Sunday Schools and in Church in almost every part of the country and in most of the different denominations, and the consequent materialistic outlook and unrest of the masses. Doesn't this seem to imply," he asked, "that we are not using the right methods for the times?" The modern child-centred outdoor activities of Guiding and Scouting (as opposed, it was implied, to the outdated and adult-oriented goals of elementary and Sunday schools) would prevent "primitive savagery" by appealing to young people's "inward desire to learn and to do, not through the application from without of dogmatic instruction in theory."

In this article the Chief Scout recommended nature study (as opposed to "dogmatic" theology) as a way to nurture religious feeling among girls and young women.[25] Nature study, he insisted, was preferable to "the formal Sunday respect paid to the Deity" because it offered "a genuine interest for the young when ... properly encouraged." By camping, hiking, and observing the outdoors, Baden-Powell claimed, Guides could acquire a range of skills that would promote world peace and help to "abolish ... the social disgraces of our time."[26]

Official Guide texts often stressed the superiority of this "natural," unstructured, and clearly gendered type of spirituality to the allegedly "dogmatic" types of nature study and religious observation that young people encountered in schools and churches. In the fourth edition of *Steps to Girl Guiding* (an abridged version of the Guide handbook produced for girls in colonial contexts), for instance, Baden-Powell contended that it was only at camp

> that one [could] really learn to study Nature in the proper way and not as you merely do it inside the school ... For the first time you live under the stars and can watch them by the hour and see what they really look like, and realize what an enormous expanse of almost endless space they cover ... You realize perhaps for the first time the enormous work of God.[27]

On the one hand, then, Guide discourse presented camping, woodcraft, and nature study as refreshingly uncomplicated avenues towards spirituality and reverence for modern girls and young women from a range of geographic and religious contexts. On the other hand, however, the movement's emphasis on inclusiveness and natural spirituality was often paralleled by formal Protestant religious observances and – as exemplified by the existence of an abridged Guide handbook for "less advanced" girls – a continuing belief in white Britain's global "civilizing mission." Guiding in general and its outdoor activities in particular were characterized by a tension between the movement's borderless, egalitarian spiritual ideal and the power of organized Christianity – a religion that, with widely varying effects, was intimately bound up with Anglo-American imperial expansion.

Formal Christian rituals, including prayers, hymns, and communion, were part of the Guide camp experience for many girls and young women in Canada, India, and England during the 1920s and 1930s.[28] These activities doubtless meant different things in different metropolitan and colonial contexts, but the fact that they were recommended and practised in Guide camps across the British Empire is worthy of comment. An article published in the *Guider* in 1933 stressed the importance of these observances and claimed that camp was "a good place to start" girls' Christian instruction. This piece recommended beginning all mealtimes with grace, discussing human dependence on God at campfire "pow-wows," and "thanking God for one of the things of nature each day – sunshine, water, trees, the grass and flowers, birds, the sea."[29]

The extent to which such advice was heeded or ignored depended, of course, on local contexts and the personalities of individual leaders. The women in charge of the 2nd Forest Hill Guides, a group from suburban south London who met weekly at St. George's Anglican Church, however, clearly agreed with the *Guider* that summer camp was a prime opportunity to provide modern girls with an explicitly Christian education. The Forest Hill Guides, whose nighttime hijinks at their annual camp was described in a local newspaper in 1930, spent at least one week every summer sleeping under the stars on borrowed land, usually in Sussex. While enjoying camp cookery and outdoor activities like swimming, the group always left the rustic confines of their chosen camping ground to attend Sunday services at local Anglican churches. In August 1922, for instance, their company logbook indicates that they left their campsite at the Plumpton Race Course to attend "the Communion service at All Saints at 8 a.m. and East Chiltington at 11 a.m." Eight years later, in the summer of 1930, a group of Forest Hill Guides left their camp at Sandling Park near Hythe to attend a church parade in the nearby village of Saltwood.[30]

Guides in India, a complex and religiously heterogeneous society in which Christianity played a relatively minor part, also left their camps to attend church services during the interwar years.[31] As reported by the *Guide* in 1924, a group of Guides from Nasirabad left their campsite in "an empty building at the entrance of the village of Ashapura" to attend church services on Sunday morning. Amidst their orderly work, drill practice, games, and camp cooking, the Guides also paused to listen to what one of their leaders called "a most thrilling address" by the Reverend G. Carstairs, BD, before gathering "round the fire for the camp fire ceremony and singing and comradeship of friends."[32]

Reports of religious observances at South Asian camps indicate that they did not deal solely with Christianity; some of them also emphasized tolerance and plurality as a central benefit of Guiding. One article in the internationalist

Council Fire magazine, for example, insisted that camps provided the clearest proof of what Guiding was "doing to India." There, according to the author, "you will find Hindus, Mahommedans [sic], Christians, Jains, Parsees and Jews representing the great antagonistic religions. They eat, sleep, work, play and pray together in perfect harmony. All bound by a common desire to be a friend to all, and a sister to every other guide no matter to what caste or creed she may belong."[33] A July 1930 *Guider* article by B. James, captain of a group of "twenty or so Purdah girls," described the benefits of Guide camping in similar terms. On Sunday evening at their camp site in Huttamoru, Kashmir, James wrote that

> the patrol leaders took "Guides' Own." One leader said a beautiful Urdu prayer, another led the singing, and the senior leader read St. Luke's Parable of the Sower, explaining it and interpreting it afterwards ... It was a marvelous experience, and all were amazed at her speaking. Would an English Guide be able to do this? I wonder. These three were Mohammedans.[34]

Christian ceremonies were also central to the Canadian camps organized by Monica Storrs, the British Anglican missionary who ran Guide groups among the ethnically and racially heterogeneous inhabitants of northern British Columbia in the late 1920s and early 1930s. Storrs clearly enjoyed camping, though the contrast between its outdoor hardships and her daily life in the Peace River district was not as great as it was for urban Guides and Guiders. Her diary includes detailed descriptions of several Guide camps, including one from mid-July 1931 whose activities included boat rides, swimming, campfires, and a range of Christian ceremonies. "On Sunday morning," she wrote, "we had the Service in the boat, which was the only cool place, and rather lovely and suitable. We sang quite a lot of hymns." After supper on Sunday, the Guides

> had a Campfire Service and ended with a special little ceremony adapted from the torch-lighting one sometimes used in England. We made a specially big and glowing fire to represent the Love of God, from which each Guide lit a torch to represent one of the Laws. Two of the little recruits lit theirs as Good Turns. We Guiders lit ours as the Threefold Promise and the last little girl, aged ten, lit hers for the Brownie smile. After that we laid on the firs a big white Cross to symbolize the Love of Christ and as it flamed up, sang "There Is a Green Hill Far Away." After that, each of us in turn gave back our torch to join the Cross in the fire, to represent the offering of ourselves to Our Lord, and after a few Thanksgivings as the flames sprang up and gave us new light we sang "Praise

My Soul The King of Heaven." I don't know how much it meant to the Guides. Of course you never can. But they had all shared in making the torches and the oldest leader had made the Cross so anyhow the little ceremony was very much their own.[35]

Storrs's reflections about the impact of her religious teachings – a rarity among the sources I consulted – raise important questions about how Guides in different contexts understood this side of their camp experiences. In the absence of textual records, it is tempting to speculate that, as with other aspects of Guiding, most girls took only what they chose from the movement's "nature religion" and formal Christian observances.

Storrs's relationship to her young charges – whose responses to her methods can only be guessed at – was complicated by her position as an agent of religious conversion. While she obviously believed in the child-centred methods and friendly internationalism promoted in Guide and Scout literature, her use of prayers, hymns, and crucifix-themed fire ceremonies – like her presence in the Peace River region more generally – are evidence of her belief in the importance and superiority of Anglican Christianity. It is important to note that Storrs was not alone in this respect; other Christian missionaries across the British Empire and elsewhere also used Guiding and Scouting as part of their pedagogical, community, and conversion work. Indeed, the 1928 Annual Report from the movement's Imperial Headquarters included a discussion of "Guiding as Religious Education" by the Reverend A.J.G. Seaton, BD, General Secretary of the Wesleyan Methodist Sunday School Department. In his report Seaton lauded Guiding as a valuable "factor in the religious education of youth" and reminded leaders that "the international aspects of the Guide Movement give them a wonderful opportunity of indicating that real sisterhood which is the true foundation of foreign missionary enterprise."[36] Despite its official emphasis on religious plurality and tolerance, imperial Guide headquarters forged formal alliances with a number of Protestant mission groups during the years between the two world wars. British Guide representatives attended the annual meetings of the Church Missionary Society and the Church of England Zenana Missionary Society, for example, and these groups were part of the Guide movement's group of "Affiliated and Kindred Societies," a list that also included the Girls' Friendly Society, the YWCA, the Royal Life Saving Society, the Church of England Temperance Society, the National Baby Week Council, and the Society for the Propagation of the Gospel.[37]

As Reverend Seaton correctly noted, the global expansion of Guiding in the early twentieth century was supported in some locations by Christian missions. Missionaries and church officials (a heterogeneous group, to be sure) organized dozens of Guide and Scout groups for non-white children in settler societies and dependent colonies across the British Empire. The meanings and goals of these missionary-led Guide groups would have varied considerably between Ajmer and Aklavik, but in both cases the movement's message of interracial sisterhood and religious plurality was accompanied and ultimately undermined by a degree of emphasis on conversion, coercion, and control. In mission and residential schools in Canada and India alike, the (mostly) white skin of Guide leaders gave them considerable power. As Patricia Grimshaw and Andrew May state in their work on missionaries and cultural exchange, "in many sites of empire, pale skin appeared the marker of a normative authority, of unreflective convictions of righteousness."[38] While Robert Frykenberg and others argue that not all white missionaries believed in or supported British imperialism, the fact remains that, in many colonial settings (including, I would argue, both Canada and India), missionaries and Guide leaders often "found themselves in collusion with white agendas about the control of indigenous people."[39]

This was certainly true of Monica Storrs and the other white women missionaries, several of whom were also Guide leaders in the Canadian Arctic, whose lives have been studied by Barbara Kelcey. In Canada, Christian missionaries and religious officials cooperated with the state in an effort to use formal education and organized leisure to eradicate Indigenous culture, language, religion, and lifeways. A number of the Anglican mission stations in northern Canada, the responsibility for which had been transferred from the Church Missionary Society to the Missionary Society of the Church of England in Canada by 1920, ran Guide groups for Indigenous and Inuit girls. This organization, which, as Myra Rutherdale notes, "was particularly active in promoting ideas about British colonization," sponsored Guide companies in mission and residential schools in a number of locations, including Aklavik, Shingle Point, and Hay River.[40]

In India, Guide and Bluebird groups were part of student life at schools run by the Church of England Zenana Missionary Society, the American Presbyterian Mission, the Society for Propagation of the Gospel, and the Church Missionary Society. Assimilation and cultural annihilation were not the aims of these schools (most of which did not require religious conversion), and a number of them eventually became prestigious educational institutions – several of which, like Isabella Thorburn College in Lucknow, still exist today.[41] Mission school Guide companies in India also went to camp, as demonstrated in the 1923 annual report from Imperial Headquarters, which stated that six mission schools had recently been established in the Central Provinces and claimed that "the type of Guide produced is most satisfactory." "This was very apparent," the report continued, "at the Holiday Camp held at the kind invitation of H.E. the Governor last May. The Indian Guides took their full share of work, and won the Shield presented by His Excellency for general efficiency and deportment in the camp. The heads of these various schools say that the Movement has had a distinctly good effect on the character of the girls."[42]

Gender Contradictions

The contradictions of Guide camping and woodcraft in interwar India, Canada, and England had to do with gender as well as religion. In Guide texts that were sold around the world, the Chief Scout often explained camping and woodcraft for girls less as thrilling adventures and more as sensible pastimes that would teach them femininity and domestic skills while appealing to their "natural" spiritual and maternal instincts. While claiming that spending time in nature would develop "the soul and character of the future mothers of the race," Baden-Powell also wrote that observing the outdoor world would provide every girl (implicitly white ones, in this instance) with "a right understanding of biology and her own position in the order of nature; to realize how she can be associated with the Creator in His work and how she can have her part in the romance of reproduction and the carrying on of the race; also that good motherhood is a wonderful gift of God, at once a sacred and a patriotic privilege and duty."[43]

As tempting as it might be to dismiss these thoughts as the archaic gender conservatism of a Victorian army officer, Baden-Powell was not alone in his beliefs. Numerous interwar educators, medical experts, and youth workers also claimed that domesticity, while threatening boys' development, was essential to that of girls.[44] While not as conservative as the American Camp Fire Girls (an organization whose leaders sought to use domestic work and Indian play to recapture modern girls' "primitive femininity"), Guide leaders across the British Empire did sometimes explain camping and woodcraft as activities that would teach girls conventionally feminine skills and identities.[45] British county camp adviser Iris Fazan clearly made this connection in a report written in 1929, claiming that "Guides with a home-making instinct can very quickly turn a bare tent into a 'home from home.'"[46] The authors of the 1933 handbook *Campcraft for Girl Guides* similarly claimed that outdoor life did "much to train the Guides in homecraft" and that camp was "the Guide home – a jolly out-of-doors home, where 'health and happiness, handcraft and helpfulness' hold sway, and cheerful friendliness abounds."[47] Many passages in these texts, obviously written with girls' expected maternal and domestic futures in mind, emphasized cooking, cleaning, practicality, and efficiency far more than they did excitement and adventure.

"Every part of camp training," enthused the authors of *Campcraft for Girl Guides*, "equally applicable in a home of another type."[48] Prescriptive texts published throughout the interwar years regularly reminded readers of the ways in which camping would teach skills that girls could apply in their assumed future roles as domestic managers, mothers and wives. *Campcraft for Girl Guides*, for example, also lauded "the resourcefulness and ingenuity, developed by means of gadget-making, [that would] stand a Guide in good stead in her own kitchen."[49] References to "gadget-making" (the construction of kitchen implements and small pieces of camp furniture with sticks and rope) were ubiquitous in published discussions of Guide camps from the 1920s and 1930s. In a representative *Council Fire* article entitled "How We Teach Woodcraft to Our Guides in England," British leader Nanette Bewley recommended using slender pieces of wood to make a variety of rustic domestic implements, including "grillers for toasting bread and sausages" and "pot-hooks, on which the tea-dixie can be hung."[50] This kind of activity also had a life beyond prescriptive texts; in the summer of 1929, for example, a group of cadets from Beckenham, south London, learned "all kinds of lashing and how to make various new sorts of camp gadgets. Two kinds were especially nice, a very neat sort of diagonal lashing, & a flat kind which is used for making tables, washstands etc."[51] Members of the Honesty Patrol of the 28th Winnipeg Girl Guide Company also used twigs to make brooms and cutlery racks on a weekend hike in 1927.[52]

Cleanliness, a must for modern and "civilized" mothers and housekeepers around the world, was also a hoped-for side effect of Guide camps run with "military precision." A July 1935 *Guider* article entitled "Camping and Good Citizenship," for example, opined that "if every Guide that had camp training kept food clean and fresh, what a far healthier nation we would be." The ordering and tidying of campsites, this piece insisted, was good practice for the inherently feminine task of "cleaning up ... the house to a certain standard before the other work or play is started."[53] Some Guide texts also made it clear that learning to clean up homes and campsites, a concept long associated with white superiority and European "civilization," was especially important for the British working classes and for non-white girls in colonial contexts.[54] This point appears far more often in official discussions of camping than in discussions of domesticity. The British Guide Association's 1921 annual report, for example, noted that "some people are inclined to suggest that the domestic side of a factory girl's nature is very underdeveloped, but the efficient way in which the orderly patrols worked in the camp huts, and the perfect neatness and cleanliness of the whole camp, was a proof that such criticism is not justified."[55] *Steps to Girl Guiding*, Baden-Powell's abridged Guide handbook for use in colonial contexts, similarly told its young and implicitly non-white readers that in camp, "you pick up the idea of how necessary it is to keep everything in its place, and to keep your kit and tent and ground as clean as possible; otherwise you get into a horrible state of dirt, and dirt brings flies and other inconveniences."[56] The movement's promotion of "scientific" domesticity was also embraced by some South Asian social reformers and Guide leaders. In one article, published in the *Council Fire*, "an Indian Guider" named Pushpam John argued that India's future mothers, wives and domestic managers benefited from "the obeying of whistles; the marching and standing at Colours ... the division of labour among different patrols; the making of gadgets." "A Guide camp," she insisted, "trains Guides to be good housewives and mothers. No Indian girl who has been to a Guide camp can come back without being impressed by the tidiness and cleanliness of everything about the camp."[57]

Yet, at the same time, Guide camping and outdoor activities also allowed many girls and women from across the British Empire to escape – however briefly – from domesticity and conventional feminine ideals. In her 1946 book *Here Come the Girl Guides*, Guide historian Kitty Barne argued that the first Guide camps took girls and young women "far from the Victorian ideal of girlhood."[58] Camping out, leaders knew, could be a liberating and modern experience – one through which young female citizens could challenge themselves and try out new identities. Camp life gave girls access to "traditionally male realms of adventure" – a degree of gender freedom that was embraced by many members of the movement, including a working-class girl from the Barnardo Girls' Village Home in Barkingside, Essex, who wrote in 1922 that her happiest memory of Guide camp was "of playing Robin Hood in a real forest."[59]

Interwar Guide texts also often celebrated the idea that camping gave girls a sense of independence. An article on hiking and lightweight camping published in the *Guider* in 1932, for instance, stressed "the *self-reliance* that comes from surmounting difficulties, of which opportunities abound on a good hike."[60] Reusing, being thrifty, and "doing without," all of which were central to the ethos and experience of Guide camp, acquired new importance during the Depression. In 1932, for example, the *Guider* explained square-lashing (the tying sticks together at a ninety-degree angle with twine) by saying that it "should be the first stepping stone to camping, and as camping teaches us 'to make do' with very little, so will square-lashing become a plank in the platform supporting a good citizen."[61]

The Depression, of course, also exposed the fragility of many established gender conventions, as exemplified in the story of the Guide group whose members "adopted" an unemployed miner and bought him all the equipment he needed to start a new business. Published discussions of outdoor Guide activities also sometimes revelled in the gender trouble brought about by self-reliant campers in a time of economic uncertainty; one 1930 issue of the *Guider*, for instance, acknowledged and made light of these role reversals with a photograph of two British Rangers in camp with their arms full of loaves of bread – accompanied by the caption "Breadwinners!"[62]

While camping and hiking, girls and women were responsible for their own well-being, even (perhaps especially) if it meant using physical strength and completing tasks that were usually left to boys and men. Building furniture and temporary shelters were considered particularly worthwhile pursuits, and magazine articles and handbooks urged Guide campers to become proficient users of tools – especially axes – that were often associated with masculine prowess. The reaction of some men to this "modern" development was captured in the 1934 Guide novel *Joan of Glen Garland*, when the leader of a Toronto Guide company explains to a confused father that "the girls can do carpentry work, Mr. Garland; they make their own tables and benches at camp."[63]

The Guide movement therefore promoted a pragmatic, vigorous, and even masculine vision of femininity for its young members. Some Guide leaders, like Miss Smith of the 1st Wandleton Guides in England, clearly believed that the value of Guide camping lay in its ability to "toughen" girls and young women. In an article published in the *Guider* in April 1932, Smith lamented the use of hot water bottles and actual beds at Guide camps: such unnecessary comforts, she feared, were threatening the movement's ideals by putting Guides "in danger of becoming effete." Smith's concerns, voiced at a moment that was also characterized by British fears about racial and international competition, were accompanied by the claim that "other nations" had not let themselves "drift from the old pioneer spirit of fending for [them]selves."[64]

Language is important here, and it is striking how often the authors of Guide handbooks and fiction chose to describe their subjects in masculine terms – as "woodsmen" and "handymen," for example.[65] This tendency is exemplified by a short story published in a *Collins' Girl Guides Annual* about the exploits of June Rockcliffe, a fourteen-year-old girl who lived in rural British Columbia with her English parents. June's self-reliance and Guide training become evident when she uses an axe and a saw to rescue an injured man she finds pinned under a tree in the forest. The story concludes when he praises June as "a man-size little girl," whose father "oughter be proud of her."[66] These fictional and prescriptive descriptions bear a number of similarities to the white imperial femininity that Mary Procida analyzes in her work on late colonial India. The wives of British officials, Procida argues, embraced a gendered ideal that "incorporated traditionally masculine attributes without completely eradicating fundamental gender distinctions."[67] While her work draws a stark line between colony and metropole in the late nineteenth and early twentieth centuries, my analysis of Girl Guide texts reveals the movement's emphasis on masculine femininity to have been an empire- and even worldwide phenomenon in the 1920s and 1930s.

Like its promotion of religious plurality and camp domesticity, Guiding's efforts to create a practical, nature-loving, self-reliant, and sometimes masculine identity for modern girls and young women were meant to apply equally to all of the movement's members. Yet they were also, in what by now should be a familiar pattern, sometimes given different meanings for white working-class Britons and non-white girls in colonial contexts. A number of Guide texts explained the gender freedom offered by camping as especially important and liberating for South Asian girls, who were still often portrayed in North America and Europe as oppressed and secluded child brides. Official sources, many of which were written by British women, often explained Guiding in general and camping in particular as a way to emancipate South Asian girls. In her 1926 book *The Story of a Million Girls: Guiding and Girl Scouting Around the World*, for instance, World Committee member Rose Kerr claimed that Guiding

> has enabled Indian girls, who in the whole course of history had never been allowed to come out into the open, to take up camping. There are now as gay and busy in camp, as ready to sleep in tents, and as keen on any kind of campcraft, as any girl from the Canadian West or from the great sheep-farms of Australia.[68]

Camping, Race, and National Identity

While camping and woodcraft, like domestic service games and accident play, were meant to highlight similarities between girls in India, Canada, Australia, and beyond, they were also ideologically loaded pursuits that conveyed context-specific messages about national identity and race. Published discussions of Guide camping in the 1920s and 1930s valorized Britain's ancient "racial" past, presented Canada as a healthy northern land (by appropriating "Indian" skills and ignoring Indigenous land rights), and depicted South Asia as an exotic and sometimes dangerous environment where independence (for girl campers and the Indian nation itself) was something to be avoided.

The problems of urban life and white racial "degeneration" that had concerned journalists and reformers in Edwardian England did not disappear after the end of the First World War. In some ways, in fact, they were intensified by postwar concerns about flappers and "modern girls" and by worries about the erosion of national identity and pride in an increasingly international age. H.V. Morton's *In Search of England*, an influential rural travelogue published in 1927, expressed many of the same ideas about race, nation and landscape that were published in interwar Guide texts. According to Morton,

> the "Back to the Land" cry is a perfectly sound instinct of racial survival ... If those men and women who, as my letter-bag so clearly shows, are starting out in their thousands to discover rural England will see it not merely as a pretty picture ... but as a living thing ... we may be a step nearer that ideal national life.[69]

Guide leaders similarly explained spending time in rural settings as important for English and British racial and national survival in the modern world. In the movement's 1934 annual report, for example, Rose Kerr (who by that time had become the movement's International Commissioner) wrote that patriotism seemed "to be rather under a cloud just now, because some people, perhaps the best and most idealistic of the nation, are feeling that children must not be encouraged to grow up narrowly patriotic; that they must be imbued with 'the international spirit,' and learn to love other countries besides their own." Kerr insisted that nationalism and internationalism were not incompatible (a claim that was likely not meant to apply to the troublesome "political" nationalisms of French Canada and South Asia), and held that young people "must love their own country before they can love any other." An important duty of Guides and Rangers, Kerr claimed, was therefore, "to get to know their own country" and "the glory of [their] heritage."[70]

While published in a report that covered and was sent to all member nations of the World Association of Girl Guides and Girl Scouts, Kerr's discussion of "glory" and "heritage" was really about Britain. After insisting on the importance of nurturing national pride, she praised the "unsurpassed beauty" of English poetry, urged readers to study English and Scottish painting and architecture, and referred to the importance of the British folk songs and dances that were being preserved by Cecil Sharp. But the "greatest of our possessions," she wrote, is our country itself, that exquisite scenery in which man has been a partner with nature, in which the old cottages and the trees around them are infused with the same spirit and seem designed by the same hand. Let us learn to know our country, not primarily by traveling by train or char-a-bancs to "celebrated beauty-spots" (although this may have to be done sometimes), but by going humbly on foot, in the spirit of the pilgrims, through the fields and forests that are nearest within our reach. When we have come to appreciate the beauty of our land the next step is to realize that it is a crime to do anything to spoil it, whether it be the deadly sin of building a hideous bungalow, or the slightly more venial sin of scattering our bus tickets all over the street.[71]

The old cottages, fields, and forests that Kerr hoped English Guides would come to appreciate while hiking and camping were part of what a number of scholars identify as a modern and mythical version of England: an ideal popularized in the late nineteenth and twentieth centuries that privileged the pastoral and "ancient" settings of the relatively unindustrialized south and that became more important in cultural terms as the countryside's real economic role decreased.[72] Like some aspects of Guide citizenship training, this rural ideal promoted a socially conservative vision of society — what Alun Howkins calls "an organic and natural society of ranks, and of inequality in an economic and social sense, but one based on trust, obligation and even love — the relationship between the 'good squire' and the 'honest peasant.'"[73] As J.S. Bratton shows, this vision of the English countryside was also often presented in British children's texts as a primary motive and reward for empire-building.[74]

The flora, fauna, and ideals of a rural and seemingly timeless southern England were celebrated throughout the 1920s and 1930s in articles and books published by the British Guide Association and by C. Arthur Pearson, the original publisher of *Scouting for Boys*. Many of these were written by Marcus Woodward, the author of numerous books on British plants who wrote nature columns for the *Guide*, the *Girl Guides' Gazette* and the *Scout*.[75] "The Woodcraft Trail," Woodward's monthly column in the *Girl Guides' Gazette*, featured descriptions of British plants and animals and essay contests with questions about camping and the identification of different natural species. In *The Guide Nature Book* (published in 1923), Woodward also encouraged his readers to learn about and love England by describing plants and animals as representatives of an idealized, ancient, and southern rural national ideal. "No country in the world," he insisted, "has fields like the English hayfields, fenced with ancient thorn, piled with lush grasses, and having their own birds, flowers, moths, and butterflies, their own sounds — music of whetstone on scythe — and their own scents."[76] While describing his rural walks and referring to the common fox as "a genuine Ancient Briton," Woodward highlighted the role of fumitory, or smokeflower ("found in every cornfield"), in Shakespeare's *King Lear* and in the poems of John Clare.[77]

Throughout the interwar period, Guide literature also encouraged girls and young women to practise "observant walking" in order to become what David Matless dubs "geographer-citizens."[78] Urban companies, whose material and geographical circumstances often made rural retreats difficult, were especially targeted in this respect. In July 1930, for example, the *Guider* published an article entitled "We Go Wandering – In London's Forest" by A.H. Blake, president of the London Rambling Society. Noting the difficulty of imagining a time when "you gathered wild flowers within a mile of St. Paul's, and fished for salmon in the clear flowing Thames," Blake urged modern English girls to hike in Burnham Beeches and Epping Forest. Noting the affordability of railway fares, he opined: "it is delightful that from the crowded London area one can visit these different parts of the old forest, and try to picture a time when dense forest covered this ground now traversed by roads and railways, and enjoy nature and the wild woodland almost as it was in olden times."[79]

While some urban Guide groups likely did visit Epping on company hikes, members of the Battersea Swallow Patrol opted for a different kind of Whit-Tuesday outing in April 1932. The group's logbook (kept by another, unknown member after Eileen Knapman's departure in 1930) shows that, instead of trying to recapture ancient rural England, three Swallows – Cath, Vera, and Nic – "went for a 'hike' in the City." For these three suburban ten- to sixteen-year-olds, an unsupervised day in central London was clearly more appealing than an inspirational ramble through pastoral English landscapes. Material manifestations of a great national past were not absent from the girls' urban excursion, however, as they visited a number of sites, including Smithfield Market, the Inns of Court, and St. Martins-in-the-Fields. But the modern pleasures of consumption and urban spectatorship also shaped the Swallows' day out, as they watched crowds in Trafalgar Square, walked through Soho, "pored over the bookshops" on Charing Cross Road, visited Guide headquarters near Buckingham Palace, and ate at a Lyons Corner House before returning to Victoria Station to catch the train home.[80]

Other English Guide groups, however, *did* follow the movement's exhortations to practise observant walking in more rural settings. The 2nd Forest Hill Company, whose annual summer camps included church parades and Anglican communions, visited one "ancient" rural site during their 1925 summer camp near Yarmouth on the Isle of Wight. A newspaper account of the campers' activities, preserved in the company's logbook, notes that the group spent an afternoon exploring Carisbooke, the medieval castle where Charles I had been imprisoned before his execution.[81] Three years later, in November 1928, the *Guide* magazine published a description and photographs by "a Cheshire Ranger" of "King Arthur's country" in Cornwall. Noting her disappointment with the state of the ruins of Tintagel Castle, the author wrote: "romance is still to be found in this stretch of the Cornish coast, but it lies in the azure blueness of the sea, in the roar of the fearsome Atlantic breakers, in those surprising coves that cut deeply into the cliffs, in rocky islets owned and peopled by gulls and cormorants." At the end of the article, the author encouraged all Rangers who "want[ed] to catch the spirit of King Arthur's Knighthood" to "hike or trek to Tintagel."[82]

While exploring ancient fields, forests, and castles, British Brownies, Guides, and Rangers were also encouraged through texts and activities to mimic a variety of cultural and racial "others" who were widely thought, by white people throughout the Anglo-American world, to have access to the "authentic" and "natural" world that had been lost through industrialization and urbanization. While it has mostly been discussed in the North American context, "playing Indian" was a transnational phenomenon that took place in Great Britain as well.[83] In Guiding and Scouting, British fascination with North American Aboriginal peoples (a phenomenon dating from at least the early nineteenth century) was combined with G. Stanley Hall's ideas about recapitulation, Ernest Thompson Seton's belief in the regenerative power of woodcraft and Indian play, and the racial typologies that had resulted from Baden-Powell's "two lives."[84]

In a number of texts published during the interwar years, the Chief Scout insisted that emulating "primitive" behaviours could be beneficial to white children in Britain and around the world.[85] He was especially concerned with the ways in which male "noble savages" and warriors – idealized versions of the men he had fought against during his days in the British army – could influence and inspire modern boys. While these ideas appear in a number of the texts he produced during the interwar years, they are expressed most fully in his 1936 book *Adventuring to Manhood*. "Most of the savage tribes about the world," he wrote, "go in for training their boys to be strong and brave men because the safety and welfare of their nation depend on the toughness and courage of its men, and not, as in civilized countries, on their cleverness at office work."[86] He criticized an apparent tendency "to think that the Red Indians are the only wild people who are any good ... [as] a great mistake. In different parts of the British Empire we have other races just as fine and with equally good customs and ideas."[87] Zulus, Maoris, and other "wild" peoples, most of whom who had been involved in nineteenth-century wars against the British, are all praised in this book for their hunting and fighting skills, and for their recognition of the importance of coming-of-age and initiation rituals for adolescent boys. Ultimately, though, the Chief Scout still argued that "Red Indians" were especially worthy of praise: it was because of their "toughness and courage," he contended, "that the Red Indians of America and Canada managed for a long time to hold their own against the white men, although these were armed with modern weapons."[88]

While Baden-Powell hoped that his tales of primitive courage would inspire and "toughen" urban boys and office workers, British Guide leaders and authors claimed that the masculine ideals represented by these idealized "Indians" could benefit modern girls as well. In interwar Guide discourse, these ideals were often combined with the positive qualities of authenticity and natural purity – traits that, as Philip Deloria shows, were seen less as the basis for critique and more as "the underpinning for a new, specifically modern ... identity."[89] A June 1928 article in the *Guide*, for instance, stressed that the benefits of Indian play were available to all girls, even those who lived in remote locations. While seeming to assume that the magazine's readership did not include any Indigenous children, the article asked: "Is there any Lone Guide, with or without brothers, who has not played at Red Indians in some form or another? A wigwam made of boughs and branches in summer and snow in winter, with herself within, is all that is required."[90] Nanette Bewley, the Ranger leader who had also discussed the importance of gadget-making at camp, also wrote in the *Council Fire* of Guiding's desire to tap into "the power that is common to all primitive tribes of men of reading from the book of nature."[91] Guide handbooks, periodicals, fiction, and prescriptive texts from the 1920s and 1930s often featured descriptions of North American Indigenous culture, including instructions for making "authentic Indian" handicraft, such as wampum belts, moccasins, and beadwork, and a serialized story called the "Jollydawnees," about English children playing Indian in their back gardens.

Guides in Canada also engaged in "Indian play" at camps and elsewhere in the interwar years. This, of course, was an especially complicated proposition in a white settler society in which imaginary Indians and assimilatory government policies collided with an Indigenous population whose members, contrary to contemporary expectations, were stubbornly refusing to die out.[92] As in the United Kingdom, playing Indian allowed white children and adults to appropriate and mimic Indigenous cultures in search of spiritual satisfaction, improved "racial" health, and antimodern authenticity. In the Canadian context, however, it was also about national identity, as social commentators and the leaders of youth organizations often explained woodcraft and Indian play as important parts of implicitly white Canadian children's national inheritance.[93] An article by a Toronto Ranger named Yvonne Roberts published in the *Canadian Girl Guide* in March 1925 did just this: "We owe all the skill of Wood-craft to the Indian," Roberts wrote. "We are influenced by the charm of his dress, the romances of his domains, the legends of the race. Above all we owe him the ancestry of our Dominion."[94]

Idealizing and mimicking implicitly male "Indians" was part of a process of Canadian national myth-making through which the Guide movement, like many other early twentieth-century educators, government officials, and social commentators, represented Aboriginal peoples as part of a noble but dying race. Both Baden-Powells alluded to this supposedly inevitable decline in Guide books and periodicals published during the 1920s and 1930s. In *Adventuring to Manhood*, Baden-Powell wrote that "the Red Indian warrior with his feather head-dress and buffalo hide robe was a fine picturesque figure of a man, and a keen hunter and a cunning Scout, hardy and enduring. He was a type of wild man that one could well admire. But, unfortunately, the red man of this kind is rapidly dying out."[95] These sentiments were echoed by his wife Olave in a report published in the *Girl Guides' Gazette* about their meeting with members of the Tsuu T'ina Nation on their reserve near Calgary, Alberta, in 1923:

> So many of us have read of their doings, so many of us have thought their lore should inspire us in dances and ceremonials, and very romantic and quaint these may have been in the old old days. But the actual real thing nowadays is but a travesty of what it was in days long past, and visiting their Reservations has a touch of pathos mixed with one's interest. We give them houses in which to live, whilst the teepee and God's open air are their natural dwelling places. We give them clothes to wear, schools for their children, churches for their religious worship and the race is slowly dying out and the children are kept in dozens of tuberculosis hospitals, civilization taking its toll, undoing God's creation in working out its destiny.[96]

Euro-Canadian Girl Guides, on the other hand, often played Indian at their summer camps, participating in "pow wows" and performing "Indian dances" around their camp fires. Press coverage of a camp held beside the Medway River in Ontario, for example, described an outdoor chapel the Guides had built themselves and praised the "very original stunts [that] were put on at the campfires," the most effective of which were the "Indian war dances" and

"Indian silhouettes."[97] In July 1938, campers at the Manitoba provincial camp at Ponemah on Lake Winnipeg (named for "The Land of the Hereafter" in Longfellow's poem "Hiawatha") were divided into groups named after "four Indian tribes" – the Sioux, the Assiniboine, the Chippewa, and the Mandan.[98] It must be noted that, while these and thousands of other settler girls were performing "Indian stunts" at Guide camps across the country, the Canadian government was in the process of criminalizing Indigenous ceremonial dancing, a legal process that resulted in the imprisonment of hundreds of Indigenous dancers during the first few decades of the twentieth century.[99]

The Guide movement, through its companies in residential, day, and industrial schools, was also part of this broader effort to eradicate Indigenous cultures in Canada. But, as Mary Jane McCallum shows, numerous First Nations girls used Guiding as "a means to practice 'culturally related behaviours,' and ... to continue distinct Aboriginal traditions."[100] Like the Six Nations girls who earned prizes for their needlework, many indigenous Guides used the movement's emphasis on handicrafts and "Indian lore" to create goods that they would also have produced in their own cultural environments. As McCallum argues, "Native and Inuit girls inverted and distorted [the movement's assimilatory] aims, using the Girl Guide organization to renew rather than dissolve their traditions; and as a resource that supported rather than transformed their own distinct cultures."[101]

In an essay that discusses Guiding and Scouting at Australian Aboriginal schools, Fiona Paisley notes that, while these groups supported racial hierarchies and naturalized colonialism, "indigenous accounts of being in Scout and Guide troops focus on the escape from uniformity they afforded. Where the impact of being institutionalized has been remembered by the 'stolen generations' as predominantly traumatic, Scouting and Guiding appears as fun."[102] A number of oral history interviews conducted with the survivors of Canadian residential schools similarly focus on the pleasures and pride that involvement in Guiding could bring. Marguerite Beaver, a student at the Mohawk Institute between 1940 and 1948, for example, recalled:

> Another thing we really liked – they had the Brownies and the Girl Guides. Shirley Stern was our Captain and Barbara Boddie was the Lieutenant and we used to look forward to that. And Lady Baden Powell come down there and we all went to the Tutela Park and the ones from the Mohawk Institute – I'll never forget, oh we were so proud – we won everything – the inspections for the Brownies and the Girl Guides, out of all the troops in Brantford. They used to take the ones that stayed there in the summer, they used to take them camping.

I went with them one time when they went to Chiefswood [the childhood
home of Mohawk poet E. Pauline Johnson] and we had a fabulous time.[103]

Beaver's words may be read as proof that, like many of their "Guide sisters"
across the British Empire and beyond, Indigenous girls in Canada took what
they wanted from the movement without necessarily agreeing with some its
broader ideological goals.

The Canadian landscape, a vast and varied collection of fields, mountains,
forests, rivers, and lakes, was often described in official sources as an especially
appropriate setting for Guide camping and woodcraft. These discussions,
unsurprisingly, failed to recognize that many Guide camps and hikes took place
on land from which Indigenous peoples had been forcibly evicted. Interwar
Guide texts often privileged the "pioneer" experiences and "natural" climate-
related hardiness of European settlers while obscuring the fact that many of
their outdoor skills had in fact been learned from Indigenous peoples. These
books also perpetuated the belief that (settler) Canadians' unique and hardy
nature was the direct result of this country's northern location and cold climate.[104] In her 1936 official history of international Guiding, for example, Rose
Kerr insisted that Canadian girls had "inherited from a pioneer background
a singular aptitude for campcraft, tracking, swimming, boating and winter
sports."[105]

Winter hikes and other activities were promoted in the pages of the *Canadian
Guider* throughout the interwar years. One columnist, for instance, encouraged
leaders to use the winter months to start summer camp preparations, by telling
their Guides to save money and collect canned goods and by practising fire-
lighting on half-day hikes in the snow.[106] Guide leader Olive Gallagher similarly
stressed the benefits of observant walking in winter. Canadian Guides, she
wrote, should get out into the fresh air to experience "many interesting things,"
including "the winter buds on the leafless trees; how to tell the direction of
the prevailing wind by the growth of the fir tree; the tracks of the tiny animals
and the marks of the winter birds; in fact a thousand things to see of which
you have never dreamed if you remain shut up between four walls."[107] Chilly
girls and young women should warm up, Gallagher suggested, at a post-hike
camp fire, where they could enjoy cocoa, toast, roasted apples, and "Komack
Stew," to be made from a can of tomatoes, eggs, onions, butter, salt, pepper,
and crackers.

Food plays a significant role in a number of recollections of winter outings
recorded by Canadian Guides and Guide leaders. Winnifred Thompson from
Winnipeg wrote in her patrol logbook about what must have been a frigid

tobogganing party held in January 1929: "It was very cold but most of us were warm enough, though Ida Turner froze one foot." Once they had finished sledding, the girls returned to their leader Miss Burritt's house, where they "played around for a while and then were served soup, doughnuts, cake, and fruit punch."[108] Monica Storrs's account of a winter Guide outing, attended by "ten Fort St. John Guides, the two teachers who wanted to come too, and Alice Leclerc, the French-Canadian girl who lives eleven miles from the rest," also testifies to the importance of food – and axes – to winter Guide outings. "It was a Heavenly day," she wrote, with

> brilliant sunshine ... sparkling through soaking wet snow. The two teachers, three Guides, and I came on horseback, the rest in sleighs. We found a clearing in the bush where the snow was not too deep, and there made two patrol fires. *Everybody* wanted to borrow my lovely little axe that the King's School gave me, and I had the greatest difficulty in keeping it for a moment. As it was the first day of using it properly, and as it was so busy cutting down, we christened it "Brutus." The two Patrols each brought a surprise feast, and had a race as to which would be ready first. The Canaries brought eggs and bacon and canned beans, and the Buttercups brought steak and onions and potatoes, so you can guess which Patrol won.[109]

Depictions of the South Asian landscape in interwar Guide texts, unlike many official sources dealing with that part of the world, focused primarily on white girls – the daughters of British soldiers and minor officials, whose parents were unable to afford to send them back to England to be educated.[110] A number of articles in official magazines, published during a time of white anxiety about racial privilege, physical health, and the future of the Raj, discussed the Indian landscape not as a regenerative source of identity (as was the case in Canada and England) but as a danger to be guarded against. Climate was important here, since medical experts and the British expatriate community more generally believed until at least the 1930s that prolonged exposure to India's warm weather would damage the moral and physical health of European children.[111]

British Guide leaders' concerns about mediating the effects of the movement's outdoor activities on white children in India started early and continued to be expressed in the movement's periodicals during the 1920s and 1930s. The October 1914 issue of the *Girl Guides' Gazette*, for example, featured a photograph of white Girl Guides (the Snowdrop Patrol, identified as "all children of British soldiers") in Kirkee (now Khadki), the site of a large army base in

Maharashtra. "As the sun is so hot in the day time," the photograph's caption explained, "the Guides parade in the evening."[112] Nearly twenty years later, in 1933, the *Council Fire* published a series of hints for Guide camping in India that featured similar words of caution about taking white girls out in the Indian sun. "Do not allow the Guides to go out in the heat of the day more than necessary," the article's author asserted. "Insist on topees being worn by girls who are used to them. An ordinary single fly-tent is not sun-proof, and only double fly-tents should be used. If possible, pitch your tents in the shade of trees." The article urged its implicitly white/British readers not to over-tire their Guides, and claimed:

> Westerners are often much more energetic than Indians, especially if they have not been out in India very long. A European running a camp for Indians or Anglo-Indians should be careful not to force them up to European standard of exercise. Organize your camp so that the active work comes in the cooler part of the day. Arrange for plenty of quiet occupations. Two hours' rest every day is advisable, as one hour is not sufficient in a hot country. Guard against overstrain in such things as water-carrying, digging, lifting heavy bundles of equipment, erecting screening, etc. It is very seldom advisable for Guides in India to pitch tents, which are usually large and very heavy.[113]

This article's detailed delineation of the apparent differences between Indians, Anglo-Indians, and Europeans, along with its warnings about climate, marked India out as a space that was decidedly unlike the settings of English or Canadian Guide camps. Published accounts of camps attended by girls from all of the aforementioned "racial" groups further emphasized the difference of India by describing its landscapes as exotic and extreme. A *Guider* article from June 1933 about hiking in Hyderabad is an especially clear example of this:

> As most of the Guides keep purdah we have to do our hiking in places where there is no danger of any man seeing them, so we arranged to meet on the Banjara Road. Hyderabad is surrounded by wild rocky country, and you need not go far to find a deserted place ... The rocks are most amazing, miles and miles strewn with great boulders and just enough soil to support a few small trees and prickly pear. Some of the tors are balanced on top of each other in the most fantastic way; any three of them would make a county show and picnic place in England, here they are just flung about in thousands in the most reckless manner.[114]

A letter from a group of Guides from Kalimpong, a hill station in Northern Bengal, published in the *Guider* in April 1937, makes similar – though slightly more positive – claims about the overwhelming nature of the surrounding landscape. Unusually for this type of publication, the letter neglects to mention the "racial" identities of its young authors; it does, however, point out that they (unlike their "sister Guides" in the West, it was implied) are unfamiliar with many of the trappings of modernity that were thought to have made youth camping necessary in the first place.[115] "We are handicapped in some ways," the letter states, "as most of us have never seen a train or a bus, or, of course, a ship, for our home is up on this mountain-top, surrounded by lonely valleys along whose depths rush mighty rivers fed by the eternal snows, but we have been lucky enough to see one aeroplane, Lord Clydesdale's, when he flew over Everest." Surrounded by the "gigantic snowy summits of the Himalayas," the Guides wrote:

We have no wireless sets or telephones in our houses, and we can never go to a cinema or a zoo, but in our own way we have happenings up here quite as interesting and novel: hailstorms where the hail falls as big as eggs, smashing our gardens to pieces, tearing branches and leaves from the trees ... earthquake tremors where the whole world seems to become suddenly like an agitated sea ... sunrises on the snowy peaks that are unearthly in their beauty, and moonlight nights where every tree seems alight with a thousand ghostly candles.[116]

Published descriptions of India's unearthly mountain sunrises, dramatic weather patterns, and decidedly un-British rock formations were often – unlike in Canada and England – combined with warnings about dangerous animals and men. An article entitled "Hints for Camping in the Tropics" and published in the *Council Fire*, for instance, stressed the importance of preventing snake bites. This piece advised Guide leaders to warn their campers not to disturb any "large stones under which snakes may be lurking. Insist on everybody carrying a lantern when moving about after dark. Provide every tent with a stick for killing snakes and either a lighted safety lantern outside or an electric torch, easily accessible inside. Whenever possible see that the Guides sleep off the ground."[117] (Interestingly, I found no anxious references in the *Canadian Guider* of the same period to the dangers posed by bears or wolves.) Guide magazines also occasionally published warnings about "marauders" and dishonest or violent Indian men, which supports Mary Procida's claim that "the powerful and emotive images of British women [and, I would add, children] as helpless victims of Mutiny violence shaped cultural norms ... and remained a dominant trope" among the British in India until Independence.[118] It is also clear, however, that all Guides in India – regardless of their racial identity – were thought to need protection in the outdoors. Camps in India, the *Council Fire* advised,

> must always be held on private, enclosed sites. An ancient respectable watch-man on duty at night will give a feeling of security to the Guides. Very often the police will provide a guard if asked to do so ... Pitch the sleeping tents close together, and have the Guiders' tents near to the Guides. If possible, persuade the Guides to leave their jewellery behind at home. Try not to have much money in camp, it can usually be deposited in the friendly bungalow which should be near at hand to every Guide camp. Having deposited the money, try to advertise the fact![119]

How did South Asian women explain camps and landscape to their young campers? How did girls in India understand camping and hiking with their Guide groups? Outdoor activities could also be part of social reform, a way to "modernize" Indian women and children, and to strengthen the nation. While the Guide sources I consulted often stressed exoticism and danger, it is important to note that this discourse existed alongside a more positive interpretation of the South Asian landscape in other children's texts, such as the Hindi periodicals studied by Nandini Chandra. These magazines, Chandra writes, encouraged children to go on country walks and used descriptions of healthy rural settings to produce "nationalistically-charged, indigenous narratives."[120]

Conclusion

In his 1930 critique of Scouting, Woodcraft Folk leader I.O. Evans wrote that the "Nature religion" promoted by the movement's outdoor activities "mingle[d] none too harmoniously" with its other institutional and highly organized aspects.[121] This chapter's investigation of early twentieth-century Guide camping and woodcraft reveals a number of other inharmonious minglings between religious plurality and Christian missions; an emphasis on domesticity and the promotion of feminine independence; and an insistence on similarity, adventure, and internationalism that was paralleled by gender-, class-, race-, and nation-based discussions of difference.

The girls and young women who joined Guide groups in England, Canada, and India during the 1920s and 1930s experienced these contradictions in a variety of ways, many of which are irretrievable. There remain glimpses, though, in scrapbooks, photo albums, and periodical articles, of the girls and young women who hiked, swam, cooked, and sometimes stayed up late at Guide camps across the world. Their presence serves as a reminder that, despite its conflicting and sometimes intolerant approaches to gender, class, and race, Guiding also provided space for a degree of freedom and play.

Regimentation, discourses of race and nation, and the opportunity to perform "masculine" tasks and roles were central to the Guide movement's promotion of camping and woodcraft. They were also at the heart of many of the public performances its leaders staged in England, Canada, and India throughout the interwar years.

Chapter 5

"THE MASS ORNAMENT"
Rallies, Pageantry, Exercise, and Drill

WHILE TEACHING MODERN GIRLS about camping, domesticity, and the duties of citizenship, the global Guide movement also encouraged its young members to display their skills in public. Mass public performances by Boy Scouts and Girl Guides, often called rallies or displays, were staged regularly by the leaders of both movements in England, Canada, India, and beyond throughout the interwar years. In amphitheatres and stadiums and on the grounds of governor's estates, anywhere from dozens to thousands of young people took part in public performances that included historical pageantry, physical exercise, and drill. "Impressive demonstration[s]," according to one Ottawa reporter, "of the work in which the Girl Guides, Brownies, and Rangers are engaged," these events were visually striking and carefully choreographed spectacles.[1] Favourite subjects of photojournalists and newsreel services across the British Empire and the world, rallies are also reminders that Guiding was an exercise in mass production – an adult-led attempt to standardize young bodies and characters within and across national and imperial boundaries.

Like many other aspects of the movement, interwar Guide rallies combined conservative and progressive messages about bodies, gender, race, class, nation, and empire. As historical pageantry, they supported class- and race-based hierarchies while allowing girls to act out heroic and sometimes masculine roles in public. As public demonstrations of physical culture, they celebrated the fit and docile bodies of good Guide citizens, echoed Edwardian concerns about national efficiency and racial fitness, and reflected the interwar popularity of mass exercise among modern girls and young women. And as performances of military-style marching and drill, Guide rallies were often explained as effective ways to teach obedience, physical grace, and self-control. Upending conventional definitions of military and civilian, masculine and feminine, the use of drill in Guide rallies was also a source of controversy both inside and outside the movement.

Guide rallies resembled what the German-Jewish cultural critic Siegfried Kracauer, writing in the 1920s and 1930s about mass sporting events and the synchronized movements of all-female dance troupes, called "the mass ornament" – they were public spectacles whose participants literally embodied standardization, factory production, and modernity. Kracauer left Germany in the early 1930s and later reinterpreted these phenomena as symptoms "of German society's slide towards totalitarianism and fascism."[2] There are some undeniable similarities of form between Guide rallies and the mass gatherings of fascist organizations in 1930s Germany and Italy, and my analysis also addresses this issue.

Guide performances, the results of weeks and sometimes months of preparation, were seen by the movement's leaders as vital forms of publicity. Tammy Proctor shows that, before the First World War, Guide leaders – like members of the militant suffrage movement – created spectacles and occupied public space to spread the movement's message and attract new followers.[3] The Guide movement's highly controlled use of girls' bodies in these public performances continued after 1918: "If well carried out," Olave Baden-Powell told readers of the *Girl Guides' Gazette* in 1925, rallies could "be the best propaganda."[4] She sounded a similar note in a mid-1930s discussion of rallies aimed at younger readers, writing: "[I have] often been surprised to find that although there are over three million of us in the world – counting Scouts and Guides of all nations – many grown-up people do not as yet understand this game of ours, and look upon us with vague apathy and complete lack of interest." Public performances, the Chief Guide insisted, were the perfect means to convert these apathetic and uninterested "grown-ups" to the Girl Guide cause. "So you see, Guides," she insisted, "you are doing what you might call your own advertisement! If you are doing good work and being courteous and useful, people will think well of you AND of the Movement you are in."[5]

While the motivational effect of these claims is uncertain, what is clear is that rallies were also vital sources of funds for companies across the British Empire and the world. Ticket sales from a "Grand Rally" held by Toronto Guides in 1928, for example, supported the purchase of a permanent campsite;

and in India two years later, despite "a certain amount of trouble over Guides resigning for political reasons," Guide leaders in Kashmir also held a District Rally "to raise funds for camp."[6]

In India, Canada, and England, despite (or perhaps because of) occasional "political" troubles, Guide rallies were held to mark local and organizational anniversaries, and to celebrate Empire Day and Thinking Day (22 February – the Baden-Powells' joint birthday). They were also often organized to recognize visiting dignitaries, and the Baden-Powells' diaries and published travel writing include hundreds of references to Guide and Scout performances that were held in their honour across the world. The Chief Guide's diary, for example, shows that, during their two-month visit to India in early 1937, she and her husband attended ten Guide rallies and a similar number of public Boy Scout performances as they made their way across the subcontinent. She described watching an "awfully good" Guide rally in Bombay (whose participants she estimated to number over two thousand) and, back in England that spring, she was a special guest at a Wembley Stadium Rally held in honour of the coronation of King George VI. The diary entry describing this event, which featured thirteen thousand Brownies, Guides, and Rangers, includes comments about the "excellent shows of country dancing and massed P.T. and camping" that were performed in front of an audience of sixty thousand people.[7]

In addition to pageantry, exercises, and drill, Guide rallies also often included demonstrations of "badge work" – the practical skills that good Girl Guides were expected to have mastered. At single-sex rallies (events that featured Guides and not Boy Scouts), the badge skills girls demonstrated often ran the gamut from domesticity to first aid and camping. The demonstration of badge work done by some four hundred white and Indian Guides and Bluebirds from Madras at a 1933 rally at the Wellington Gymkhana Club's Polo Ground in the Nilgiri Hills is a case in point: following the opening ceremony (which featured music from the Somerset Light Infantry), Bluebirds "daintily laid a tea table and washed up after the repast," while Guides and Rangers "rendered first aid to a fainting girl," built a trestle bridge, lit a fire, and demonstrated how to rescue children from a burning house.[8]

At mixed-sex rallies, by contrast, the badge skills that girls performed tended to be those that fitted most closely to domestic and maternal definitions of femininity.[9] At a December 1929 performance by Cubs, Scouts, Brownies, and Guides from South London, for example, the Swallow Patrol of the 8th Battersea Guide Company demonstrated their preparedness for motherhood, homecraft, and matrimony by acting out the skills they had learned for their

Laundress, Cook's, and Child Nurse badges. Eileen Knapman, the member of the Swallows who recorded their activities in a small logbook, followed her description of their domestic performances with a smug reference to her group's ability to subvert conventional gender roles and hierarchies. "The Guides," she wrote, "beat the Scouts hollow in the Team Games, much to the delight of the audience."[10]

Knapman's comment, proof that participants and audience members could derive their own meanings from these public events, does not negate the fact that Guide rallies were performances of the ideal qualities the movement's leaders saw as important for girls and young women across the world. On the one hand, as events that encouraged the public to gaze upon strong and healthy female bodies, rallies were celebrations of the new and emancipatory possibilities of modern girlhood. At the same time, however, they were public performances of domestic skills and obedience – qualities that had a longer and still powerful association with femininity. In this respect, and in their depiction of class- and race-based hierarchies, interwar Guide rallies were also often attempts to support the established social order.

As Michael Woods writes about British pageantry in the 1920s, public performances frequently demonstrated the power of elites by granting them "symbolically significant space."[11] This statement applies to interwar Guide and Scout rallies on several levels: first, these events used conventions of military and civic ritual to set apart and celebrate the members of these youth movements as ideal citizens. At the same time, however, most of them also conveyed the message that uniformed youngsters owed respect and deference to their guests of honour, a group that variously included the Baden-Powells, Guide and Scout officials, members of the British royal family, politicians, judges, the rulers of Indian princely states, and the viceroy and vicereine of India. The importance ascribed to these high-status adults is evident in a number of places: in the descriptions of these events published in annual reports, for example, and the many photographs and newsreels of Guides saluting and being inspected by elite men and women. These public figures were usually seated on raised platforms, a spatial arrangement that marked them out as both separate from the audience and – literally – above the girls whose performances they were there to watch. Guide performances in interwar Canada, England, and India, then, emphasized social hierarchy, discipline, and physical strength. They also prompted both positive and negative responses from participants and observers, and were used in support of a range of local, national, and imperial projects.

Historical Pageantry

Interwar Guide rallies, particularly in Britain and the dominions, often included historical pageants. Idealized performances of the imagined pasts of local, national, and imperial communities, these pageants featured groups of girls acting out historical episodes – many of which included well-known heroic and mythical characters. In this respect, interwar Guide performances owed much to the genre of historical pageantry that had been made popular in early twentieth-century Britain, Canada, and the United States by Louis Napoleon Parker and Frank Lascelles.[12] This Edwardian form of pageantry, as Deborah Sugg Ryan observes, "became popular at a time when questions of democracy, the franchise and citizenship were acute."[13] A critical examination of the Guide pageants held during the interwar years reveals that their organizers were motivated by a similar set of conservative concerns about modern girlhood, class conflict, the maintenance of social hierarchies, and the future of the British Empire.

Like their predecessors in the late nineteenth and early twentieth centuries, many of the pageants performed by English Guides during the 1920s and 1930s were based on the assumption that national identity was rooted in local, and often rural, history.[14] This belief, of course, shaped the Guide movement's approach to outdoor pursuits, too; just as the president of the London Rambling Society had encouraged girls and young women to discover that city's "ancient" past by walking in Epping Forest, so the organizers of the East London Guide Pageant, held in June 1926, sought to "show the people of East London – Scouts, Guides, parents, and friends ... what famous history was staged in their midst." Held over two evenings in the East End, then for several more at the Royal Horticultural Hall in Westminster, the rally also aimed to raise money "to find and furnish a permanent camping-place for the Guides of East London, where those who otherwise could not afford it may be taken in and given a real holiday in the country they so seldom see."[15]

Like many other English Guide performances, the East London Pageant included Romans, royalty, and lessons about the importance of accepting a hierarchically organized society. Described in the *Girl Guides' Gazette* as an attempt to highlight the "colourful history" that was hidden by the "grime and sordid drabness" of "the slums of East London to-day," the performance featured Guides in a number of imagined scenes from the region's history, including Britons and Romans camping in Stepney fields, St. Augustine preaching to Anglo-Saxons, and the building of the Tower of London. In the pageant's climactic scene, set during the Peasant's Revolt of 1381, a group of East End

Guides reenacted the final violent confrontation that took place between the Revolt's leader, Wat Tyler, and King Richard II on the Mile End Road. Presenting the killing of Tyler as a cause for celebration less than a month after the end of the 1926 General Strike, the East London Pageant delivered an unmistakable message about the costs of rebellion. At the same time, like so many other examples of Guide practice from the interwar years, it also raises questions about how these working-class girls and their parents understood and responded to the pageant and its depiction in the press.

While the East London Pageant painted an alternately condescending and pastoral picture of the place of working-class culture in England's past and present, it was also an attempt to inculcate patriotism with the use of local history. This emphasis on imagined local pasts characterized numerous other English Guide performances, including the 1931 Hertfordshire Guide Rally. This display included a "Pageant of the Hertfordshire Highways" – an imagined journey through time that, like the East London Pageant, began with the Romans. Accompanied by musicians from the Royal College of Music, the Hertfordshire Guides began their pageant by reenacting the surrender of Celtic warrior Cassivellanus and his men to Julius Caesar in 54 BC. Held on the grounds of Hatfield House, the estate where the young Elizabeth Tudor had lived in semi-captivity for several years during her sister Mary's reign, the pageant also portrayed King Edward I and Queen Eleanor on the road to nearby Hertford Castle in "1285 or Thereabouts" as well as the moment in 1558 when Elizabeth I learned that she had become Queen.[16] After several other episodes featuring merchants, agricultural labourers, and "vagabonds," the pageant ended on a comedic note, with a scene in which the "Famous [eighteenth-century] Highwayman" Dick Turpin displayed an "occasional lapse into good nature" by helping a young couple to elope.[17]

Highwaymen, kings, queens, vagabonds, and rebels – in serious and comic Guide pageants, all of these parts were played by girls. In this respect Guide performances stood apart from other mixed-sex historical pageants, in which female participants were often limited to allegorical and domestic roles.[18] In fact, English Guide pageants often displayed the same emphasis on chivalry, risk-taking, and masculine femininity that characterized the movement's approach to citizenship and camping.

In *Scouting for Boys*, Baden-Powell claimed that St. George, the dragon-slaying patron saint of England, was also a model for modern boys and young men.[19] He made no similar mention of chivalric behaviour for girls in the Guide handbook, but some of the movement's female leaders clearly believed that the myth of St. George contained ideals that were relevant for girls as well.

While the protagonists of several Guide novels dreamed of being knights and rescuing princesses, dozens of English girls acted out these roles in pageant performances during the interwar years.

Guides from Leicester, for example, braved a rainy day in July 1931 to perform physical drill, team games, and "a very dramatic rendering of the legend of St. George" before an audience that included Princess Mary, Princess Royal, who had been named Honorary President of the British Girl Guides in 1920.[20] That same year, a rally featuring some seven thousand Essex Guides included a pageant in which "a Princess" was tied to a stake and "left to the mercy" of a dragon. After "a fierce battle," the girl performing as St. George killed the dragon before "claim[ing] the Princess as his [her] bride ... amid the cheers of the crowd."[21] The 1937 coronation rally at Wembley Stadium featured yet another version of this narrative: there, a dragon "made up of about a hundred Brownies" tried to devour a princess but "was foiled," according to the movement's annual report, "by a gallant St. George mounted on a hobby horse."[22] These performances, orchestrated on one level to create feelings of national pride, also let girls embody daring heroes and act out scenes of independence and adventure – albeit in ways that ultimately reinforced existing cultural scripts about active masculinity and passive femininity.

Whereas English Guide pageants tended to concentrate on chivalry and place-based histories, their Canadian equivalents often skimmed over local pasts in order to focus on a "colony-to-nation" progress narrative. Most Guide pageants in interwar Canada, like the historical performances that marked the 1908 Tercentenary of Quebec and the 1927 Diamond Jubilee of Confederation, were essentially celebrations of settler colonialism. At public performances across the country during the 1920s and 1930s, Brownies, Guides, and Rangers acted out scenes that focused on European exploration, conflicts with and the eventual disappearance of "Indians," and the westward growth of white settlement.[23] These Canadian Guide pageants, which glorified French and British heroes and heroines while portraying Indigenous people as alternately childlike and dangerous, were – like their counterparts in Britain – characterized by varying degrees of anachronism and historical wishful thinking.

Of the thousands of Canadian girls and young women who donned period costumes and performed both male and female roles in Guide pageants during the 1920s and 1930s, several hundred were featured in a rally staged on a Saturday afternoon in April 1923 at Massey Hall in Toronto. This performance was held in honour of Olave Baden-Powell, who had travelled Canada with her husband to attend the triennial conference of the National Council of Education, a group of Anglo-Canadian educational, business, and religious leaders who promoted a conservative vision of citizenship, schooling, and national unity.[24] In an article describing this visit to Canada, the Chief Guide sought to explain the country's "many political, social, religious and national problems" to the readers of the *Girl Guides' Gazette*. Her interpretation of these problems, which had much in common with the ideals of the National Council of Education, focused particularly on what she called "the large influx of 'non-English-speaking' peoples from central Europe who come to make their livings" and "the perpetual attraction of city life and crowds and cinemas that prevents people settling contentedly on land to farm."[25]

While praising the healthy, rural, and assimilatory leisure pursuits offered by Canadian Guide leaders, Olave Baden-Powell also described the Massey Hall Rally. She devoted particular attention to a pageant of Canadian history in which "Guides, dressed in the costumes of the times, came on to the stage and acted scenes ... of [the] bravery and conquests that brought the Dominion within the British Empire."[26] The performance that had so impressed the Chief Guide consisted of seven consecutive tableaux, each one portraying a successive phase in what Torontonian Guide leaders, like many of their contemporaries, saw as Canada's inevitable march towards British settlement. Each scene was acted out silently by the adolescent members of various Ranger companies, while a series of explanatory poems was read by a Guide leader named Mrs. L. Ballantyne. In the first tableau, entitled "Jacques Cartier, Followers, Priests, Sailors, [and] Soldiers meet the Indians," girls acted out a sixteenth-century scene of contact between Indigenous people and the French, which was explained in verse as the moment that fuelled Cartier's "desire to come again / to civilize the land." Next, a different group of costumed Rangers pantomimed the experiences of the seventeenth-century French explorer Samuel de Champlain, his missionary followers, and "Indians" as they "push[ed] farther west into Canada."[27] These scenes, which celebrated the "heroic age" of European exploration, fulfilled a double function in 1920s Toronto: they expressed imperialist sentiment and a belief in racial hierarchy, while also celebrating national unity and progress.[28]

The next part of the pageant, "Madelaine Vercheres" [sic], gave the audience its first glimpse of white female heroism as yet more Rangers acted out what would have been a well-known story to many Canadians: fourteen-year-old Madeleine de Verchères's successful defence, in 1692, of her family's Quebec fort against an Iroquois attack.[29] Mrs. Ballantyne's narration of this event, which focused on a white girl's violent triumph over "great hordes of painted Indians" in "war canoes" east of Montreal (provided for the Massey Hall performance "by Gilbert Deane, of Deane's Sunnyside Pleasure Boats"), both demonized Indigenous peoples and stressed the importance of agency and duty for young white women. This part of the Toronto pageant also echoed other published Guide texts in its depiction of Madeleine de Verchères as a model of loyalty and selflessness whose daring deeds, it was hoped, might appeal to cinema-loving twentieth-century girls and young women. According to several chapters in an anthology entitled *The Guiding Book*, the feminine bravery displayed by heroines like Verchères and Grace Darling were of particular importance to modern girls, whose work and leisure pursuits often placed them "side by side with men." One chapter in *The Guiding Book*, on "Loyalty," singled out de Verchères as a particularly inspirational role model – a loyal and courageous girl who had enough "imagination ... to see beyond the band of angry Indians to a white man's Christian country that she must save."[30]

The Toronto Rangers' representation of Madeleine de Verchères and her Iroquois foes was followed by a "street scene" tableau in which girls pretended to be "Indians, Squaws, Coureurs des Bois, Seyniers [sic], Ladies, Trappers, Monks, Nuns, Etc., in Montreal of Old." From there, the pageant moved on to what was likely the best-known historical example of white feminine heroism in the Canadian past: Laura Secord's trek across enemy lines during the War of 1812. Courage in the face of danger, a key concept in Guide citizenship training, was at the heart of this particular scene, as Mrs. Ballantyne's narration informed the audience: "With every crackling twig, her heart within her started / Lest it be a wandering enemy or Indian." Like the interwar Victoria Day parades that have been studied by Katie Pickles, this Girl Guide pageant and others liked it silenced Indigenous narratives and replaced them with "Anglo-Celtic spectacles that imposed the meanings of the colonizer."[31]

The final tableau presented to the Toronto audience, most of whom had paid a modest admission fee to support Guide activities in Ontario, was a reenactment of early "pioneer life." Especially to be celebrated as nation- and empire-builders, as Mrs. Ballantyne's verse made clear, were the "United Empire Loyalists that ever / Clung to Britain and the British land, / And the Pioneers who cleared the forests / Mile on mile where now fair homesteads stand." This interpretation of British settlement recalls the early twentieth-century vogue for "Empire Romance" novels – pro-imperialist texts in which, as Barbara Bush notes, virtuous white womanhood was used to represent the importance of the white Dominions, "reflecting women's central role in 'domesticating the heart of the wild,' taming marauding 'frontier masculinities,' and securing the stability of racial purity of the white Empire."[32]

This final scene, a celebration of the hardiness, "racial" pedigree, and imperial loyalty of nineteenth-century white settlers, was also the only one without any Indigenous characters. Whereas previous scenes had depicted the Aboriginal inhabitants of northern North America as alternately threatening and colourful reminders of Canada's early modern colonial past, there was literally no place for them in a nation of cleared forests and "fair" pioneer homesteads. Olave Baden-Powell noticed this as well, and wrote in the *Girl Guides' Gazette* that, along with conquest and settlement, the Massey Hall pageant also depicted "the passing of the Red Indian."[33] Despite the combined efforts of church and state, Indigenous peoples in interwar Canada were neither "passing" nor "dying out" – and I suspect that this is one instance in which the age of the participants limited possibilities for resisting or reshaping the narrative. Unlike the Indigenous adult participants in the Quebec tercentenary celebrations, who performed their own version of "Indianness" despite a different script having been written for them, the young performers at Massey Hall (few, if any, of whom were Aboriginal) were given little choice in the matters of participation and role assignment.[34]

Did South Asian Guide rallies also include historical pageants? What kinds of messages would Guide pageantry in interwar India have conveyed about the past? These questions are difficult, if not impossible, to answer since the archival collections of Girl Guiding UK, the British Library, and the Bharat Scouts and Guides include no programs or promotional material from Guide performances in the years before Independence. Pageantry (as opposed to exercise and badge work) is also virtually absent from visual and textual depictions of the Indian Guide rallies that exist in annual reports and scrapbooks.

The only reference to South Asian historical pageantry I have been able to locate comes from the pages of the *Guide* magazine, which reprinted a speech made by Olave Baden-Powell at a 1937 rally held on the grounds of the Government House in Nagpur, which was attended by numerous high-ranking leaders of the Indian Guide movement, including Chief Commissioner Mrs. Carey Morgan and Provincial Commissioners from Maharashtra, Bengal, the United Provinces, Hyderabad, and the Punjab. Yet instead of celebrating local, imperial, or national heroes, this event reenacted the founding and growth of the Guide movement in India. "You have seen depicted by one of your companies, the history of the Guide Movement in India," the Chief Guide told the assembled girls. "Aren't you proud to feel that it was in your Province that the seed was first sown?" Those first Guides, she said, "were the pioneers and the origin of a sisterhood which now numbers about 40,000 already in this great and wonderful country of India."[35] How, if at all, did the pageant deal with the fact that the first Indian Guide company, formed in nearby Jabalpur, was only open to girls with British parents? While no record remains of the intentions of this pageant's organizers (or of the identities of the girls involved), it is possible that the decision to tell an organizational story instead of an imperial, national, or local one was an attempt to preempt or avoid questions about nationalism and the power imbalances inherent in British rule.

Exercise

In addition to using pageantry to narrate local, national, and organizational pasts in ways that often supported social hierarchies, Guide rallies were also intended as proof of the movement's ability to produce strong, docile, and uniformly healthy young female bodies. As mass demonstrations of physical culture, these events both reflected and contributed to Guiding's vision of healthy citizenship, which intersected with a broader understanding, new in the interwar years, of fit and active female bodies as emblems of modernity.[36] The Guide movement's promotion of exercise, which challenged an older understanding of intense physical activity as unsuitable for girls, was also often explained as a way to ensure the physical fitness of future mothers, their putative children, and the body politic – though, as was the case with the movement's citizenship training initiatives, some Indian Guiders explained physical culture as a way to strengthen a national, rather than an imperial, community.

While the movement's emphasis on mass exercise intensified in the mid- to late 1930s in the midst of concerns about the discipline and physical prowess of young people in fascist countries and perceived competition from groups like the British National Council of Girls' Clubs and the Women's League of Health and Beauty, physical fitness and public displays of young female bodies in motion had been part of Guiding's program since its inception. Along with "Character and Intelligence," "Skill and Handicraft," and "Service for Others and Fellowship," the fourth object of Guide training as outlined in the Guide handbook was "Physical Health and Hygiene, through development up to standard by games and exercises designed for the purpose" – a reflection of the movement's origins in early twentieth-century white/British fears about racial degeneration.[37]

In this respect, Guiding's emphasis on training and strengthening bodies was part of a set of globally circulating discourses and practices that emphasized physical culture.[38] It also gave girls in England, India, Canada, and beyond age- and gender-specific messages about the importance of physical training. Olave Baden-Powell, for example, articulated the movement's conservatively modern understanding of games, exercises, and the value of girls' bodies especially clearly in a speech at the "Girl Guide Victory Rally" held at the Royal

Albert Hall in London in November 1919. After praising the Guide movement's wartime promotion of obedience, helpfulness, and feminine self-control, she also noted that girls and young women had recently "realize[d] that physical fitness is not the prerogative of manhood." Sports, swimming, camping, and physical culture, she insisted, were as central to the Guides as they were to the Scouts – but they also needed to be practised correctly, in order to prevent physically strong modern girls from "becom[ing] tom-boys."[39]

This association of physical culture with conventional definitions of femininity, visible in performances of nursing and domestic skills at rallies, was also echoed in other published discussions of girlhood and Guiding during the interwar years. The author of an article entitled "Physical Training" published in the *Canadian Guider* in 1936, for example, explained the value of exercise with reference to maternity and domesticity:

> To the motherly girl may occur the value of a sound, active, healthy body able to carry all the demands made on it. She wants to play games and run races with possible small sons and daughters of the future; and wants to be able to get through the week's wash and the day's work and have time and energy to enjoy the evenings, and be able to "do things and go places" with her husband as well as create for him and her children a peaceful atmosphere of calm and the contented enjoyment of home life.[40]

The real value of physical training, according to this article, lay not in the salubrious and non-commercial leisure activities it offered girls in the present, but rather in the healthy and harmonious home lives it promised to husbands and children in the future. Yet this imagined future, which stressed white racial fitness, domestic harmony, and imperial stability, was not used universally to explain the importance of exercise for modern girls. In South Asia, some of the movement's supporters also understood Guiding as a way to strengthen girls' bodies not for the British Empire but for the Indian nation.

Because of its perceived effectiveness as a nationalist pursuit, training for motherhood, and a means to strengthen the British Empire, physical culture played a central part in the dozens of Guide rallies that were held across Canada, India, and the UK during the interwar years. Yet while prescriptive discussions of the individual and collective benefits of exercise abound in the movement's textual archives, it is more difficult to discern what exactly was involved in the mass demonstrations of physical training that were regularly featured at Guide rallies. A program from the 16th Annual Montreal Guide Rally, held in May 1938, includes references to a number of physical pursuits, including bowling, tennis, sprinting, baseball, rowing, and a "Good Posture Competition."[41] Other textual sources include less information: the section on Assam in the Guide Association's 1927 report, for example, notes only that on Empire Day that year, "the Shillong and Khesi Guides and Bluebirds had sports and a tea."[42] Photograph albums provide some further clues about the types of exercises undertaken by rally participants; one album in the south Indian city of Bangalore, for example, includes a photo captioned "Practising for the Rally" – an image in which Guides from the Methodist-run Baldwin Girls' High School are shown making "human pyramids" outdoors on the grass.[43]

Guide rallies also often included folk dancing, a form of physical activity that was used by schoolteachers and informal educators across early twentieth-century Britain and the dominions to cultivate patriotism, encourage physical fitness, and build support for the British Empire.[44] Like pageantry, folk dancing also conveyed specific messages about national and racial belonging; Stanley Hall, for example, insisted that folk dances were good for children because they were "moral, social, and aesthetic forces, condensed expressions of ancestral and racial traits."[45]

Guide performances in England often featured dances from across the British Isles, many of which had been recorded by Cecil Sharp and popularized by the English Folk Dance Society. The 1932 Essex Rally, in addition to the story of St. George and the dragon, also included performances of Irish and Welsh Jigs, Scottish Eightsome Reels, and an "Old English Sword Dance."[46] Folk dancing also figures prominently in a five-minute-long British Pathé newsreel about a 1937 Guide rally in Torquay. In this film, a series of panning shots reveals thousands of spectators in the stands as well as Brownies and Guides dancing in groups of two and in circles, performing what the narrator identifies as the Durham Reel, Norfolk Long Dance, and Circassian Circle. The film also shows thousands of Guides marching past and saluting the Princess Royal, and features several scenes of Rangers in short tunics doing can-can kicks and running in place – movements that owed more to keep-fit movements and the Hollywood films of Busby Berkeley than to an imagined rural past or the "ancestral and racial" traits imagined by Stanley Hall.[47]

Canadian Guides also performed British and Scandinavian folk dances alongside more "modern" forms of mass exercise at public events throughout the interwar years. A rally held at Toronto's University Arena in 1932, for example, included a "Demonstration of Physical Education" and Swedish and Danish dances, while the program from a 1936 rally held in London, Ontario, included references to "Danish Exercises" and "Country Dancing."[48] Other Canadian rally programs referred to dances from Sweden, Finland, Switzerland,

and the Netherlands – a reflection, perhaps, of immigration patterns and of "northern" racial nationalism.[49]

The group exercises and folk dances girls performed at rallies in Canada and England, adult-led efforts to discipline and shape young bodies, were political projects meant to celebrate modern girlhood while strengthening national-imperial patriotism and white racial pride. Exercise and dance were also practised – both in public and at weekly meetings – by Girl Guides in interwar India, and the form and meaning of these pursuits reflected the contradictions between colonizing and nationalist Guide ideals. On the one hand, Guiding's promotion of physical culture for Indian girls was about disciplining colonized bodies and training young people to support the British Empire;[50] on the other hand, exercise and folk dançe could reflect national pride and anti-colonial sentiments.[51] This is also an opportunity to include girls in the scholarly conversation about physical culture in late colonial India as, currently, the historiography focuses on boys and men.[52]

At a rally in Bombay held in honour of the Baden-Powells' 1937 visit to India, 2,500 Guides and Rangers, most of whom wore bright blue saris with white blouses, performed a demonstration of physical culture "on Indian lines" that included relay races, ball games, and a marching drill representing the map of India. In an article about the event published in the *Guide* magazine, the Chief Guide described a folk dance performed by Guides from the princely state of Sangli as "an old Indian form of exercise ... [that] is most vigorous and graceful."[53] Girls from the princely state of Baroda, she noted, provided a "most effective display" of a drill with lathis, fighting sticks that had been used for centuries in rural South Asian martial arts and that were also wielded by the British Indian police against crowds at nationalist and other demonstrations. Significantly, military drill and lathi training for young people were also used in the 1930s by the Rashtriya Swayamsweak Sangh, a Hindu paramilitary organization whose leaders, inspired by Hitler and especially Mussolini, believed that uniforms and martial training could strengthen and bring order to the Indian nation.[54]

Printed programs, press coverage, and photo albums all provide valuable insights into the adult ideals and local practices that shaped the interwar Guide movement's approach to physical culture. While these sources tend to reveal little about the girls who were at the heart of these performances, there are a few indications of how individual Guides understood and reacted to rallies in general and mass exercise in particular. Eileen Knapman, the south London girl who mocked Guiding's emphasis on child nursing and ambulance training in the pages of her patrol's logbook, took a similarly satirical approach in her descriptions of folk dancing. Instead of feeling racial pride or musing about international sisterhood, Knapman seems to have felt slightly embarrassed by her role in a "Scandinavian Dance" performance at a Guide display in 1929. "The dresses were very pretty," she wrote, "& the dancing well in time. We got an 'encore,' but, I must say that the performers made a very undignified exit, the second time. They seemed rather glad to go!"[55]

Despite the Swallow Patrol's "undignified exit" and evident relief at the end of their performance, the next year Knapman and her fellow Guides "strain[ed] ... [their] legs and memories in Country Dancing, for ... five weeks" to prepare for a bigger springtime rally. Her logbook describes this perform-ance as follows: "We did our dancing on hard, non-grassy ground, and were feebly applauded – not on account of our dancing, oh no – but because of the few visitors. We began well by winning the first race in grand style, but, unfortunately, here our skill ended. We think it was probably something to do with the ice-cream and lemonade stall in the corner!"[56] This account is ac-companied by a drawing of two uniformed Guides, one of whom is holding an ice-cream cone. A rare example of a youthful response to the Guide movement's emphasis on exercise and public performance, Knapman's logbook presents a different understanding of Guide rallies than do newspaper articles, news-reels, and the movement's official records. Instead of precise movements, docile bodies, and national/racial pride, for example, the Swallow Patrol logbook emphasizes undignified exits and performers who were glad to leave, feeble ap-plause and small audiences instead of large and enthusiastic crowds, and girls running races because they wanted ice-cream and lemonade – not because they wanted to strengthen their physiques or promote the Guide movement.

Drill

While military-style marching and drill seem not to have played too large a part in Eileen Knapman's public Guide performances (her logbook includes only two brief references to a "march past" and "Company drill"), these physical pursuits were central to thousands of other girls' experiences of Guide meetings and rallies during the 1920s and 1930s.[57] The meanings of duty, disci-pline, and drill were also at the heart of a heated scholarly debate in the 1980s, in which several historians disagreed about whether the early twentieth-century Scouts and Guides could be characterized as "militaristic."[58] This earlier work focused mainly on boys, and privileged the Edwardian era and the First World War. It also, as Brad Beaven and Carey Watt point out, set up a false opposition between civilian society/citizenship and militarism.[59]

Baden-Powell himself often used this binary to explain the importance of the Scouts and Guides, and – from the mid-1930s on – to attempt to distance them from fascist youth groups. While discussing the importance of outdoor life and exercise in remedying the "lamentably low" standard of British "physical soundness" in 1934, for example, he insisted that the aim of Guiding was "non-military, but to make healthy citizens." Revealing a fascination with fascism (and particularly its ability to create and showcase strong and muscular bodies) that was shared by many of his contemporaries, the Chief Scout wrote in the same passage: "Mussolini has shown how by proper organization it is possible within a generation completely to alter for the better the health and stamina of a nation. Hitler is organizing the training of the German youth with the same intent. In both cases the training is imposed obligatorily and with military aims."[60]

Despite the claim, repeated by Baden-Powell and other leaders throughout the interwar years, that Guiding and Scouting were "non-military" and therefore unlike fascist youth groups, all of these movements were adult-led body projects whose physical practices and stated goals had much in common with those of modern armies.[61] Just as leaders' emphasis on the "apolitical" nature of Guiding sat uneasily beside what was actually a quite clearly defined official vision of politics and citizenship, so did repeated assertions about the movement's "non-martial" nature fail to alter the fact that, like fascist youth groups, the Scouts and Guides used uniforms and drill to promote discipline, efficiency, and obedience among young people. Baden-Powell's youth movements, of course, were far from alone in their use of marching and military-style exercises; as Franziska Roy and other scholars observe, schoolteachers and youth leaders in India, Canada, and England also employed paramilitary techniques throughout the first few decades of the twentieth century.[62] Guiding's use of these physical training methods is further evidence of the movement's modern gender conservatism: one the one hand, marching and drill gave girls a chance to use their bodies in ways that had for centuries been restricted to men and boys; on the other hand, while it blurred the lines between military and civilian, masculine and feminine, Guide drill was also often explained as an effective way to impart such stereotypically desirable feminine traits as obedience, physical grace, and self-control.[63]

Throughout the 1920s and 1930s, Guide prescriptive texts explained drill as a valuable physical pursuit for modern girls across the world – a way to discipline and strengthen young female bodies and characters while, it was hoped, creating feelings of pride and group loyalty. In the pages of the Guide handbook, for example, Baden-Powell explained:

Guides drill in order to enable them to be moved quickly from one point to another in good order. Drill also sets them up, and makes them smart and quick. It strengthens the muscles which support the body, and by keeping the body upright the lungs and heart get plenty of room to work, and the inside organs are kept in the proper position for good digestion of food, and so on.[64]

He repeated these assertions in *Drill for Girl Guides*, an instructional pamphlet for leaders that included commands for infantry drills (forming fours and the like) as well as more advanced marching patterns that were recommended for public performances. First published in 1924 and reprinted several times throughout that decade, this text also asserted that drill would improve modern girls' "discipline and esprit-de-corps."[65] The publication of this pamphlet, which included a number of commands from the British Army Drill Book, reflects an increased emphasis on military-style physical culture in official Guide discourse from the mid-1920s on.[66]

Encouraging team spirit and discipline through marching and drill seems to have been important to a number of Guide leaders, some of whom discussed the value of these pursuits in the pages of the *Guider* in the early 1930s. A 1931 article on "The Teaching of Simple Drill" by M.L. Martin, for example, agreed with the Chief Scout that drill was useful when taking large groups of girls to public places. Aside from this practical benefit, Martin and other Guide leaders imagined that teaching modern girls to march, salute, stand at attention, and obey commands would help to stabilize what seemed like an increasingly shaky local, national, and imperial social order. In this respect, many rally organizers hoped that drill – like historical pageantry – would foster respect and reverence for social hierarchies. As John McNeill argues in his study of dance and drill in human history, "public rituals involving rhythmic movement" have been used in complex societies for centuries "to confirm constituted authorities."[67]

Unlike fascist Germany and Italy, where young people were expected to follow and revere a single charismatic leader, the authority Guides were meant to respect was more diffuse: a group that, broadly defined, consisted of adults and girls' social superiors. Respecting authority the Girl Guide way required both self-control and a willingness to sublimate individual desires for the sake of the group. In her *Guider* article on "Teaching Simple Drill," for instance, M.L. Martin insisted that drill would bring social benefits because it gave girls few opportunities for individualism. Company drill, she wrote, "provides an excellent form of team work, because the success of the whole depends entirely upon the perfect co-operation of every part." "Slack, untidy drill," Martin went on, was essentially useless because it had "no value as discipline."[68] In an article published in the *Guider* in 1933, A.M. Maynard, a Guide leader and author of several prescriptive books, claimed that if drill "is done well and smartly the public are favourably impressed and the girls feel a pride in their company." Along with pride and the possibility of public approval, Maynard further insisted that the benefits of drill included "silence – alertness – [and] fun."[69]

Articles like these, which described the apparent physical and social benefits of drill while insisting that silence and alertness could be "fun," were not the only discussions of drill published in Guide periodicals during the 1930s. Throughout that decade, they were often juxtaposed with letters to the editor in which disappointed leaders lamented the apparently poor marching skills and physical discipline of various groups of Guides and Brownies. Josephine H. Potter of the 3rd Marylebone Brownie Pack, for instance, complained in 1935 that Girl Guide drill was "getting appalling." "There is something beautiful in the bodies of girls moving with rhythm and grace," she wrote, "but the general parades that have been organized lately have no idea how to keep straight lines."[70] Similarly, in 1934, a Guider from Cheshire wrote:

> The other Sunday afternoon I was in Liverpool when a number of Guides (roughly between fifty and a hundred) passed me, carrying their colours and apparently bound for a church service. They walked along in fours, out of time, out of line and looking all round them. I was horrified to think of the impression non-Guiders must have received. When a large number of Guides are to be moved, especially in a town, the only way is by marching and surely the fact that we deny being a military movement does not stop us from learning to march smartly. Might I make a plea for better marching? I know it makes a big difference with the impression outsiders get of the movement.[71]

In 1936, another anonymous leader criticized the disorderly public presence of "many of our English Guides" by comparing them to the Bund Deutscher Mädel (BDM), the girls' wing of the Hitler Youth movement: "We in this country could learn many things from the Germans, in the same way as the Guide movement could learn from the Bund Deutscher Mädel ... There must be something in their training which we lack, that instills such a sense of responsibility in them."[72]

Correspondents like these believed that marching and drill created impressive public spectacles; taught discipline, rhythm, and grace; and were important ways to broaden the Guide movement's influence. Yet not everyone agreed that drill was a good thing for modern girls, and the issue was debated publicly in the popular press and Guide publications at several points during the late 1920s and 1930s. The first stirrings of controversy occurred in the summer of 1928, when the British *Evening Standard* published a full-page story with a headline claiming that Guiding was "Making Little Girls into Soldiers."[73]

Written by an anonymous "Guider," the piece deplored the movement's apparent lack of spontaneity and described it as "a hard and fast, cut and dried curriculum, in which the individual is merged in the company, over-drilled, over-officered, over-organized, and – at fifteen – fed up!"[74] Rebutting one common justification for Guide drill, the author insisted that "there is no need to move a handful of girls on the lines laid down for moving thousands of troops." The creative and plucky Edwardian Girl Scout of the movement's early days, it appeared, had been replaced by "a well-trained, ever-drilled, demure young person, ever-conscious of her appearance and entirely dependent on the orders and arrangings of an older person." The root of the problem, the article insisted, was the movement's unnecessary militarization of modern girlhood: "Real Army drill, drawn from the King's Regulations. Right dress! Eyes right! On parade! Salute! Form fours, all by numbers, every little Guide grave as a judge, and the officer shouting her commands with all the air of a drill sergeant in the Grenadier Guards. Capital training in obedience, no doubt."[75]

Baden-Powell, unsurprisingly, contested these claims in a letter to the editor of the *Evening Standard*. His rebuttal, reprinted in the *Guider*, asserted that Guiding was not "out to make soldiers of the girls." Instead of stressing militarism and obedience, the Chief Scout insisted that the movement was actually "a game, a comradeship of fun and laughter through which ... the girl emerges a happy, healthy, helpful citizen."[76] This published disagreement about the aims and methods of Guiding, which reflected divergent views about the value of drill, also reveals a broader clash between different ideas about age- and gender-appropriate behaviour. Should modern girls be loyal and obedient, or should they be spontaneous adventurers? Could they ever be both?

This conflict between the desire for order and a belief in the importance of spontaneity, which reflected broader concerns about girlhood, modernity, and social change, continued to animate discussion among Guide leaders into the 1930s. Another debate, this time about the movement's use of military-style march-pasts and salutes at Guide events, took place in the pages of the *Guider* in 1936. It was started by a leader named C. Godden, who spoke out against "marching-past" in a letter to the editor: "it has always seemed to me most unfortunate that this feature of a military review should so often be included in the programme for a Guide Rally."[77] Godden's complaint prompted a flurry of responses from Guiders eager to defend march-pasts and (sometimes) militarism. Lily Lyons, for example, asked: "As to the military aspect, is it such a terrible crime to emulate the services? NO! NO! NO! I come from a military stock, and I resent this attitude, as would any other Guider who has always been brought up in these traditions."[78] In April 1936, "a London Guider" suggested: "the Guiders who decry the March Past at our Rallys [sic] are thinking rather more of their own feelings in this matter than the thrill it affords to the Guides." "I well remember," she wrote, "my intense excitement and pride, first as a Guide and then as a Patrol Leader, when my company took part in a 'March Past' in a big rally at Chester it was the supreme moment of the afternoon. In the March Past one seemed to realize the greatness and the 'oneness' of the movement."[79] In their attempts to articulate the benefits and drawbacks of marching and militarism, the authors of these letters all fail to mention fascism – a surprising omission, given that marching, saluting, drill, and displays of uniformed bodies were at the heart of public events in fascist Germany and Italy during this period, and they were also central to the activities of the British Union of Fascists.

Regardless of Guiders' published disagreements about the use and purpose of drill, many of the benefits it promised – self-control, loyalty, and the ability to follow orders – were widely seen as qualities worth encouraging in all young people. They were also at the heart of settler attempts to control, shape, and civilize the bodies and lifeways of Indigenous peoples in Canada. For girls at residential schools, the Guide movement's colonizing project included drill as well as uniforms, cleanliness training, marching, and saluting the Union Jack. While some Indigenous Guides (the company at the Mohawk Institute in Brantford, for example) participated in public displays and competitions with settler girls, many others only practised drill at their weekly meetings.[80]

The logbook kept by Rosina Hobbs, an Anglican missionary who organized Guide and Brownie groups at St. Peter's Residential School at Hay River in the Canadian Northwest Territories in the mid-1930s, provides evidence of the regularity with which the members of one group of Indigenous Guides were expected to use their bodies in marching and drill.[81] Of a Guide meeting held on 4 June 1935, Hobbs wrote: "after a good practice of drill, we revised the reef knot & learned to bandage a sprained ankle & carry a helpless patient." Her weekly entries feature numerous references to activities like "Company Drill & forming fours," and the meeting held on 23 April 1936, according to Hobbs, included "drill, games, tracking signs, singing, a talk on the Health Rule of Cleanliness & the Story of St. George."[82]

The Anglo-Canadian girls of the 21st Winnipeg Guide Company also drilled and marched during their weekly meetings at St. Alban's Anglican Church. Yet, unlike the Hay River Guides, whose geographical isolation kept them from participating in rallies, the St. Alban's Guides also practised drill in order to perform in public. Winnifred Thompson, the Guide whose logbook detailed this group's activities in the late 1920s, noted in October 1928 that her group was learning "a unique fancy drill" for a display later that fall.[83] Thompson's weekly entries over the next several months emphasize the amount of time that was devoted to drill practice with the ultimate goal of public perform-ance: "we had no time in patrol corners as usual but spent most of the time in drill and songs" (29 October); "learnt drill and songs as usual" (5 November); "preparations for the display as usual" (26 November). Of 3 December, which Thompson dubbed "the fatal night of the display," she noted that the Guides' opening ceremony, "drill and ambulance work were ... pretty good," though "the singing should have been better." Her account also reveals that the dis-play achieved its promotional and fundraising aims as the company "made $12.16 from the collection" and enrolled six new Guides. Did Patrol Leader Thompson's experience as a performer bring her into touch, as some leaders suggested, with "the greatness and oneness" of Guiding? Did it shape her thoughts about the importance of hierarchy, obedience, and self-control?

These are fragmentary glimpses of how girls themselves experienced march-ing and drill, and it behooves us to think about them critically and carefully. Further fragments of other girls' responses may be found in such visual sources as a photograph album depicting a 1933 Empire Day Guide rally in the Nilgiri Hills. Featuring some four hundred British, Indian, and Anglo-Indian Guides and Bluebirds, this rally was a public event at which girls exhibited their first aid and rescue skills, built a trestle bridge, laid a British-style tea table, and demonstrated fire-lighting. Held outdoors before a sizable crowd on the polo grounds of the Wellington Gymkhana Club, it was one of many Empire Day rallies and parades through which British Guide leaders in locations including Assam, Baluchistan, and Bangalore sought to promote imperial loyalty among ethnically and religiously diverse groups of girls.[84] The creator of the album, whose identity was not recorded but who I suspect was a local Guide leader, pasted in numerous snapshots of girls saluting the Union Jack and the event's guests of honour, a list that included several Guide Commissioners and the wife of the Governor of Madras. Accompanied by handwritten captions, many of these photos focus on marching girls and are similar in composition to the images of rallies that were reproduced in Guide publications and the popular press. One of these images, entitled "St. George's Homes Guides March Past,"

Order and disorder at a Canadian Brownie and Guide rally held in honour of the Baden-Powells. *Archives of the National Council of the Girl Guides of Canada – Guides du Canada, APH #724*

shows several dozen Guides holding Union Jack flags and marching away from the photographer in neat lines. Another photograph, however, demonstrates that not all Guide performers' movements were consistently orderly and precise. Accompanied by the caption "Blue Birds 'fly past'! In every direction," this image shows groups of youngsters (British and Anglo-Indian girls wearing white dresses and topees, and South Asian ones in light-coloured blouses and long dark skirts) looking, walking, and mostly running in different directions. Some girls are laughing, and others are holding hands in small groups. A photograph from the Canadian Girl Guide archives in Toronto captures a similar scene, in which some members of a group of Brownies encircling Robert and Olave Baden-Powell at an outdoor rally are spaced unevenly and colliding into each other – to the consternation of a Scout leader who has turned to look at them.

These photographs are evidence of the difference between prescription and practice, and of the ways in which ritual spaces can facilitate the pursuit of diverse and sometimes competing interests.[85] Their preservation in albums and archives – and the South Asian Bluebird leader's indulgent choice of words and emphasis – also suggests that some of the adults who organized Guide performances enjoyed and may occasionally have encouraged such youthful scenes of play and disorder.

By contrast, press coverage of Guide rallies (both positive portrayals and critiques like the one published in the *Evening Standard*) often emphasized the success of the movement in encouraging discipline and self-control among girls. In a range of settings, journalists often singled out the martial side of Guiding's body project for special praise. A newspaper article about the 1933 Madras Empire Day Rally, pasted along with photos in the pages of the aforementioned album, stated that the British and Anglo-Indian Guides from the Laidlaw Memorial School at St. George's Homes in Ketti "were exceptionally well-drilled," and it praised Capt. Miss Dunhill, leader of a company of poor and orphaned Anglo-Indian girls from the Mountain Home School in Coonoor, for "the very efficient display given by her girls."[86]

Canadian newspapers similarly reserved special praise for the Guide movement's marching girls. One Ottawa journalist, also writing in 1933, claimed that a rally of some eight hundred Guides at Lansdowne Park Coliseum had been "carried out smartly and efficiently." The article stated that the Guides' march-past and salute to Lady Bessborough (wife of the governor general of Canada) were particularly impressive as the girls' "movements were concerted [and] brisk and their responses to the command were prompt and soldierly."[87] The *Hamilton Spectator* sounded a similar note in its coverage of a 1933 rally held in Wentworth, Ontario: "Deeply impressive was the taking of the salute at the opening of the performance, the hundreds of blue-frocked girls marching with military precision before their chief commissioner, after which the companies were massed, with the colour parties in the center, for the breaking of the flag."[88] "Soldierly," "well-drilled," and "military" – these adjectives were employed regularly by journalists in interwar India and Canada to praise the Guide movement and its young members. As terms with a long history of masculine connotations, their use also indicates a degree of public approval for the movement's blurring – within the confined space of the rally ground – of conventional boundaries between masculine and feminine, civilian and martial.

Conclusion

Harold Stovin's 1935 book *Totem: The Exploitation of Youth*, a left-wing critique of organized youth movements, condemned the Scouts and Guides as enemies of spontaneity and individuality. By joining these organizations, Stovin insisted, "the poorer youth of this country – euphemistically known as 'Young England' – are to be cajoled into an artfully concealed and elaborately camouflaged variation on the Hitler-Jugend or the Italian Balilla."[89] Baden-Powell, in fact, had met with Mussolini in Italy in 1933 and described him in the pages of the *Scouter* magazine as "a very charming, humorous and human man."[90] The Chief Scout, whose initial excitement about the Balilla and Hitler Jugend has been attributed to "confusion," "blindness," and "a hatred of communism," was not alone in his admiration for the discipline and strength that European fascism had apparently been able to instill in young people.[91] Some Guide leaders also shared his enthusiasm, while staying silent about the violence and intolerance that characterized these movements. The many similarities in form and discourse between the Scouts, Guides, and fascist groups are jarring to twenty-first-century eyes. Yet, instead of insisting on the ideological opposition between these youth movements, it might make more sense to understand them as different points on a continuum – what Franziska Roy refers to as a "common grammar" of physical discipline and a desire for racial regeneration that reached across national and political boundaries.[92]

At the heart of these commonalities – and of interwar Guiding's use of the mass ornament – was a desire for order in what seemed an increasingly uncertain and disorderly world. By staging historical pageants in Canada, England, and (to a lesser extent) India, Guide leaders asked girls to celebrate and perform social hierarchies based on class and race. Group exercise demonstrations, which linked Edwardian fears of racial degeneration with modernity and mass culture, were consistently lauded for their role in strengthening future mothers. Marching and drill, meanwhile, earned praise from journalists and Guiders across the British Empire for their apparent ability to teach modern girls about the importance of obedience, self-control, and respect for authority.

Yet these physical pursuits could also carry different, more emancipatory messages. Playing kings, knights, and explorers in historical pageants – like marching and practising military-style drill – gave some girls (temporary) access to what had conventionally been masculine identities and ways of occupying space. Building a fit and healthy body – and using it in mass public demonstrations – also included girls in a transnational physical culture movement that celebrated feminine strength and modernity. At the same time, the girls who performed in rallies interpreted these events in widely different ways – an important reminder that, despite adult debates about militarism and obedience, modern girls took their own meanings from the Guide movement's official scripts. These tensions – between emancipation and hierarchy as well as between official discourse and individual response – also characterized interwar Guiding's efforts to create an imperial and international sisterhood of girls.

Chapter 6

IMPERIAL AND INTERNATIONAL SISTERHOOD
Possibilities and Limits

THE GUIDE MOVEMENT'S OFFICIAL scripts, while offering both emancipatory and conservative possibilities to girls at rallies and public performances, also emphasized imperial and international cooperation. In July 1925, for instance, the editors of the *Girl Guides' Gazette* sought to demonstrate the appeal of Guiding to girls across the British Empire and the world with a glossy centre section featuring photographs of uniformed Girl Guides in thirteen different contexts, including Canada, South Africa, India, Australia, and Singapore. This celebratory pictorial shows girls with very different life experiences and identities participating in the activities that defined Girl Guiding during most of the twentieth century: camping, playing games, and learning first aid. Accompanying this photographic evidence of the Guide movement's global reach were several brief articles, all of which stressed the imperial *and* international nature of the diverse and benevolent "sisterhood" that the movement's leaders sought to create. Former British prime minister H.H. Asquith, one of several prominent men asked to contribute to this special issue of the magazine, used his article to describe the post-Great War British Empire as a "great, worldwide, peace-loving partnership" whose leaders wanted neither to acquire territory nor to rule "alien populations." Instead, Asquith wrote that the role of the Empire – and, it was implied, of the diverse girls and women who inhabited it – was to raise "the level of common opportunity" for all people and "to draw closer the bond of affection and confidence within its parts."[1]

Similar ideas were expressed by members of the Guide movement from across the Empire throughout the interwar years. A reader named Edith

Lyttleton, for example, wrote to the editor of the *Guider* in March 1929 that, since

the future Peace of the World depends on the attitude of the young of all races towards each other, depends also upon the understanding of other peoples, other customs, other ideals than our own, I would urge Rangers to try and learn as much as they can about foreign countries, and to welcome any opportunities for getting to know individuals of a different race.[2]

The next year, Toronto teenager Margaret Warren wrote in the *Canadian Girl Guide* that she and her contemporaries were "citizens not only of Canada but of the British Empire and the World. We might almost say, from the viewpoint of an inhabitant of some celestial sphere, that we are citizens first of the World, then of the British Empire and Canada, Ontario and Toronto." Responsible girl citizens, Warren wrote, should balance these various identities, "follow the events of the world, learn about the people of other countries and races, and their history, their customs and their thoughts."[3] At a 1934 Guide rally in the Indian princely state of Mysore, the Yuvarani of Mysore, a prominent figure in Indian Guiding, expressed a similar understanding of the movement's benefits. She explained to the assembled spectators:

by the joining together of children of different types, of different classes, of different races and of different religions on an equal footing, a greater understanding of one another is inculcated among them and a tolerant and benevolent sympathy is developed which should in time do much to ensure the peace which is so much desired in all countries of the world to-day.[4]

Fostering friendliness, cooperation, and sisterly goodwill across all kinds of boundaries was a central goal of Guiding during the 1920s and 1930s.[5] Touted in official publications as a "junior League of Nations" and a "happy empire family," the Guide movement was effectively an early non-governmental organization – one that, unlike many twenty-first century NGOs, defined itself as "apolitical" while buttressing British imperial power in often quite conservative ways.[6]

Unlike some other Western-based international organizations that were founded in the late nineteenth century, the Guide movement only adopted the language of internationalism and experienced real global membership growth after the First World War.[7] This fits with Frank Trentmann's argument that the traumas of the Great War caused many in Britain and the dominions

to critique the nation-state and "turn to the British Empire as a historic building block in the creation of a new transnational framework of governance and
cultural solidarity," and it supports Akira Iriye's claim that it was only during
the 1920s that Western cultural internationalists began to think more about a
type of "global internationalism, embracing different races and peoples."[8]

This chapter focuses on the conservative modernity of Guiding's imperial
and international ideals and practices in England, Canada, India, and beyond
during the interwar years. To begin with, I examine how the movement used
familial metaphors and organizational changes, travel, buildings, philanthropy,
and the mass media to promote a friendly, peaceful, and egalitarian sisterhood
that transcended the lines of empire, nation, and race. The second part of the
chapter argues that these optimistic efforts – like so many other of the movement's goals – were ultimately hampered by material constraints and by the
persistence of hierarchical racial thinking.

Familial Metaphors and Organizational Changes

Interwar Guiding's official commitment to imperial internationalism was especially obvious at the discursive level, as exemplified by its persistent emphasis on international and/or imperial sisterhood. The fourth part of the
Guide Law, other sections of which mandated courtesy, obedience, cheerfulness, and thrift, stated: "A Guide is a friend to all, and a sister to every other
Guide, no matter to what creed, country, or class the other belongs."[9]

The use of familial metaphors to explain global power relations and the
work of imperialist and international voluntary organizations was not a new
development in the interwar years, but the international imperial family imagined by Guide leaders during the 1920s and 1930s differed in several significant ways from its Victorian and Edwardian predecessors.[10] Whereas earlier
organized women had emphasized hierarchical networks of British imperial
sisterhood, the interwar Guide movement sought to maintain these links while
working within what its leaders explained as a more egalitarian and international context.[11]

Especially important to this discourse of Guide sisterhood was the movement's much-emphasized commitment to familial egalitarianism regardless
of race, nationality, and religion. This stance, a shift from earlier, more hierarchical views of racial and cultural difference and power relations, was a
product of post-First World War internationalism, the ideals embodied by the
League of Nations, and shifting power relations within the British Empire. The
Guide movement's zealous promotion of cheerful sisterhood and internation-

alism is exemplified by an address made to the Chief Guide at a "Guiding Round the World" pageant performed at a rally of 9,000 Guides at Knole Park in Kent in July 1936. In this recitation, the text of which was reprinted in the event's souvenir program, the Guides promised to "pledge ourselves anew to link our creeds, our races and our nationalities in one great garland of happiness and peace for the adornment of the world."[12]

This conception of international Guiding as an egalitarian, happy, and peace-loving sisterhood of girls and women both within and beyond the British Empire led its leaders to institute a number of organizational changes in the movement after the First World War. Until that point, the establishment of a Guide company had been a relatively informal affair – women would order materials from London, start holding meetings, and, eventually, sometimes not for several years, register their group with Guide headquarters. This loosely organized process meant that the activities offered to girls in Brownie, Guide, and Ranger groups varied greatly in different national and local contexts, and were determined largely by the personalities and interests of individual leaders. In 1918, however, Olave Baden-Powell – in her new position as Chief Guide – established an imperial council with the aim of promoting "mutual interest and sympathetic understanding throughout the empire."[13] The Imperial Council, like its sister Guide organization the International Council (a body representing nations outside the British Empire), was essentially a corresponding society, in which elite women living in London wrote to and advised Guide leaders in their "special part[s] of the Empire" and the world.[14]

The rapid expansion of international Guiding after the First World War meant that the International and Imperial Councils' limited and Anglo-centric system of governance, in which elite London-based women wrote and received letters about Guiding in different parts of the world, was soon seen by many women as insufficient. From 1920 on, Guide leaders from Britain and around the world began to organize and attend imperial and international meetings in order to compare their experiences and pedagogical techniques. Such meetings did not completely replace the movement's reliance on an elite network of English-speaking white women; the pages of Olave Baden-Powell's diary from the 1920s and 1930s, for instance, contain many references to London tea parties and lunches attended by wealthy Guide officials from across the British Empire.[15]

The First International Conference for Guiders was held in 1920 at St. Hugh's College, Oxford, and was attended by delegates and visitors from Belgium, China, Czechoslovakia, Denmark, Holland, Italy, Liberia, Poland, Portugal, Romania, Russia, Serbia, Sweden, and the United States. This was

followed two years later by a combined imperial and international conference in 1922 at Newnham College, Cambridge. The Third International Conference, which was combined with the first World Camp for Girl Guides, was
attended in July 1924 by 1,100 representatives from thirty countries. The Fourth
International Conference – a reflection of the growing power of the United
States and American Girl Scouting – was held two years later in the United
States at Camp Edith Macy in New York State. This conference partially reflected the desire, expressed by Baden-Powell and numerous Guide leaders
during the interwar years, for the construction of a global Anglo-Saxon alliance
between Europe, the dominions, and the United States that, as Proctor writes,
"could bring peace to the world on British terms."[16]

This 1926 International Conference – the first to be held outside the United
Kingdom – also highlighted the problems that could be caused by the Guide
movement's official practice of dividing the world into the discrete categories
of "imperial" and "foreign/international" since Canada, defined by Guide headquarters as an "imperial" nation but close to the United States in geographical
and cultural terms, was only allowed to attend as a non-voting visitor.

Partly because of the confusion caused by the distinction between "imperial"
and "international" at the Fourth International Conference in 1926, Guide
representatives from twenty-eight countries, including Britain, India, and
Canada, approved the dissolution of the International and Imperial Councils
at the 1928 World Conference in Hungary. In place of these two corresponding societies-cum-governing bodies, the women approved the creation of a
more unified, formal, and bureaucratic governing organization: the World
Association of Girl Guides and Girl Scouts. This decision was explained in
official WAGGGS publications as the result of these women's desire for "closer
organization, in which each country should take part, on an equal footing,
and should have a share of determining the policy on the whole."[17]

At first glance, this attempt to encourage communication and equality in
policy making sounds very different from the jingoistic expansionism that
characterized much British Victorian thinking on imperial and international
questions. But WAGGGS's desire to promote "unity of purpose and common
understanding in the fundamental principles of Guiding and Girl Scouting
throughout the world" may also be seen as an attempt by the movement's
metropolitan leaders to regulate Guide activities in different countries while
preventing the formation of unofficial and potentially subversive groups.[18] The
establishment of rival or unaffiliated youth organizations like the socialist and
co-educational Woodcraft Folk in England, French Catholic Guides in Canada, and the Seva Samiti Guides in India threatened several of the movement's

ideological goals. While similar in form to the Girl Guides, these groups encouraged girls to embrace concepts and ways of life – including socialism, co-education, and French-Canadian and Indian nationalism – that opposed the official Guide vision of girlhood and the global social order. While leaders like the Chief Guide derided them as "separatist" and "political," WAGGGS also sought to combat the threat these groups posed to Guide membership numbers. The women who were at the centre of the Guide movement's international growth during the interwar years clearly knew that the organization – and their places within it – depended on the money generated by membership fees and sales of official Guide-related goods to the "sisterhood" of Girl Guide consumers around the world. In a letter to the Canadian Chief Commissioner about Catholic French-Canadian Guiding, Olave Baden-Powell, who tried desperately to keep worldwide Guiding under British control, sought to put the threat posed by rival French Catholic Guide groups in a broader context. Separate and ideologically antagonistic organizations, she wrote, were "so distressful and worrying, when you see what happens for instance in South Africa with the formation of the 'Voortrekkers' (the ultra Dutch Dutch Movement, imitating Guideing [sic] but twisting it for political ends) the 'Home Daughters' in Estonia, and the 'Seva Samiti Guides' in India."[19]

A Utopian Vision:
International and Imperial Gatherings and Properties

While deriding rival groups for their lack of originality and apparently "political" motivations, the Chief Guide and WAGGGS also promoted the notion that modern girls had a duty to learn about people from other races and nations (and it is worth noting that the two terms were often used interchangeably) because it would be good for society in the future. If girls followed "Guide principles" in this way, the implicit promise was that there would be an end to racial prejudice, an increase in cross-cultural understanding, and, last but not least, world peace.

In some respects, Guiding's promotion of imperialism and internationalism was a utopian project – a normative, prescriptive, and future-oriented attempt to create a standardized and useful group of young female citizens.[20] "Desire and design, harmony and hope," qualities that Krishan Kumar shows to be central to utopian thinking, were also at the heart of many of the Guide movement's ideologies and practices. They are especially evident in the many international camps and conferences the movement held for girls and adult leaders from the early 1920s on.[21]

These camps and conferences gave some girls and women the opportunity to travel internationally and forge personal connections with their sister Guides across the boundaries of nation, race, and religion. The most highly publicized international Guide events were the movement's Imperial and World Camps and Conferences, semi-annual events at which girls and women from different countries came together with the aim of promoting tolerance and sisterly friendship. Unlike the societies in which girls and women spent their daily lives, imperial and world Guide events were utopian spaces: small, temporary, highly organized all-female ideal cities whose inhabitants were meant to work together in affective and material ways to produce a better world.

The first World Camp for Girl Guides, held in conjunction with the Third International Conference for Guide Leaders, took place at Foxlease, the British Guide estate in the New Forest, in 1924. Many smaller international Guide gatherings were also held in a variety of locations during the 1920s and 1930s. Geography often played a determining role in these events, as companies mixed with groups from neighbouring nations regardless of the presence or absence of British imperial ties. Twenty-four Canadian Girl Guides from Walkerville, Ontario, joined a company of American Girl Scouts for a mother-daughter banquet in Detroit, Michigan, in 1933 – an event whose internationalist goals seem to have been similar to the ones promoted at a camp for English, French, and Belgian Guides held in Normandy during the summer of 1922.[22] The camp in Normandy, which included a daily parade featuring each country's flag and national anthem, had been planned primarily to "eliminate the fear that Guides of other nations might have of different ideals."[23] Seven years later, British Guides joined girls from sixteen other European countries at another international camp in Bierville, run by the Eclaireuses de France.[24] The report about the camp published in the *Council Fire* stressed the importance of the friendships that developed there, asking:

> Isn't that perhaps the right kind of feeling with which to be left? – of wanting to see more of each other? For nations are only collections of human beings, and once we discover that we are, at bottom, very much alike, and that our differences are only interesting, not alien, then surely we have discovered something of the secret of Friendship.[25]

In the mid- to late 1930s, some British Guiders expressed similar sentiments about the youth movements in Nazi Germany. One leader, V.E. Powell from Lyndhurst, wrote in a prize-winning 1937 essay that was published in the *Guider*:

Nowadays there seems no end to the descriptions of Rover and Ranger tours through Germany. They made friends with German boys and girls and found young Nazis, however Nationalistic in their training, are very friendly and welcoming. Is it not possible that in sending our Scouts and Guides to Germany to make friends with the Hitler Jugend, we are doing more in the cause of peace than any International camps confined to our own members can do? We can learn certain things from the Hitler Jugend – hard work, enthusiasm, endurance – and in return we may sow amongst them the seeds of friendship with other countries.[26]

Minutebooks from the Guide Movement's International Committee, a small London-based group chaired by International Commissioner Rose Kerr, provide further evidence of some British Guiders' desire to create personal, affective links with members of the Bund Deutscher Mädel. Between 1936 and mid-1939, a period marked by the Nazis' violent persecution of German Jews and invasion of Czechoslovakia, the Guide International Committee received an "increased number of applications" from British companies asking for introductions to BDM groups.[27] The committee responded to these applications not by discouraging them, but by recommending that invitations not be sent on Guide notepaper and insisting that the organizers of any Guide-BDM correspondence or exchanges be undertaken "unofficially" and by leaders in their capacity as "private citizens."[28]

Relatively few of these hoped-for Guide-BDM exchanges seem to have taken place, though a company from West Surrey, aided by the Anglo-German Kameradschaft, did host a group of BDM girls at a camp in London in the spring of 1939. Were the initiators of these exchanges internationalist women who hoped to avoid war through personal contact and appeasement? Or might they have sympathized with the anti-Semitism and militarized discipline of National Socialism? While the motives of individual Guide leaders are difficult – and sometimes impossible – to recover, these episodes do undermine Rosenthal and Jeal's claims that Baden-Powell and the Scouts and Guides stopped pursuing relationships with the Hitler Jugend and BDM in 1937–38.[29]

Regardless of the political context of their travels, the girls and women who attended international gatherings were encouraged to perform and explain their cultural and national identities for each other through structured activities like folk dance displays and round-table talks as well as through more informal discussions and socializing. Imperial and world camps and conferences, like the movement's other smaller international exchanges, were based on an assumption that underlay much of the movement's work in the interwar years: that in order to contribute to world peace and to succeed as modern citizens, domestic managers, mothers, and paid workers, modern girls needed to learn about and compare themselves with girls from other countries. These comparisons, it was hoped, would highlight similarities of age and gender while encouraging girls and young women to disregard differences of culture, geography, religion, and race.[30] International camping played a less significant role in South Asian Guiding during the 1920s and 1930s, although the annual All-India Guide Camp was frequently explained as a way to help girls from different parts of India's large and diverse population to look beyond the categories of race, caste, and religion.

Imperial and international Guide events were also contact zones, sites of encounter and interaction in which girls and women with widely varying subject positions and experiences of international relations and the British imperial project came together in sometimes fruitful and sometimes uncomfortable ways.[31] Official publications, unsurprisingly, often stressed the importance of these friendly cross-cultural gatherings. In the movement's 1934 annual report, for instance, Baden-Powell wrote that,

> thanks to the personal contacts thus established, not only are the eyes of youth opened to the fact that foreigners are not so very foreign after all, but personal friendships have been started and then maintained by means of correspondence or return visits, and the leaders have found themselves united and inspired in a great common interest.[32]

At the Ninth World Conference, held in Stockholm in 1936, Madeleine Beley, chair of the international movement's leader training subcommittee, similarly insisted on the importance of personal contact to the movement's stated aims of familial tolerance and understanding. "One realizes," she said in a talk that was later published in the *Council Fire*, "that it is chiefly by knocking about among people of different races in their own countries that individuals can get their corners rubbed off and their prejudices melted."[33]

This process of "rubbing off" and "melting" was the goal of one cross-border gathering that produced an especially rich set of records: the 1928 Imperial Camp for Overseas Guiders. Held at Foxlease and attended by several hundred women from locations, including the dominions, Malta, Gibraltar, India, Tasmania, and the British Isles, this was also the event at which the elderly Agnes Baden-Powell, having been relegated to the sidelines of the movement by her sister-in-law Olave, was forced to observe the proceedings while hiding behind some shrubbery.[34] A report about the camp published in the *Council Fire* celebrated the diversity and connectedness of the camp's participants by citing the presence of campers clad in different national uniforms, including a South Asian Guide Captain in a "coloured sari," as sources of internationalist inspiration and as proof of "how rapidly Guiding is growing in the East as well as in the West."[35]

Official coverage of these events, while commenting on "exotic" uniforms and celebrating Guiding's growing global influence, provides few details about the activities that took place and how participants responded to them. In the case of the 1928 Imperial Camp, however, this problem is partly solved by the existence of a logbook kept by Elsie Berger, the captain of two Guide companies in north London. Describing her impressions of the camp's first communal supper, consumed under a canopy of beech trees in the New Forest, Berger marvelled at the fact that many of the over three hundred campers "seem[ed] to have arrived from all parts of the Empire."[36] The logbook describes her conversations with women from Scotland, Australia, and Barbados, and depicts a camp fire speech made by the Chief Guide that, Berger wrote, made "us feel the very spirit of friendliness and cooperation in the vast [Girl Guide] sisterhood."[37] The participants at this camp followed a "militarily precise" and busy schedule: cooking breakfast, saluting the Union Jack, learning woodcraft skills so that they could supervise camps and test Guides for related badges, attending Sunday mass at Lyndhurst Church, entertaining Princess Mary (president of the British Guide Association), swimming, and "discovering many good specimens of plants and insects" while hiking.

Berger's account provides one example of a positive individual response to interwar Guiding's efforts to create an imperial sisterhood. It is also proof that these efforts, like WAGGGS more generally during this period, were largely dominated by white women. This demographic fact – and the uncomfortable questions it sometimes raised – was made even clearer in a *Council Fire* article written by Patricia Richards, a white member of the Indian Girl Guide Executive Committee who had represented India at the 1930 World Conference at Foxlease. There, Richards wrote, other delegates asked her "why India was not represented by Indian ladies." Recognizing that her presence (along with that of other white "Indian" leaders) "gave the impression that Guiding in India was not really an Indian movement," she sought to set the record straight in print by stating: "It is true that Guiding was introduced into India by Europeans, and that the Commissioners and trainers are still mainly Europeans,

A group of mostly white Guide leaders and one Indian Guider at an international gathering, early 1930s. *Archives of the National Council of the Girl Guides of Canada – Guides du Canada, Imperial and International Guiding Album*

though by no means entirely so. But the Association in India is now more than three-quarters pure Indian."

Richards, like a number of other white women internationalists during this period, tried to explain her continued attempts to speak for Indian women by citing economic constraints and the orientalist idea that eastern women, while gradually "awakening" to Western-style feminism, necessarily remained a bit behind.[38] "Women's education in India and a broadly national outlook," she wrote, "are of very recent growth. Only a very few exceptional Indian ladies could do more than represent their own community." With regard to the 1930 World Conference, Richards claimed that it had simply been impossible to find

an Indian lady who had time to spare and who was in a position to pay her own expenses. There are no available Guide funds in India for sending delegates to Europe or America. Still we must hope that a truly Indian delegate will enjoy the hospitality of Poland in 1932, and perhaps some day the World Conference will be held in Asia.[39]

Richards's ill-considered words proved prophetic, as an Indian Guider named Julie Sen attended the 1932 World Conference in Poland.[40] As the 1930s progressed, Western "Indian" representatives like Patricia Richards were increasingly replaced, at WAGGGS gatherings and at the conventions of other women's international organizations, by Indian delegates – but the overall face of these events remained overwhelmingly white.[41]

Including settler societies like Canada in this analysis also highlights international Guiding's silence about Indigenous women and girls. As Fiona Paisley says of the Pan-Pacific Women's Association, "women identified as belonging to cultures lower down on the civilizational scale, namely, indigenous women in settler societies, were deemed indefinitely outside" the purview of interwar white women's internationalism.[42] Would the prize-winning Indigenous Canadian Guides from the Blood and Six Nations of the Grand Reserves have felt themselves to be a part of this side of the movement?

The generalizations made by Patricia Richards and many other white members of the global Guide sisterhood were named and critiqued in a 1936 *Council Fire* article entitled "Guiding and Mutual Understanding" by Sherene Rustomjee, a Parsi Guide leader from Bombay who had attended multiple Guide training sessions in England and Europe.[43] While she left far fewer traces of her experiences than did the Indian travellers studied by Antoinette Burton, her article functions as a rebuttal of sorts – an explicit challenge to the movement's self-congratulatory and mostly white imperial internationalists to rethink their assumptions about "other" populations and parts of the world.[44] "It has been amazing to me," she wrote, "to find in the course of my visits to Europe how little people know of India, its peoples and its distances. This must be true of other countries too. Perhaps this lack of knowledge is the result of our present systems of education; let us, anyhow, get to know each other better through Guiding." Guides and Rangers, Rustomjee suggested, "might be able to form study groups, and to investigate racial problems; they could widen their knowledge by reading books and newspapers of other countries, not only Guide literature."[45]

As Rustomjee's article indicates, long-distance travel of the sort often required to attend international meetings could be an unsettling experience – one that often forced individuals to think about the British Empire and their own racialized identities in new ways.[46] The vast majority of the documents I consulted are frustratingly silent about this issue – a gap that, I suspect, is partly due to the lack of curiosity Rustomjee identified and partly a result of the fact that relatively few documents created by pre-Independence Indian Guide leaders have survived.

One observation I am able to make, however, is that many of the movement's imperial and international meetings were only tangentially about girls; many of them, after all, were events organized by and for adult women. Ida von Herrenschwand, the Swiss woman who ran Our Chalet (the international Guide house in Adelboden, Switzerland) from its opening in 1932 until the early 1950s, emphasized this point in a passage in her memoir about attending her first international conference in 1930. "Having joined Guiding only in 1929," she wrote, "I had never had the opportunity of meeting Guiders or Commissioners of other countries, and great was my surprise to see so many great, middle-aged and elderly ladies ornamented with silver and golden cords, cocked hats and some with dangling fishes on their uniforms."[47] Many of these "middle-aged" and "elderly" Guide internationalists, of course, were members of the movement's global community of single women (see Chapter 2). Unlike many of Guiding's younger members, for whom it played a relatively small part in their journey to adulthood, Guide internationalists often saw these events as chances to promote and sometimes alter Baden-Powell's original ideals while catching up with their global social network. Fiona Paisley writes about the romantic and sexual possibilities offered by international women's meetings; it is, I think, worth wondering about the extent to which similar possibilities increased the zeal of some Guide leaders.[48]

The adult women in charge of global Guiding also sought to include girls from around the world in their imperial and international project by explaining the movement's property holdings and furnishings, along with its fundraising efforts to pay for buildings, furnishings, and upkeep, as another way of creating feelings of international and imperial sisterhood. The architecture and furnishings at Foxlease, the sixty-five-acre Hampshire estate where many cross-border Guide events were held, were discussed in annual reports, magazines, and books as material proof of the success of the movement's friendly imperial and international ideals. Each room in the estate's main house was furnished with donations from Guide groups from across the British Empire and the world. These included rugs from India, a desk from New Zealand, and cottage furniture from Canada. Alice Behrens, the first Guider-in-Charge at Foxlease, boasted in 1924 that, in the front hall alone, visitors could see the global Guide family represented by "the carpet from Halifax, the clock from Gloucestershire, the gong from Egypt, [and] the table and chairs from China."[49] The obvious and growing political and economic influence of the United States and its Girl Scout movement was epitomized by a four-bedroomed cottage furnished by the American Girl Scouts that was "known as 'The Link' (between England and America)."[50]

Foxlease, South Aspect.

The house at Foxlease, the British Guide Association's estate in the New Forest, furnished by Guides from across the British Empire and the world. *Archives of the National Council of the Girl Guides of Canada – Guides du Canada, Imperial and International Guiding Album*

A Canadian Guider who had attended the 1924 World Camp wrote in the *Girl Guides' Gazette* that she was "proud to think that each room has been furnished by a different country." Visiting Foxlease, she claimed, made her feel thrilled to belong to "an organization that has spread itself over the face of the whole globe, every individual member of which has the same laws and codes, each furthering the great cause and promoting an advance in all spheres, bringing a higher sense of honour and integrity into every condition of life."[51] Lillian Picken, a Guide leader and Protestant missionary sponsored by the American Board of Commissioners for Foreign Missions who worked in Maharashtra, western India, also rhapsodized about her visit to Foxlease in a letter penned in August 1929. Calling the "South African" room (where she slept) "the loveliest room in the house," Picken insisted that Foxlease was the material representation of "a sisterhood that transcends all class and racial barriers and draws us together in deepest fellowship."[52]

Similar terms were also used to explain the construction and use of Our Chalet, the international Guide house in Adelboden, Switzerland, that was purchased for the World Association of Girl Guides and Girl Scouts by Helen Storrow (another wealthy American woman) in the early 1930s. Ida von

"For the promotion of guiding and good will between nations": The dining room at Our Chalet in Adelboden, Switzerland, c.1932. *Archives of the National Council of the Girl Guides of Canada – Guides du Canada, Imperial and International Guiding Album*

Herrenschwand, who ran Our Chalet from 1932 to 1952, remembered the chalet as being full of "no end of things to admire," including "the old Swiss cupboard bought out of the gift of the Connecticut Girl Scouts; the lovely rug sent by the Swedish Flickscout Raad; the arm-chairs from Holland; the American Room and the library furnished with old Swiss furniture given by British Commissioners; the cutlery from England and France; the china from the Swiss Guides; [and] the Polish beds."[53]

Guide leaders and official publications insisted that the feelings of pride and connectedness expressed by visitors to Foxlease and Our Chalet were available to all members of the movement and not just to the relatively few women and girls who had the time and means to see their international furnishings in person. Girls and young women from across the Empire and the world were urged to donate money to pay for the upkeep of these properties – an undertaking that metropolitan leaders insisted would make them feel they had a personal and material stake in the success of the movement's international vision. While touring Canada in 1923, for example, Olave Baden-Powell claimed to have been struck by Canadian Guides' "intense interest" in Foxlease and "in the voluntary share that they are all able to take" in its furnishing and decoration.[54]

Donating money in support of international Guide properties was especially encouraged every 22 February on "Thinking Day." Thinking Day, the Baden-Powells' joint birthday, was promoted in Guide periodicals and speeches as a chance for "all those thousands upon thousands of girls of different races, of different nations, scattered in every part of this enormous world, [to] send ... their kind thoughts to one another."[55] During the early 1930s, the movement established the Thinking Day Fund and encouraged every girl to add a financial donation to their sisterly thoughts. In 1935, for example, the monies raised on Thinking Day were used to help pay for the upkeep of Our Chalet.[56] While published appeals for Thinking Day funds stressed the voluntary nature of these suggested contributions, there remained an element of coercion, the impact of which was felt especially keenly by poor families (especially during the Depression) and by Guide groups in non-Western countries. This is particularly evident in the minutes of a meeting of the Indian Guide movement's Headquarters Executive Committee held in Lahore in November 1933, one of the few such documents to have survived. At this meeting, the committee recommended that the friendly international spirit of Thinking Day be developed, but it did not approve of any further financial demands being made on Indian Guides. "Individuals wishing to contribute may do so," the committee decided, "but Provinces are asked to let the Honorary General Secretary know of any sums sent to the World Bureau. As several Provinces find it very difficult to meet the capitation fee and World Quota, they are reminded that it is imperative that these be paid before other collections are made."[57]

Further financial pressures, which were likely met with similar responses in India and elsewhere, were also placed on Guides in the early 1930s in connection with the construction of the movement's new Imperial Headquarters building at 17–19 Buckingham Palace Road.[58] The movement's 1930 annual report explained:

> Guiders and Guides in the British Overseas Dominions and Colonies number not quite a quarter of those in the British Isles, and there must be thousands who have little hope of seeing the new building for themselves, or being welcomed within its doors. Far from being deterred by this, however, they are wholeheartedly giving their time, energy and money to the scheme, and showing what sheer loyalty to the Guide cause can do, without hope of visual benefit.

Girls and young women, the report stated, could sponsor bricks for 2s.6d each, windows for sums ranging from £5 to £50, and entire rooms at the new head-quarters building for £500 to £1,000. The importance of these donations was further described as follows:

> Many counties in the British Isles have arranged to provide special parts and their Guides and Brownies are invited to build a piece of wall in their county's room, corridor or landing. Thus, when a Guider or Guide from any part of the country visits Headquarters she has a special feeling of pride when she walks upstairs to a landing, and from a detailed plan can see that Leicestershire – her own county – has provided the money to pay for that part of the building. A child from South Africa has brought her parents to the new building in order to see the room which all the Guides of the Union have worked to provide. Hong Kong Guiders call in to enquire where the cupboards are, which their £30 donation has bought. These were found on the top floor outside the restau-rant, where are also the Argentine Window and the Gold Coast Door and a number of other parts belonging to Overseas Guides, or Guides in Foreign Lands. Graphic descriptions of a room with a fireplace have been sent to the Guides and Bluebirds of India who are very proud to feel that they are providing £500 to pay for it.[59]

Inclusion, Exclusion, and the Mass Media

These efforts to promote imperial and international Guide links through fundraising, furnishings, and buildings, while motivated by a genuine concern for inclusiveness and cross-cultural understanding, could also be quite exclusionary. While more accessible than ever before, long-distance travel remained a costly luxury during the interwar years and was an unimaginable expense for thousands of families who had trouble even finding the funds to buy Guide uniforms or donate on Thinking Day. Experiences like the World Camps, so central to the Guide movement's vision of a familial imperial internationalism, were in reality only available to a minority of girls during this period of global economic uncertainty. The members of Guide and Ranger companies based in urban factories, like the two works companies led by J.M. Marsh in Warring-ton, England, would have had trouble affording travel expenses, and would almost certainly have been unable to take the time off work in order to attend these international gatherings.[60] International travel and fellowship were simi-larly out of the question for the many girls and young women who belonged to Guide companies in medical, regulatory, or colonizing institutions. Earning badges and attending company meetings – as opposed to internationalism or "friendly imperialism" – were almost certainly what defined Guiding for the young members of the women's prison company in Lahore, India; the Mary Wilson Tuberculosis Sanatorium Company in Tilannia, Rajputana, India; and the All Saints Mission School Company in Aklavik in the Northwest Territories of Canada.[61] While badge work and company meetings were important for all Guides, in terms of the movement's internationalist vision, it is clear that some "Guide sisters" were more equal than others.

The "tension between the ideal of inclusiveness and the reality of exclusiveness" that characterized much early twentieth-century women's internationalism was a defining feature of interwar Guiding.[62] Unsurprisingly, though, it was seldom mentioned in official Guide publications and organizational records – likely because the women who produced these texts were often the ones who had the means and time to attend the movement's various international meetings. However, the October 1930 issue of the *Council Fire* includes a rare but telling reflection on the fact that most girls would never have the opportunity to travel to different countries or befriend distant "Guide sisters" at international camps. The author of the article, Miss S.J. Warner, a staff member at the Guide Association's newly opened World Bureau in central London, lamented the fact that, despite the formation of WAGGGS and the institution of regular international meetings for women and girls, "unfortunately much of our international unity rests on theory." Noting the centrality of international gatherings to Guiding's ideological emphasis on cooperation and friendly sisterhood, Warner expressed concern that "comparatively few of our members will ever be able to take part" in these types of activities.[63]

As a paid employee of a voluntary organization whose international activities often depended on the unpaid work done by elite women, Warner might occasionally have been left out of the movement's internationalist vision herself – and could therefore have been more conscious of the processes of inclusion and exclusion that inevitably accompanied Guiding's imperial and transnational activities. Privileged by her metropolitan location, she also clearly recognized the role played by geography in determining attendance at international Guide meetings. Urging readers to think of "troops of Girl Scouts in the Middle-West of the United States, miles away from the sea-board ... of the companies in the provinces of France ... [and] of the numbers of children in little England who will never be able to go abroad," she insisted that Guiding must try harder to bring its international message to these children since they, too, will "be voting, thinking citizens, and will have influence over the destinies of their countries."[64]

Having taken the unusual step of acknowledging the fact that most members of the global "Guide sisterhood" were being left out of the movement's most significant imperial and international initiatives, Warner suggested one possible solution to this problem of exclusivity: that more of the movement's "international work must rest on the power of the pen, and on the broadcast word."[65] The "power of the pen," as exercised through publishing and personal correspondence, was also central to the Guide movement's attempt to spread its message of imperial and international sisterhood throughout the interwar years. The various official periodicals to which members of different ages were urged to subscribe during the 1920s and 1930s frequently encouraged girls and young women to think of themselves as members of an imperial and international imagined community. Featured stories in the *Girl Guides' Gazette*, for instance, discussed "The First All-Island Rally in Ceylon," the Baden-Powells' visits to Canada, and Guide camps in Rhodesia.[66] The *Canadian Guider* often published similar articles; the May 1934 issue, for example, included descriptions of the All-India Guide Training Camp that had been held in Lahore the previous summer and of an embroidered banner that had been sent to Guides in India from a United Church company in Winnipeg.[67] Subjects discussed in the *Council Fire*, the movement's most explicitly internationalist periodical (featuring articles in English, French, and German), included the 1st Purulia Leper Company in India, the Baden-Powells' travels in the Mediterranean, and the Inuit Guides and Brownies in the Canadian Arctic.[68]

Guide periodicals, along with annual reports and handbooks, suggested a range of activities to encourage feelings of international and imperial sisterhood among girls who were unable to travel. "What yarns can be constructed for company meetings," the Chief Guide proclaimed, "with tales of Guides in a different country each week! What a chance for the gaining of an Interpreter's Badge, where the Guide magazines of different countries can be read and translated by an ambitious Guide!"[69] Guides in sixteen different countries were also depicted in a series of lantern slides (available by mail order for a small fee) advertised in the *Girl Guides' Gazette* in the mid-1920s. The advertisement for the slides described several of them using nation- and race-based stereotypes:

The sturdy Czechs boldly sent thirty plates through the post, and not one of them was broken. The Swiss sent small negatives carefully labeled and names, and so did the French. From India and Burma came large square photos of very active Guides in white uniform, cooking, carrying stretchers, tying their tenderfoot knots, etc. The United States thoughtfully sent lantern slides, and coloured ones at that.[70]

Lantern slides and magazine articles, like the activities of the American armchair travel clubs studied by Kristin Hoganson, provided readers with a popular geography that let them feel included in the movement's culture of international travel.[71] Yet the opportunities for fictive travel provided by Guiding can also be seen as exercises in ethnographic classification, which emphasized difference as they generalized about Guide groups from "exotic" locales.

Guide periodicals also encouraged girls and women to experience world travel vicariously by reading. The May 1935 issue of the *Canadian Guider*, for example, recommended a number of books for girls "who are interested in learning more about the life in other countries, or who are corresponding through the Canadian Post Box with Guides in other lands."[72] This list consisted of novels and autobiographical accounts by men and women whose lives exemplified the border-crossing and multiple identities of the "international current" in early twentieth-century life. *Charlotte Lowensköld*, a novel by the Swedish Nobel Prize-winning writer Selma Lagerlof, was the only European book on the list, and the rest of the recommended texts may be seen as proof of the continuing importance of orientalism to twentieth-century internationalism. They included two books by white American women based on their experiences in China (*East Wind, West Wind* by Pearl Buck and Nora Waln's *The House of Exile*) as well as texts by writers from India, Japan, and China: Dhan Gopal Mukerji's *Caste and Outcast*, Etsu Sugimoto's *A Daughter of the Samurai*, and *Kow-Tow* by Princess Der Ling.

Personal correspondence also played a part in interwar Guiding's utopian vision of imperial and international cooperation. Beginning in the early 1920s, Brownies, Guides, and Rangers were urged to make contact with their sister Guides around the world through a headquarters-sponsored letter exchange program called the Post Box. Through the Post Box, girls were encouraged to write to Guide headquarters requesting a pen friend from a distant part of the globe; the program then provided them with the address of a girl from another country in the hopes of encouraging the development of imperial and/or international friendships. This attempt to strengthen the sisterly ties of Guiding in imperial and global terms was lauded in the 1924 Canadian Girl Guide Association Council Annual Report as a "means by which Canadian Guides may correspond with other Guides in distant parts of the world and more especially in parts of the Empire and by this means realize more fully the large sisterhood to which they belong."[73] According to this report, Canadian Guides corresponded with girls in Australia, New Zealand, India, the United States, South Africa, Jamaica, and, especially, the United Kingdom. The Indigenous Guides from St. Peter's School in Hay River, Northwest Territories, for example, corresponded with girls in England and Wales.[74]

Stories celebrating the potential of the post to connect girls from different lands also appeared often in Guide periodicals as proof of the movement's international success and as incentives for other girls to join. The March 1929 issue of the *Council Fire* describes a friendship between an English and an Indian Ranger who met on board a ship to Australia: "The Indian one, on hearing where the other came from, said, 'Oh, I've got a little match-box painted by a North Cumberland Guide,' sent [to] me at Foxlease."[75]

But even official Guide publications and efforts to encourage the global exchange of letters and gifts were sometimes unable to reach or include certain groups of girls, since not all members of the Guide sisterhood spoke or read the same language, and some girls and women, of course, were unable to read at all. The language issue was especially politically charged in Canada, as many members of that country's French Catholic population saw the English language as an unwelcome after-effect of the British conquest of Quebec in 1759. Many French-Canadian girls could read only in French, as some of their parents and teachers saw the language spoken by Protestant anglophones as a threat to French Catholic culture in Canada. Sylvie Taschereau, the district commissioner of the Quebec Guides whose "political" leanings so concerned the movement's anglophone leaders, chose to solve French-Canadian Guides' translation problems and avoid Anglo-Canadian cultural influence by using the prescriptive literature produced by the Guides de France instead of the English-language texts (many of which were published in Britain) used by the Canadian Girl Guides Association.[76]

Literacy and translation also posed problems for the Guide movement in late colonial India. The diffusion of its program and internationalist ideals was hampered by the existence of so many vernacular languages; of those women and girls who knew how to read, many did so in languages other than English, which made translation an issue of considerable concern. On the occasion of the British Princess Mary's wedding in 1922, the Maharaja of Jaipur donated one thousand pounds to the Guide Association in India, the interest from which was used "for the translation of the English publications into different Indian languages."[77] This interest in translation was not limited to the Princely States; in Bombay Presidency, for instance, information on Girl Guiding was translated into Marathi and Gujarati in 1923.[78] Translation work continued during the 1920s and into the 1930s, although, as indicated by the international section of the British Guide Association's 1930 annual report, it was a slow process plagued by difficulties that at times "seem[ed] almost insuperable."[79]

These difficulties included a lack of financial resources with which to pay translators, but the biggest issue of all – and the one that British Guide leaders were the most reluctant to discuss in print – was Indian nationalism. In the same 1930 annual report that discussed translation, the District Commissioner for Kashmir reported "a certain amount of trouble over Guides resigning for political reasons," a representative from Bihar and Orissa noted "trouble in one company on the question of loyalty," and the regional reports from Bengal and the Central Provinces noted that "political unrest" had led to the suspension or disbandment of several companies.[80] These were not the first instances of South Asian Guides acting in support of the popular movement to free India from its colonial ties to Britain. In 1928, for instance, senior students at the non-denominational Brahmo Girls' School in Calcutta refused to make the Guide promise of loyalty to the King-Emperor.[81] Perhaps unsurprisingly, this telling incident was not mentioned in the 1928–30 WAGGGS biennial report. But the fact that it is discussed in the official history of South Asian Guiding written by Guider Lakshmi Mazumdar in 1968 reveals the importance of these acts of resistance. Despite – or perhaps because of – these girls' expressions of dissatisfaction with colonial rule and Guiding's insistence on loyalty to Britain, the British-based international movement's official translation efforts in South Asia continued. *Steps to Girl Guiding in India*, the abridged version of the Guide handbook produced for use in colonial contexts, was published in Hindi, Kanarese, and Gujarati by 1930, and translation work was also begun that year on the Bluebird handbook.[82]

A revealing contrast to the British-based Guide movement's insistence on translating handbooks into South Asian languages in the midst of anti-colonial ferment is the case of Girl Guide companies in Canadian Indigenous day and residential schools. These institutions, in which hunger and violence often coexisted with lessons and extracurricular activities like the Guides, separated Indigenous children from their families and cultures in the hope of transforming them into docile English-speaking citizens and workers. The Canadian Scouts and Guides did not provide programs and literature in Indigenous languages to these children because these would have undermined the Dominion government's attempt to assimilate them into Euro-Canadian society. Material considerations also obviously influenced this decision, as Guide companies in residential schools were funded by the federal Department of Indian Affairs.[83]

The international Guide movement's familial vision, which applied in very different and sometimes flawed ways to girls in various colonial settings, was also promoted, as Miss Warner had suggested, through the broadcast word. Guide leaders, like many other cultural internationalists during the 1920s and 1930s, were enthusiastic about the potential of modern mass media to unite young female citizens across the boundaries of age, race, geography, and class.[84] The Guide films and radio programs that were released during the interwar years often dealt with imperial and global themes, and frequently depicted big international events that most girls would have missed. The British-made film *Girl Guides to the Fore* was brought to Canada for two months in 1922 and was shown from Nova Scotia to British Columbia.[85] A two-reel film of the 1924 World Camp at Foxlease was "shown extensively" throughout Britain and in Brussels and Cologne, and copies were also sold to Guide groups in Canada and the United States.[86] Three years later, in November and December 1927, the film of an international Guide camp in Geneva was shown at the Metropolitan Theatre in downtown Winnipeg.[87] As with so many other aspects of the movement, its use of the cinema raises important but largely unanswerable questions about reception. How many times was each film shown? How many girls and young women attended each showing, and what did they think of the messages contained in each film? Did they prefer Guide films or Hollywood movies? The young people Guiding hoped to reach with these films were sophisticated consumers of modern media who would have recognized the didactic and "character-building" intent of Guide movies and radio programs. As one English Guide wrote in her logbook about *Girl Guides to the Fore*: "we witnessed some very thrilling episodes in the life of a girl guide in a foreign country [but] (we all wondered if there ever had lived a girl who was such and [sic] ideal Guide)."[88]

The Guide movement also used radio, with similarly uncertain results, to reach out to its million and a half members, especially during the 1930s. The Chief Scout and the Chief Guide, for example, regularly addressed the members of their youth movements on the BBC Home, Empire, and International Services during the 1930s.[89] Guide publications also discussed other radio programs (particularly those involving the British monarchy) as important links between far-flung members of the imperial Guide sisterhood. As Rose Kerr commented in the movement's 1934 annual report:

> It is only at certain moments that we realize fully the greatness of our privilege in belonging to the British Commonwealth of Nations. Such a moment must have come to all of us last Christmas Day, as we listened to the broadcast greetings from one member of the family to another all round the world, and finally as we listened in tense silence to the measured, majestic words of our King, in

whom are summed up all the aspirations and ideals of the nation, in whom we have a symbol on which to place our loyalty and our trust.[90]

The coronation of King George VI in 1937 was similarly seen and used by many Guide leaders as a chance to cement the movement's international and especially imperial bonds across all kinds of borders. A number of events were held in honour of the new monarch in England, including a coronation camp attended by nearly 500 girls from the United Kingdom and "almost all of the colonies and Dominions," a display of Guides on the coronation parade route, a service in Westminster Abbey attended by 4,000 international Scouts and Guides, and a "monster rally" featuring 1,600 young participants at Wembley Stadium.[91] A number of radio broadcasts were also made to describe these events and encourage girls to feel a part of the coronation celebrations.

But these new means of mass communication, which brought Guiding's imperial internationalist vision to tens of thousands of girls around the world, were still not enough to reach all the girls and women who wore Brownie, Guide, and Ranger uniforms during the 1920s and 1930s. Radio programs, for example, were only effective if listeners understood the language being broadcast, lived within range of wireless signals, and had access to a radio, either in their parents' home or in someone else's.[92] The ease and speed with which radio could connect listeners in remote locations to more populated parts of the world also sometimes undermined broadcasters' efforts to create feelings of family and community. Barbara Kelcey, for instance, demonstrates that radio shows from southern Canada, broadcast in the Arctic from the mid-1930s on, actually increased some white women's feelings of isolation and loneliness.[93] Material considerations also constrained the effectiveness of the cinema as an internationalist Guiding propaganda tool – buying tickets required disposable income, and theatres were far more common in cities and the industrialized west than they were elsewhere. Regardless of these limitations, though, Guide films and radio broadcasts still reached more girls and women than could ever have hoped to attend a world camp or similar international gathering. How this vast and varied audience understood the movement's media messages, however, is far more difficult to determine.

The Persistence of Racial Hierarchies

The Guide movement's varied attempts to include girls and women who, for reasons of class, culture, and geography, were left out of its imperial and international gatherings during the 1920s and 1930s were significant, as they reached thousands of girls who would otherwise have had little or no sense of belonging to a modern global sisterhood. But these efforts were paralleled and sometimes undermined by a different vision of imperial internationalism – one that still bore traces of older, more conservative and hierarchical ways of thinking about race. This less inclusive aspect of the movement is especially evident in published accounts of the Chief Scout and Chief Guide's world travels, as well as in newspaper articles and fiction.

Through mass media, consumer culture, and travel, Olave and Robert Baden-Powell sought to fashion an image of themselves as the benevolent parents of a worldwide family of youthful Scouts and Guides. In this respect, the Chief Scout and Chief Guide, who travelled nearly nonstop during the 1920s and 1930s, were agents of what Robert Clarke calls "celebrity colonialism": modern media stars whose lives and achievements served, in sometimes contradictory ways, as endorsements of "imperial and colonial institutions and practices."[94] While touring the world to promote and monitor the growth of Guiding and Scouting, the Baden-Powells and other British leaders celebrated the geographical and cultural breadth of both movements, while continuing to insist on metropolitan control and the existence of real differences between "races." As the Chief Scout wrote upon his return from one of his many world tours in the early 1930s, the global and imperial expansion of the Girl Guides provided the

> most encouraging proof of the innate vitality of the Movement, and of its appeal to untutored as well as the educated races. To see with one's own eyes the effects of Guiding, not merely in great industrial centres, but in such isolated communities as, say, the Malay States and the Pacific Islands, as well as in the outposts of Newfoundland, and prairie settlements of Canada, is to gain a new view-point such as could not be got from merely reading reports, and one which cannot fail to develop the highest hopes and confidence in the possibilities which yet lie before the Movement.[95]

In her 1936 book *The Story of a Million Girls: Guiding and Girl Scouting around the World*, British Guide official Rose Kerr similarly praised Guiding's worldwide reach, while insisting on the continued importance of the movement's metropolitan centre: "The term 'British Guides' is a wide one and includes girls of many different countries and types. They speak many different languages, but they all make the same Promise, and follow the rules of the Guide game as laid down by British Imperial Headquarters."[96]

Like the early twentieth-century white international feminists studied by Charlotte Weber, the Baden-Powells both indulged in and rebutted common nation- and race-based stereotypes when describing their travels.[97] In magazine articles and books published throughout the interwar years, they used images and words to represent and produce the British Empire and the world for the members of their youth movements. While more tempered than their unpublished writings, these texts nonetheless epitomize the uneasy relationship that existed between interwar Guiding's emphasis on sisterly affection and tolerance and a way of seeing the world that still differentiated between "untutored" and "educated" races.

This often contradictory modern approach to imperial internationalism is characterized by the content of *Guide Links*, a 1936 collection of essays originally published in the *Guide* magazine by Chief Guide Olave Baden-Powell. These essays concern her and her husband's visits to Scout and Guide companies around the world. The essay about their travels in Canada, for example, features several positive (though still decidedly paternalistic) descriptions of their encounters with Indigenous people, including the dances done by "a group of real live Red Indians" at a 1923 Guide and Scout rally in Calgary, Alberta, and the ceremony in which the Chief Guide was named an honorary member of the Alberta-based Tsuu T'ina (then known as Sarcee) Nation.[98] Yet the Chief Guide also sought to explain Canada to Guides from other countries by referring to early European settlers' "considerable trouble with the Red Indians" and the legacy of "many unhappy conflicts between the native Redskin and the conquering white race."[99] The Chief Guide's assumptions about "native Redskins" and the "conquering white race" undermine her youth movement's official support of interracial cooperation in obvious ways. Her claims, which were based on an understanding of Canada as a "white" nation whose Indigenous inhabitants were weak and likely to die out, bore some significant similarities to the ideas that underpinned the Canadian state's Indian policy during the 1920s and 1930s.

This uneasy mix of calls for sisterhood and international tolerance with uninformed statements about racial and cultural "others" also appeared in contemporary newspapers as well Guide fiction and prescriptive literature published in or dealing with England, Canada, and India. In August 1937, several months after Baden-Powell's controversial remarks about Indian Scouting, the Girl Guide column in the *Toronto Daily Star* published an article about an "interesting correspondence" between Florence Joyce of the 37th Toronto Guide Company and Merlyn Cross, an "English girl who was born in India" and belonged to the 1st Calcutta Guides.[100] Summarizing several of Merlyn's letters to her Canadian Guide "sister," the article discusses the Baden-Powells' recent visit to India and describes the Guide rallies that were frequently held at "the compound of Belvedere House, Calcutta, India, the home of the Viceroy."[101] This exchange of letters was, on the one hand, exactly the type of international success story that the organizers of the Post Box had hoped for. On the other hand, it was also an exclusive exchange between two white girls that did little to challenge the belief, expressed by Merlyn, that "the Hindoos have many queer customs."[102]

The fact that a similar belief about the "queerness" of non-European cultures continued to influence some aspects of Guiding during the apparently familial and internationalist 1920s and 1930s is also evident in a number of the novels and short stories about Girl Guides that were published during these two decades. While most novels about Guides and Guiding were not published by the Guide Association, they were often reviewed and advertised in official magazines like the *Girl Guides' Gazette* and the *Guide*. Many of these novels were quite innovative in gender terms, allowing their female protagonists the kind of freedom and agency that had previously only been available to the boy heroes in Victorian adventure fiction. They were generally far less progressive, however, when it came to matters of race. One especially pertinent example is Janet Aldis's *A Girl Guide Captain in India*, published in 1922 by the Methodist Publishing House in Madras. The Guide captain of the book's title is an English girl who moves from London to India with her parents. While describing the "queer experiences, odd sights, weird sounds, and odours of the far east," she notes that "the [Guide] movement has taken hold here among Indian girls as well as Europeans" and starts a company at her school, which is attended exclusively by girls of British descent.[103] The South Asian people encountered by the novel's English protagonists are generally not fellow members of the interwar "Guide family"; instead, they are characters like the "picturesque" labourer who invites them for a tour of a tea factory on behalf of the estate's British manager.[104] Like many other interwar Guide novels, *A Girl Guide Captain in India* concludes with a triumphant Guide and Scout rally. At this point in the story, the narrator makes a significant comparison, noting that the excited behaviour of the Scouts and Guides while waiting for the rally to begin "was like playing a delightful game of Red Indians."[105]

"Playing [North American] Indian" through camping and woodcraft was a central part of the Guide game around the world. While imaginary North American Indians were to be admired and emulated, some interwar Guide fiction gave young readers the message that real Indigenous people were to be feared or laughed at. The 1923 *Collins' Girl Guide Annual*, for instance, featured a short story about two British girls who get lost in the wintry backwoods of Canada and take shelter in a cabin there, only to be surprised by the Indigenous man whose home they had entered and who had returned "a maniac from drink."[106] This troubling depiction of a moment of contact between British-born girls and an Indigenous man reveals the enormous gulf between discourse and experience that Indigenous Girl Guides would have faced during the 1920s and 1930s. Like *A Girl Guide Captain in India*, this story – with its exclusively white protagonists and occasionally racist assumptions – shows that the published word also had the power to undermine the interwar Guide movement's official attempts to create bonds of familial tolerance and affection between girls.

Conclusion

In the second WAGGGS biennial report, published in 1932, World Association Chairwoman Dame Katharine Furse acknowledged the existence of "serious obstacles to the progress of international thinking" and insisted that all members of the Guide movement must learn "to know and to love, as equal friends, all our neighbours of all creeds, all races, all colours, and all nationalities."[107] The vision of imperial internationalism that Guiding promoted during the 1920s and 1930s did go some way towards the realization of Furse's tolerant and friendly familial ideal. In discursive terms, the movement encouraged girls and young women from around the world to think of each other as sisters belonging to a benevolent empire family and a junior League of Nations. This emphasis on interconnectedness was also reflected in a series of organizational changes, the most significant of which was the formation of WAGGGS in 1928. International and imperial camps and gatherings, dozens of which were held during the interwar years, let some Guides travel to different countries and meet girls and young women from other parts of the British Empire and elsewhere. Published accounts of these events and coverage of Guide activities in different national contexts went some way towards including the girls and young women who were left out of these events, as did the movement's Post Box letter exchange program and its use of cinema and radio.

Yet the Guide movement's attempts to create a benevolent, egalitarian imperial and international family were ultimately limited by a number of practical difficulties. Class and economic considerations were an especially powerful impediment. Many girls and young women had to struggle to afford Guide uniforms, and the experience of world camps (and even smaller international ones) were only available to an elite minority. Material constraints did more than limit Guides' access to travel and international fellowship: limited funds – especially in the context of the Depression – also meant that many girls and women did not have regular access to Guide radio programs, films, and magazines. Finally, the creation of an imperial/international Guide sisterhood was also limited by differing levels of literacy and by divisions of language, as translating official Guide texts was an expensive and often time-consuming endeavour.

The creation of a worldwide Guide sisterhood was also complicated by the international movement's active support of the British Empire, an entity that (despite interwar assertions to the contrary) was intimately linked to inequality, violence, and hierarchical racial thinking. As Simon Potter argues, networks of mass media in the nineteenth- and twentieth-century British Empire, while creating communities, also worked "to help to sustain pervasive, hierarchical, and oppressive structures of imperial and settler dominance."[108] Recurrent references in official and unofficial Guide texts to threatening Indigenous men, "queer hindoo customs," and the "conquering white race," for example, reveal an uneasy balance between inclusivity and exclusivity – a tension that also characterized a number of other imperial/international voluntary organizations. The pervasiveness of these assumptions, combined with the international movement's Anglo-centric organization, led groups of girls and young women – French-Canadian Guides and the Calcutta Brahmo Girls' School company, for instance – either to attempt to reject British-based international Guiding altogether or to insist that they be included on their own terms. Much of this changed during and after the Second World War as Guide groups around the world shifted their attention to the war effort, and it became increasingly difficult to believe in any sort of international or imperial family. But during the interwar years, a brief period when a friendly British Empire and League of Nations-style internationalism seemed possible (to some people), Girl Guide programs and ideology tried – with only partial success – to create a diverse, interracial, connected, and egalitarian sisterhood of girls and young women.

CONCLUSION

IN THE SUMMER OF 1939, as the outbreak of a second world war seemed increasingly likely, the World Association of Girl Guides and Girl Scouts clung to its international ideals by holding a two-week World Camp for Girl Guides in Gödöllö, Hungary.[1] Dubbed "Pax Ting" (translated variously as "peace rally" or "peace gathering"), the event was attended by nearly four thousand girls and women from across the British Empire and the world.[2] According to letters written by Alison Duke, the twenty-four-year-old Cambridge-educated Guide captain in charge of the camp's British contingent, the girls and women in attendance took part in camp fire singing, a "Keep Fit display," folk dancing, and patriotic drills. They enjoyed a boat trip on the Danube and attended "an open-air Protestant church service" in Hungarian and English.[3] White internationalists' fascination with "Eastern" women and their clothes, a constant at earlier, Western-dominated international Guide gatherings, shaped the events at Pax Ting as well; one account published in the *Council Fire* noted that, "on Visitors' Day the Indian Guider, in her attractive sari, received so much attention from the public and press that she finally had to be removed to the hospital tent for her own protection."[4]

Yet this camp was also different from its predecessors, as it was held at a moment when the friendly ideals of international Guiding and the League of Nations could clearly be seen to have failed. The over 200 British Guides and leaders who attended Pax Ting, like many of the camp's other European participants, travelled to Hungary by train – a journey that took them through

Germany as well as other territories that had recently been annexed by the Nazis. In a letter dated 29 July 1939, Duke, whose leadership position on this trip was due to her fluency in German, described the border-crossing difficulties her group encountered during this time of international hostility. The "journey was great fun but rather lively for me," she wrote, "as I had to keep running up and down the train to deal with officials who were sometimes rather angry with me!" Some border crossings, Duke's letters reveal, were eased for the British Guides by members of the Bund Deutscher Mädel.[5]

A report about the journey published in the *Council Fire* one month after war had been declared also highlighted the helpfulness and friendliness of the BDM; on the Belgian-German border, the report stated, "we were met at 3 a.m. by a Leader of the Bund Deutscher Mädel, who had come from Cologne on purpose to help us. She travelled with us to Cologne, and on the platform we found a group of BDM to greet us ... At other places on the journey we were also received by the BDM with great cordiality."[6] The BDM and the Guides were, of course, not strangers at this point; a number of British Guide leaders had sought to arrange exchanges with the BDM during the late 1930s, a group of English Guides wrote to BDM girls through the WAGGGS Post Box in 1938 (though the British International Committee had told the Guides *not* to discuss "politics"), and a group of BDM girls attended a Surrey Guide camp and visited the movement's Imperial Headquarters in London as "unofficial" guests in the summer of 1939.[7]

By December 1939, however, relations between British-based international Guiding and Nazi Germany had cooled considerably. The movement's annual report for that year, for example, stated:

> Hitler knew how important it was to train the youth of Germany to his own advantage; if his training had inculcated Guide and Scout ideals instead of blind hero worship and fiery nationalism, much of the present misery in the world would have been prevented. Let us in this country realize, too, the importance of training the youth of our nation, for they are our future citizens, and on their shoulders will rest the future of our Empire.[8]

The outbreak of the Second World War posed significant challenges to WAGGGS's internationalist efforts. The World Bureau (as WAGGGS headquarters was also known) continued to operate in London, but "as a precaution" its leaders set up a second office in New York.[9] The fourth WAGGGS biennial report, published in the spring of 1940, stated of Our Chalet in Switzerland: "We do not know whether the Chalet is open or closed ... We do not know how long it may be before Our Chalet can again open its doors to the Guides and Girl Scouts of all countries, but we know that when it does, the same spirit of friendship, generosity, peace, and goodwill will be there."[10] The World Bureau continued to publish the *Council Fire* throughout the war, and the Post Box continued to connect girl correspondents from different countries – although its administrators noted that Guides in Nazi-occupied Finland and Poland had ceased to respond to their pen pals' letters.[11] Imperial connections, which often took a backseat to more pressing discussions of the war in Europe, remained important to Guiding's pen-pal program and to its sense of mission throughout the conflict. The movement's 1939 annual report, for example, proudly claimed that "the Dominions and India still send names, and enthusiastic letters have come from Canada and South Africa saying how quickly and regularly the mails and cargoes arrive there, and how anxious the Guides are to help the Empire's war effort, and to hear what the Guides in England are doing."[12]

As in the First World War, voluntary war work and its attendant focus on national interests replaced pacifism and internationalism as the focus of Guiding for many girls and women.[13] Katharine Furse, who by this point had stepped down as president of WAGGGS, lamented this shift in an article entitled "The World Association in War Time" that was published in the October 1939 issue of the *Council Fire*. "I would have liked," she wrote, "to see our World Association on as neutral a basis as the International Red Cross Society at Geneva or the League of Red Cross Societies which had its headquarters in Paris, but with our Promise of loyalty to country this cannot be, and each individual Girl Guide and Girl Scout is now faced with deciding for herself what part she is to take in the struggle."[14] Individual Guides in Canada, England, and India served their countries and the Allied war effort in a number of ways: by knitting and sewing, collecting scrap metal, donating clothes and goods for child refugees, growing fruit and vegetables, and providing child care for women employed in war-related industries. Guides in Britain also volunteered at train stations during the evacuation of urban children, helped to equip and maintain army carrier pigeons, and put their first aid skills to use during the Blitz. Guides from across the Empire also raised funds for the war effort, as when girls from Canada, India, South Africa, New Zealand, and several other colonial locations purchased a lifeboat and two air ambulances for Allied forces in 1940.[15]

The internment of thousands of Japanese Canadians after the attack on Pearl Harbor significantly undermined the claims about equality and sisterhood that had been made by Canadian Guide leaders during the 1920s and 1930s.

Perhaps because of the movement's emphasis on fostering understanding and goodwill between nations and "races," the British Columbia Security Commission, the administrative body in charge of evacuation and internment, asked Canadian Guide headquarters to send a representative to start Guiding in internment camps – an undertaking that, it was hoped, would improve morale while somehow making the girls more "Canadian."[16] Margaret Hannah and Doris Illingworth, the two white women chosen for the task, described their work in a letter in 1943:

> We go into the various camps, 4,000 in one, 3,000 in another and so on, and we collect possible Japanese Guiders. So far we have made contact with five old Rangers from Vancouver, most useful. We give concentrated training classes, enroll a few, and then usually run the first open meeting for the Guides and leave them to carry on, and we plan to return in the Spring to give further help. It is late for these parts, heavy snow ... in Sandon a Buddhist Japanese lassie met us, beaming, she had collected 50 Guides, and some 10 possible Guiders and had told them they now belonged to a world-wide movement, and they must not let it down, nay, could not let it down! ... These Japs feel Canadian, they talk of "those darned Japs," and they take the first promise most willingly and seriously. We don't much like them as a nation, but we do like individuals, and these poor children are nothing, suspect of Canada, and suspect of Japan, and when they go to Japan are kept under surveillance by the Gestapo, and other Japs dare not be friendly.[17]

Guide groups also continued to operate (clandestinely, and under threat of severe punishment) in Nazi concentration camps and in Changi Prison in Singapore, where many British and European nationals were imprisoned for the duration of the war.[18]

The notion that all Guides belonged to a benevolent worldwide sisterhood also influenced the movement's wartime and postwar relief work, the most dramatic manifestation of which was the Guide International Service (GIS), a humanitarian relief agency made up primarily of Rangers and Guide leaders. As Phyllis Stewart Brown wrote in the official history of the GIS, Guiding had provided women and older adolescent girls with a particular set of skills that could be useful in wartime: "many Guiders were experienced in organizing and staffing large camps, with a minimum of equipment; numbers were used to co-operation with fellow Guiders of other nations; all were used to working in some form of team."[19] Thousands of young women volunteered, but as Tammy Proctor points out, "those chosen typically had good camping and Guiding credentials, with widespread experience in first aid, cooking, outdoor life, and special skills (language, medical training etc)."[20] Guide fundraising efforts in the British Empire and the United States paid for the scheme, while the British army provided team members' room, board, transport, and uniforms. Training began in Britain in 1942, and it included hauling carts across rough terrain and serving tea to patients at a mental hospital "to get exposure to mental illness and distress."[21]

The first GIS team, known as RRUY7, took a troopship to Egypt in 1944. They underwent further training there and began their relief work in civil war-torn Greece in January 1945. This team included Alison Duke, the woman who had translated for angry German officials onboard the train to Pax Ting in 1939. Duke, who had studied Classics at Cambridge (where she would later lecture in the subject and serve as a Life Fellow at Girton College), acted as interpreter and Greek tutor.[22] The members of RRUY7 provided food, clothing, and medical assistance to displaced civilians in difficult and often dangerous conditions. All in all, there were thirteen teams of GIS relief workers in Europe and Asia during the mid- to late 1940s. (British teams served primarily in Greece, Germany, and the Netherlands, while those from Australia and New Zealand served mostly in Singapore and Malaya.)

The shape of Guiding, significantly altered by the conditions of wartime, was further changed by the resignation and deaths of many of the movement's most influential leaders. Katharine Furse, for example, whose internationalist vision and involvement with the League of Nations had moulded WAGGGS since its founding in 1928, stepped down as president of that organization in 1938. Three years later, in 1941, Baden-Powell died in Kenya. Although he was never the sole author of Guide policy, Guide leaders from around the world sought to remain true to his vision while also teaching their girls with the "most modern methods." This concern with following Baden-Powell's ideals faded considerably after the end of the Second World War, when new prescriptive literature was introduced in many national contexts. Rose Kerr, the British Guide leader and former international commissioner whose official histories and articles about global Guiding have been cited throughout this book, died in 1944. Agnes Baden-Powell, who had been relegated to the sidelines of the movement for most of the 1920s and 1930s, died one year later, in 1945.

Olave Baden-Powell, grief-stricken by her beloved husband's death, did not attend his military funeral in Kenya. She sailed for England in 1942 and was immediately confronted with the war's destruction and upheaval: she saw several ships destroyed by German torpedoes while en route, was unable to return to her house in Hampshire, as it had been occupied by the Canadian army, and walked alone from Victoria station past Guide headquarters in London, where she was shocked at the damage done by German bombs.[23] She continued to revere her "beloved Scout" and spent the rest of her life trying to carry on the work he had started.[24] She travelled the world for much of the next thirty years and was an honoured guest at Guide and Scout camps and rallies in dozens of different countries. She was also present at the openings of two new WAGGGS world centres (proof, perhaps, that the movement was becoming less focused on Europe and North America): Our Cabaña in Cuernavaca, Mexico, in 1957, and Sangam in Pune, India, in 1966.[25] She stopped travelling due to ill health in 1970 and died in England at the age of eighty-eight in 1977. Her ashes were flown to Kenya, which had achieved its independence from Britain in 1963, and were buried in her husband's grave. Tim Jeal writes that "the presence of a vast crowd of Africans including leading members of the Kenyan government at her funeral service in All Saints Cathedral, Nairobi, was perfectly natural – but extraordinary, too, in view of her husband's activities in Ashanti and Matabeleland."[26]

India, of course, had severed its ties with Britain in 1947. Four years later, the leaders of Scouting and Guiding there decided to form a single national organization: the Bharat Scouts and Guides. Until that time, Indian Guiding in schools had been mostly restricted to the daughters of what mid-twentieth-century leader Lakshmi Mazumdar called "comparatively more well-to-do and progressive families." That changed as the Bharat Scouts and Guides expanded during the decades after Independence, and in the late 1960s Mazumdar noted the movement's success at reaching out to a broader social spectrum and to girls and boys from rural and semi-rural areas. She explained this change as partly the result of the decision to merge the Scouts and Guides but also as a consequence of the change in the country's political and social conditions in the postwar and post-Independence period.[27] South Asian Guide leaders continued to promote feelings of friendliness and tolerance after the devastation of Partition, and Julie Sen, who had represented India at the Seventh World Conference in Poland in 1932, was the first Indian Guider to be elected to the WAGGGS World Committee at the Twelfth World Conference held in 1948.[28]

Throughout the rest of the twentieth century, the global Guide movement sought to remain true to many of its founding values while seeking to reinvent itself in response to a range of social and political changes, including the end of the British Empire, the Cold War, an expanding and shifting youth culture, television, second-wave feminism, co-education, and the internet. In 1954, for instance, the name of Imperial Headquarters was changed to Commonwealth Headquarters. English-Canadian Guiding officially affiliated with its French

Catholic counterpart in 1939, and the numbers of companies in residential schools attended by Indigenous children increased until assimilatory education was halted by the federal government in the late twentieth century. While its founding and early growth were tied to British imperialism, the Guide movement's organizational structure and broad emphasis on sisterhood, combined with the loss during the 1940s of most of its first generation of leaders (all of whom had been born in the nineteenth century), meant that the gradual dismantling of Britain's empire was not a significant disjuncture for global Guiding. Membership numbers in many former colonies – particularly in Africa and Asia – increased during the second half of the twentieth century, and Guide leaders at WAGGGS and in a range of national contexts came to see remaining relevant in the face of changing youth cultures as the movement's most pressing concern.

In 2010, the hundredth anniversary of the founding of the Guide movement, there were 10 million Girl Guides and Girl Scouts in 146 countries – a significant increase over the interwar years, and a reflection in particular of Guiding's popularity in the twenty-first-century global south.[29] The Bharat Scouts and Guides, whose membership has increased exponentially since the early 1950s, currently organizes a number of activities, including camping, polio vaccination campaigns, and computer literacy training.[30] Girl Guiding UK, unlike its co-educational Indian counterpart, proudly emphasizes its single-sex nature at numerous points on its website, proclaiming, for example, that "Guiding lets girls think, learn and develop without having to put up with boys trying to be the centre of attention all the time!"[31] Guiding also remains a single-sex organization in Canada, and, like Girl Guiding UK, its website reflects a not-always successful desire to compete with twenty-first-century media and youth culture: "Guiding is more than crafts, camping and cookies. Some of the badges and challenges girls work on today include Career Awareness, Streetwise, Saving Water, Fashion, Eating Local, Cultural Awareness, Inventing, Money Talk and Business Communications."[32]

To honour the "plucky" Edwardian girls who had dressed in Scout uniforms at the Crystal Palace Rally in 1909, Girl Guiding UK commissioned two female artists to design a new maze on the Palace grounds in south London. Officially opened in 2009, it features ten granite monoliths bearing symbols related to Guiding and the natural world. On 5–6 September 2009, 7,000 British Guides made a pilgrimage of sorts to the place where the first "Girl Scouts" had joined Baden-Powell's Boy Scout rally in 1909, where they took part in "outdoor adventures [and] performing arts workshops" and watched "a star-studded evening concert." Over 600 other events also took place that weekend across the United Kingdom, including a gathering of over 8,500 girls in Heaton Park in Manchester.[33]

The movement's centenary was celebrated on a relatively smaller scale elsewhere in the world. Forty-eight thousand Canadian Guides, for instance, participated in a "National Rally Day" on 15 May 2010. This coast-to-coast celebration started "with sunrise ceremonies in Newfoundland," included nature activities, tug-of-wars, birthday cake, and a "flash mob dance," and it concluded with "a gigantic sleepover in Vancouver."[34] I have been unable to find any references to similar celebrations in India; the Bharat Scouts and Guides seem to have celebrated the anniversary of the movement in 2009, one hundred years from the founding of the first Boy Scout troop in India.

WAGGGS, which still runs an international pen pal program – administered by Girl Guiding UK – also organized three years of Guiding centenary celebrations, from 2010 to 2012. These events included a series of Young Women's World Forums, held in 2010 in the United Kingdom; in 2011 simultaneously at all four World Centres; and in 2012 in the United States – discussion groups at which Guides from around the world met to discuss the United Nations' Millennium Development Goals and how to achieve them.[35] The World Association's engagement with the UN, a legacy of Guiding's earlier commitment to the League of Nations and politically engaged citizenship, continues today. One example of this is WAGGGS's sponsorship of two "UN Teams": groups of former Guides and Girl Scouts living in New York and Paris who represent Guiding and the interests of girls and young women at United Nations meetings while learning more about the ideals and workings of the UN.[36]

❧ • ☙

JOAN FOSTER, THE PROTAGONIST of Margaret Atwood's novel *Lady Oracle*, was a Brownie. The book's early chapters, which focus on Joan's girlhood in mid-twentieth-century Toronto, describe Tuesday evenings of "rituals and badges and the sewing on of buttons" amidst "clouds of church-basement dust." Joan, who was sometimes bullied by Brownies from a wealthier neighbourhood, "liked wearing the same baggy uniform with its odd beret and tie." She also, like many of the girls and young women discussed in this book, did not accept all of the movement's rituals and teachings at face value. Of Joan's kind and enthusiastic Brownie leader, Atwood writes:

> It was hard to believe that an adult, older than my mother even, would actually squat on the floor and say things like "tu-whit, Tu-whoo" and "When Brownies make their fairy ring, They can magic everything!" Brown Owl acted as if she

believed all this, and thought that we did too. This was the novelty: someone even more gullible than I was. Occasionally I felt sorry for her, because I knew how much pinching, shoving and nudging went on during Thinking Time and who made faces behind Brown Owl's back when we were saying, "I promise to do my duty to God and the King and to help others every day, especially those at home."[37]

The girls discussed in this book, who in symbolic and practical terms were at the heart of many anxious discussions about the future of the British Empire and the world, also used some aspects of Guiding for their own purposes, while laughing at or rejecting others. Examples in this book include the Battersea Guides, who chose a day out in London over a healthy country hike; the Calcutta Guides, who refused to promise to serve the King-Emperor; and the Indigenous Guides in Canada, who earned badges and won prizes for producing traditional crafts in settings that were meant to assimilate them. Eileen Knapman's jokes about the seriousness with which her Guide leaders tried to teach scientific child care, like the Peace River Guides' laughter at Monica Storrs's domestic advice and health rules, provide further proof of modern girls' agency. But these examples, while important, play a relatively small part in the chorus of largely adult voices that comprises early twentieth-century Guiding's archival record.

Guiding, an organization that appealed to women and girls from a range of national, colonial, and "racial" backgrounds during the 1920s and 1930s, was a source of conflicting messages about age, gender, class, race, empire, and internationalism. On the one hand, it combined Victorian and Edwardian ideas about maternal, domestic, and marital instincts and duty with a concern for teaching girls the most modern and scientific ways to look after children, houses, and husbands. The movement's consistent emphasis on homekeeping, motherhood, and matrimony was the result of adult anxieties about racial, national, and imperial health; about girls' leisure and employment choices; and about the impact of the modern world on a supposedly natural gender order and social hierarchy. It also stressed similarities of age and gender by encouraging girls and young women in very different settings to perform the same kinds of gendered emotional and practical labour.

At the same time, Guiding's insistence on the importance of heterosexuality and the private sphere was paralleled and sometimes undermined by its promotion of bravery, independence, physical strength, and female masculinity. While practising for their Child Nurse badges and learning the correct way to set a table, many girls would have come into contact with unmarried Guide leaders – women whose lives did not include men and motherhood, some of whom had little time for the dictates of domesticity. The interwar Guide movement also encouraged girls to think of themselves as citizens; to educate themselves about local, national, and global political systems; and to acquire skills that would help them find paid work or run for public office. It encouraged them to strengthen their bodies and to act decisively and courageously in dangerous situations. Modern girls, many official texts insisted, were self-reliant citizens who could handle axes and other tools, had more in common with knights than princesses, and should think nothing of saving the lives and economic fortunes of men and boys.

The movement's leaders in England, Canada, and India also promoted a friendly familial version of international and imperial relations. With sometimes varying motives, they encouraged girls to think of themselves as members of a global family, whose well-being they could ensure through social service. At the same time, adult Guide leaders told girls from all backgrounds to look for God in nature and encouraged them to strengthen and display their bodies at public performances of pageantry, physical culture, and drill. The movement also encouraged modern girls and young women from England, Canada, and India to make connections with their international and imperial Guide sisters by attending cross-border camps, financing the furnishing and upkeep of international properties, reading about and writing to girls in distant places, and following the movement's radio and cinema programs.

These efforts were partly a reflection of the widespread desire to build a friendly and tolerant international community to prevent the horrors of another global war. But they also worked (in perhaps less explicit but no less powerful ways) to shore up older ideas about race- and class-based hierarchies and the British "civilizing mission." Guiding's definition of citizenship as a series of responsibilities and privileges, like many of its historical pageants, supported rather than challenged existing social divisions and hierarchies. Its emphasis on similarity across borders was undermined by the tendency of many metropolitan leaders to dismiss or ignore challenges to the British Empire and their "non-political" youth organization, and by its official silence about the many women around the world who were still excluded from the franchise. In Canada, white women saw the movement as a way to assimilate Indigenous peoples and non-British immigrants; in India, it was represented by white women as a way to "happify" and liberate oppressed Indian girls. At the same time, however, Guiding was also embraced by a group of educated Indian women who used it as a way to modernize their nation's girls. These complexities show that women and girls' relationship to Guiding does not need to be understood as either supportive or oppositional; instead, it could be – and often was – partial, changing, and contradictory.

ঙ • ঙ

DID THE INTERWAR GUIDE movement succeed in its multifaceted, future-oriented attempts to promote peace, shore up the British Empire, and shape modern girls' lives? Despite their combined efforts during the 1920s and 1930s, Scouting and Guiding were not enough to prevent the Second World War, the end of the League of Nations, and the dismantling of Britain's empire. It is more difficult to assess the effects of Guide training on the private and public lives of the hundreds of thousands of women in England, Canada, and India who belonged to the movement during the years between the two world wars. Did its former members remember and/or apply the movement's teachings about scientific motherhood, politically engaged but non-political citizenship, exercise, and tolerant sisterhood as they transitioned into adulthood? How did women from across the social and geographical spectrum experience and remember the movement's continued support of class-based and racial hierarchies?

The answers to these questions are beyond the reach of this study, and they still await their historian. However, what this book *does* show is that the history of modern girlhood, like the history of imperialism, is a story of conflict over autonomy and self-determination. In England, Canada, and India during the 1920s and 1930s, debates about young women reflected broader concerns about futurity, emancipation, and dependence in individual and collective terms. They were also always influenced by the constructed categories of race and class, and were shaped by local circumstances and the ideas and responses of individual women and girls. The history of girlhood and Guiding intersects with a vast array of historiographies, and it is a reminder of the ways that conventional archives continue to privilege the voices of white, elite, and middle-class adults from the metropole. Considering archival silences alongside textual and photographic sources in a multi-sited study of the world's largest voluntary organization for girls highlights the multiplicity of imperial girlhoods that were prescribed and lived across England, Canada, and India during the 1920s and 1930s, while reminding us of the power imbalances that continue to shape the lives of girls and young women around the world.

NOTES

Several sections of this book are based on the following previously published material: Kristine Alexander, "Can the Girl Guide Speak? The Perils and Pleasures of Looking for Children's Voices in Archival Research," *Jeunesse: Young People, Texts, Cultures* (Summer 2012): 132–44; Kristine Alexander, "Similarity and Difference at Girl Guide Camps in England, Canada and India," in *Scouting Frontiers: Global Youth in the Scout Movement's First Century*, ed. Tammy Proctor and Nelson Block (Newcastle-Upon-Tyne: Cambridge Scholars Press, 2009), 104–18; Kristine Alexander, "Canadian Girls, Imperial Girls, Global Girls: Race, Nation and Transnationalism in the Interwar Girl Guide Movement," in *Within and Without the Nation: Canadian History as Transnational History*, ed. Karen Dubinsky, Adele Perry, and Henry Yu (Toronto: University of Toronto Press, 2015), 276–92; Kristine Alexander, "The Girl Guide Movement and Imperial Internationalism in the 1920s and 1930s," *Journal of the History of Childhood and Youth* 2, 1 (Winter 2009): 37–63.

INTRODUCTION

1 Guide groups (officially called "companies") were divided into "patrols" of four to eight girls. Each patrol chose its own leader.
2 Girl Guiding UK Archives (London), 8th Battersea Company Swallow Patrol Diary, 1928–30, October 1928.
3 Archives of the Manitoba Council of the Girl Guides of Canada – Guides du Canada (Winnipeg), Nightingale Patrol Logbook, 1928–29, 22 October 1928.
4 Girl Guiding UK Archives (London), Logbook, All-India Guide Camp, Belvedere, Calcutta, January 1929.
5 Girl Guiding UK Archives (London), *Girl Guides Annual Report, 1934*, 10.
6 Kristine Moruzi, *Constructing Girlhood through the Periodical Press, 1850–1915* (Farnham, Surrey: Ashgate, 2012); Tamara Myers, *Caught: Montreal's Modern Girls and the Law, 1869–1945* (Toronto: University of Toronto Press, 2006); Carolyn Strange, *Toronto's Girl*

Problem: The Perils and Pleasures of the City, 1880–1930 (Toronto: University of Toronto Press, 1995); Kathy Peiss, *Cheap Amusements: Working Women and Leisure in Turn-of-the-Century New York* (Philadelphia: Temple University Press, 1986).

7 Jane Nicholas, *The Modern Girl: Feminine Modernities, Bodies, and Commodities in the 1920s* (Toronto: University of Toronto Press, 2014); Catherine Driscoll, "Girls Today: Girls, Girl Culture, and Girl Studies," *Girlhood Studies* 1, 1 (Summer 2008): 13–32; Adrian Bingham, *Gender, Modernity, and the Popular Press in Inter-War Britain* (Oxford: Clarendon Press, 2004).

8 On the Modern Girl, see, for instance, Nicholas, *Modern Girl*; Su Lin Lewis, "Cosmopolitanism and the Modern Girl: A Cross-Cultural Discourse in 1930s Penang," *Modern Asian Studies* 43, 6 (2009): 1385–419; Alys Eve Weinbaum et al., *The Modern Girl around the World: Consumption, Modernity and Globalization* (Durham and London: Duke University Press, 2008).

9 Frederick Cooper, *Colonialism in Question: Theory, Knowledge, History* (Berkeley: University of California Press, 2005), 113, 115.

10 Daniel Gorman, *The Emergence of International Society in the 1920s* (Cambridge: Cambridge University Press, 2012), 2.

11 Significant works in this area include Richard Ivan Jobs and David M. Pomfret, eds., *Transnational Histories of Youth in the Twentieth Century* (New York: Palgrave Macmillan, 2015); Sara Fieldston, *Raising the World: Child Welfare in the American Century* (Cambridge, MA: Harvard University Press, 2015); Mischa Honeck and Gabriel Rosenberg, "Transnational Generations: Organizing Youth in the Cold War," *Diplomatic History* 38, 2 (2014): 233–39; Jennifer Helgren, "'Homemaker Can Include the World': Female Citizenship and Internationalism in the Camp Fire Girls," in *Girlhood: A Global History*, ed. Jennifer Helgren and Colleen A. Vasconcellos (New Brunswick, NJ: Rutgers University Press, 2010), 304–21.

12 On girls/girlhood and the British Empire, see Kristine Moruzi and Michelle Smith, eds., *Colonial Girlhood in Literature, Culture and History, 1840–1950* (Basingstoke: Palgrave Macmillan, 2014); Michelle J. Smith, *Empire in British Girls' Literature and Culture: Imperial Girls, 1880–1915* (New York: Palgrave Macmillan, 2011); J.S. Bratton, "British Imperialism and the Reproduction of Femininity in Girls' Fiction, 1900–1930," in *Imperialism and Juvenile Literature*, ed. Jeffrey Richards (Manchester: Manchester University Press, 1989), 195–215. Important works in the history of women and interwar internationalism include Fiona Paisley, *Glamour in the Pacific: Cultural Internationalism and Race Politics in the Women's Pan-Pacific* (Honolulu: University of Hawaii Press, 2009); Angela Woollacott, "Inventing Commonwealth and Pan-Pacific Feminisms: Australian Women's Internationalist Activism in the 1920s–30s," in *Feminisms and Internationalism*, ed. Mrinalini Sinha, Donna J. Guy, and Angela Woollacott (Oxford: Blackwell, 1999), 81–104; Leila J. Rupp, *Worlds of Women: The Making of an International Women's Movement* (Princeton: Princeton University Press, 1998).

13 Manu Goswami, "Imaginary Futures and Colonial Internationalisms," *American Historical Review* 117, 5 (December 2012): 1461–85.

14 Lee Edelman, *No Future: Queer Theory and the Death Drive* (Chapel Hill: Duke University Press, 2004).

15 Fiona Paisley, "Childhood and Race: Growing Up in the Empire;" in *Gender and Empire*, ed. Philippa Levine (Oxford: Oxford University Press, 2004), 246. One recent MA thesis

begins to address this question: Sally K. Stanhope, "'White, Black, and Dusky': Girl Guiding in Malaya, Nigeria, India, and Australia from 1909–1960" (MA thesis, Georgia State University, 2012).

16 Tammy M. Proctor, *Scouting for Girls: A Century of Girl Guides and Girl Scouts* (Santa Barbara, CA: ABC-Clio, 2009); Allen Warren, "Citizens of the Empire: Baden-Powell, Scouts and Guides, and an Imperial Ideal," in *Imperialism and Popular Culture*, ed. John M. MacKenzie (Manchester: Manchester University Press, 1986), 236; Tammy M. Proctor, "Scouts, Guides and the Fashioning of Empire, 1919–39," in *Fashioning the Body Politic: Dress, Gender, Citizenship*, ed. Wendy Parkins (Oxford and New York: Berg, 2002), 130.

17 Some recent examples: Benjamin Rene Jordan, *Modern Manhood and the Boy Scouts of America: Citizenship, Race, and the Environment, 1910–1930* (Chapel Hill: University of North Carolina Press, 2016); Jialin Christina Wu, "'A Life of Make-Believe': Being Boy Scouts and 'Playing Indian' in British Malaya, 1910–1942," *Gender and History* 26, 3 (November 2014): 589–619; Timothy H. Parsons, *Race, Resistance, and the Boy Scout Movement in British Colonial Africa* (Athens: Ohio University Press, 2004).

18 My thinking about archives owes much to Nupur Chaudhuri, Sherry J. Katz, and Mary Elizabeth Perry, eds., *Contesting Archives: Finding Women in the Sources* (Urbana-Champaign: University of Illinois Press, 2012); Ann Laura Stoler, *Along the Archival Grain: Epistemic Anxieties and Colonial Common Sense* (Princeton: Princeton University Press, 2008); Antoinette Burton, ed., *Archive Stories: Facts, Fictions, and the Writing of History* (Durham and London: Duke University Press, 2005); Antoinette Burton, *Dwelling in the Archive: Women Writing House, Home and History in Late Colonial India* (New York: Oxford University Press, 2003); Carolyn Steedman, *Dust: The Archive and Cultural History* (Manchester: Manchester University Press, 2001).

19 Alison Light, *Forever England: Femininity, Literature and Conservatism between the Wars* (London and New York: Routledge, 1991), 19. Tammy Proctor also makes this point about British Guiding and Scouting in the interwar years. See Tammy M. Proctor, *On My Honour: Scouts and Guides in Interwar Britain* (Philadelphia: American Philosophical Society, 2002).

20 Jane Nicholas, "Gendering the Jubilee: Gender and Modernity in the Diamond Jubilee of Confederation Celebrations, 1927," *Canadian Historical Review* 90, 2 (June 2009): 247–74; Katie Pickles, "The Old and New On Parade: Mimesis, Queen Victoria, and Carnival Queens on Victoria Day in Interwar Victoria," in *Contact Zones: Aboriginal and Settler Women in Canada's Colonial Past*, ed. Myra Rutherdale and Katharine Pickles (Vancouver: UBC Press, 2005), 272–91; Jon Lawrence, "Paternalism, Class, and the British Path to Modernity," in *The Peculiarities of Liberal Modernity in Imperial Britain*, ed. Simon Gunn and James Vernon (Berkeley and Los Angeles: University of California Press, 2011), 147.

21 Proctor, *On My Honour*, 3.

22 Thanks to Corrie Decker for encouraging me to think more about the connections between conservative and colonial modernity.

23 Tony Ballantyne, *Webs of Empire: Locating New Zealand's Colonial Past* (Vancouver: UBC Press, 2014); Alan Lester, "Imperial Circuits and Networks: Geographies of the British Empire," *History Compass* 4, 1 (2006): 124–41; Philippa Levine, *Prostitution, Race, and Politics: Policing Venereal Disease in the British Empire* (New York and London: Routledge, 2003).

24 Ann Curthoys and Marilyn Lake, "Introduction," in *Connected Worlds: History in Transnational Perspective* (Canberra: Australian National University E-Press, 2005), 5.

25 C.A. Bayly, Sven Beckert, Matthew Connelly, Isabel Hofmeyr, Wendy Kozol, and Patricia Seed, "AHR Conversation: On Transnational History," *American Historical Review* 111, 5 (December 2006): 1448.

26 Mark-Anthony Falzon, "Introduction – Multi-Sited Ethnography: Theory, Praxis and Locality in Contemporary Research," in *Multi-Sited Ethnography: Theory, Praxis and Locality in Contemporary Research*, ed. Mark-Anthony Falzon (Farnham: Ashgate, 2009), 1.

27 For more on this, see Kristine Alexander, "Can the Girl Guide Speak? The Perils and Pleasures of Looking for Children's Voices in Archival Research," *Jeunesse: Young People, Texts, Cultures* 4, 1 (Summer 2012): 132–44.

28 Mary Jo Maynes, "Age as a Category of Historical Analysis: History, Agency, and Narratives of Childhood," *Journal of the History of Childhood and Youth* 1, 1 (Winter 2008): 116.

29 This problem has attracted some attention in the United Kingdom, most notably through the Database of Archives of Non-Governmental Organizations (DANGO), an Arts and Humanities Research Council-funded project based at the University of Birmingham. DANGO's main focus, however, is on the "new social movements" of the 1950s, 1960s, and 1970s, so it is not especially concerned with Guide sources from the early twentieth century.

30 Laura E. Nym Mayhall, "Creating the Suffragette Spirit: British Feminism and the Historical Imagination," in *Archive Stories: Facts, Fictions, and the Writing of History*, ed. Antoinette Burton (Durham and London: Duke University Press, 2005), 236.

31 Dany Maneely, Girl Guiding UK Head of Projects and Programs, e-mail message to author, 9 March 2015.

32 Girl Guiding UK Archives (London), India Folder, Ethel M. White, "Guiding in the Punjab." Sanjay Seth also highlights the small percentage of Indian girls attended these schools, writing that "the quinquennial survey of education for 1927–37 found that only 14 percent of girls who enrolled in school proceeded to even reach the fourth grade, completion of which was conventionally defined as the minimal requirement for attaining literacy, and on the eve of Independence there were only 232,000 girls in high schools, compared to almost two million boys." See Sanjay Seth, *Subject Lessons: The Western Education of Colonial India* (Chapel Hill, NC: Duke University Press, 2007), 157.

33 Lakshmi Mazumdar, ed., *A Dream Came True* (New Delhi: The Bharat Scouts and Guides, 1997), 38.

34 Alexander, "Can the Girl Guide Speak?"

35 Light, *Forever England*, 13; Ruth Roach Pierson, "Experience, Difference, Dominance and Voice in the Writing of Canadian Women's History," in *Writing Women's History: International Perspectives*, ed. Karen Offen, Ruth Roach Pierson, and Jane Rendall (Bloomington and Indianapolis: Indiana University Press, 1991), 94.

36 I have chosen to end this study in 1939 primarily because of the significant organizational and program changes that were caused by the Second World War. Further changes during the 1940s and after were caused by Baden-Powell's death in 1941 and the achievement of Indian independence in 1947.

CHAPTER 1: GUIDING'S BEGINNINGS

1 For more on this, see Allen Warren, "Baden-Powell: Two Lives of a Hero, or Two Heroic Lives?" in *Heroic Reputations and Exemplary Lives*, ed. Geoffrey Cubitt and Allen Warren

(Manchester: Manchester University Press, 2000), 123–41; William Hillcourt and Olave Baden-Powell, *Baden-Powell: The Two Lives of a Hero* (New York: Putnam, 1964); M. Drewery, *Baden-Powell: The Man Who Lived Twice* (London: Hodder and Stoughton, 1975).

2 Partha Chatterjee, *The Nation and Its Fragments: Colonial and Postcolonial Histories* (Princeton: Princeton University Press, 1993). See also Catherine Hall, *Civilising Subjects: Metropole and Colony in the English Imagination, 1830–1867* (London: Polity, 2002).

3 See Sarah Carter, *The Importance of Being Monogamous: Marriage and Nation Building in Western Canada to 1915* (Edmonton: University of Alberta Press, 2008); Adele Perry, *On the Edge of Empire: Gender, Race, and the Making of British Columbia, 1849–1871* (Toronto: University of Toronto Press, 2001).

4 Carol Dyhouse, *Girls Growing Up in Late Victorian and Edwardian England* (London, Boston, and Henley: Routledge and Kegan Paul, 1981), 2–12.

5 Nineteenth-century girl readers' preference for boys' books is discussed in Gillian Avery, *Childhood's Pattern: A Study of the Heroes and Heroines of Children's Fiction, 1770–1950* (London: Hodder and Stoughton, 1975), 6–7.

6 Tim Jeal, *Baden-Powell: Founder of the Boy Scouts* (New Haven and London: Yale University Press, 1989), 36. Jeal notes that, despite his apparent enjoyment of public school life, Baden-Powell had relatively few close friends.

7 Martin Green, *Dreams of Adventure, Deeds of Empire* (New York: Basic Books, 1979), 3; Hall, *Civilising Subjects*, 27.

8 John Tosh, "Imperial Masculinity and the Flight from Domesticity in Britain 1880–1914," in *Gender and Colonialism*, ed. Timothy P. Foley, Lionel Pilkington, Sean Ryder, and Elizabeth Tilley (Galway: Galway University Press, 1995), 72–85.

9 Thomas Pakenham, *The Boer War* (New York: Random House, 1979), 425 and 429.

10 Quoted in Paula Krebs, *Gender, Race, and the Writing of Empire: Public Discourse and the Boer War* (Cambridge: Cambridge University Press, 1999), 16.

11 Graham Dawson, *Soldier Heroes: British Adventure, Empire and the Imagining of Masculinities* (London: Routledge, 1994), 2.

12 Quoted in Elleke Boehmer, "Introduction," *Scouting for Boys: The Original 1908 Edition* (Oxford: Oxford University Press, 2005), xxiv.

13 Almeric William Fitz Roy, *Report of the Interdepartmental Committee on Physical Deterioration* (London: Printed for H.M. Stationery Office, 1904).

14 Dyhouse, *Girls Growing Up*, 118. See also Gail Bederman, *Manliness and Civilization: A Cultural History of Gender and Race in the United States, 1880–1917* (Chicago: University of Chicago Press, 1995), 94.

15 Mariana Valverde, *The Age of Light, Soap, and Water: Moral Reform in English Canada, 1885–1925* (Toronto: McClelland and Stewart, 1991).

16 John Springhall, *Youth, Empire, and Society* (London: Croom Helm, 1977), 16.

17 Anna Davin, "Imperialism and Motherhood," *History Workshop Journal* 5, 1 (Spring 1978): 10.

18 Dyhouse, *Girls Growing Up*, 92.

19 Paisley, "Childhood and Race," 244–45.

20 Carol Devens, "'If We Get the Girls, We Get the Race': Missionary Education of Native American Girls," *Journal of World History* 3, 2 (1992): 219–37.

21 Mariana Valverde, "When the Mother of the Race Is Free: Race, Reproduction and Sexuality in First-Wave Feminism," in *Gender Conflicts: New Essays in Women's History*, ed. Franca Iacovetta and Mariana Valverde (Toronto: University of Toronto Press, 1992), 11.

22 Antoinette Burton, *Burdens of History: British Feminists, Indian Women, and Imperial Culture, 1865–1915* (Chapel Hill and London: University of North Carolina Press, 1994). The figure of the Hindu woman was also, as Antoinette Burton has shown, at the heart of many early British feminists' claims to autonomous citizenship.

23 Kenneth W. Jones, *Socio-Religious Reform Movements in British India* (Cambridge: Cambridge University Press, 1989); Michelle Elizabeth Tusan, "Writing *Stri Dharma*: International Feminism, Nationalist Politics, and Women's Press Advocacy in Late Colonial India," *Women's History Review* 12, 4 (December 2003): 623–49; Aparna Basu and Bharati Ray, *Women's Struggle: A History of the All India Women's Conference, 1927–1990* (New Delhi: Manohar Publications, 1990).

24 This article is discussed as proof of Baden-Powell's lack of militarist motivation in Martin Dedman, "Baden-Powell, Militarism, and the 'Invisible Contributors' to the Boy Scout Scheme, 1904–1920," *Twentieth Century British History* 4, 3 (1993): 204–5.

25 Quoted in Dedman, "Baden-Powell," 210.

26 Ibid.

27 Brian Morris, "Ernest Thompson Seton and the Origins of the Woodcraft Movement," *Journal of Contemporary History* 5, 2 (1970): 183–94; H. Allen Anderson, "Ernest Thompson Seton and the Woodcraft Indians," *Journal of American Culture* 8, 1 (1985): 43–50.

28 Jeal, *Baden-Powell*, 353. This is also discussed in Jon Savage, *Teenage: The Creation of Youth Culture, 1875–1945* (London: Viking Penguin, 2007), 83.

29 Dedman, "Baden-Powell," 214. Dedman notes that, while Baden-Powell seldom acknowledged the sources of his ideas, he had to seek permission from Kipling and his publisher to print extracts from *The Jungle Book* and *Kim*.

30 Timothy H. Parsons, "Een-Gonyama Gonyama! Zulu Origins of the Boy Scout Movement and the Africanisation of Imperial Britain," *Parliamentary History* 27, 1 (2008): 62.

31 Boehmer, "Introduction," xxx.

32 Jeal, *Baden-Powell*, 396; Springhall, *Youth, Empire and Society*, 68.

33 Michael Rosenthal, *The Character Factory: Baden-Powell's Boy Scouts and the Imperative of Empire* (New York: Pantheon Books, 1986).

34 This narrative about the first "Girl Scouts," which emphasizes girls' agency, has served for most of the Guide organization's history as a myth of origins explaining the movement's beginnings.

35 Proctor, *Scouting for Girls*, 4–5. See also Sarah Mills, "Scouting for Girls? Gender and the Scout Movement in Britain," *Gender, Place and Culture* 18, 4 (2011): 537–56.

36 Rose Kerr, *The Story of the Girl Guides* (London: The Girl Guides Association, 1937), 35.

37 Ibid., 30.

38 The American arm of the Girl Guides, established by Juliette Gordon Low, is known as the Girl Scouts. Low's decision to use the name "Girl Scout" was met with hostility and outrage by Boy Scout officials in ways that illustrate the very real issues of gender and power that were at stake in naming these organizations. For more on this, see Mary Aickin Rothschild, "To Scout or to Guide? The Girl Scout-Boy Scout Controversy, 1912–1941," *Frontiers* 6, 3 (1981): 115–21; Susan A. Miller, "Trademark: Scout," in *Scouting Frontiers:*

Youth and the Scout Movement's First Century, ed. Nelson R. Block and Tammy M. Proctor (Newcastle-Upon-Tyne: Cambridge Scholars' Press, 2009), 28–41.

39　Sally Mitchell, *The New Girl: Girls' Culture in England, 1880–1915* (New York: Columbia University Press, 1995), 105.

40　Quoted in Proctor, *On My Honour*, 22.

41　Kitty Barne, *Here Come the Girl Guides* (London: The Girl Guides Association, 1946), 15.

42　Of early Guide texts, for example, Carol Dyhouse writes that "at times Agnes's cloying emphasis on femininity became absurd." See Dyhouse, *Girls Growing Up*, 111.

43　Agnes Baden-Powell and Robert Baden-Powell, *Pamphlet A: Baden-Powell Girl Guides, a Suggestion for Character Training for Girls* (1909), 5.

44　Agnes Baden-Powell and Robert Baden-Powell, *Pamphlet B: Baden-Powell Girl Guides, a Suggestion for Character Training for Girls* (1909), 16.

45　Agnes Baden-Powell and Robert Baden-Powell, *Pamphlet A*, 7.

46　Agnes Baden-Powell and Robert Baden-Powell, *The Handbook for Girl Guides: How Girls Can Help Build the Empire* (London: Thomas Nelson and Sons, 1912), vii.

47　Ibid., 34. See also Michelle Smith, "Be(ing) Prepared: Girl Guides, Colonial Life, and National Strength," *Limina: A Journal of Historical and Cultural Studies* 12 (2006): 1–11.

48　For more on these early Guide texts, see Michelle J. Smith, *Empire in British Girls' Literature and Culture: Imperial Girls, 1880–1915* (New York: Palgrave Macmillan, 2011), chap. 5.

49　Agnes Baden-Powell and Robert Baden-Powell, *How Girls Can Help*, 291.

50　Ibid., 286.

51　For more on this, see Colin Coates and Cecilia Morgan, *Heroines and History: Representations of Madeleine de Verchères and Laura Secord* (Toronto: University of Toronto Press, 2002).

52　Agnes Baden-Powell and Robert Baden-Powell, *How Girls Can Help*, 288–90.

53　Archives of the Ontario Council of the Girl Guides of Canada – Guides du Canada, scrapbook no. 11, Program for Evening Entertainment by the Toronto Girl Guides and the St. John Ambulance Brigade.

54　Scout Association Archives (Gilwell Park), Diaries of Olave St. Clair Soames, 3 January 1912.

55　Scout Association Archives (Gilwell Park), Diaries of Olave St. Clair Soames, 1912–13.

56　This point is also made in Adrian Bingham, *Gender, Modernity, and the Popular Press in Inter-War Britain* (Oxford: Clarendon Press, 2004).

57　For more on this, see Janet Lee, "A Nurse and a Soldier: Gender, Class and National Identity in the First World War Adventures of Grace McDougall and Flora Sandes," *Women's History Review* 15, 1 (2006): 83–103.

58　Richard A. Voeltz, "'The Antidote to Khaki Fever'? The Expansion of the British Girl Guides during the First World War," *Journal of Contemporary History* 27, 4 (1992): 627–38.

59　Rose Kerr, *The Story of a Million Girls: Guiding and Girl Scouting around the World* (London: The Girl Guides Association, 1936), 18.

60　*Girl Guides' Gazette* XVI (April 1915): 10.

61　Archives of the National Council of the Girl Guides of Canada – Guides du Canada (Toronto), scrapbook, 1912–61, clipping from the *Toronto Daily Star*, 8 March 1918. See also Kristine Alexander, "An Honour and a Burden: Canadian Girls and the Great War," in *A Sisterhood of Suffering and Service: Canadian and Newfoundland Girls and Women and the First World War*, ed. Sarah Glassford and Amy Shaw (Vancouver: UBC Press, 2012), 173–94.

62 This task had originally been given to Boy Scouts, but their "mischievous" behaviour meant that they were replaced by Girl Guides in September 1915. Tammy Proctor, *Female Intelligence: Women and Espionage in the First World War* (New York: New York University Press, 2003), 58–59.

63 Erez Manela, *The Wilsonian Moment: Self-Determination and the International Origins of Anticolonial Nationalism* (Oxford: Oxford University Press, 2007).

64 Scout Association Archives (Gilwell Park), Diaries of Olave Baden-Powell, 10 March 1913.

65 Jeal, *Baden-Powell*, 471–77.

66 Scout Association Archives (Gilwell Park), Diaries of Olave Baden-Powell, 14 July 1928.

67 Olave Baden-Powell, *Training Girls as Guides: Hints for Commissioners and All Who Are Interested in the Welfare and Training of Girls* (London: C. Arthur Pearson Ltd., 1919), 13–15.

68 Ibid., 66 and 69.

69 Robert Baden-Powell, *Girl Guiding: A Handbook for Brownies, Guides, Rangers, and Guiders* (London: C. Arthur Pearson Ltd., 1931), 6.

70 Ibid.

71 Robert Baden-Powell, *Girl Guiding*, 9.

72 Kerr, *Story of the Girl Guides*, 29.

73 Olave Baden-Powell, *Training Girls as Guides*, 15.

74 Ibid., 16.

75 Robert Baden-Powell, *Girl Guiding*, 184.

76 Olave Baden-Powell, *Training Girls as Guides*, 15.

77 Robert Baden-Powell, *Girl Guiding*, 17.

78 Ibid., 51.

79 Ibid., 179.

80 The Girl Guide Promise and Law were the same in most contexts; girls in India were required to promise to do their duty to the King-Emperor. See Robert Baden-Powell, *Girl Guiding*, 51.

81 Timothy H. Parsons, "The Consequences of Uniformity: The Struggle for the Boy Scout Uniform in Colonial Kenya," *Journal of Social History* 40, 2 (Winter 2006): 361–83.

82 Tammy Proctor argues that, in interwar Britain, the Scouts and Guides offered "a seductive consumer paradise to members." See Tammy Proctor, "(Uni)forming Youth: Girl Guides and Boy Scouts in Britain, 1908–1939," *History Workshop Journal* 45 (1998): 104.

83 The 1930 Biennial Report of the World Association of Girl Guides and Girl Scouts notes the existence of established Guide movements in the following countries: Australia, Belgium, Canada, China, Czechoslovakia, Denmark, Egypt, Estonia, France, Great Britain, Hungary, Iceland, India, Japan, Latvia, Liberia, Lithuania, Luxembourg, Netherlands, New Zealand, Norway, Poland, South Africa, Suomi-Finland, Sweden, Switzerland, the United States, and Yugoslavia. This list continued to increase throughout the 1930s. Membership numbers in the three countries upon which I focus are quoted as follows: Canada (population 9 million): 24,529 in 1927, 28,234 in 1929 (increase of 3,705); Great Britain and Ireland (population 47.5 million): 433,283 in 1927, 518,826 in 1929 (increase of 85,543); India (population 320 million): 13,979 in 1927, 18,970 in 1929 (increase of 4,991). WAGGGS Archives (London), *World Girl Guides and Girl Scouts First Biennial Report: July 1st 1928 to June 30th 1930 and General Historical Sketch*.

84 The *Times* (London), 15 March 1928, 9. I believe this to be a reflection of the fact that girls and young women continued during the interwar years to have fewer leisure options than did their brothers.

85 Proctor, *On My Honour*, 2.

86 Ibid., 5 and 46.

87 For more on the Scouts and strike-breaking in the United States, see Stephen Harlan Norwood, *Strike-Breaking and Intimidation: Mercenaries and Masculinity in Twentieth-Century America* (Durham: University of North Carolina Press, 2002), 11.

88 Barne, *Here Come the Girl Guides*, 22. For similar reactions to Boy Scouting, see, for example, Stephen Humphries, *Hooligans or Rebels? An Oral History of Working-Class Childhood and Youth 1889–1939* (Oxford: Basil Blackwell, 1981), 134–35.

89 On formally political youth groups, see Stephen Heathorn and David Greenspoon, "Organizing Youth for Partisan Politics in Britain, 1918–c. 1932," *Historian* 68, 1 (Spring 2006): 89–119. On the Woodcraft Folk, see Mary Davis, *Fashioning a New World: A History of the Woodcraft Folk* (Loughborough: Holyoake Books, 2000); David Prynn, "The Woodcraft Folk and the Labour Movement, 1925–1970," *Journal of Contemporary History* 18, 1 (1983): 79–95; I.O. Evans, *Woodcraft and World Service: Studies in Unorthodox Education – An Account of the Evolution of the Woodcraft Movements* (London: Noel Douglas, 1930). On cooperative youth groups, see Selina Todd, "Pleasure, Politics and Co-operative Youth: The Interwar Co-operative Comrades' Circles," *Journal of Co-operative Studies* 32, 2 (September 1999): 129–45.

90 On the CGIT, see M. Lucille Marr, "Church Teen Clubs, Feminized Organizations? Tuxis Boys, Trail Rangers, and Canadian Girls in Training, 1919–1939," *Historical Studies in Education* 3, 2 (1991): 249–67; Veronica Strong-Boag, *The New Day Recalled: Lives of Girls and Women in English Canada, 1919–1939* (Toronto: Copp Clark Pitman, 1988), 28–29; Margaret Prang, "'The Girl God Would Have Me Be': The Canadian Girls in Training, 1915–1939," *Canadian Historical Review* 66, 2 (1985): 154–84. On left and working-class youth groups, see Rhonda L. Hinther, "Raised in the Spirit of Class Struggle: Children, Youth and the Interwar Ukrainian Left in Canada," *Labour/Le Travail* 60 (Fall 2007): 43–76; Ester Reiter, "Camp Naivelt and the Daughters of the Jewish Left," in *Sisters or Strangers? Immigrant, Racialized and Ethnic Women in Canadian History*, ed. Marlene Epp, Franca Iacovetta, and Frances Swyripa, 365–80 (Toronto: University of Toronto Press: 2004). On L'Action catholique, see Louise Bienvenue, *Quand la jeunesse entre en scène: L'Action catholique avant la Révolution tranquille* (Montréal: Boréal, 2003).

91 *Collins' Girl Guides Annual* (London: Collins' Clear-Type Press, n.d. [late 1920s–early 1930s]), 57.

92 There are no published studies of French Canadian Guiding. But for the Scouts, see James Trepanier, "Building Boys, Building Canada: The Boy Scout Movement in Canada, 1908–1970" (PhD diss., York University, 2015); Pierre Savard, "Une jeunesse et son Église: Les scouts routiers, de la crise à la Révolution tranquille," *Les cahiers des Dix* 53 (1999): 117–59; "L'implantation du scoutisme au Canada français," *Les cahiers des Dix* 43 (1983): 207–62; "Affrontements de nationalisms aux origines du scoutisme canadien-français," *Mémoires de la Société royale du Canada* 17 (1979): 41–56.

93 Canadian Brownies, Guides, and Rangers numbered 55,921 in 1937–38. Archives of the National Council of the Girl Guides of Canada – Guides du Canada (Toronto), *The Canadian Council of Girl Guides Inc. Annual Reports, Year Ending April 1st 1938*, 9.

94 Katie Pickles, *Female Imperialism and National Identity: Imperial Order Daughters of the Empire* (Manchester: Manchester University Press, 2002).

95 See David Cannadine, *Ornamentalism: How the British Saw Their Empire* (Oxford: Oxford University Press, 2002), chap. 3.

96 *Girl Guides' Gazette* X, 118 (October 1923): 232.

97 Mary Jane McCallum, "To Make Good Canadians: Girl Guiding in Indian Residential Schools" (MA thesis, Trent University, 2002); J.R. Miller, *Shingwauk's Vision: A History of Native Residential Schools* (Toronto: University of Toronto Press, 1997), 277–80; Elizabeth Graham, ed., *The Mush Hole: Life at Two Indian Residential Schools* (Waterloo, ON: Heffle Publishing, 1997). While Guiding and Scouting began in some residential schools in the 1920s, McCallum's thesis concentrates mainly on the post-First World War period.

98 *Council Fire* XIII, 2 (April 1938): 21.

99 Carey A. Watt, "The Promise of 'Character' and the Spectre of Sedition: The Boy Scout Movement and Colonial Consternation in India, 1908–1921," *South Asia* 29, 2 (1999): 37–62; Carey A. Watt, *Serving the Nation: Cultures of Service, Association, and Citizenship in Colonial India* (New Delhi: Oxford University Press, 2005).

100 Timothy Parsons makes a similar argument about the Scouts and Guides in colonial Kenya. See Timothy H. Parsons, "The Limits of Sisterhood: The Evolution of the Girl Guide Movement in Colonial Kenya," in *Scouting Frontiers: Youth and the Scout Movement's First Century*, ed. Nelson R. Block and Tammy M. Proctor (Newcastle-Upon-Tyne: Cambridge Scholars Publishing, 2009), 144.

101 For more on the Seva Samiti, see Watt, *Serving the Nation*, 215–17.

102 Girl Guiding UK Archives (London), India Folder, Report: "Early Days of Guiding in India."

103 Quoted in Lakshmi Mazumdar, ed., *A Dream Came True* (New Delhi: The Bharat Scouts and Guides, 1997), 80.

104 Girl Guiding UK Archives (London), *The Girl Guides Association (Incorporated by Royal Charter) Fifteenth Annual Report and Balance Sheet of the Committee of the Council for the Year ending December 31st, 1929*, 141; *The Girl Guides Association Fifteenth Annual Report and Balance Sheet, Year Ending December 31st, 1935*, 173.

105 *Council Fire* VI, 3 (n.d.): 40. Guide membership in late colonial India was significantly smaller than in Britain, the United States, and the dominions, with 18,970 members in 1929, and 38,129 in 1935. Girl Guiding UK Archives (London), *The Girl Guides Association Fifteenth Annual Report, and Balance Sheet, Year ending December 31st, 1929*, 141; *The Girl Guides Association Fifteenth Annual Report and Balance Sheet, Year ending December 31st, 1935*, 173.

106 Sanjay Seth, *Subject Lessons: The Western Education of Colonial India* (Chapel Hill, NC: Duke University Press, 2007), 157.

107 Satadru Sen, *Colonial Childhoods: The Juvenile Periphery of India, 1850–1945* (London: Anthem Press, 2005), 5.

108 Mazumdar, *Dream Came True*, 81.

109 Margaret Cousins Memorial Library, All-India Women's Conference (Delhi). *Report: All-India Women's Conference on Educational Reform, 5–8 January, 1927*, 11 and 54.

110 *Indian Ladies' Magazine* III, 7 (February 1930): 333–34.

111 Watt, *Serving the Nation*, 117–18; Watt, "Promise of 'Character' and the Spectre of Sedition," note 1.

112 Mrinalini Sinha, *Specters of Mother India: The Global Restructuring of an Empire* (Durham and London: Duke University Press, 2006).
113 Scout Association Archives (Gilwell Park), Diaries of Olave Baden-Powell, 9 February 1937.
114 Ibid., 28 March 1937.
115 Mazumdar, *Dream Came True*, 38.
116 Ibid.
117 Quoted in Mazumdar, *Dream Came True*, 116.
118 Ibid., 117.
119 This controversy is also discussed briefly in Thomas R. Metcalf, *Ideologies of the Raj* (Cambridge: Cambridge University Press, 1994), 219–20.
120 In 1950, three years after Independence, all existing Scout and Guide groups in India were amalgamated into a single co-educational organization, the Bharat Scouts and Guides.
121 The Baden-Powells' cottage, named "Paxtu" (a play on the Latin word for "peace"), was located on the grounds of the Outspan Hotel, a property owned by Eric Sherbrooke Walker (Baden-Powell's first private secretary and an early Scout inspector). The cottage is still there and is now a small Scouting museum.
122 *Council Fire* XIII, 4 (October 1938): 54.

Chapter 2: Guiding Girls toward the Private Sphere

1 *Council Fire* III, 8 (January 1928): 34.
2 The literature on these subjects is vast. Studies that were particularly useful to this project include Anna Davin, "Imperialism and Motherhood," *History Workshop Journal* 5, 1 (1978): 9–65; Carol Dyhouse, "Working Class Mothers and Infant Mortality in England, 1895–1914," *Journal of Social History* 12 (1978): 121–42; Margaret Jolly, "Introduction: Colonial and Postcolonial Plots in Histories of Maternities and Modernities," in *Maternities and Modernities: Colonial and Postcolonial Experiences in Asia and the Pacific*, ed. Kalpana Ram and Margaret Jolly (Cambridge: Cambridge University Press, 1998), 1; Nita Kumar, "Mothers and Non-Mothers: Gendering the Discourse of Education in South Asia," *Gender and History* 17, 1 (2005): 154–82; Dipesh Chakrabarty, "The Difference-Deferral of a Colonial Modernity: Public Debates on Domesticity in British Bengal," in *Tensions of Empire: Colonial Cultures in a Bourgeois World*, ed. Frederick Cooper and Ann Laura Stoler (Berkeley: University of California Press, 1997), 373–405; Samita Sen, "Motherhood and Mothercraft: Gender and Nationalism in Bengal," *Gender and History* 5 (Summer 1993): 231–43; Indira Chowdhury-Sengupta, "Mother India and Mother Victoria: Motherhood and Nationalism in Nineteenth-Century Bengal," *South Asia Research* 12, 1 (May 1992): 20–37; Partha Chatterjee, "The Nationalist Resolution of the Women's Question," in *Recasting Women: Essays in Indian Colonial History*, ed. Kumkum Sangari and Sudesh Vaid (New Brunswick, NJ: Rutgers University Press, 1990), 233–53; Dagmar Engels, "The Limits of Gender Ideology: Bengali Women, the Colonial State, and the Private Sphere, 1890–1930," *Women's Studies International Forum* 12, 4 (1989): 425–37.
3 Dena Attar, *Wasting Girls' Time: The History and Politics of Home Economics* (London: Virago, 1990); Carol Dyhouse, *Girls Growing Up in Late Victorian and Edwardian England* (London, Boston, and Henley: Routledge and Kegan Paul, 1981).
4 Susan Kingsley Kent, *Making Peace: The Reconstruction of Gender in Interwar Britain* (Princeton: Princeton University Press, 1993); Brian Harrison, *Prudent Revolutionaries:*

Portraits of British Feminists between the Wars (Oxford: Clarendon Press, 1987), 1; Diana Pedersen, "'Keeping Our Good Girls Good': The YWCA and the 'Girl Problem,' 1870–1930," *Canadian Woman Studies* 7, 4 (Winter 1986): 20–24.

5 Mary Hancock, "Gendering the Modern: Women and Home Science in British India," in *Gender, Sexuality and Colonial Modernities,* ed. Antoinette Burton, 148–60 (London and New York: Routledge, 1999); Birgitte Søland, *Becoming Modern: Young Women and Reconstruction of Womanhood in the 1920s* (Princeton: Princeton University Press, 2000), chap. 6; Judith E. Walsh, *Domesticity in Colonial India: What Women Learned When Men Gave Them Advice* (London: Rowman and Littlefield, 2004).

6 *Council Fire* XIII, 4 (October 1938): 63.

7 Robert Baden-Powell, *Girl Guiding: A Handbook for Brownies, Guides, Rangers, and Guiders* (London: C. Arthur Pearson Ltd., 1931), 163.

8 Ibid., 160.

9 Olave Baden-Powell, *Training Girls as Guides: Hints for Commissioners and All Who Are Interested in the Welfare and Training of Girls* (London: C. Arthur Pearson Ltd., 1919), 19.

10 Philippa Mein Smith, *Mothers and King Baby: Infant Survival and Welfare in an Imperial World, Australia 1880–1950* (London: Macmillan, 1997), 10. Mein Smith notes that, in these places, "infant mortality rates halved between the end of the nineteenth century and the 1920s, and again by the 1940s." On declining British infant mortality during the Great War, see J.M. Winter, "The Impact of the First World War on Civilian Health in Britain," *Economic History Review* 30, 3 (1977): 493.

11 *Girl Guides' Gazette* IX, 104 (August 1922): 146.

12 Mein Smith, *Mothers and King Baby,* xv.

13 Mary Ellen Kelm, *Colonizing Bodies: Aboriginal Health and Healing in British Columbia, 1900–1950* (Vancouver: UBC Press, 1998), 61. See also Cynthia Comacchio, *The Infinite Bonds of Family: Domesticity in Canada, 1850–1940* (Toronto: University of Toronto Press, 1999), 52.

14 These concerns about climate and health are discussed in greater detail in Chapter 4. On the legal construction of the figure of the "infanticidal Indian woman," see Padma Anagol, "The Emergence of the Female Criminal in India: Infanticide and Survival under the Raj," *History Workshop Journal* 53, 1 (2002): 73–93; Malavka Kasturi, "Law and Crime in India: British Policy and the Female Infanticide Act of 1870," *Indian Journal of Gender Studies* 1, 2 (1994): 169–93.

15 Sen, "Motherhood and Mothercraft," 235.

16 *Girl Guides' Gazette* IX, 104 (August 1922): 146.

17 Robert Baden-Powell, *Girl Guiding,* 184–85.

18 *Girl Guides' Gazette* IX, 97 (January 1922): 13.

19 Ibid., 9.

20 A.M. Maynard, *An A.B.C. of Guiding* (London: The Girl Guides Association, 1935), 64.

21 Sheila Rowbotham, *Good Girls Make Good Wives: Guidance for Girls in Victorian Fiction* (Oxford: Basil Blackwell, 1989).

22 *Council Fire* XIII, 4 (October 1938): 69.

23 *Girl Guides' Gazette* IX, 97 (January 1922): 14.

24 Ibid., 9.

25 Robert Baden-Powell, *Girl Guiding,* 159.

26 Veronica Strong-Boag, "Intruders in the Nursery: Childcare Professionals Reshape the Years One to Five, 1920–1940," in *Childhood and Family in Canadian History*, ed. Joy Parr (Toronto: McClelland and Stewart, 1982), 166.
27 *Girl Guides' Gazette* IX, 97 (January 1922): 9.
28 Quoted in Mein Smith, *Mothers and King Baby*, 98.
29 Interestingly, interwar Guide texts paid little attention to the fact that many girls had likely looked after younger siblings or neighbourhood children.
30 Quoted in Cathy Urwin and Elaine Sharland, "From Bodies to Minds in Childcare Literature: Advice to Parents in Interwar Britain," in *In the Name of the Child: Health and Welfare, 1880–1940*, ed. Roger Cooter (London and New York: Routledge, 1992), 178.
31 For more on the connections between time and colonization in settler societies, see Giordano Nanni, *The Colonisation of Time: Ritual, Routine and Resistance in the British Empire* (Manchester: Manchester University Press, 2012).
32 Quoted in Chakrabarty, "Difference-Deferral of a Colonial Modernity," 396.
33 Chakrabarty, "Difference-Deferral of a Colonial Modernity," 393.
34 Criminal tribes were nomadic communities seen as "hereditarily criminal" by the British and whose lives were regulated by the Criminal Tribes Act, 1871 (revised and made applicable to the whole of British India in 1911). Like the Girl Guides, the Salvation Army also sought to reform members of these groups by teaching them "appropriate" ideas about gender and work. See, for example, Meena Radhakrishna, *Dishonoured by History: "Criminal Tribes" and British Colonial Policy* (Hyderabad: Orient Longman, 2001).
35 *Guider* XXVI, 2 (February 1939): 40.
36 *Girl Guiding*, for example, recommends exercises and lots of water to ensure a "punctual daily move [sic] of bowels." Baden-Powell, *Girl Guiding*, 119.
37 *Guide* XVIII, 30 (3 November 1938): 937.
38 Strong-Boag, "Intruders in the Nursery," 164.
39 Mein Smith, *Mothers and King Baby*, 101.
40 Sinha, *Specters of Mother India*.
41 Antoinette Burton, *Dwelling in the Archive: Women Writing House, Home and History in Late Colonial India* (New York: Oxford University Press, 2003), 67.
42 Helen Rappaport, *Encyclopedia of Women Social Reformers, Volume 1* (Santa Barbara, CA: ABC-Clio, 2001), 661–62. Thanks to Mary Jane Mossman for alerting me to this connection.
43 See also Ishita Pande, "Coming of Age: Law, Sex, and Childhood in Late Colonial India," *Gender and History* 24, 1 (April 2012): 205–30.
44 Girl Guiding UK Archives (London), *The Girl Guides Association (Incorporated by Royal Charter) Thirteenth Annual Report and Balance Sheet of the Committee of the Council for the Year ending December 31st, 1927*, 117.
45 *Council Fire* IX, 4 (October 1934): 144.
46 *Girl Guides' Gazette* XII, 155 (November 1926): 339.
47 Rudyard Kipling, *Kim* (Oxford: Oxford World's Classics, 1998), chap. 9. Several of the women who volunteer at the Ontario Council Guide Archives in Toronto remembered using Kim's game with their Guides during the 1970s and 1980s.
48 *Girl Guides' Gazette* X, 118 (October 1923): 222.
49 Margaret M. Russell, ed., *The Mauve Games Book for Cripple, Hospital, Blind, Deaf and Post Guide Companies* (London: The Girl Guide Association, n.d.), 40.

50 Archives of the Manitoba Council of the Girl Guides of Canada – Guides du Canada (Winnipeg), Marjorie Hoskins Folder, Marjorie Hoskins scrapbook, clippings – 1938–39, "Rangers Hear How to Make Layettes," *Winnipeg Tribune*, 30 April 1938.

51 Girl Guiding UK Archives (London), *The Girl Guides Association (Incorporated by Royal Charter) Fourteenth Annual Report and Balance Sheet of the Committee of the Council for the Year ending December 31st, 1928*, 98. The report says little else about the competition, though I suspect the winning company may have been from the St. Paul's residential school in Cardston, Alberta.

52 Kristin Burnett, *Taking Medicine: Women's Healing Work and Colonial Contact in Southern Alberta, 1880–1930* (Vancouver: UBC Press, 2010).

53 Quoted in Elizabeth Graham, ed., *The Mush Hole: Life at Two Indian Residential Schools* (Waterloo, ON: Heffle Publishing, 1997), 145.

54 Alison Norman, "Race, Gender, and Colonialism: Public Life among the Six Nations of Grand River, 1899–1939" (PhD diss., Ontario Institute for Studies in Education, University of Toronto, 2010), 118–21.

55 National Baby Week was originally a British concern, born out of elite anxieties about infant (and therefore white/"racial") health during the First World War. Support for Britain's National Baby Week increased after the end of the war, and Martin Pugh notes that "by 1921[,] the National Baby Week Council had over a million members and a thousand local committees [including many working-class women] organizing baby shows and competitions, pram parades, slide lectures and child welfare exhibitions." See Martin Pugh, *Women and the Women's Movement in Britain, 1914–1999*, 2nd ed. (Houndmills and London: Macmillan, 2000), 89. See also J.M. Winter, "The Impact of the First World War on Civilian Health in Britain," *Economic History Review* 30, 3 (1977): 498.

56 *Girl Guides' Gazette* X, 115 (July 1923): 153.

57 Ibid., V, 54 (June 1918): 81; IX, 101 (May 1922): 82; XI, 123 (March 1924): 59.

58 Ibid., IX, 104 (August 1922): 146.

59 See also Miriam Forman-Brunell, *Babysitter: An American History* (New York: NYU Press, 2010).

60 Girl Guiding UK Archives (London), 8th Battersea Company Swallow Patrol Diary, 1928–30, 23 January 1928.

61 J. Alex Robinson, "The Homemakers," in *The Guiding Book*, ed. Ann Kindersley (London: Hodder and Stoughton, n.d.), 83.

62 Ann Kindersley, ed., *The Guiding Book* (London: Hodder and Stoughton, n.d.), 83.

63 Ibid., 86.

64 Olave Baden-Powell, *Training Girls as Guides*, 36.

65 Ibid., 37.

66 Archives of the Ontario Council of the Girl Guides of Canada – Guides du Canada (Toronto), scrapbook: Early History of Toronto Girl Guides, press clipping: "Toronto Girl Guides Push Rapidly Ahead: 'Finest Thing Going,' Says Capt. Head, Instructor of Officers. Leaders Are Needed: It Gives Halo of Romance to the Every-Day Tasks," *Toronto Star Weekly*, 19 February 1921.

67 According to the *Oxford English Dictionary*, a hussif is "a woman (usually, a married woman) who manages or directs the affairs of her household; the mistress of a family; the wife of a householder. Often (with qualifying words), a woman who manages her household with skill and thrift, a domestic economist." See http://dictionary.oed.com.

68 Dyhouse, *Girls Growing Up*, 80.
69 Olave Baden-Powell, *Training Girls as Guides*, 15.
70 *Girl Guides' Gazette* VIII, 85 (January 1921): 10. Mrs. Fryer was likely Joan Fryer (nee Denny Cooke), who ran a Guide company in a munition factory in Coventry during the First World War, and later co-authored *The Extension Book* for Guide leaders (see note 83).
71 While similar concerns were expressed by some elite white women in interwar Canada, and one of the aims of education for Indigenous girls was to create skilled and docile domestic servants, these issues do not appear in the Canadian texts I consulted.
72 Selina Todd, *Young Women, Work and Family in England, 1918–1950* (Oxford and New York: Oxford University Press, 2005), 11.
73 Olave Baden-Powell, *Training Girls as Guides*, 16.
74 Robert Baden-Powell, *Girl Guiding*, 13.
75 Girl Guiding UK Archives (London), *Girl Guides Annual Report, 1933*, 11.
76 Maynard, *A.B.C. of Guiding*, 129.
77 *Girl Guides' Gazette* IX, 105 (September 1922): 162; XI, 121 (January 1924): 4; XI, 123 (March 1924): 61.
78 Robert Baden-Powell, *Girl Guiding*, 22.
79 Ibid., 17.
80 Ibid., 24.
81 Ibid., 40.
82 Tammy Proctor writes that the Domestic Service badge (introduced in 1917) was one of the most popular Guide badges in the interwar years. See Tammy M. Proctor, *Scouting for Girls: A Century of Girl Guides and Girl Scouts* (Santa Barbara, CA: ABC-Clio, 2009), 37.
83 Vera Cleeve and Joan Fryer, eds., *The Extension Book* (London: The Girl Guides Association, 1936), 172.
84 Russell, *Mauve Games Book*, 89.
85 *Collins' Girl Guides Annual* (London and Glasgow: Collins' Clear-Type Press, 1923), 222.
86 *Guide* XVIII, 43 (2 February 1939): 1351.
87 Engels, "Limits of Gender Ideology," 432.
88 L.K. Trotter and O.I. Crosbie, *Team Games for Girl Guides* (Essex, England, 1923), 39.
89 Vivien Rhys Davids, *Brownie Games* (London: The Girl Guides Association, 1931), 29.
90 Archives of the Manitoba Council of the Girl Guides of Canada – Guides du Canada (Winnipeg), Nightingale Patrol Logbook, 1928–29, 15 December 1928 and 14 January 1929.
91 Girl Guiding UK Archives (London), 8th Battersea Company Swallow Patrol Diary, 1928–30.
92 Monica Storrs, *God's Galloping Girl: The Peace River Diaries of Monica Storrs, 1929–1931*, ed. W.L. Morton (Vancouver: UBC Press, 1979), 61–62.
93 Ibid., 73.
94 Anne McClintock, *Imperial Leather: Race, Gender, and Sexuality in the Colonial Contest* (New York: Routledge, 1995), 208. On domesticity and cleanliness in settler societies, see Paige Raibmon, "Living on Display: Colonial Visions of Aboriginal Domestic Spaces," *BC Studies* 140 (Winter 2003–04): 69–89.
95 Girl Guiding UK Archives (London), Logbook presented to Miss Watson, Bangalore District Commissioner, 1932–34.
96 Sarah Carter, *The Importance of Being Monogamous: Marriage and Nation Building in Western Canada to 1915* (Edmonton: University of Alberta Press, 2008); Bettina Bradbury, "Colonial

Comparisons: Rethinking Marriage, Civilization and Nation in Nineteenth-Century White Settler Societies," in *Rediscovering the British World*, ed. Phillip Buckner and R. Douglas Francis (Calgary: University of Calgary Press, 2005), 135–58; Adele Perry, "Metropolitan Knowledge, Colonial Practice, and Indigenous Womanhood: Missions in Nineteenth-Century British Columbia," in *Contact Zones: Aboriginal and Settler Women in Canada's Colonial Past*, ed. Katie Pickles and Myra Rutherdale (Vancouver: UBC Press, 2005), 115–22; Stephanie Coontz, *Marriage, a History: From Obedience to Intimacy, or How Love Conquered Marriage* (New York: Viking, 2005); Adele Perry, *On the Edge of Empire: Gender, Race, and the Making of British Columbia, 1849–1871* (Toronto: University of Toronto Press, 2001); Nancy F. Cott, *Public Vows: A History of Marriage and the Nation* (Cambridge, MA, and London: Harvard University Press, 2000).

97 *Council Fire* XI, 4 (October 1936): 25.
98 Comacchio, *Infinite Bonds of Family*, 74. See also Carolyn Strange, *Toronto's Girl Problem: The Perils and Pleasures of the City, 1880–1930* (Toronto: University of Toronto Press, 1995), 9; Veronica Strong-Boag, *The New Day Recalled: Lives of Girls and Women in English Canada, 1919–1939* (Toronto: Copp Clark Pitman, 1988).
99 Penny Tinkler, *Constructing Girlhood: Popular Magazines for Girls Growing Up in England, 1920–1950* (London: Taylor and Francis, 1995), 3.
100 Walsh, *Domesticity in Colonial India*.
101 *Indian Ladies' Magazine* VIII, 1 (January–February 1935): 58 (emphasis in original).
102 *Girl Guides' Gazette* 72 (December 1919): 154–55.
103 Robert Baden-Powell, *Girl Guiding*, 177.
104 Ibid., 178.
105 Girl Guiding UK Archives (London), *Girl Guides Annual Report, 1933*, 11.
106 Olave Baden-Powell, *Training Girls as Guides*, 17.
107 Ibid.
108 Tammy M. Proctor, *On My Honour: Scouts and Guides in Interwar Britain* (Philadelphia: American Philosophical Society, 2002), 113. Proctor writes: "just as the Chief Guide and Chief Scout maintained a companionate marriage, so should boys and girl aim to cooperate and complement each other's skills."
109 Archives of the National Council of the Girl Guides of Canada – Guides du Canada (Toronto), *The Canadian Council of the Girl Guides Association (Inc.) Annual Reports, 1925*, 7.
110 Burton, *Dwelling in the Archive*, 10. Chakrabarty, "Difference-Deferral of a Colonial Modernity," 373–74. Chakrabarty notes that the British in India promoted "the idea that husbands and wives should be friends/companions in marriage. It reflected the well-known Victorian patriarchal ideals of 'companionate marriage' that the British introduced into India in the nineteenth century and that many Bengali male and female reformers embraced with great zeal."
111 *Indian Ladies' Magazine* VIII, 6 (November-December 1935): 184–85.
112 Agnes Baden-Powell and Robert Baden-Powell, *The Handbook for Girl Guides: How Girls Can Help Build the Empire* (London: Thomas Nelson and Sons, 1912), 340. The passage states that "all secret bad habits are evil and dangerous, lead to hysteria and lunatic asylums, and serious illness is the result, so if you have any sense and courage you will throw off such temptation at once ... Evil practices do not face an honest person; they lead you on to blindness, paralysis, and loss of memory."
113 Robert Baden-Powell, *Girl Guiding*, 51.

114 Sally Alexander, "The Mysteries and Secrets of Women's Bodies: Sexual Knowledge in the First Half of the Twentieth Century," in *Modern Times: Reflections on a Century of English Modernity*, ed. Mica Nava and Alan O'Shea (London: Routledge, 1996), 161–74; Kate Fisher, *Birth Control, Sex, and Marriage in Britain, 1918–1960* (Oxford: Oxford University Press, 2006), chap. 1.

115 Beth Bailey, *From Front Porch to Back Seat: Courtship in Twentieth-Century America* (Baltimore: The Johns Hopkins University Press, 1989).

116 Proctor, *On My Honour*, 115.

117 Quoted in Proctor, *On My Honour*, 118.

118 Sheila Jeffreys, *The Spinster and Her Enemies: Feminism and Sexuality, 1880–1930* (London: Pandora, 1985); Alison Oram, "Repressed and Thwarted, or Bearer of the New World? The Spinster in Inter-War Feminist Discourses," *Women's History Review* 1, 3 (September 1992): 413–33.

119 Rosemary Auchmuty, "You're a Dyke, Angela! Elsie J. Oxenham and the Rise and Fall of the Schoolgirl Story," in *Not a Passing Phase: Reclaiming Lesbians in History, 1840–1945* (London: The Women's Press, 1989), 119–40.

120 *Canadian Guider* 6, 1 (January 1937): 3. Sharon Wall has shown that similar concerns about the "pathological" nature of crushes were also expressed by the organizers of girls' summer camps in interwar Ontario. See Sharon Wall, *The Nurture of Nature: Childhood, Antimodernism, and Ontario Summer Camps, 1920–55* (Vancouver: UBC Press, 2010), 204.

121 Martha Vicinus, *Independent Women: Work and Community for Single Women, 1850–1920* (Chicago and London: University of Chicago Press, 1985), 291.

122 Proctor, *Scouting for Girls*, 57.

123 Ibid.

124 Tone Hellesund, "Queering the Spinsters: Single Middle-Class Women in Norway, 1880–1920," *Journal of Homosexuality* 54, 1–2 (April 2008): 21–48.

125 Monica Storrs, *God's Galloping Girl: The Peace River Diaries of Monica Storrs, 1929–1931*, ed. W.L. Morton (Vancouver: UBC Press, 1979), 21.

126 Myra Rutherdale, *Women and the White Man's God: Gender and Race in the Canadian Mission Field* (Vancouver: UBC Press, 2002), 69. Rutherdale notes that Storrs and Harmer shared a bedroom, and she also discusses the close emotional and physical relationships of other female missionaries in the Canadian North.

127 Fiona Paisley, "Performing 'New Zealand': Maori and Pakeha Delegates at the Pan-Pacific Women's Conference, Hawai'i, 1934," *New Zealand Journal of History* 38, 1 (2004): 25.

128 Proctor, *Scouting for Girls*, 57.

129 Ibid., 57–58.

130 Kitty Barne, *Here Come the Girl Guides* (London: The Girl Guides Association, 1946), 24.

131 Ellen Jordan, "'Making Good Wives and Mothers'? The Transformation of Middle-Class Girls' Education in Nineteenth-Century Britain," *History of Education Quarterly* 31, 4 (Winter 1991): 443.

CHAPTER 3: WE MUST GIVE THE MODERN GIRL A TRAINING
IN CITIZENSHIP

1 Girl Guiding UK Archives (London), *The Girl Guides' Annual Report, 1925*, 23–24.

2 Ibid., *1919*, 24.

3 Archives of the Ontario Council of the Girl Guides of Canada – Guides du Canada (Toronto), scrapbook no. 11, press clipping from an unknown, undated newspaper: "Empire's Chief Girl Guide: Lady Baden-Powell Addresses Woman's Canadian Club."

4 *Canadian Guider* 2, 1 (January 1934): 4.

5 *Indian Ladies' Magazine* I, 3 (October 1927): 37.

6 Ibid., III, 7 (February 1930): 334.

7 Archives of the World Association of Girl Guides and Girl Scouts (London), *The World Association of Girl Guides and Girl Scouts Fifth Biennial Report: 1st July, 1936 to 30th June, 1938*, 88.

8 Keith McClelland and Sonya Rose, "Citizenship and Empire, 1867–1928," in *At Home with the Empire: Metropolitan Culture and the Imperial World*, ed. Catherine Hall and Sonya O. Rose (Cambridge: Cambridge University Press, 2006), 276–77.

9 Carey A. Watt, *Serving the Nation: Cultures of Service, Association, and Citizenship in Colonial India* (New Delhi: Oxford University Press, 2005), 15.

10 T.H. Marshall, *Citizenship and Social Class* (London and Concord, MA: Pluto Press, 1992).

11 For more on this distinction, see Margot Canaday, *The Straight State: Sexuality and Citizenship in Twentieth-Century America* (Princeton: Princeton University Press, 2009), 8.

12 The historical literature on women/gender and citizenship in Britain and its empire is vast. On citizenship and the woman suffrage movement in Britain, see Laura E. Nym Mayhall, *The Militant Suffrage Movement: Citizenship and Resistance in Britain, 1860–1930* (New York: Oxford University Press, 2003). On British citizenship and the First World War, see Nicoletta F. Gullace, *"The Blood of Our Sons": Men, Women, and the Regeneration of British Citizenship during the Great War* (New York: Palgrave Macmillan, 2002); Susan Pedersen, "Gender, Welfare and Citizenship in Britain during the Great War," *American Historical Review* 95, 4 (October 1990): 983–1006. Also relevant is Sonya O. Rose, *Which People's War? National Identity and Citizenship in Britain, 1939–1945* (New York: Oxford University Press, 2003). On British women and citizenship in the interwar period, see Sue Innes, "Constructing Women's Citizenship in the Interwar Period: The Edinburgh Women Citizens' Association," *Women's History Review* 13, 4 (2004); Catriona Beaumont, "Citizens Not Feminists: The Boundary Negotiated between Citizenship and Feminism by Mainstream Women's Organizations in England, 1928–39," *Women's History Review* 9, 2 (2000): 411–29. On white settler and Indigenous women in the dominions, see Patricia Grimshaw, "Settler Anxieties, Indigenous Peoples, and Women's Suffrage in the Colonies of Australia, New Zealand, and Hawaii, 1889–1902," *Pacific Historical Review* 69, 4 (2000): 553–72; Marilyn Lake, "'The Inviolable Woman: Feminist Conceptions of Citizenship, 1900–1940," in *Feminism: The Public and the Private*, ed. Joan Landes (Oxford: Oxford University Press, 1998), 223–40; Marilyn Lake, "Between Old Worlds and New: Feminist Citizenship, Nation and Race, the Destabilisation of Identity," in *Suffrage and Beyond: International Feminist Perspectives*, ed. Caroline Daley and Melanie Nolan (Auckland: Auckland University Press and Pluto Press, 1994), 277–94; Fiona Paisley, "Citizens of Their World: Australian Feminism and Indigenous Rights in the International Context, 1920s and 1930s," *Feminist Review* 58 (1998): 66–84. On citizenship in Canada, see Veronica Strong-Boag, "'The Citizenship Debates': The 1885 Franchise Act," in *Contesting Canadian Citizenship: Historical Readings*, ed. Dorothy E. Chunn and Robert Menzies (Peterborough, ON: Broadview Press, 2002), 69–94. On India, see Mrinalini Sinha, *Specters of Mother India: The Global Restructuring of an Empire* (Durham and London: Duke University Press, 2006). Sinha

argues that the global controversy that followed the 1927 publication of Katherine Mayo's *Mother India* created a brief moment in which Indian women were constituted as "paradigmatic citizen-subjects" (197).

13 Antoinette Burton, *Burdens of History: British Feminists, Indian Women, and Imperial Culture, 1865–1915* (Chapel Hill and London: University of North Carolina Press, 1994); Mrinalini Sinha, *Colonial Masculinity: The "Manly Englishman" and the "Effeminate Bengali" in the Late Nineteenth Century* (Manchester: Manchester University Press, 1995).

14 Sinha, *Specters of Mother India;* Robin Jarvis Brownlie, "'A Better Citizen Than Lots of White Men': First Nations Enfranchisement – An Ontario Case Study, 1918–1940," *Canadian Historical Review* 87, 1 (March 2006): 29–53; Laura Tabili, *We Ask for British Justice: Workers and Racial Difference in Late Imperial Britain* (Ithaca: Cornell University Press, 1994).

15 Daniel Gorman, *Imperial Citizenship: Empire and the Question of Belonging* (Manchester and New York: Manchester University Press, 2006), 20.

16 *Girl Guides' Gazette* XII, 133 (January 1925): 16.

17 *Guider* XVI, 182 (February 1929): 38.

18 *Canadian Girl Guide* (September 1930): 12.

19 Quoted in Martin Pugh, *Women and the Women's Movement in Britain, 1914–1999*, 2nd ed. (Houndmills and London: Macmillan, 2000), 75.

20 *Indian Ladies' Magazine* IV, 4 (November 1930): 216.

21 *Girl Guides' Gazette* XI, 123 (March 1924): 61.

22 *Girl Guides' Gazette* IX, 106 (October 1922): 195.

23 Ibid., XI, 122 (February 1924): 40.

24 Ibid., XII, 135 (March 1925): 65.

25 Girl Guiding UK Archives (London), 2nd Forest Hill Company Logbook, 4 May 1934.

26 Patricia Grimshaw, "Reading the Silences: Suffrage Activists and Race in Nineteenth-Century Settler Societies," in *Women's Rights and Human Rights: International Historical Perspectives*, ed. Patricia Grimshaw, Katie Holmes, and Marilyn Lake (Basingstoke and New York: Palgrave, 2001), 31.

27 Stephen Heathorn, *For Home, Country, and Race: Constructing Gender, Class, and Englishness in the Elementary School, 1880–1914* (Toronto, Buffalo, and London: University of Toronto Press, 2000), 25–29.

28 Lydia Murdoch, *Imagined Orphans: Poor Families, Child Welfare and Contested Citizenship in London* (New Brunswick, NJ: Rutgers University Press, 2006), 45.

29 Angela Woollacott, "Inventing Commonwealth and Pan-Pacific Feminisms: Australian Women's Internationalist Activism in the 1920s–30s," in *Feminisms and Internationalism*, ed. Mrinalini Sinha, Donna J. Guy, and Angela Woollacott (Oxford: Blackwell, 1999), 93 and 84. This egalitarianism leads Woollacott to label the BCL as a "Commonwealth feminist" (as opposed to "imperial feminist") organization.

30 See Dominique Marshall, "Peace, War and the Popularity of Children's Rights in Public Opinion, 1919–1959: The League of Nations, the United Nations and the Save the Children International Union," in *Children and War: An Anthology*, ed. James Marten (New York: New York University Press, 2002), 184–99; Dominque Marshall, "The Formation of Childhood as an Object of International Relations: The Child Welfare Committee and the Declaration of Children's Rights of the League of Nations," *International Journal of Children's Rights* 7, 2 (1999): 103–47.

31 *Guider* (August 1933): 312.

32 Jessica Harland-Jacobs, *Builders of Empire: Freemasonry and British Imperialism, 1717–1927* (Chapel Hill: University of North Carolina Press, 2007), 284. J. Brian Harrison, in an article on the Girls' Friendly Society, similarly writes that "conservatism, like liberalism or socialism, has always profited by its connections with sympathetic but ostensibly non-political groups." See Brian Harrison, "For Church, Queen and Family: The Girls' Friendly Society, 1874–1920," *Past and Present* 61, 1 (1973): 107.

33 Watt, *Serving the Nation*, 215–16. Watt mentions the Seva Samiti Guides at several points in his study, but I have been unable to find any more information about them.

34 Scout Association Archives (Gilwell Park), Diary of Olave St. Clair Soames, 25 February 1937 and 8 March 1937.

35 Girl Guiding UK Archives (London), India Folder, Letter to Phyllis [?] from Olave Baden-Powell, March 18 1938.

36 Archives of the World Association of Girl Guides and Girl Scouts (London), *The World Association of Girl Guides and Girl Scouts Fourth Biennial Report: 1st July, 1936 to 30th June, 1938*, 137.

37 Girl Guiding UK Archives (London), Canada Folder, *Chief Guide's Report on Canada, 1935*. Quebec's French Catholic Guides did not officially join the anglophone-led Girl Guides of Canada until 1939.

38 Girl Guiding UK Archives (London), Canada Folder, letter from Sarah Warren (Chief Commissioner, Canada) to Olave Baden-Powell, 21 September 1937.

39 Ibid., copy of letter from Olave Baden-Powell to Sarah Warren (Chief Commissioner, Canada), 6 October 1937.

40 Tammy Proctor, "'A Separate Path': Scouting and Guiding in Interwar South Africa," *Comparative Studies in Society and History* 42, 3 (2000): 605–31; Deborah Gaitskell, "Upward All and Play the Game: The Girls' Wayfarer Association in the Transvaal, 1925–1974," in *Apartheid and Black Education: The Education of Black South Africans*, ed. Peter Kallaway (Johannesburg: Raven Press, 1984), 222–64.

41 Naomi Whelpton and Kitty Streatfeild, *Rangers* (London: C. Arthur Pearson Ltd., 1926), 16.

42 Robert Baden-Powell, *Girl Guiding: A Handbook for Brownies, Guides, Rangers and Guiders* (London: C. Arthur Pearson Ltd., 1931), 9.

43 Ibid., 30.

44 Robert Baden-Powell, *Girl Guiding: A Handbook for Brownies, Guides, Rangers, and Guiders* (London: C. Arthur Pearson Ltd., 1938), 123.

45 Monica Storrs, *God's Galloping Girl: The Peace River Diaries of Monica Storrs, 1929–1931*, ed. W.L. Morton (Vancouver: UBC Press, 1979), 69.

46 Ibid., 83 (emphasis in original).

47 Girl Guiding UK Archives (London), *Girl Guides Annual Report, 1923*, 3; Girl Guiding UK Archives (London), 8th Battersea Company Swallow Patrol Diary, 1928–30, 2 November 1929.

48 Archives of the Manitoba Council of the Girl Guides of Canada – Guides du Canada (Winnipeg), "Guide Districts Hold Annual Field Days," clipping from the *Winnipeg Tribune*, 15 October 1938; Girl Guiding UK Archives (London), *Girl Guides Annual Report, 1926*, n.p.

49 Archives of the Manitoba Council of the Girl Guides of Canada – Guides du Canada (Winnipeg), Nightingale Patrol Logbook, 1928–29, 14 January 1929.

50 Watt, *Serving the Nation.*
51 Carey Watt, "Education for National Efficiency: Constructive Nationalism in North India, 1909–1916," *Modern Asian Studies* 31, 2 (May 1997): 339–74; Joseph S. Alter, *The Wrestler's Body: Identity and Ideology in North India* (Berkeley: University of California Press, 1992); John Rosselli, "The Self-Image of Effeteness: Physical Education and Nationalism in Nineteenth-Century Bengal" *Past and Present* 86 (February 1980): 121–48.
52 *Indian Ladies' Magazine* I, 7 (February 1928): 171–72.
53 Ibid., II, 1 (August 1928): 43.
54 Christine Kotchemidova, "From Good Cheer to 'Drive-By Smiling': A Social History of Cheerfulness," *Journal of Social History* 39, 1 (Fall 2005): 8.
55 Robert Baden-Powell, *Girl Guiding*, 51.
56 R. Tyacke, *Into a Wider World: Talks with Rangers and Cadets* (London: The Religious Tract Society, 1927), 77.
57 *Council Fire* IV, 3 (July 1929): 22.
58 Ibid.
59 *Girl Guides' Gazette* IX, 106 (October 1922): 189.
60 Kotchemidova discusses cheerfulness as an American phenomenon and contrasts it with the "un-cheerful" emotional culture of continental Europe. As the preceding paragraph demonstrates, by the early twentieth century, England and Canada also subscribed to this hegemonic emotional style.
61 Sara Ahmed, *The Promise of Happiness* (Durham and London: Duke University Press, 2010), 128.
62 *Guider* XXI, 241 (January 1934): 2.
63 *Guider* XXIV, 281 (May 1937): 176.
64 For more on Smiles, see Asa Briggs, "Samuel Smiles: The Gospel of Self-Help," *History Today* 37 (May 1987): 37–43. Carey Watt notes the influence among early twentieth-century Indian social reformers of "the ideas of J.S. Mill, Samuel Smiles' doctrine of self-help, Charles Darwin, and Herbert Spencer's notions of social Darwinism and social efficiency." See Watt, *Serving the Nation*, 33. On the use of Smiles's concepts of duty and obedience in colonial India, see also Ranajit Guha, "Dominance without Hegemony and Its Historiography," in *Subaltern Studies VI: Writings on South Asian History and Society*, ed. Ranajit Guha (Delhi: Oxford University Press, 1989), 250–53.
65 Anna Davin, "Imperialism and Motherhood," *History Workshop Journal* 5, 1 (1978): 52.
66 Frank Trentmann, "After the Nation-State: Citizenship, Empire and Global Coordination in the New Internationalism, 1914–1930," in *Beyond Sovereignty: Britain, Empire and Trans-nationalism, c. 1880–1950*, ed. Kevin Grant, Philippa Levine, and Frank Trentmann (Houndmills, Basingstoke: Palgrave Macmillan, 2007), 49.
67 *Girl Guides' Gazette* X, 113 (May 1923): 89.
68 Archives of the National Council of the Girl Guides of Canada – Guides du Canada, Annual Reports, Year Ending April 1st 1936, The Canadian Council of the Girl Guides Association, Inc., 7.
69 *Indian Ladies' Magazine* V, 12 (November–December 1932): 578–79.
70 Robert Baden-Powell, *Girl Guiding*, 9.
71 Robert Baden-Powell, *Steps to Girl Guiding: An Abridged Edition of the Official Handbook*, 4th edition (London: C. Arthur Pearson Ltd., n.d.), 7.

72 Mrs. Isabel Jacobs, "Social Organizations for Adolescent Girls," in *The New Survey of London Life and Labour, vol. 9, Life and Leisure,* ed. Sir Hubert Llewellyn Smith (London: P.S. King and Son Ltd., 1935), 201.

73 *Canadian Guider* 4, 5 (September 1936): 3.

74 *Guider* XVI, 190 (October 1929): 307.

75 *Council Fire* XI, 4 (October 1936): 35.

76 *Guider* XVI, 190 (October 1929): 307.

77 Ibid.

78 Katie Pickles, *Female Imperialism and National Identity: Imperial Order Daughters of the Empire* (Manchester: Manchester University Press, 2002), 40.

79 Archives of the Manitoba Council of the Girl Guides of Canada, Marjorie Hoskins Folder, Marjorie Hoskins scrapbook, clippings – 1920s, "Progress of Guides Highly Recommended."

80 Provincial Archives of Manitoba (Winnipeg), Girl Guides – Manitoba Council, 1926–83, P 3467, Manitoba Council of the Girl Guides of Canada, 1925–28, minute book, 14 May 1928.

81 John Herd Thompson, "Canada and the 'Third British Empire,' 1901–1939," in *Canada and the British Empire,* ed. Phillip Buckner (New York: Oxford University Press, 2008), 101–2. Bonnie MacQueen's article on Guiding in British Columbia, on the other hand, discusses such companies as examples of ethnic segregation. See Bonnie MacQueen, "Domesticity and Discipline: The Girl Guides in British Columbia, 1910–1943," in *Not Just Pin Money: Selected Essays on the History of Women's Work in British Columbia,* ed. Barbara K. Latham and Roberta J. Pazdro (Victoria: Camosun College, 1984), 221–36.

82 Girl Guiding UK Archives (London), *Girl Guides Annual Report, 1935,* 159.

83 Ibid., *1933,* 152; *Council Fire* IX, 2 (April 1934): 95.

84 *Council Fire* VIII, 1 (January 1933): 6.

85 My thinking about this issue is indebted to Daniel Coleman's work on white civility, Julie Evans's discussion of property- and state assistance-based restrictions on the franchise, and Alice Kessler-Harris's work on the ways in which employment works "as a boundary line demarcating different kinds of citizenship." See Daniel Coleman, *White Civility: The Literary Project of English Canada* (Toronto: University of Toronto Press, 2006), 32; Julie Evans et al., *Equal Subjects, Unequal Rights: Indigenous Peoples in British Settler Colonies, 1830–1910* (Manchester: Manchester University Press, 2003), 51; Alice Kessler-Harris, *In Pursuit of Equity: Women, Men, and the Quest for Economic Citizenship in Twentieth-Century America* (Oxford and New York: Oxford University Press, 2001), 4 and 12–13.

86 *Indian Ladies' Magazine* I, 3 (October 1927): 37.

87 *Times of London,* "Girlhood of India: Lady Baden-Powell on the Guide Movement," 30 May 1921.

88 *Council Fire* IX, 4 (October 1934): 114.

89 Carolyn Strange, *Toronto's Girl Problem: The Perils and Pleasures of the City, 1880–1930* (Toronto: University of Toronto Press, 1995), 191. Strange notes that the ability of women (especially those who were single or working-class) "to choose healthy leisure pursuits was increasingly touted [during the interwar years] as the hallmark of feminine citizenship." Selina Todd makes a similar point about the British context, writing that, between 1918 and 1950, "young women's particular unwillingness to engage in organized leisure was interpreted as selfish and potentially immoral." See Selina Todd, *Young Women, Work and Family in England, 1918–1950* (Oxford and New York: Oxford University Press, 2005), 215.

90 Strange, *Toronto's Girl Problem*, 5.

91 Olave Baden-Powell, *Training Girls as Guides: Hints for Commissioners and All Who Are Interested in the Welfare and Training of Girls* (London: C. Arthur Pearson Ltd., 1919), 13–15.

92 Claire Langhamer, *Women's Leisure in England, 1920–60* (Manchester and New York: Manchester University Press, 2000), 49–50.

93 Girl Guiding UK Archives (London), 1st Foots Cray Company Record Book.

94 Langhamer, *Women's Leisure in England*, 76.

95 Jill Julius Matthews, "They Had Such a Lot of Fun: The Women's League of Health and Beauty between the Wars," *History Workshop* 30, 1 (Autumn 1990): 27.

96 Quoted in Tammy M. Proctor, *On My Honour: Scouts and Guides in Interwar Britain* (Philadelphia: American Philosophical Society, 2002), 118. Proctor states that mixed-sex socializing between Guide/Scout and Ranger/Rover groups gradually increased in interwar Britain. I have found several similar references in my own research, but this development seems not to have affected Guiding in Canada and India to a similar extent.

97 Joan Harley, "Report of an Enquiry into the Occupations, Further Education, and Leisure Interests of a Number of Girl Wage-Earners from Elementary and Central Schools in the Manchester District, with Special Reference to the Influence of School Training on Their Use of Leisure" (MEd thesis, University of Manchester, 1937), 84.

98 Ibid., 95.

99 Provincial Archives of Manitoba (Winnipeg), Girl Guides – Manitoba Council, 1926–1983, P 3467, Girl Guides Winnipeg Division Minute Book, 1926–31, 17 February 1931.

100 Robert Baden-Powell, *Girl Guiding*, 40.

101 Ibid., 134; *Guider* XXII, 268 (April 1936), 112.

102 Roger Cooter, "The Moment of the Accident: Culture, Militarism and Modernity in Late-Victorian Britain," in *Accidents and History: Injuries, Fatalities and Social Relations*, ed. Roger Cooter and Bill Luckin (Amsterdam and Atlanta: Rodopi, 1997), 123–24. Cooter defines this as a Victorian phenomenon that had largely disappeared by 1918 – a contention that is difficult to maintain after having considered the interwar Girl Guides.

103 Cooter, "Moment of the Accident," 125.

104 Anne Summers, *Angels and Citizens: British Women as Military Nurses, 1854–1914* (London: Routledge and Kegan Paul, 1988).

105 Robert Baden-Powell, *Girl Guiding*, 54.

106 Ibid., 149.

107 Ibid., 154.

108 Archives of the Manitoba Council of the Girl Guides of Canada – Guides du Canada (Winnipeg), Nightingale Patrol Logbook, 1928–29.

109 Girl Guiding UK Archives (London), 8th Battersea Company Swallow Patrol Diary, 1928–30, 4 June 1928.

110 Storrs, *God's Galloping Girl*, 60.

111 Girl Guiding UK Archives (London), *Our Chalet, 1932–1992* (Cambridge, UK: World Association of Girl Guides and Girl Scouts, 1992), 25.

112 *Guider* XIV, 219 (March 1932): 81–82.

113 Girl Guiding UK Archives (London), logbook presented to Miss Watson, Bangalore District Commissioner, 1932–34; Logbook: Empire Day Rally, Nilgin Division, Madras Province (Southern India), 1933.

114 Watt, *Serving the Nation*, 117–18. Interestingly, Watt supports his argument with the following example: A Grand Rally in Allahabad in 1921, at which "scouts played Indian games, formed pyramids, gave first-aid demonstrations, and engaged in sword play, fire brigade and rescue work. Indian Sister Scouts and girl guides, on the other hand, were 'a delightful spectacle' in green saris and they 'gave a special display of home nursing, first aid, cooking, drill, etc.'" He further explains this performance by claiming that "there were very real limits. The skills learned still related to the domestic sphere."

115 Girl Guiding UK Archives (London), *Girl Guides Annual Report, 1919*, 14.

116 Hugh Cunningham, *Grace Darling: Victorian Heroine* (London: Hambledon Continuum, 2007); Colin Coates and Cecilia Morgan, *Heroines and History: Representations of Madeleine de Verchères and Laura Secord* (Toronto: University of Toronto Press, 2002); Kristine Moruzi, *Constructing Girlhood through the Periodical Press, 1850–1915* (Farnham, Surrey: Ashgate, 2012), chap. 7; John Price, "'Heroism in Everyday Life': The Watts Memorial for Heroic Self Sacrifice," *History Workshop Journal* 63 (Spring 2007): 255–78.

117 Shobna Nijhawan, "Hindi Children's Journals and Nationalist Discourse, 1910–1930," *Economic and Political Weekly* 39, 33 (2004): 3726; Nandini Chandra, "The Pedagogic Imperative of Travel Writing in the Hindi World: Children's Periodicals, 1920–1950," *South Asia* 30, 2 (August 2007): 311.

118 Girl Guiding UK Archives (London), *Girl Guides Annual Report, 1919*, 14; *Girl Guides Annual Report, 1920*, 31. Descriptions of Guide rescues in annual reports and periodicals during this period are considerably longer than their counterparts in Boy Scout texts.

119 Girl Guiding UK Archives (London), *Girl Guides Annual Report, 1922*, 48; Girl Guiding UK Archives (London), *Girl Guides Annual Report, 1924*, 51.

120 Mary Cadogan and Patricia Craig, *You're a Brick, Angela: A New Look at Girls' Fiction from 1839 to 1975* (London: Victor Gollancz Ltd., 1976), 149 and 156.

121 Carol Dyhouse, *Girls Growing Up in Late Victorian and Edwardian England* (London, Boston, and Henley: Routledge and Kegan Paul, 1981), 2.

122 Girl Guiding UK Archives (London), *Girl Guides Annual Report, 1920*, 31.

123 Ibid., *1933*, 38–39. See also Christopher Love, "Swimming, Service to the Empire and Baden-Powell's Youth Movements," *International Journal of the History of Sport* 24, 5 (2007): 682–92.

124 *Guide* (16 February 1939): 1417.

125 Lucy Delap, "'Thus Does Man Prove His Fitness to Be the Master of Things': Shipwrecks, Chivalry and Masculinities in Nineteenth- and Twentieth-Century Britain," *Cultural and Social History* 3, 1 (2006): 1–30.

126 Archives of the World Association of Girl Guides and Girl Scouts, *The World Association of Girl Guides and Girl Scouts Second Biennial Report: July 1st 1930 to June 30th 1932*, 20; Mrs. Janson Potts, *Hints on Girl Guide Tests: Tenderfoot, Second Class, First Class and Able Sea Guide* (Glasgow: Brown, Son and Ferguson Ltd., 1939), 3. Jane Mackay and Pat Thane have also noted the appearance of heroic "girl knight" characters in British girls' fiction after the First World War. See Jane Mackay and Pat Thane, "The Englishwoman," in *Englishness: Politics and Culture*, ed. Robert Colls and Phillip Dodd (London: Routledge, 1986), 221–22.

127 Mary Lean, *Joan of Glen Garland: A Canadian Girl Guide Story* (London: The Girls Own Paper Office, 1934): 138.

128 *Guide* 8, 25 (13 October 1928): 773.

129 *Guide* 8, 30 (17 November 1928): 937–938.

130 See John E. Kendle, *The Round Table Movement and Imperial Union* (Toronto and Buffalo: University of Toronto Press, 1975).
131 Girl Guiding UK Archives (London), *Girl Guides Annual Report, 1934*, 12.
132 Ken Osborne, "Public Schooling and Citizenship Education in Canada," *Canadian Ethnic Studies* 32, 1 (2000): 5.

CHAPTER 4: MOULDING BODIES AND IDENTITIES IN THE OUTDOORS

1 *Council Fire* VII, 3 (1932): 45; *Guider* XVII, 196 (April 1930): 132–34; *Guider* XX, 234 (June 1933): 219–220; *Guider* XX, 237 (September 1933): 353; *Council Fire* III, 9 (April 1928): 47.
2 See, for instance, T.J. Jackson Lears, *No Place of Grace: Antimodernism and the Transformation of American Culture, 1880–1920* (New York: Pantheon Books, 1981); Patricia Jasen, *Wild Things: Nature, Culture, and Tourism in Ontario, 1790–1914* (Toronto: University of Toronto Press, 1995); Peter J. Schmitt, *Back to Nature: The Arcadian Myth in Urban America* (New York: Oxford University Press, 1969). See also Sharon Wall, *The Nurture of Nature: Childhood, Antimodernism, and Ontario Summer Camps, 1920–55* (Vancouver: UBC Press, 2010), chap. 1.
3 *Guider* XV, 169 (January 1928): 13.
4 David I. Macleod, *Building Character in the American Boy: The Boy Scouts, YMCA, and Their Forerunners, 1870–1920* (Madison: University of Wisconsin Press, 1983), 247.
5 Archives of the Ontario Council of the Girl Guides of Canada – Guides du Canada (Toronto), scrapbook on early history of Toronto Girl Guides, press clipping: "A Model Guide Camp Goes Like Clock Work: Military Precision Prevails, with Provision for Work, Study and Play," *Toronto Star Weekly*, 16 July 1921.
6 Monica Storrs, *God's Galloping Girl: The Peace River Diaries of Monica Storrs, 1929–1931*, ed. W.L. Morton (Vancouver: UBC Press, 1979), 135.
7 Archives of the Manitoba Council of the Girl Guides of Canada – Guides du Canada (Winnipeg), Marjorie Hoskins scrapbook – 1920s, press clipping from unknown, undated newspaper: "Ponemah Beach Camp for Girl Guides Opened: Advance Guard of Holiday Seekers Report Hectic First Night Out."
8 Girl Guiding UK Archives (London), 2nd Forest Hill Company [London] Logbook, 1930, press clipping from unknown, undated newspaper: "Girl Guide Camp."
9 *Campcraft for Girl Guides* (London: The Girl Guides Association, 1933), 9.
10 Macleod, *Building Character in the American Boy*, 247; *How Guides Camp* (London: The Girl Guides Association, 1935), 5.
11 *How Guides Camp* (London: The Girl Guides Association, 1935), 4–5.
12 *Times of London*, 21 August 1930; *Times of London*, 20 August 1932.
13 Girl Guiding UK Archives (London), camps box, file: Camping Memorabilia, 1911 on, *The Girl Guides Association and the National Council of Girls' Clubs: Chigwell Row Camping Ground, Chigwell Row, Chigwell, Essex [and] The Shaws Camping Ground, Cudham Lane, Cudham, near Sevenoaks, Kent. Particulars of Camping Arrangements.* This undated pamphlet reminded leaders that "first aid and medical treatment are available, but no responsibility can be taken for any accident or illness arising during or resulting from any camp. Guiders and Leaders in charge are strongly advised to enter into the insurance scheme as arranged by the Girl Guides Association and the National Council of Girls' Clubs."
14 *Guider* XVIII, 209 (May 1931): 167.

15 Ibid., XIV, 219 (March 1932): 81. The article does not mention how, or if, the camp's organizers accommodated religious and caste requirements.

16 Girl Guiding UK Archives (London), *Girl Guides Annual Report,* 1922, 24.

17 *Guider* XVII, 196 (April 1930): 116.

18 Girl Guiding UK Archives (London), *Girl Guides Annual Report,* 1922, 24.

19 Girl Guiding UK Archives (London), logbook: "Lady Hayward from the Satara Camp Guides, September 1925."

20 *Girl Guides' Gazette* X, 117 (September 1923): 209.

21 *Canadian Guider* I, 1 (January 1932): 8.

22 *Guide* IV, 12 (5 July 1924): 183.

23 *Council Fire* V, 4 (October 1930): 59–60.

24 On this issue in Canada, see David Marshall, *Secularizing the Faith: Canadian Protestant Clergy and the Crisis of Belief, 1850–1940* (Toronto: University of Toronto Press, 1992). Sharon Wall also discusses YMCA and CGIT summer camps as responses to secularization. See Wall, *Nurture of Nature,* 34; Sharon Wall, "Totem Poles, Teepees and Token Traditions: 'Playing Indian' at Ontario Summer Camps, 1920–1955," *Canadian Historical Review* 86, 3 (September 2005): 513–44.

25 *Girl Guides' Gazette* VIII, 85 (January 1921): 5.

26 Robert Baden-Powell, *Girl Guiding: A Handbook for Brownies, Guides, Rangers, and Guiders* (London: C. Arthur Pearson Ltd., 1931), 117.

27 Robert Baden-Powell, *Steps to Girl Guiding: An Abridged Edition of the Official Handbook,* 4th edition (London: C. Arthur Pearson Ltd., n.d.), 19.

28 It is important to note, however, that Christian religious ceremonies did not take place at all Guide camps. Jewish companies in Canada and Britain, for example, while stressing the importance of "God," would have dealt with these matters somewhat differently, as did the leaders of Hindu and Muslim groups in South Asia.

29 *Guider* XX, 239 (November 1933): 431.

30 Girl Guiding UK Archives (London), 2nd Forest Hill Company Logbook.

31 For more on Christianity in colonial India, see Robert Eric Frykenberg, "Christian Missions and the Raj," in *Missions and Empire,* ed. Norman Etherington (Oxford: Oxford University Press, 2005), 107–31.

32 *Guide* IV, 19 (23 August 1924): 334.

33 *Council Fire* VII, 4 (1932): 106.

34 *Girl Guides' Gazette* XVII, 199 (July 1930): 238.

35 Storrs, *God's Galloping Girl,* 219.

36 Girl Guiding UK Archives (London), *The Girl Guides Association (Incorporated by Royal Charter) Fourteenth Annual Report and Balance Sheet of the Committee of the Council for the Year ending December 31st, 1928,* 19–21.

37 Girl Guiding UK Archives (London), *Girl Guides Annual Report, 1934,* 36; *Girl Guides Annual Report, 1933,* 40.

38 Patricia Grimshaw and Andrew May, "Reappraisals of Mission History: An Introduction," in *Missionaries, Indigenous Peoples and Cultural Exchange,* ed. Patricia Grimshaw and Andrew May (Eastbourne: Sussex Academic Press, 2010), 2; Robert Eric Frykenberg, "Christian Missions and the Raj," in *Missions and Empire,* ed. Norman Etherington (Oxford: Oxford University Press, 2005), 107–31.

39 Grimshaw and May, "Reappraisals of Mission History," 2.

40 Myra Rutherdale, *Women and the White Man's God: Gender and Race in the Canadian Mission Field* (Vancouver: UBC Press, 2002), xix and 47.

41 Norman Etherington, "Education and Medicine," in *Missions and Empire*, ed. Norman Etherington (Oxford: Oxford University Press, 2005), 266. Maina Chawla Singh's work on the relationships between American Christian missionaries and their Hindu and Muslim pupils at mission schools, based on interviews with former students, shows that many Indian women remembered their mission school years fondly and could recall little of the denominational or Christian side of their education. See Maina Chawla Singh, *Gender, Religion, and "Heathen Lands": American Missionary Women in South Asia 1860s–1940s* (New York and London: Garland, 2000).

42 Girl Guiding UK Archives (London), *The Girl Guides' Annual Report, 1923*, 272.

43 *Girl Guides' Gazette* VIII, 85 (January 1921): 4; Robert Baden-Powell, *Girl Guiding*, 197.

44 Leslie Paris, *Children's Nature: The Rise of the American Summer Camp* (New York: New York University Press, 2008), 46.

45 This point is also made in Laureen Ann Tedesco, "A Nostalgia for Home: Daring and Domesticity in Girl Scouting and Girls' Fiction, 1913–1933" (PhD diss., Texas A&M University, 1999); Wall, *Nurture of Nature*, 191. On the Camp Fire Girls, see Mary Jane McCallum, "The Fundamental Things: The Camp Fire Girls and Authenticity, 1910–20," *Canadian Journal of History* 40, 1 (April 2005): 45–66; Jennifer Hillman Helgren, "Inventing American Girlhood: Gender and Citizenship in the Twentieth Century Camp Fire Girls" (PhD diss., Claremont Graduate University, 2005); Paris, *Children's Nature*; and Susan A. Miller, *Growing Girls: The Natural Origins of Girls' Organizations* (New Brunswick, NJ: Rutgers University Press, 2007).

46 *Guider* XVI, 184 (April 1929): 101.

47 *Campcraft for Girl Guides* (London: The Girl Guides Association, 1933), 11 and 91–92.

48 Ibid., 92.

49 Ibid.

50 *Council Fire* (n.d.; likely VI, no. 3), 51.

51 Girl Guiding UK Archives (London), 1st Beckenham Cadets Logbook, May – August 1929, 20 June 1929, and 29 June 1929.

52 Archives of the Manitoba Council of the Girl Guides of Canada – Guides du Canada (Winnipeg), *Honesty Patrol Logbook*, 28th Girl Guide Company, Winnipeg, 1927–28, 15 October 1927.

53 *Guider* XXII, 259 (July 1935): 294.

54 Inderpal Grewal, *Home and Harem: Nation, Gender, Empire, and the Cultures of Travel* (Durham and London: Duke University Press, 1996); Anne McClintock, *Imperial Leather: Race, Gender, and Sexuality in the Colonial Contest* (New York: Routledge, 1995); D.A. Lorimer, *Colour, Class and the Victorians: English Attitudes to the Negro in the Mid-Nineteenth Century* (Leicester: Leicester University Press, 1978).

55 Girl Guiding UK Archives (London), *Girl Guides Annual Report, 1921*, 18.

56 Robert Baden-Powell, *Steps to Girl Guiding*, 18.

57 *Council Fire* VI, 3 (no date): 42.

58 Kitty Barne, *Here Come the Girl Guides* (London: The Girl Guides Association, 1946), 59.

59 Paris, *Children's Nature*, 128; *Girl Guides' Gazette* X, 110 (February 1923): 36.

60 *Guider* XIV, 218 (February 1932): 43.

61 Ibid., 219 (March 1932): 96.

62 *Guider* XVII, 196 (April 1930): 115.
63 Mary Lean, *Joan of Glen Garland: A Canadian Girl Guide Story* (London: The Girls Own Paper Office, 1934), 35.
64 *Guider* XIX, 220 (April 1932): 133–34.
65 Ibid., XXIV, 279 (March 1937): 78; XIV, 218 (February 1932): 43. See also Paris, *Children's Nature*, 129.
66 *Collins' Girl Guides Annual* (London: Collins' Clear-Type Press, no date), 186.
67 Mary A. Procida, *Married to the Empire: Gender, Politics, and Imperialism in India, 1883–1947* (Manchester: Manchester University Press, 2002), 137.
68 Rose Kerr, *The Story of a Million Girls: Guiding and Girl Scouting around the World* (London: The Girl Guides Association, 1936), 225.
69 Quoted in David Matless, *Landscape and Englishness* (London: Reaktion Books, 1998), 66. Matless notes that twenty-six editions of the book had been published by 1939.
70 Girl Guiding UK Archives (London), *Girl Guides Annual Report, 1934*, 18.
71 Ibid., 1934, 20.
72 Martin J. Wiener, *English Culture and the Decline of the Industrial Spirit, 1850–1980*, 2nd ed. (Cambridge: Cambridge University Press, 2004); W.G. Hoskins, *The Making of the English Landscape* (London: Penguin, 1991); Alun Howkins, "The Discovery of Rural England," in *Englishness: Politics and Culture*, ed. Robert Colls and Philip Dodd (London: Routledge, 1986), 80.
73 Howkins, "Discovery of Rural England," 80. See also Stephen Heathorn, *For Home, Country, and Race: Constructing Gender, Class, and Englishness in the Elementary School, 1880–1914* (Toronto, Buffalo, and London: University of Toronto Press, 2000), 152.
74 J.S. Bratton, "Of England, Home, and Duty: The Image of England in Victorian and Edwardian Fiction," in *Imperialism and Popular Culture*, ed. John M. MacKenzie (Manchester: Manchester University Press, 1986), 78.
75 See, for example, Marcus Woodward, *Nature's Merry-Go-Round* (London: C. Arthur Pearson Ltd., 1929); Marcus Woodward, *How to Enjoy Wild Flowers* (London: Hodder and Stoughton, 1927).
76 Marcus Woodward, *The Guide Nature Book: A Naturalist's Notebook for Girl Guides* (London: C. Arthur Pearson Ltd., 1923), 20.
77 Woodward, *Guide Nature Book*, 43.
78 Matless, *Landscape and Englishness*, 77. Matless makes this point about the English Boy Scouts in the interwar years.
79 *Guider* XVII, 199 (July 1930): 240.
80 Girl Guiding UK Archives (London), Guide Association Archives, 8th Battersea Company Swallow Patrol Diary, 1928–30, 12 April 1932.
81 Girl Guiding UK Archives (London), 2nd Forest Hill Company Logbook, 1925.
82 *Guide* 8, 30 (17 November 1928): 934–35.
83 For more on "playing Indian," see: Jay Mechling, "'Playing Indian' and the Search for Authenticity in Modern White America" *Prospects* 5, 17 (1980): 17–33; Philip J. Deloria, *Playing Indian* (New Haven: Yale University Press, 1998); Mary Jane McCallum, "The Fundamental Things: Camp Fire Girls and Authenticity, 1910–1920," *Canadian Journal of History* 40, 1 (April 2005): 45–66; Daniel Francis, *The Imaginary Indian: The Image of the Indian in Canadian Culture* (Vancouver: Arsenal Pulp Press, 1992); Wall, "Totem Poles"; Paris, *Children's Nature*, 208.

84 On British attitudes towards Indigenous peoples, see Kate Flint, *The Transatlantic Indian, 1776–1930* (Princeton: Princeton University Press, 2009); Cecilia Morgan, "'A Wigwam to Westminster': Performing Mohawk Identity in Imperial Britain, 1890s–1990s," *Gender and History* 15, 2 (August 2003): 319–41.

85 Jialin Christina Wu, "'A Life of Make-Believe': Being Boy Scouts and 'Playing Indian' in British Malaya, 1910–1942," *Gender and History* 26, 3 (November 2014): 589–619.

86 Robert Baden-Powell, *Adventuring to Manhood* (London: C. Arthur Pearson Ltd., 1936), 67.

87 Ibid., 77.

88 Ibid., 67.

89 Deloria, *Playing Indian*, 103.

90 *Guide* 8, 7 (9 June 1928): 203.

91 *Council Fire* VI, 3 (n.d.): 51.

92 See E. Brian Titley, *A Narrow Vision: Duncan Campbell Scott and the Administration of Indian Affairs in Canada* (Vancouver: UBC Press, 1986); and Hugh Shewell, *"Enough to Keep Them Alive": Indian Welfare in Canada, 1873–1965* (Toronto: University of Toronto Press, 2004).

93 Wall, "Totem Poles," 530. See also Wall, *Nurture of Nature*, 50.

94 *Canadian Girl Guide* (March 1925): 15.

95 Robert Baden-Powell, *Adventuring to Manhood*, 67.

96 *Girl Guides' Gazette* X, 115 (July 1923): 158.

97 Archives of the Ontario Council of the Girl Guides of Canada – Guides du Canada, Mrs. Routledge's scrapbook (1930s), undated article from unknown Toronto newspaper: "Girl Guides Had Big Time at Camp on Medway River."

98 Archives of the Manitoba Council of the Girl Guides of Canada – Guides du Canada, Marjorie Hoskins scrapbook, 1938–39, "Girl Guides," *Winnipeg Tribune*, 23 July 1938.

99 Constance Backhouse, *Colour-Coded: A Legal History of Racism in Canada, 1900–1950* (Toronto, Buffalo, and London: University of Toronto Press, 1999), 63 and 100. See also Katherine Pettipas, *Severing the Ties That Bind: Government Repression of Indigenous Religious Ceremonies on the Prairies* (Winnipeg: University of Manitoba Press, 1994); and Wall, "Totem Poles," 539.

100 McCallum, "To Make Good Canadians," 156; Celia Haig-Brown, *Resistance and Renewal: Surviving the Indian Residential School* (Vancouver: Arsenal Pulp Press, 1998). See also Jennifer Helgren, "Native American and White Camp Fire Girls Enact Modern Girlhood, 1910–39," *American Quarterly* 66, 2 (June 2014): 333–60.

101 Mary Jane McCallum, "To Make Good Canadians: Girl Guiding in Indian Residential Schools" (MA thesis, Trent University, 2002), 157. McCallum, whose work focuses mostly on the post-Second World War period, also notes that Indigenous Guides used money earned from the sale of their "Guide" crafts to support their own communities as well as Guide activities. In 1944, for example, a group of Maliseet Guides used the money they had earned from selling knitted goods to buy a movie projector for their village hall.

102 Fiona Paisley, "Childhood and Race: Growing Up in the Empire," in *Gender and Empire*, ed. Philippa Levine (Oxford: Oxford University Press, 2004), 255.

103 Elizabeth Graham, ed., *The Mush Hole: Life at Two Indian Residential Schools* (Waterloo, ON: Heffle Publishing, 1997), 386. This book also includes excerpts from reports written by the principal of the Mohawk Institute during the 1920s and 1930s that discuss the positive impact of Guiding on female students; unfortunately, most of the interviews cover a slightly later time period.

104 Carl Berger, "The True North Strong and Free," in *Nationalism in Canada*, ed. Peter Russell (Toronto: McGraw-Hill, 1966), 3–26.

105 Kerr, *Story of a Million Girls*, 29–30.

106 *Canadian Guider* 1, 7 (January 1933): 5.

107 Ibid.

108 Archives of the Manitoba Council of the Girl Guides of Canada – Guides du Canada (Winnipeg), Nightingale Patrol Logbook, 10 January 1929.

109 Storrs, *God's Galloping Girl*, 81–82.

110 Elizabeth Buettner writes that the educational (and, I would add, extracurricular) experiences of those white girls and adolescents who were not sent back to Britain for schooling are "underdocumented since many schools they attended were small-scale and are now defunct." See Elizabeth Buettner, *Empire Families: Britons and Late Imperial India* (Oxford and New York: Oxford University Press, 2004), 18.

111 David M. Pomfret, *Youth and Empire: Trans-Colonial Childhoods in British and French Asia* (Stanford: Stanford University Press, 2016); Buettner, *Empire Families*, 23–26; Dane Kennedy, *The Magic Mountains: Hill Stations and the British Raj* (Berkeley: University of California Press, 1996); Dane Kennedy, "The Perils of the Midday Sun: Climatic Anxieties in the Colonial Tropics," in *Imperialism and the Natural World*, ed. J.M. MacKenzie (Manchester: Manchester University Press, 1990), 118–40. See also Nupur Chaudhuri, "Memsahibs and Motherhood in Nineteenth-Century India," *Victorian Studies* 31, 4 (1988): 532–33.

112 *Girl Guides' Gazette* 1, 10 (October 1914): 9.

113 *Council Fire* VII, 3 (1932): 44.

114 *Guider* XX, 234 (June 1933): 219.

115 The first schools in Kalimpong were established in the nineteenth century by Scottish missionaries for white children, but by the interwar years there were also schools for Anglo-Indian and Indian boys and girls.

116 *Guider* XXIV, 280 (April 1937): 130.

117 *Council Fire* VII, 3 (1932): 45.

118 Procida, *Married to the Empire*, 111.

119 *Council Fire* VII, 3 (n.d.): 45; *Council Fire* VI, 3 (n.d.): 44.

120 Nandini Chandra, "The Pedagogic Imperative of Travel Writing in the Hindi World: Children's Periodicals, 1920–1950," *South Asia* 30, 2 (August 2007): 316–17.

121 I.O. Evans, *Woodcraft and World Service: Studies in Unorthodox Education – An Account of the Evolution of the Woodcraft Movements* (London: Noel Douglas, 1930), 167–69.

CHAPTER 5: THE MASS ORNAMENT

1 Archives of the Ontario Council of the Girl Guides of Canada – Guides du Canada (Toronto), "Monster Rally Is Held By Girl Guides When Their Work Reviewed," press clipping from an unknown newspaper dated 13 May 1933 in Mrs. Routledge's scrapbook.

2 Siegfried Kracauer, *The Mass Ornament: Weimar Essays*, edited and translated by Thomas Y. Levin (Cambridge, MA: Harvard University Press, 1995).

3 Tammy Proctor, *On My Honour: Scouts and Guides in Interwar Britain* (Philadelphia: American Philosophical Society, 2002), 68.

4 *Girl Guides' Gazette* XII, 140 (August 1925): 227.

5 Olave Baden-Powell, *Guide Links* (London: C. Arthur Pearson, 1936), 88.

6 Archives of the Ontario Council of the Girl Guides of Canada – Guides du Canada (Toronto), special events box, rallies and march pasts folder, Program: "Grand Rally, Toronto Division Girl Guides," University Arena, 28 April, 1928. 14; Girl Guiding UK Archives (London), *The Girl Guides Association (Incorporated by Royal Charter) Sixteenth Annual Report and Balance Sheet of the Committee of the Council for the Year ending December 31st, 1930.* Report from Kashmir, India. n.p. The participation of college and high school students in processions and demonstrations in Kashmir during the spring of 1930 is discussed in Ravinderjit Kaur, *Political Awakening in Kashmir* (Delhi: S.B. Nangia, 1996), 118–22.

7 Scout Association Archives (Gilwell Park), Diaries of Olave (St. Clair Soames) Baden-Powell, 29 January, 1937 and 5 June, 1937.

8 Girl Guiding UK Archives (London), Guide Association Archives, no. 11908. Logbook, Empire Day Rally, Nilgiri Division, Madras Province (Southern India), 1933. Press clipping from unknown newspaper: "Empire Day Rally at Wellington: Lady Beatrix Inspects Guides and Blue Birds."

9 Strictly enforced gender divisions also characterized the mixed-sex marches and tableaux organized by other late nineteenth- and early twentieth-century British and dominion youth organizations, as shown in Simon Sleight, *Young People and Public Space in Melbourne, 1870–1914* (Farnham, Surrey: Ashgate, 2013), 198.

10 Girl Guiding UK Archives (London), 8th Battersea Company Swallow Patrol Diary, 1928–30, 10 December 1929.

11 Michael Woods, "Performing Power: Local Politics and the Taunton Pageant of 1928," *Journal of Historical Geography* 25, 1 (1999): 58.

12 H.V. Nelles, *The Art of Nation-Building: Pageantry and Spectacle at Quebec's Tercentenary* (Toronto: University of Toronto Press, 2000); David Glassberg, *American Historical Pageantry: The Uses of Tradition in the Early Twentieth Century* (Chapel Hill and London: University of North Carolina Press, 1990).

13 Deborah Sugg Ryan, "'Pageantitis': Frank Lascelles' 1907 Oxford Historical Pageant, Visual Spectacle and Popular Memory," *Visual Culture in Britain* 8, 2 (Winter 2007): 63–82.

14 Paul Readman, "The Place of the Past in English Culture, c. 1890–1914," *Past and Present* 186 (February 2005): 176.

15 *Girl Guides' Gazette* XIII, 150 (June 1926): 163.

16 Guiding UK Archives (London), Festival and Rally Program Collection, "Hertfordshire Girl Guides' County Rally and Pageant, Hatfield Park, 13 June 1931," 15–17.

17 Ibid., 19.

18 Jane Nicholas, "Gendering the Jubilee: Gender and Modernity in the Diamond Jubilee of Confederation Celebrations, 1927," *Canadian Historical Review* 90, 2 (June 2009): 249; David Glassberg, *American Historical Pageantry: The Uses of Tradition in the Early Twentieth Century* (Chapel Hill and London: University of North Carolina Press, 1990), 39.

19 Robert Baden-Powell, *Scouting for Boys: The Original 1908 Edition,* ed. Elleke Boehmer (Oxford: Oxford University Press, 2005), 214.

20 *Guider* XIX, 219 (March 1932): 100.

21 Girl Guiding UK Archives (London), Festival and Rally Program Collection, Program: Essex Girl Guides Rally, 2 July 1932, Thorndon Park, Brentwood.

22 Girl Guiding UK Archives (London), *The Girl Guides Association Twenty-Third Annual Report and Balance Sheet of the Committee of the Council for the Year ending December 31st, 1937,* 12.

23 Nicholas, "Gendering the Jubilee"; Nelles, *Art of Nation-Building*, chap. 7; Robert Cupido, "Appropriating the Past: Pageants, Politics, and the Diamond Jubilee of Confederation," *Journal of the Canadian Historical Association* 9 (1998): 155–86.

24 Ken Osborne, "'Where Are the Ancient Pieties and Loyalties of the Race?' A 1923 Report on Teaching Civics," *Canadian Social Studies* 36, 1 (Fall 2001), https://sites.educ.ualberta.ca/css/Css_36_1/CLvoices_from_the_past.htm.

25 *Girl Guides' Gazette* X, 115 (July 1923): 157.

26 Ibid.

27 Ibid.

28 Cupido, "Appropriating the Past," 155–86.

29 Colin M. Coates and Cecilia Morgan, *Heroines and History: Representations of Madeleine de Verchères and Laura Secord* (Toronto: University of Toronto Press, 2002).

30 Roger Mackarness, "Loyalty," in *The Guiding Book*, ed. Ann Kindersley (London: Hodder and Stoughton Ltd., n.d.), 50; Mary I. Houston, "On the Wings of Imagination," in *The Guiding Book*, ed. Ann Kindersley (London: Hodder and Stoughton Ltd., n.d.), 66.

31 Katie Pickles, "The Old and New on Parade: Mimesis, Queen Victoria, and Carnival Queens on Victoria Day in Interwar Victoria," in *Contact Zones: Aboriginal and Settler Women in Canada's Colonial Past* (Vancouver: UBC Press, 2005), 275.

32 Barbara Bush, "Gender and Empire: The Twentieth Century," in *Gender and Empire*, ed. Philippa Levine (Oxford: Oxford University Press, 2004), 86–87.

33 *Girl Guides' Gazette* X, 115 (July 1923): 157.

34 Nelles, *Art of Nation-Building*, 164–93.

35 Girl Guiding UK Archives (London), India Folder, speech delivered by Lady Baden-Powell at the Girl Guides Rally held at 5:00 p.m. on Monday, 22 February 1937, in the Government House, Nagpur.

36 Charlotte MacDonald, "Body and Self: Learning to Be Modern in 1920s–1930s Britain," *Women's History Review* 22, 2 (2013): 267–79; Ina Zweiniger-Bargielowska, "The Making of a Modern Female Body: Beauty, Health and Fitness in Interwar Britain," *Women's History Review* 20, 2 (April 2011): 299–317; Jill Julius Matthews, "They Had Such a Lot of Fun: The Women's League of Health and Beauty between the Wars," *History Workshop Journal* 30, 1 (1990): 22–54.

37 Robert Baden-Powell, *Girl Guiding: A Handbook for Brownies, Guides, Rangers, and Guiders* (London: C. Arthur Pearson Ltd., 1931), 9.

38 Carey Watt, "'No Showy Muscles': The Boy Scouts and the Global Dimensions of Physical Culture and Bodily Health in Britain and Colonial India," in *Scouting Frontiers: Youth and the Scout Movement's First Century*, ed. Nelson R. Block and Tammy M. Proctor (Newcastle-Upon-Tyne: Cambridge Scholars Press, 2009), 121–42.

39 Girl Guiding UK Archives (London), Rally and Festival Program Collection, Program: Girl Guide Victory Rally, Royal Albert Hall, 4 November 1919.

40 *Canadian Guider* 4, 2 (March 1936): 3.

41 Archives of the Ontario Council of the Girl Guides of Canada – Guides du Canada (Toronto), Special Events Box, Rallies and March Pasts Folder, Program: 16th Rally of the Montreal Division Girl Guides, Montreal Forum, 14 May 1938.

42 Girl Guiding UK Archives (London), *The Girl Guides Association (Incorporated by Royal Charter) Thirteenth Annual Report and Balance Sheet of the Committee of the Council for the Year ending December 31st, 1927*, 111.

43 Girl Guiding UK Archives (London), Logbook presented to Miss Watson, Bangalore District Commissioner, 1932–34.
44 Anne Bloomfield, "Drill and Dance as Symbols of Imperialism," in *Making Imperial Mentalities: Socialization and British Imperialism*, ed. J.A. Mangan (Manchester: Manchester University Press, 1990), 84.
45 Quoted in Bloomfield, "Drill and Dance as Symbols of Imperialism," 84.
46 Girl Guiding UK Archives (London), Festival and Rally Program Collection, Essex Girl Guides Rally, 2 July 1932, Thorndon Park, Brentwood.
47 "The Princess Royal at Torquay, 1937," http://www.britishpathe.com/video/the-princess-royal-at-torquay/query/%22girl+guide%22.
48 Archives of the Ontario Council of the Girl Guides of Canada – Guides du Canada (Toronto), Special Events Box, Rallies and March Pasts Folder, Program: Grand Rally – Toronto Division Girl Guides, University Arena, 8 April 1932; Archives of the Ontario Council of the Girl Guides of Canada – Guides du Canada (Toronto), Special Events Box, Rallies and March Pasts Folder, Program: Middlesex-Elgin Divisional Girl Guides Rally, Queen's Park, London, Ontario, Saturday, 26 May 1934.
49 Archives of the Ontario Council of the Girl Guides of Canada – Guides du Canada (Toronto), Special Events Box, Rallies and March Pasts Folder, Program: 16th Rally of the Montreal Division Girl Guides, Montreal Forum, 14 May 1938; Carl Berger, "The True North Strong and Free," in *Nationalism in Canada*, ed. Peter Russell (Toronto: McGraw-Hill, 1966), 3–26.
50 Sudipa Topdar, "Knowledge and Governance: Political Socialization of the Indian Child within Colonial Schooling and Nationalist Contestations in India, 1870–1925" (PhD diss., University of Michigan, 2010), chap. 3; Satadru Sen, "Schools, Athletes and Confrontation: The Student Body in Colonial India," in *Confronting the Body: The Politics of Physicality in Colonial and Post-Colonial India*, ed. James H. Mills and Satadru Sen (London: Anthem Press, 2004), 58–79.
51 Franzisca Roy, "International Utopia and National Discipline: Youth and Volunteer Movements in Interwar South Asia," in *The Internationalist Moment: South Asia, Worlds, and World Views*, ed. Ali Raza, Franziska Roy, and Benjamin Zachariah (Delhi: Sage, 2015), 150–87.
52 See, for example, the work of Satadru Sen, Carey Watt, Joseph Alter, and John Rosselli.
53 *Guide* XVII, 6 (20 May 1937): 164.
54 Marzia Casolari, "Hindutva's Foreign Tie-Up in the 1930s: Archival Evidence," *Economic and Political Weekly* 35, 4 (22 January 2000): 218–28.
55 Girl Guiding UK Archives (London), 8th Battersea Company Swallow Patrol Diary, 1928–30, 12 December 1929.
56 Ibid., 14 June 1930.
57 Ibid., 23 April 1928 and 14 June 1930.
58 See, for example, John Springhall, "Debate: Baden-Powell and the Scout Movement before 1920: Citizen Training or Soldiers of the Future?" *English Historical Review* 102, 405 (October 1987): 934–42; Anne Summers, "Scouts, Guides, and VADs: A Note in Reply to Allan Warren," *English Historical Review* 102, 405 (October 1987): 943–47; Allan Warren, "Sir Robert Baden-Powell, the Scout Movement and Citizen Training in Great Britain, 1900–1920," *English Historical Review* 101, 399 (April 1986): 376–98.
59 Carey Watt, "'No Showy Muscles': The Boy Scouts and the Global Dimensions of Physical Culture and Bodily Health in Britain and Colonial India," in *Scouting Frontiers: Youth and*

the Scout Movement's First Century, ed. Nelson R. Block and Tammy M. Proctor (Newcastle-Upon-Tyne: Cambridge Scholars Press, 2009), 130–31; Brad Beaven, *Leisure, Citizenship, and Working-Class Men in Britain, 1850–1945* (Manchester: Manchester University Press, 2005), 95–96.

60 Girl Guiding UK Archives (London), *Girl Guides Annual Report, 1934,* 10.

61 Joan Jacobs Brumberg, *The Body Project: An Intimate History of American Girls* (New York: Random House, 1997). The literature on fascist youth groups is vast. Relevant texts include Michael H. Kater, *Hitler Youth* (Cambridge, MA: Harvard University Press, 2006); Dagmar Reese, *Growing Up Female in Nazi Germany,* translated by William Templar (Ann Arbor: University of Michigan Press, 2006); Victoria De Grazia, *How Fascism Ruled Women: Italy, 1922–1945* (Berkeley: University of California Press, 1993).

62 Franzisca Roy, "International Utopia and National Discipline: Youth and Volunteer Movements in Interwar South Asia," in *The Internationalist Moment: South Asia, Worlds, and World Views,* ed. Ali Raza, Franziska Roy, and Benjamin Zachariah (Delhi: Sage, 2015), 165; Mark Moss, *Manliness and Militarism: Educating Young Boys in Ontario for War* (Don Mills, ON: Oxford University Press, 2001); Bloomfield, "Drill and Dance as Symbols of Imperialism."

63 Charlotte MacDonald, "Putting Bodies on the Line: Marching Spaces in Cold War Culture," in *Sites of Sport: Space, Place, Experience,* ed. Patricia Vertinsky and John Bale (London and New York: Routledge, 2004), 93.

64 Robert Baden-Powell, *Girl Guiding,* 79.

65 *Drill for Girl Guides* (London: The Girl Guides Association, 1932), 4.

66 See, for example, "Simple Drill: The Formation of a Horse-Shoe without Colours," in *Guider* XVIII, 206 (February 1931): 50.

67 William H. McNeill, *Keeping Together in Time: Dance and Drill in Human History* (Cambridge, MA: Harvard University Press, 1995), 66.

68 *Guider* XVIII, 215 (November 1931): 417.

69 Quoted in *Guider* XX, 236 (August 1933): 314.

70 *Guider* XXII, 259 (July 1935): 314.

71 *Guider* XXI, 248 (August 1934): 330.

72 *Guider* XXIII, 273 (September 1936): 362.

73 *Evening Standard,* 15 May 1928.

74 Ibid.

75 Ibid.

76 Reprinted in *Guider* XV, 175 (July 1928), n.p.

77 *Guider* XXIII, 267 (March 1936): 96.

78 *Guider* XXIII, 268 (April 1936): 136.

79 Ibid.

80 Alison Norman, "Race, Gender and Colonialism: Public Life among the Six Nations of Grand River, 1899–1939" (PhD diss., University of Toronto, 2010), 180.

81 For more on this group of Guides and Brownies, see Kristine Alexander, "Picturing Girlhood and Empire," in *Colonial Girlhood in Literature, Culture and History, 1840–1950,* ed. Kristine Moruzi and Michelle Smith (Basingstoke: Palgrave Macmillan, 2014), 197–213.

82 Anglican Church of Canada, General Synod Archives (Toronto), Logbook of the First Hay River Guide Company, 1934–36, 4 June 1935, 17 October 1935, 23 April 1936.

83 Archives of the Manitoba Council of the Girl Guides of Canada – Guides du Canada, Nightingale Patrol Logbook, 1928–29, 9 October 1928.

84 References to Empire Day rallies in these three places appear regularly in the Guide Association's Annual Reports throughout the 1920s and 1930s. See, for instance, *Girl Guides Annual Report, 1925*, 276; *Girl Guides Annual Report, 1933*, 164–66.

85 Alan Trevithick, "Some Structural and Sequential Aspects of the British Imperial Assemblages at Delhi: 1877–1911," *Modern Asian Studies* 24, 3 (1990): 562.

86 Girl Guiding UK Archives (London), "Empire Day Rally at Wellington: Lady Beatrix Inspects Guides and Blue Birds," press clipping from an unknown, undated newspaper in Logbook, Empire Day Rally, Nilgiri Division, Madras Province (Southern India), 1933.

87 Archives of the Ontario Council of the Girl Guides of Canada – Guides du Canada, "Lady Bessborough Takes Salute at Girl Guide Rally: Nearly 800 Members of Movement Give Fine Demonstration of Training They Have Received," press clipping from an unknown newspaper dated 13 May 1933 in Mrs. Routledge's scrapbook.

88 Archives of the Ontario Council of the Girl Guides of Canada – Guides du Canada, Special Events Box, Rallies and March Pasts Folder, "District Guides Hold Grand Rally: Hundreds Take Part in Program – Chief Commissioner for Dominion Present," *Hamilton Spectator*, 21 April 1933.

89 Harold Stovin, *Totem: The Exploitation of Youth* (London: Methuen and Co. Ltd., 1935), 7–8.

90 Quoted in WAGGGS Archives (London), *The World Association of Girl Guides and Girl Scouts Third Biennial Report: 1st July, 1932 to 30th June, 1932*, 49.

91 Tim Jeal, *Baden-Powell: Founder of the Boy Scouts* (New Haven and London: Yale University Press, 1989), 544–45.

92 Roy, "International Utopia and National Discipline," 186.

CHAPTER 6: IMPERIAL AND INTERNATIONAL SISTERHOOD

1 *Girl Guides' Gazette* XII, 138 (July 1925): n.p.

2 *Guider* XVI, 183 (March 1929): 82.

3 *Canadian Girl Guide* (September 1930): 13.

4 *Indian Ladies' Magazine* VII, 1 (January–February 1934): 332.

5 It was also, as several scholars have noted, central to the Boy Scout movement. See, for example, Scott Johnston, "Courting Public Favour: The Boy Scout Movement and the Accident of Internationalism, 1907–29," *Historical Research* 88, 241 (August 2015): 508–29; Mischa Honeck, "An Empire of Youth: American Boy Scouts in the World, 1910–1960," *Bulletin of the German Historical Institute* 52 (Spring 2013): 95–112; Eduard Vallory, *World Scouting: Educating for Global Citizenship* (Basingstoke: Palgrave, 2012). See also the chapters by Elena Jackson Albarrán and Christina Wu in Richard Ivan Jobs and David M. Pomfret, eds., *Transnational Histories of Youth in the Twentieth Century* (New York: Palgrave Macmillan, 2015).

6 This point was inspired by Harald Fischer-Tiné, "Global Civil Society and the Forces of Empire: The Salvation Army, British Imperialism and the 'Pre-History' of NGOs (c. 1880–1920)," in *Competing Visions of World Order: Global Moments and Movements, 1880s–1930s*, ed. Sebastian Conrad and Dominic Sachsenmaier (London: Palgrave Macmillan, 2007), 53.

7 Daniel Laqua, *The Age of Internationalism and Belgium, 1880–1930: Peace, Progress and Prestige* (Manchester: Manchester University Press, 2015). See also Daniel Laqua, ed.,

Internationalism Reconfigured: Transnational Ideas and Movements between the World Wars (London and New York: I.B. Tauris, 2011).

8 Frank Trentmann, "After the Nation-State: Citizenship, Empire and Global Coordination in the New Internationalism, 1914–1930," in *Beyond Sovereignty: Britain, Empire and Transnationalism, c. 1880–1950,* ed. Kevin Grant, Philippa Levine, and Frank Trentmann (Houndmills, Basingstoke: Palgrave Macmillan, 2007), 46; Akira Iriye, *Cultural Internationalism and World Order* (Baltimore: Johns Hopkins University Press, 1997), 43; Daniel Gorman, *The Emergence of International Society in the 1920s* (Cambridge: Cambridge University Press, 2012). The work of Angela Woollacott and, especially, Fiona Paisley on women and internationalism has also been helpful here.

9 Robert Baden-Powell, *Girl Guiding: The Official Handbook* (London: C. Arthur Pearson Ltd., 1938), 54. For a different analysis of the movement's rhetoric of sisterhood, see Janice N. Brownfoot, "Sisters under the Skin: Imperialism and the Emancipation of Women in Malaya, c. 1891–1941," in *Making Imperial Mentalities: Socialisation and British Imperialism,* ed. J.A. Mangan (Manchester: Manchester University Press, 1990), 46–73. Timothy Parsons shows how African Scouts used the Fourth Scout Law (about brotherhood) to challenge racial discrimination. See Timothy Parsons, *Race, Resistance, and the Boy Scout Movement in British Colonial Africa* (Athens: Ohio University Press, 2004).

10 Antoinette Burton, *Burdens of History: British Feminists, Indian Women, and Imperial Culture, 1865–1915* (Chapel Hill and London: University of North Carolina Press, 1994); Julia Bush, *Edwardian Ladies and Imperial Power* (London and New York: Leicester University Press, 2000).

11 This shift also occurred in a number of other women's organizations during the interwar years and is discussed in Fiona Paisley's work on the Pan-Pacific Women's Association as well as in Angela Woollacott, "Inventing Commonwealth and Pan-Pacific Feminisms: Australian Women's Internationalist Activism in the 1920s–30s," in *Feminisms and Internationalism,* ed. Mrinalini Sinha, Donna J. Guy, and Angela Woollacott, 81–104 (Oxford: Blackwell, 1999). See also Marie Sandell, *The Rise of Women's Transnational Activism: Identity and Sisterhood between the World Wars* (London and New York: I.B. Tauris, 2015).

12 Girl Guiding UK Archives (London), Festival and Rally Program Collection, Program: Kent County Rally, Knole Park, Sevenoaks (by kind permission of Lord Sackville), Saturday, 11 July 1936; *Guider* XXIII, 274 (October 1936): 361.

13 Archives of the World Association of Girl Guides and Scouts (London), *World Association of Girl Guides and Girl Scouts First Biennial Report: July 1st 1928 to June 30th 1930 and General Historical Sketch,* 2.

14 Girl Guiding UK Archives (London), *The Girl Guides' Annual Report, 1921,* 54.

15 An example from March 1929: "Mrs. Duggan (Prov. Com. for Quebec), Mrs. Green (Com. in Nigeria), Mrs. Clarke (Com. in Northern Rhodesia) and Mrs. Francis (Commissioner in British Guiana) to lunch with me at the Rubens [Hotel]." See Scout Association Archives (Gilwell Park), Diary of Olave (St. Clair Soames) Baden-Powell, 19 March 1929.

16 Tammy M. Proctor, *On My Honour: Scouts and Guides in Interwar Britain* (Philadelphia: American Philosophical Society, 2002), 131.

17 Archives of the Ontario Council of the Girl Guides of Canada – Guides du Canada (Toronto), *The World Association of Girl Guides and Girl Scouts,* 4th ed. (London: WAGGGS, 1951), 2.

18 Ibid.

19 Girl Guiding UK Archives (London), Canada Folder, copy of letter dated 6 October 1937 from Olave Baden-Powell to Sarah Warren (Canadian Chief Commissioner).

20 Ruth Levitas, "The Imaginary Reconstitution of Society, or, Why Sociologists and Others Should Take Utopia More Seriously," lecture, University of Bristol, 24 October 2005. http://www.bristol.ac.uk/media-library/sites/spais/migrated/documents/inaugural.pdf; Peter Kraftl, "Young People, Hope and Childhood-Hope," *Space and Culture* 11 (2008): 81–92.

21 Krishan Kumar, *Utopianism* (Minneapolis: University of Minnesota Press, 1991), 9.

22 Robarts Library, University of Toronto, *Historical Sketch of Guiding in Canada*, 11.

23 *Girl Guides' Gazette*, IX, 106 (October 1922): 188.

24 The Eclaireuses were a French interdenominational girls' organization; they were paralleled in many ways by the Catholic Guides de France. For more on the Guides de France, see Marie-Thérèse Cheroutre, *Le scoutisme au féminin: Les guides de France, 1923–1998* (Paris: Les éditions du cerf, 2002).

25 *Council Fire* IV, 4 (October 1929): 28.

26 *Guider* XXIV, 279 (March 1937): 92.

27 Girl Guiding UK Archives (London), International Committee Minute Book, December 1935–May 1938, 12 April 1937.

28 Ibid., 13 May 1936, 14 October 1936, and 12 December 1938.

29 Tim Jeal, *Baden-Powell: Founder of the Boy Scouts* (New Haven and London: Yale University Press, 1989), 547; Michael Rosenthal, *The Character Factory: Baden-Powell's Boy Scouts and the Imperative of Empire* (New York: Pantheon Books, 1986), 277.

30 Penny Tinkler shows that British Girl Guides were encouraged to compare themselves to "enemy" girls and Guides from allied nations during the Second World War, but my research so far has made it clear that comparisons between British and "colonial" Guides (and between Guides in different colonial locations) were both made and encouraged in Guide publications during the 1920s and 1930s. See Penny Tinkler, "English Girls and the International Dimensions of British Citizenship in the 1940s," *European Journal of Women's Studies* 8, 1 (2001): 77–94. International Guiding (especially in the post-Second World War period) is also discussed in Tammy M. Proctor, *Scouting for Girls: A Century of Girl Guides and Girl Scouts* (Santa Barbara, CA: ABC-Clio, 2009), chap. 6.

31 My thinking here draws on Mary Louise Pratt, *Imperial Eyes: Travel Writing and Transculturation* (London and New York: Routledge, 1992), 7.

32 Girl Guiding UK Archives (London), *Girl Guides Annual Report, 1934*, 12.

33 *Council Fire* XI, 4 (October 1936): 30.

34 Describing the Imperial Camp in her diary, the Chief Guide comments: "Had rather a difficult time owing to Robin's sister Agnes turning up and going about making trouble." See Scout Association Archives (Gilwell Park), Diary of Olave (St. Clair Soames) Baden-Powell, 14 July 1928.

35 *Council Fire* III, 3 (December 1928): 66. Fiona Paisley has shown that white delegates at Pan-Pacific Women's Association conferences similarly often commented on Asian women's dress. See Fiona Paisley, "Cultivating Modernity: Culture and Internationalism in Feminism's Pacific Age," *Journal of Women's History* 14, 3 (Autumn 2002): 116.

36 Girl Guiding UK Archives (London), no. 11845, Logbook: 1928 Imperial Camp at Foxlease by Captain Elsie Berger, 11 July 1928.

37 *Council Fire* III, 3 (December 1928): 66.
38 As Leila Rupp argues, the "dominant discourse within the transnational [women's] organizations – what has been called 'feminist orientalism' – lauded 'Western' societies as the pinnacle of progress for women in contrast to backward, repressive 'Eastern' ways. The very constructs of 'West' and 'East,' of course, polarized the world in a way that had little to do with geography and obscured the much more complex hierarchical rankings embodied in the dominant assumptions about progress, civilization, and the emancipation of women." See Leila J. Rupp, "Challenging Imperialism in International Women's Organizations, 1888–1945," *NWSA Journal* 8 (Spring 1996): 10.
39 *Council Fire* VI, 3 (n.d.): 40.
40 Lakshmi Mazumdar, *A Dream Came True* (New Delhi: The Bharat Scouts and Guides, 1997), 9.
41 Sumita Mukherjee, "The All-Asian Women's Conference 1931: Indian Women and Their Leadership of a Pan-Asian Feminist Organization," *Women's History Review* 26, 3 (2017): 13.
42 Paisley, "Cultivating Modernity," 126.
43 According to the 1935 Imperial Headquarters annual report, "Miss Rustomjee went to England on leave in order to refresh her training, and while there, attended the International Training at Adelboden and represented India at the Round Table Conference of Trainers. Her close touch with Imperial Headquarters and the experience gained at Trainings, both in England and the Continent[,] has proved most valuable to the Presidency. Miss Rustomjee returned after having gained the Red Cord Diploma." See Girl Guiding UK Archives (London), *Girl Guides Annual Report*, 1935, 178.
44 Antoinette Burton, *At the Heart of the Empire: Indians and the Colonial Encounter in Late Victorian Britain* (Berkeley: University of California Press, 1998).
45 *Council Fire* XI, 1 (January 1936): 10.
46 This statement, of course, applies especially to girls and women from the "peripheries." See Burton, *At the Heart of the Empire*; Angela Woollacott, *"To Try Her Fortune in London": Australian Women, Colonialism, and Modernity* (New York: Oxford University Press, 2001); Cecilia Morgan, "'A Wigwam to Westminster': Performing Mohawk Identity in Imperial Britain, 1890s–1990s," *Gender and History* 15, 2 (August 2003): 319–41.
47 Falk (Ida von Herrenschwand), *The Story of Our Chalet* (London: The World Association of Girl Guides and Girl Scouts, 1952), 4.
48 Fiona Paisley, "Glamour in the Pacific: Cultural Internationalism and Maori Politics at Pan-Pacific Women's Conferences in the 1950s," *Pacific Studies* 29, 1 / 2 (December 2006): 54–81. See also Verta Taylor and Leila J. Rupp, "Loving Internationalism: The Emotion Culture of Transnational Women's Organizations, 1888–1945," *Mobilization: An International Journal* 7, 2 (2002): 141–58.
49 Girl Guiding UK Archives (London), *The World Camp: Foxlease 1924* (London: The Girl Guides Association, 1924), 25.
50 *Girl Guides' Gazette* X, 117 (September 1923): 208.
51 *Girl Guides' Gazette* XI, 129 (September 1924): 249.
52 Yale Divinity School Archives, Lillian Picken Papers, RG 159, box 1, file 1: "Circular Letters Feb 1928–Aug 1930," letter dated 31 August 1929.
53 Falk, *The Story of Our Chalet*, 9.
54 *Girl Guides' Gazette* X, 116 (August 1923): 181.

55 Girl Guiding UK Archives (London), India Folder, speech delivered by Lady Baden-Powell at the Girl Guides Rally held at 5:00 p.m. on Monday, 22 February 1937, in the Government House, Nagpur.

56 *Canadian Guider* 3, 1 (January 1935): 2. "This is a voluntary contribution and one cent from each Guide in the Company is suggested as a suitable amount."

57 "Mrs. Chatterjee proposed: 'That the Chief Commissioner be asked to write to the Director of the World Bureau explaining India's financial difficulties.' Seconded by Mrs. Conran Smith, carried." See Girl Guiding UK Archives (London), minutes of meetings of the Indian Headquarters Executive Committee of the Girl Guides held at Lahore, 13–15 November 1933.

58 This building is still the headquarters of Girl Guiding UK.

59 This report states that the appeal to fund the construction of a new imperial headquarters (the estimated cost of which was seventy-four thousand pounds) was launched on 1 March 1929 and had reached forty-four thousand pounds by 1930. It outlines donations and loans from British businessmen, the Carnegie Trust, the Court of Common Council, the Orient Steam Navigation Company, and nine "prominent City of London Companies." Girl Guiding UK Archives (London), *The Girl Guides Association (Incorporated by Royal Charter) Sixteenth Annual Report and Balance Sheet of the Committee of the Council for the Year ending December 31st, 1930*, 18–20.

60 *Girl Guides' Gazette* IX, 103 (July 1922): 129.

61 Girl Guiding UK Archives (London), *The Girl Guides Association (Incorporated by Royal Charter) Eighteenth Annual Report and Balance Sheet of the Committee of the Council for the Year ending December 31st, 1932*, 160–68; Mary Jane McCallum, "To Make Good Canadians: Girl Guiding in Indian Residential Schools" (MA thesis, Trent University, 2002).

62 Leila Rupp, *Worlds of Women: The Making of an International Women's Movement* (Princeton: Princeton University Press, 1998), 52.

63 *Council Fire* V, 4 (October 1930): 99.

64 Ibid.

65 Ibid.

66 *Girl Guides' Gazette* X, 113 (May 1923): 99; X, 115 (July 1923): 156; X, 117 (September 1923): 203.

67 *Canadian Guider* 2, 3 (May 1934): 2; *Canadian Guider* 3, 4 (July 1935): 2.

68 *Council Fire* XI, 2 (April 1936): 13; IX, 3 (July 1934), 104; XIII, 2 (April 1938): 21.

69 Archives of the World Association of Girl Guides and Girl Scouts (London), *The World Association of Girl Guides and Girl Scouts Second Biennial Report: July 1st 1930 to June 30th 1932*, 16.

70 *Girl Guides' Gazette* XI, 132 (December 1924): 327.

71 Kristin L. Hoganson, *Consumers' Imperium: The Global Production of American Domesticity, 1865–1920* (Durham: University of North Carolina Press, 2007).

72 *Canadian Guider* 3, 3 (May 1935): 2.

73 Archives of the National Council of the Girl Guides of Canada – Guides du Canada (Toronto), *Canadian Council of the Girl Guides Association (Incorporated) Annual Report 1924*, 12.

74 Anglican Church of Canada, General Synod Archives (Toronto), Logbook of the First Hay River Guide Company, 1934–36, 14 June 1935 and 16 August 1935.

75 *Council Fire* IV, 2 (March 1929): 16.

76 Girl Guiding UK Archives (London), Canada Folder, "Extract from a letter from Lady Baden-Powell." [Likely 1935]

77 Mazumdar, *Dream Came True*, 83. This donation also testifies to the Guide movement's success in gaining the support of local elites, especially in the Princely States.

78 Girl Guiding UK Archives (London), *Girl Guides' Annual Report, 1923.* 269.

79 Girl Guiding UK Archives (London), *The Girl Guides Association (Incorporated by Royal Charter) Sixteenth Annual Report and Balance Sheet of the Committee of the Council for the Year ending December 31st, 1930*, 139.

80 Ibid., 138–47.

81 Mazumdar, *Dream Came True*, 85.

82 Ibid., 139.

83 McCallum, "To Make Good Canadians," 94.

84 Iriye, *Cultural Internationalism and World Order*, 69–70; Diana Selig, "World Friendship: Children, Parents, and Peace Education in America between the Wars," in *Children and War: A Historical Anthology*, ed. James Marten (New York and London: New York University Press, 2002), 135–46.

85 Archives of the National Council of the Girl Guides of Canada – Guides du Canada (Toronto), "Canadian Council, Girl Guides Association Annual Meeting, April 1923: Report of Organizing Secretary."

86 Girl Guiding UK Archives (London), *Girl Guides Annual Report, 1924*, 46.

87 Provincial Archives of Manitoba (Winnipeg), Girl Guides – Manitoba Council, 1926–1983, P 3467, Manitoba Council of the Girl Guides of Canada, 1925–28, minute book, 2 November 1927.

88 2nd Caversham Company Logbook, 12 December 1922. Quoted in Proctor, *Scouting for Girls*, 107.

89 A quote from the Chief Guide's diary in November 1933: "Ran up to London just to Broadcast from the BBC about Guides for ten minutes to India and the East. Marvellous thing to be able to talk to them like that!" See Scout Association Archives (Gilwell Park), Diary of Olave (St. Clair Soames) Baden-Powell, 4 November 1933.

90 Girl Guiding UK Archives (London), *Girl Guides Annual Report, 1934*, 20.

91 Girl Guiding UK Archives (London), *The Girl Guides Association Twenty-Third Annual Report and Balance Sheet of the Committee of the Council for the Year ending December 31st, 1937*, 12–13.

92 Neil Sutherland notes, for example, that, while radios were common in urban homes in interwar Canada, they remained relatively rare in a number of rural settings. See Neil Sutherland, "Popular Media in the Culture of English-Canadian Children in the Twentieth Century," *Historical Studies in Education/Revue d'histoire de l'éducation* 14, 1 (2002): 27.

93 Barbara Kelcey, *Alone in Silence: European Women in the Canadian North before 1940* (Montreal and Kingston: McGill-Queen's University Press, 2001), 32. Simon Potter also argues that the BBC's Empire Service failed to meet "the diverse expectations of audiences in different parts of the British world." See Simon J. Potter, "Who Listened When London Called? Reactions to the BBC Empire Service in Canada, Australia and New Zealand, 1932–1939," *Historical Journal of Film, Radio and Television* 28, 4 (October 2008): 475–87.

94 Robert Clarke, "The Idea of Celebrity Colonialism: An Introduction," in *Celebrity Colonialism: Fame, Power and Representation in Colonial and Postcolonial Cultures*, ed. Robert Clarke (Newcastle-Upon-Tyne: Cambridge Scholars Publishing, 2009), 1.

95 Girl Guiding UK Archives (London), *Girl Guides Annual Report*, 1935, 9–10.
96 Rose Kerr, *The Story of a Million Girls: Guiding and Girl Scouting around the World* (London: The Girl Guides Association, 1936), 28.
97 Charlotte Weber, "Unveiling Scheherazade: Feminist Orientalism in the International Alliance of Women, 1911–1950," *Feminist Studies* 27, 1 (2001): 125–27.
98 Olave Baden-Powell, *Guide Links* (London: C. Arthur Pearson Ltd., 1936), 151–53.
99 Ibid., 171.
100 The article's references to Merlyn's national-racial identity as well as her place of birth are proof of the complexities of racial categorization in late colonial India.
101 Archives of the Ontario Council of the Girl Guides of Canada – Guides du Canada (Toronto), scrapbook kept by Mrs. Verna Conant, 1909–36, "Indian Viceroy's Compound Rendezvous of Girl Guides: Toronto Girl Recipient of Interesting Correspondence from Guides in Calcutta," *Toronto Daily Star*, 27 August 1937.
102 Ibid.
103 Janet Aldis, *A Girl Guide Captain in India* (Madras: Methodist Publishing House, 1922), 1.
104 Ibid., 97. In this respect, they resemble the Victorian and Edwardian texts discussed in Kathryn Castle, *Britannia's Children: Reading Colonialism through Children's Books and Magazines* (Manchester: Manchester University Press, 1996).
105 Aldis, *Girl Guide Captain in India*, 245.
106 *Collins' Girl Guides Annual* (London and Glasgow: Collins' Clear-Type Press, 1923), 166.
107 Archives of the World Association of Girl Guides and Girl Scouts (London), *The World Association of Girl Guides and Girl Scouts Second Biennial Report: July 1st 1930 to June 30th 1932*, 7.
108 Simon Potter, "Webs, Networks, and Systems: Globalization and the Mass Media in the Nineteenth- and Twentieth-Century British Empire," *Journal of British Studies* 46 (July 2007): 638.

CONCLUSION

1 Unlike the movement's Imperial and International Conferences for leaders, World Camps for girls were not (and still are not) held at regular intervals. The first two were held at Foxlease in 1924 and at Camp Edith Macy in New York State in 1926.
2 The countries represented included England, Scotland, Ireland, Wales, Malta, India, Australia, New Zealand, Bermuda, Hong Kong, Kenya, Denmark, Norway, Suomi-Finland, the Netherlands, France, Switzerland, Poland, Estonia, and Lithuania.
3 Girl Guiding UK Archives (London), World Camps Box, letter dated 2 August 1939 from Miss Alison Duke (German interpreter) to Miss Gaskell and Company.
4 *Council Fire* XIV, 4 (October 1939): 52.
5 Girl Guiding UK Archives (London), World Camps Box, letter dated 29 July 1939 from Miss Duke (German Interpreter) to Miss Gaskell and Company. "At Cologne we had an unexpected surprise as we were received in state by the Hitler Youth girls!"
6 *Council Fire* XIV, 4 (October 1939): 55.
7 Girl Guiding UK Archives (London), International Committee Minute Book, June 1938–May 1945, 14 November 1938. This minute book also discusses the committee's efforts to reach out to fascist and communist youth groups in Italy and Russia.

8 Girl Guiding UK Archives (London), *The Girl Guides Association (Incorporated by Royal Charter) Twenty-Fifth Annual Report and Balance Sheet of the Committee of the Council for the Year ending December 31st, 1939*, 9.

9 Tammy H. Proctor, *Scouting for Girls: A Century of Girl Guides and Girl Scouts* (Santa Barbara, CA: PBC-Clio, 2009), 78.

10 WAGGGS Archives (London), *The World Association of Girl Guides and Girl Scouts Fourth Biennial Report: 1st July, 1938 to 30th June, 1940*, 26.

11 Girl Guiding was outlawed in Nazi-occupied territories. Guide groups from a number of European countries lost contact with WAGGGS during the war, including Poland, Bohemia, Moravia, the Baltic states, Denmark, Norway, Netherlands, Belgium, France, and Luxembourg.

12 Girl Guiding UK Archives (London), *The Girl Guides Association (Incorporated by Royal Charter) Twenty-Fifth Annual Report and Balance Sheet of the Committee of the Council for the Year ending December 31st, 1939*, 36.

13 See Janie Hampton, *How the Girl Guides Won the War* (London: HarperCollins, 2010).

14 *Council Fire* XIV, 4 (October 1939): 49.

15 Proctor, *Scouting for Girls*, 80–84. For more on Canadian Guide activities during the Second World War, see Dorothy Crocker, *All about Us: A Story of the Girl Guides of Canada* (Toronto: Girl Guides of Canada, 1990), 25–27.

16 For a brief discussion of Girl Scouting at Japanese internment camps in the United States, see Stephanie Bangarth, *Voices Raised in Protest: Defending North American Citizens of Japanese Ancestry, 1942–49* (Vancouver: UBC Press, 2008), 148–49.

17 Girl Guiding UK Archives (London), Canada Folder, extract of letter dated January 1943 from Miss Hannah and Miss Illlingworth to Miss Paterson about Guiding at Japanese Internment Camps.

18 Proctor, *Scouting for Girls*, 85.

19 Phyllis Stewart Brown, *All Things Uncertain: The Story of the GIS* (London: The Girl Guides Association, 1966), 11.

20 Proctor, *Scouting for Girls*, 88.

21 Ibid. These first trainees were from the United Kingdom, Australia, and New Zealand.

22 http://www.girton.cam.ac.uk/fellows-and-staff/life-fellows/alison-duke/. Duke, who remained involved with the Guide movement for most of her life, also never married.

23 Tim Jeal, *Baden-Powell: Founder of the Boy Scouts* (New Haven and London: Yale University Press, 1989), 566.

24 According to Tim Jeal, the Chief Guide never accepted her husband's death and she consoled herself by seeking "messages" from him through two mediums from 1942 on. Jeal writes that Baden-Powell "would have been appalled had he ever known that it would one day be asserted that he predicted the arrival of 'much higher grades of beings' in flying saucers. Nor would he have relished reports of his conversations with George VI and Christ." See Jeal, *Baden-Powell*, 574.

25 For more on Our Cabaña, see Marcia Chatelain, "International Sisterhood: Cold War Girl Scouts Encounter the World," *Diplomatic History* 38, 2 (2014): 261–70.

26 Jeal, *Baden-Powell*, 577. For more on the Scout movement in Kenya during decolonization, see Timothy H. Parsons, "No More English Than the Postal System: The Kenya Boy Scout Movement and the Transfer of Power, 1956–1964," *Africa Today*, 51, 3 (2005); Timothy H. Parsons, *Race, Resistance, and the Boy Scout Movement in British Colonial Africa* (Athens:

Ohio University Press, 2004).

27 Lakshmi Mazumdar, ed., *A Dream Came True* (New Delhi: The Bharat Scouts and Guides, 1997), 92–93.

28 Ibid., 89.

29 See https://www.wagggs.org/en/about-us/who-we-are/. Membership numbers in Canada and the United Kingdom, in contrast to India, have never again reached the highs achieved in the 1920s and 1930s.

30 See http://www.bsgindia.org.

31 See http://www.girlguiding.org.uk/about_us/what_makes_guiding_special.aspx.

32 See http://www.girlguides.ca/en/who_we_are.

33 *Girlguiding UK Today* 5 (Autumn 2009).

34 http://www.girlguides.ca/web/uploads/File/Focus_Newsletter/focus_spring_2010.pdf.

35 These goals, determined in 2000–01, are: eradicate extreme poverty and hunger; achieve universal primary education; promote gender equality and empower women; reduce child mortality; improve maternal health; combat HIV/AIDS, malaria, and other diseases; ensure environmental sustainability; and develop a global partnership for development. See http://www.un.org/millenniumgoals.

36 See https://www.wagggs.org/en/what-we-do/speak-out/get-involved/un-teams/.

37 Margaret Atwood, *Lady Oracle* (Toronto: McClelland and Stewart, 1976), 56.

BIBLIOGRAPHY

ARCHIVAL SOURCES

All-India Women's Conference Library and Archives (Delhi)
    Annual Reports
    Conference Reports

Anglican Church of Canada, General Synod Archives (Toronto)
    Logbook of the First Hay River Guide Company, 1934–36

Archives of the Manitoba Council of the Girl Guides of Canada – Guides du Canada
    (Winnipeg)
    Oral History Collection
    Photograph Collection
    Scrapbook Collection

Archives of the Ontario Council of the Girl Guides of Canada – Guides du Canada
    (Toronto)
    Collection of Rally Programs
    Scrapbook Collection

Archives of the National Council of the Girl Guides of Canada – Guides du Canada
    (Toronto)
    Annual Reports
    Dominion Secretary's Reports
    Photograph Collection
    Scrapbook Collection

Archives of the New Brunswick Council of the Girl Guides of Canada (St. John)
    Scrapbook Collection

Archives of the World Association of Girl Guides and Girl Scouts (London)
  Biennial Reports of the World Association of Girl Guides and Girl Scouts

Girl Guiding UK Archives (London)
  Annual Reports
  Collection of Rally Programs
  Correspondence
  Guide Company Record Books
  Logbook and Diary Collection
  Photograph Collection
  Scrapbook Collection
  World Camps Collection

Glenbow Archives Photographic Collection

Provincial Archives of Manitoba (Winnipeg)
  Manitoba Council Minutebooks
  Annual Reports

Scout Association Archives (Gilwell Park, UK)
  Diaries of Olave (St. Clair Soames) Baden-Powell

Yale Divinity School (New Haven, Connecticut)
  Lillian Picken Papers

PERIODICALS AND NEWSPAPERS

Canadian Girl Guide
Canadian Guider
Council Fire
Indian Ladies' Magazine
Girl Guides' Gazette
Guide
Guider
Scouter
Times of London

OTHER SOURCES

Ahmed, Sara. *The Promise of Happiness*. Durham and London: Duke University Press, 2010.
Aldis, Janet. *A Girl Guide Captain in India*. Madras: Methodist Publishing House, 1922.
Alexander, Kristine. "Can the Girl Guide Speak? The Perils and Pleasures of Looking for Children's Voices in Archival Research." *Jeunesse: Young People, Texts, Cultures* 4, 1 (Summer 2012): 132–44.
—. "The Girl Guide Movement and Imperial Internationalism in the 1920s and 1930s." *Journal of the History of Childhood and Youth* 2, 1 (2009): 37–63.
—. "An Honour and a Burden: Canadian Girls and the Great War." In *Canadian and Newfoundland Women and the First World War*, ed. Sarah Glassford and Amy Shaw, 173–94. Vancouver: UBC Press, 2012.

—. "Une pédagogie des rôles sociaux dans le guidisme Canadien anglophone." In *Guidisme, scoutisme et coeducation: Pour une histoire de la mixité dans les mouvements de jeunesse*, ed. Thierry Scaillet, Sophie Wittemans, and Françoise Rosart, 195–210. Louvain-la-Neuve, Belgium: Bruylant-Academia, 2006.

—. "Picturing Girlhood and Empire: The Girl Guide Movement and Photography." In *Colonial Girlhood in Literature, Culture and History, 1840–1950*, ed. Kristine Moruzi and Michelle Smith, 197–213. Basingstoke: Palgrave Macmillan, 2014.

—. "Similarity and Difference at Girl Guide Camps in England, Canada and India." In *Scouting Frontiers: Youth and the Scout Movement's First Century*, ed. Nelson R. Block and Tammy M. Proctor, 106–20. Cambridge: Cambridge Scholars Publishing, 2009.

Alexander, Sally. "The Mysteries and Secrets of Women's Bodies: Sexual Knowledge in the First Half of the Twentieth Century." In *Modern Times: Reflections on a Century of English Modernity*, ed. Mica Nava and Alan O'Shea, 161–74. London: Routledge, 1996.

Alter, Joseph S. *The Wrestler's Body: Identity and Ideology in North India*. Berkeley: University of California Press, 1992.

Anagol, Padma. "The Emergence of the Female Criminal in India: Infanticide and Survival under the Raj." *History Workshop Journal* 53 (2002): 73–93.

Anderson, E.M. *Practical Camp Cookery for Guides and Guiders*. Glasgow: Brown, Son and Ferguson, 1936.

Anderson, H. Allen. "Ernest Thompson Seton and the Woodcraft Indians." *Journal of American Culture* 8, 1 (1985): 43–50.

Anonymous. *Campcraft for Girl Guides*. London: The Girl Guides Association, 1933.

Anonymous. *Collins' Girl Guides Annual*. London: Collins' Clear-Type Press, n.d.

Anonymous. *Drill for Girl Guides*. London: The Girl Guides Association, 1932.

Anonymous. *How Guides Camp*. London: The Girl Guides Association, 1935.

Anonymous. *Our Chalet, 1932–1992*. Cambridge: The World Association of Girl Guides and Girl Scouts, 1992.

Anonymous. *The Story of Our Chalet, Olave House, Our Cabaña: Three World Centres for Girl Guides and Girl Scouts*. London: The World Association of Girl Guides and Girl Scouts, 1961.

Anonymous. *The World Camp: Foxlease 1924*. London: The Girl Guides Association, 1924.

Appadurai, Arjun. *Modernity at Large: Cultural Dimensions of Globalization*. Minneapolis: University of Minnesota Press, 1996.

Attar, Dena. *Wasting Girls' Time: The History and Politics of Home Economics*. London: Virago, 1990.

Atwood, Margaret. *Lady Oracle*. Toronto: McClelland and Stewart, 1976.

Auchmuty, Rosemary. "You're a Dyke, Angela! Elsie J. Oxenham and the Rise and Fall of the Schoolgirl Story." In *Not a Passing Phase: Reclaiming Lesbians in History 1840–1945*, ed. The Lesbian History Group, 119–40. London: The Women's Press, 1989.

Avery, Gillian. *Childhood's Pattern: A Study of the Heroes and Heroines of Children's Fiction, 1770–1950*. London: Hodder and Stoughton, 1975.

Backhouse, Constance. *Colour-Coded: A Legal History of Racism in Canada, 1900–1950*. Toronto, Buffalo, and London: University of Toronto Press, 1999.

Baden-Powell, Agnes, and Robert Baden-Powell. *Pamphlet A: Baden-Powell Girl Guides, a Suggestion for Character Training for Girls*, 1909.

–. *Pamphlet B: Baden-Powell Girl Guides, a Suggestion for Character Training for Girls*, 1909.

Baden-Powell, Agnes. *The Handbook for Girl Guides: How Girls Can Help Build the Empire*. London: Thomas Nelson and Sons, 1912.

Baden-Powell, Olave. *Window on My Heart: The Autobiography of Olave, Lady Baden-Powell as Told to Mary Drewery*. London: Hodder and Stoughton, 1973.

–. *Guide Links*. London: C. Arthur Pearson Ltd., 1936.

–. *Training Girls as Guides: Hints for Commissioners and All Who Are Interested in the Welfare and Training of Girls*. London: C. Arthur Pearson Ltd., 1919.

Baden-Powell, Robert. *Adventuring to Manhood*. London: C. Arthur Pearson Ltd., 1936.

–. *Girl Guiding: A Handbook for Brownies, Guides, Rangers and Guiders*. London: C. Arthur Pearson Ltd., 1938.

–. *Girl Guiding: A Handbook for Brownies, Guides, Rangers and Guiders*. London: C. Arthur Pearson Ltd., 1931.

–. *Brownies or Blue Birds: A Handbook for Young Girl Guides*. London: C. Arthur Pearson Ltd., 1920.

–. *Steps to Girl Guiding: An Abridged Edition of the Official Handbook*. London: C. Arthur Pearson Ltd., n.d.

Bailey, Beth. *From Front Porch to Back Seat: Courtship in Twentieth-Century America*. Baltimore: Johns Hopkins University Press, 1989.

Baker, H.R. *The Common Birds of Ooty, Coonoor and Kotagiri, Written for the Girl-Guides*. Ootacamund, India: Ootacamund and Nilgiri Press, 1921.

Ballantyne, Tony. *Webs of Empire: Locating New Zealand's Colonial Past*. Vancouver: UBC Press, 2014.

Ballantyne, Tony, and Antoinette Burton. "Introduction: Bodies, Empires, and World Histories." In *Bodies in Contact: Rethinking Colonial Encounters in World History*, ed. Tony Ballantyne and Antoinette Burton, 1–16. Durham, NC: Duke University Press, 2005.

Bangarth, Stephanie. *Voices Raised in Protest: Defending North American Citizens of Japanese Ancestry, 1942–49*. Vancouver: UBC Press, 2008.

Bannerji, Himani. "Age of Consent and Hegemonic Social Reform." In *Gender and Imperialism*, ed. Clare Midgley, 21–44. Manchester: Manchester University Press, 1998.

Barlow, Tani E., Madeleine Yue Dong, Uta G. Poiger, Priti Ramamurthy, Lynn M. Thomas, and Alys Eve Weinbaum. "The Modern Girl around the World: A Research Agenda and Preliminary Findings." *Gender and History* 17, 2 (2005): 245–94.

Barne, Kitty. *Here Come the Girl Guides*. London: The Girl Guides Association, 1946.

Basu, Aparna, and Bharati Ray. *Women's Struggle: A History of the All India Women's Conference, 1927–1990*. New Delhi: Manohar Publications, 1990.

Baughan, Emily. "'Every Citizen of Empire Implored to Save the Children!' Empire, Internationalism and the Save the Children Fund in Interwar Britain." *Historical Research* 86, 231 (2013): 116–37.

Bayly, C.A., Sven Beckert, Matthew Connelly, Isabel Hofmeyr, Wendy Kozol, and Patricia Seed. "AHR Conversation: On Transnational History." *American Historical Review* 111, 5 (2006): 1441–64.

Beaumont, Catriona. "Citizens Not Feminists: The Boundary Negotiated between Citizenship and Feminism by Mainstream Women's Organizations in England, 1928–39." *Women's History Review* 9, 2 (2000): 411–29.

Beaven, Brad. *Leisure, Citizenship, and Working-Class Men in Britain, 1850–1945.* Manchester: Manchester University Press, 2005.

Berger, Carl. "The True North Strong and Free." In *Nationalism in Canada,* ed. Peter Russell, 3–26. Toronto: McGraw-Hill, 1966.

Bederman, Gail. *Manliness and Civilization: A Cultural History of Gender and Race in the United States, 1880–1917.* Chicago: University of Chicago Press, 1995.

Bienvenue, Louise. *Quand la jeunesse entre en scène: L'Action catholique avant la Révolution tranquille.* Montréal: Boréal, 2003.

Bingham, Adrian. *Gender, Modernity, and the Popular Press in Inter-War Britain.* Oxford: Clarendon Press, 2004.

–. "Stop the Flapper Vote Folly: Lord Rothermere, the *Daily Mail,* and the Equalization of the Franchise 1927–28." *Twentieth Century British History* 13, 1 (2002): 17–37.

Bloomfield, Anne. "Drill and Dance as Symbols of Imperialism." In *Making Imperial Mentalities: Socialisation and British Imperialism,* ed. J.A. Mangan, 74–95. Manchester: Manchester University Press, 1990.

Boehmer, Elleke. "The Text in the World, the World through the Text: Robert Baden-Powell's *Scouting for Boys.*" In *Ten Books That Shaped the British Empire: Creating an Imperial Commons,* ed. Antoinette Burton and Isabel Hofmeyr, 131–52. Durham and London: Duke University Press, 2014.

–. "Introduction." *Scouting for Boys: The Original 1908 Edition,* xi–xxxix. Oxford: Oxford University Press, 2005.

Bradbury, Bettina. "Colonial Comparisons: Rethinking Marriage, Civilization and Nation in Nineteenth-Century White Settler Societies." In *Rediscovering the British World,* ed. Phillip Buckner and R. Douglas Francis, 135–58. Calgary: University of Calgary Press, 2005.

Bratton, J.S. "British Imperialism and the Reproduction of Femininity in Girls' Fiction, 1900–1930." In *Imperialism and Juvenile Literature,* ed. Jeffrey Richards, 195–215. Manchester: Manchester University Press, 1989.

–. "Of England, Home, and Duty: The Image of England in Victorian and Edwardian Fiction." In *Imperialism and Popular Culture,* ed. John M. MacKenzie, 73–93. Manchester: Manchester University Press, 1986.

Briggs, Asa. "Samuel Smiles: The Gospel of Self-Help." *History Today* 37 (May 1987): 37–43.

Brown, Phyllis Stewart. *All Things Uncertain: The Story of the GIS* London: The Girl Guides Association, 1966.

Brownfoot, Janice N. "Sisters under the Skin: Imperialism and the Emancipation of Women in Malaya, c. 1891–1941." In *Making Imperial Mentalities: Socialisation and British Imperialism,* ed. J.A. Mangan, 46–73. Manchester: Manchester University Press, 1990.

Brumberg, Joan Jacobs. *The Body Project: An Intimate History of American Girls.* New York: Random House, 1997.

Buckley, Suzann. "Ladies or Midwives? Efforts to Reduce Infant and Maternal Mortality." In *A Not Unreasonable Claim: Women and Reform in Canada, 1880s–1920s,* ed. Linda Kealey, 131–50. Toronto: Women's Press, 1979.

Buettner, Elizabeth. *Empire Families: Britons and Late Imperial India.* Oxford and New York: Oxford University Press, 2004.

Burgess, E.M.R. *The Girl Guide Book of Recreation.* Glasgow: Brown, Son & Ferguson Ltd., 1934.

Burnett, Kristin. *Taking Medicine: Women's Healing Work and Colonial Contact in Southern Alberta, 1880–1930.* Vancouver: UBC Press, 2010.

Burton, Antoinette. *Dwelling in the Archive: Women Writing House, Home and History in Late Colonial India.* New York: Oxford University Press, 2003.

—. "Who Needs the Nation? Interrogating 'British' History." In *Cultures of Empire: A Reader,* ed. Catherine Hall, 137–53. Manchester: Manchester University Press, 2000.

—. *At the Heart of the Empire: Indians and the Colonial Encounter in Late Victorian Britain.* Berkeley: University of California Press, 1998.

—. *Burdens of History: British Feminists, Indian Women, and Imperial Culture, 1865–1915.* Chapel Hill and London: University of North Carolina Press, 1994.

Burton, Antoinette, ed. *Archive Stories: Facts, Fictions, and the Writing of History.* Durham and London: Duke University Press, 2005.

Bush, Barbara. "Gender and Empire: The Twentieth Century." In *Gender and Empire,* ed. Philippa Levine, 77–111. Oxford: Oxford University Press, 2004.

Bush, Julia. *Edwardian Ladies and Imperial Power.* London and New York: Leicester University Press, 2000.

Cadogan, Mary, and Patricia Craig. *You're a Brick, Angela: A New Look at Girls' Fiction from 1839 to 1975.* London: Victor Gollancz Ltd., 1976.

Canaday, Margot. *The Straight State: Sexuality and Citizenship in Twentieth-Century America.* Princeton: Princeton University Press, 2009.

Cannadine, David. *Ornamentalism: How the British Saw Their Empire.* Oxford: Oxford University Press, 2002.

Carter, Sarah. *The Importance of Being Monogamous: Marriage and Nation Building in Western Canada to 1915.* Edmonton: University of Alberta Press, 2008.

Casolari, Marzia. "Hindutva's Foreign Tie-Up in the 1930s: Archival Evidence." *Economic and Political Weekly* 35, 4 (2000): 218–28.

Castle, Kathryn. *Britannia's Children: Reading Colonialism through Children's Books and Magazines.* Manchester: Manchester University Press, 1996.

Chakrabarty, Dipesh. "The Difference-Deferral of a Colonial Modernity: Public Debates on Domesticity in British Bengal." In *Tensions of Empire: Colonial Cultures in a Bourgeois World,* ed. Frederick Cooper and Ann Laura Stoler, 373–405. Berkeley: University of California Press, 1997.

Chandra, Nandini. "The Pedagogic Imperative of Travel Writing in the Hindi World: Children's Periodicals, 1920–1950." *South Asia* 30, 2 (2007): 293–325.

Chatelain, Marcia. "International Sisterhood: Cold War Girl Scouts Encounter the World." *Diplomatic History* 38, 2 (2014): 261–70.

Chatterjee, Partha. *The Nation and Its Fragments: Colonial and Postcolonial Histories.* Princeton: Princeton University Press, 1993.

—. "The Nationalist Resolution of the Women's Question." In *Recasting Women: Essays in Indian Colonial History,* ed. Kumkum Sangari and Sudesh Vaid, 233–53. New Brunswick, NJ: Rutgers University Press, 1990.

Chaudhuri, Nupur, Sherry J. Katz, and Mary Elizabeth Perry, eds. *Contesting Archives: Finding Women in the Sources.* Urbana-Champaign: University of Illinois Press, 2012.

Chaudhuri, Nupur. "Memsahibs and Motherhood in Nineteenth-Century India." *Victorian Studies* 31, 4 (1988): 517–35.

Cheroutre, Marie-Thérèse. *Le scoutisme au féminin: Les guides de France 1923–1998*. Paris: Les éditions du cerf, 2002.

Chowdhury-Sengupta, Indira. "Mother India and Mother Victoria: Motherhood and Nationalism in Nineteenth-Century Bengal." *South Asia Research* 12, 1 (May 1992): 20–37.

Clark, Ruth (Minobi). *Camp Fire Training for Girls*. London: C. Arthur Pearson Ltd., 1919.

Clarke, Robert. "The Idea of Celebrity Colonialism: An Introduction." In *Celebrity Colonialism: Fame, Power and Representation in Colonial and Postcolonial Cultures*, ed. Robert Clarke, 1–12. Newcastle-Upon-Tyne: Cambridge Scholars Publishing, 2009.

Cleeve, Vera, and Joan Fryer, eds. *The Extension Book*. London: The Girl Guides Association, 1936.

Coates, Colin, and Cecilia Morgan. *Heroines and History: Representations of Madeleine de Verchères and Laura Secord*. Toronto: University of Toronto Press, 2002.

Coleman, Daniel. *White Civility: The Literary Project of English Canada*. Toronto: University of Toronto Press, 2006.

Comacchio, Cynthia. *The Dominion of Youth: Adolescence and the Making of a Modern Canada, 1920–1950*. Waterloo, ON: Wilfrid Laurier University Press, 2006.

—. *The Infinite Bonds of Family: Domesticity in Canada, 1850–1940*. Toronto: University of Toronto Press, 1999.

Coontz, Stephanie. *Marriage, a History: From Obedience to Intimacy, or How Love Conquered Marriage*. New York: Viking, 2005.

Cooper, Frederick. *Colonialism in Question: Theory, Knowledge, History*. Berkeley: University of California Press, 2005.

Cooter, Roger. "The Moment of the Accident: Culture, Militarism and Modernity in Late-Victorian Britain." In *Accidents and History: Injuries, Fatalities and Social Relations*, ed. Roger Cooter and Bill Luckin, 107–57. Amsterdam and Atlanta: Rodopi, 1997.

Cott, Nancy F. *Public Vows: A History of Marriage and the Nation*. Cambridge, MA and London: Harvard University Press, 2000.

Crocker, Dorothy. *All about Us: A Story of the Girl Guides of Canada*. Toronto: Girl Guides of Canada, 1990.

Cubitt, Geoffrey. "Introduction: Heroic Reputations and Exemplary Lives." In *Heroic Representations and Exemplary Lives*, ed. Geoffrey Cubitt and Allen Warren, 1–15. Manchester: Manchester University Press, 2000.

Cunningham, Hugh. *Grace Darling: Victorian Heroine*. London: Hambledon Continuum, 2007.

Cupido, Robert. "Appropriating the Past: Pageants, Politics, and the Diamond Jubilee of Confederation." *Journal of the Canadian Historical Association* 9 (1998): 155–86.

Curthoys, Ann, and Marilyn Lake. "Introduction." In *Connected Worlds: History in Transnational Perspective*, ed. Ann Curthoys and Marilyn Lake, 5–20. Canberra: Australian National University E-Press, 2005.

Davidson, H.B. *Pat of Whitehouse: A Story of Girl Guides*. London and NY: Macmillan, 1924.

Davies, Andrew. *Leisure, Gender and Poverty: Working-Class Culture in Salford and Manchester, 1900–39*. Buckingham and Philadelphia: Open University Press, 1992.

Davin, Anna. "Imperialism and Motherhood." *History Workshop Journal* 5, 1 (1978): 9–65.

Davis, Mary. *Fashioning a New World: A History of the Woodcraft Folk.* Loughborough: Holyoake Books, 2000.

Dawson, Graham. *Soldier Heroes: British Adventure, Empire and the Imagining of Masculinities.* London: Routledge, 1994.

Dedman, Martin. "Baden-Powell, Militarism, and the 'Invisible Contributors' to the Boy Scout Scheme, 1904–1920." *Twentieth Century British History* 4, 3 (1993): 201–23.

de Grazia, Victoria. *How Fascism Ruled Women: Italy, 1922–1945.* Berkeley: University of California Press, 1993.

Delap, Lucy. "'Thus Does Man Prove His Fitness to Be the Master of Things': Shipwrecks, Chivalry and Masculinities in Nineteenth- and Twentieth-Century Britain." *Cultural and Social History* 3, 1 (2006): 45–74.

Deloria, Philip J. *Playing Indian.* New Haven: Yale University Press, 1998.

Devens, Carol. "'If We Get the Girls, We Get the Race': Missionary Education of Native American Girls." *Journal of World History* 3, 2 (1992): 219–37.

Dodd, Danne. "Advice to Parents: The Blue Books, Helen MacMurchy, MD, and the Federal Department of Health, 1920–34." *Canadian Bulletin of Medical History* 8 (1991): 203–30.

Drewery, M. *Baden-Powell: The Man Who Lived Twice.* London: Hodder and Stoughton, 1975.

Driscoll, Catherine. *Girls: Feminine Adolescence in Popular Culture and Cultural Theory.* New York: Columbia University Press, 2013.

—. "Girls Today: Girls, Girl Culture, and Girl Studies." *Girlhood Studies* 1, 1 (Summer 2008): 13–32.

Dyhouse, Carol. *Girls Growing Up in Late Victorian and Edwardian England.* London, Boston, and Henley: Routledge and Kegan Paul, 1981.

—. "Working Class Mothers and Infant Mortality in England, 1895–1914." *Journal of Social History* 12 (1978): 121–42.

Edelman, Lee. *No Future: Queer Theory and the Death Drive.* Chapel Hill: Duke University Press, 2004.

Engels, Dagmar. "The Limits of Gender Ideology: Bengali Women, the Colonial State, and the Private Sphere, 1890–1930." *Women's Studies International Forum* 12, 4 (1989): 425–37.

Etherington, Norman. "Education and Medicine." In *Missions and Empire,* ed. Norman Etherington, 261–84. Oxford: Oxford University Press, 2005.

Evans, I.O. *Woodcraft and World Service: Studies in Unorthodox Education – An Account of the Evolution of the Woodcraft Movements.* London: Noel Douglas, 1930.

Evans, Julie, Patricia Grimshaw, David Philips, and Shurlee Swain. *Equal Subjects, Unequal Rights: Indigenous Peoples in British Settler Colonies, 1830–1910.* Manchester: Manchester University Press, 2003.

Falk (Ida von Herrenschwand). *The Story of Our Chalet.* London: The World Association of Girl Guides and Girl Scouts, 1952.

Falzon, Mark-Anthony. "Introduction – Multi-Sited Ethnography: Theory, Praxis and Locality in Contemporary Research." In *Multi-Sited Ethnography: Theory, Praxis and Locality in Contemporary Research,* ed. Mark-Anthony Falzon, 1–24. Farnham: Ashgate, 2009.

Fieldston, Sara. *Raising the World: Child Welfare in the American Century.* Cambridge, MA: Harvard University Press, 2015.

Fischer-Tiné, Harald. "Global Civil Society and the Forces of Empire: The Salvation Army, British Imperialism and the "Pre-History" of NGOs (c. 1880–1920)." In *Competing Visions of World Order: Global Moments and Movements, 1880s–1930s,* ed. Sebastian Conrad and Dominic Sachsenmaier, 29–68. London: Palgrave Macmillan, 2007.

Fisher, Kate. *Birth Control, Sex, and Marriage in Britain, 1918–1960.* Oxford: Oxford University Press, 2006.

Fitz Roy, Almeric William. *Report of the Interdepartmental Committee on Physical Deterioration.* London: Printed for H.M. Stationery Office, 1904.

Flint, Kate. *The Transatlantic Indian, 1776–1930.* Princeton: Princeton University Press, 2009.

Forbes, Geraldine. *Women in Colonial India: Essays on Politics, Medicine and Historiography.* New Delhi: Chronicle Books, 2005.

—. *Women and Modern India.* Cambridge: Cambridge University Press, 1996.

Forman-Brunell, Miriam. *Babysitter: An American History.* New York and London: New York University Press, 2009.

Francis, Daniel. *National Dreams: Myth, Memory, and Canadian History.* Vancouver: Arsenal Pulp Press, 1997.

—. *The Imaginary Indian: The Image of the Indian in Canadian Culture.* Vancouver: Arsenal Pulp Press, 1992.

Frykenberg, Robert Eric. "Christian Missions and the Raj." In *Missions and Empire,* ed. Norman Etherington, 107–31. Oxford: Oxford University Press, 2005.

Furse, Katharine. *Hearts and Pomegranates: The Story of Forty-Five Years, 1875–1920.* London: Peter Davies, 1940.

Gaitskell, Deborah. "Upward All and Play the Game: The Girls' Wayfarer Association in the Transvaal, 1925–1974." In *Apartheid and Black Education: The Education of Black South Africans,* ed. Peter Kallaway, 222–64. Johannesburg: Raven Press, 1984.

Ghosh, Durba. "National Narratives and the Politics of Miscegenation: Britain and India." In *Archive Stories: Facts, Fictions, and the Writing of History,* ed. Antoinette Burton, 27–44. Durham and London: Duke University Press, 2005.

Gillis, John R. *Youth and History: Tradition and Change in European Age Relations, 1770-Present.* New York: Academic Press, 1974.

Glassberg, David. *American Historical Pageantry: The Uses of Tradition in the Early Twentieth Century.* Chapel Hill: University of North Carolina Press, 1990.

Gorham, Deborah. *The Victorian Girl and the Feminine Ideal.* Bloomington: Indiana University Press, 1982.

Gorman, Daniel. *The Emergence of International Society in the 1920s.* Cambridge: Cambridge University Press, 2012.

—. *Imperial Citizenship: Empire and the Question of Belonging.* Manchester: Manchester University Press, 2006.

Goswami, Manu. "Imaginary Futures and Colonial Internationalisms." *American Historical Review* 117, 5 (December 2012): 1461–85.

Graham, Elizabeth, ed. *The Mush Hole: Life at Two Indian Residential Schools.* Waterloo, ON: Heffle Publishing, 1997.

Grant, Kevin, Philippa Levine, and Frank Trentmann. "Introduction." In *Beyond Sovereignty: Britain, Empire and Transnationalism c. 1880–1950,* ed. Kevin Grant, Philippa

Levine, and Frank Trentmann, 1–15. Houndmills, Basingstoke: Palgrave Macmillan, 2007.

Green, Martin. *Dreams of Adventure, Deeds of Empire.* New York: Basic Books, 1979.

Grewal, Inderpal. *Home and Harem: Nation, Gender, Empire, and the Cultures of Travel.* Durham and London: Duke University Press, 1996.

Grimshaw, Patricia. "Reading the Silences: Suffrage Activists and Race in Nineteenth-Century Settler Societies." In *Women's Rights and Human Rights: International Historical Perspectives,* ed. Patricia Grimshaw, Katie Holmes, and Marilyn Lake, 31–48. Basingstoke and New York: Palgrave, 2001.

–. "Settler Anxieties, Indigenous Peoples, and Women's Suffrage in the Colonies of Australia, New Zealand, and Hawaii, 1889–1902." *Pacific Historical Review* 69, 4 (2000): 553–72.

Grimshaw, Patricia, and Andrew May. "Reappraisals of Mission History: An Introduction." In *Missionaries, Indigenous Peoples and Cultural Exchange,* ed. Patricia Grimshaw and Andrew May, 1–9. Eastbourne: Sussex Academic Press, 2010.

Guha, Ranajit. "Dominance eithout Hegemony and Its Historiography." *Subaltern Studies VI: Writings on South Asian History and Society,* 210–309. Delhi: Oxford University Press, 1989.

Gullace, Nicoletta F. *"The Blood of Our Sons": Men, Women, and the Regeneration of British Citizenship during the Great War.* New York: Palgrave Macmillan, 2002.

Haig-Brown, Celia. *Resistance and Renewal: Surviving the Indian Residential School.* Vancouver: Arsenal Pulp Press, 1998.

Hall, Catherine. *Civilising Subjects: Metropole and Colony in the English Imagination, 1830–1867.* Chicago and London: University of Chicago Press, 2002.

Hampton, Janie. *How the Girl Guides Won the War.* London: HarperCollins, 2010.

Hancock, Mary. "Gendering the Modern: Women and Home Science in British India." In *Gender, Sexuality and Colonial Modernities,* ed. Antoinette Burton, 148–60. London and New York: Routledge, 1999.

Hargrave, John. *The Great War Brings It Home: The Natural Reconstruction of an Unnatural Existence.* London: Constable and Company Ltd., 1919.

Harland-Jacobs, Jessica. *Builders of Empire: Freemasonry and British Imperialism, 1717–1927.* Chapel Hill, NC: University of North Carolina Press, 2007.

Harley, Joan. "Report of an Enquiry into the Occupations, Further Education, and Leisure Interests of a Number of Girl Wage-Earners from Elementary and Central Schools in the Manchester District, with Special Reference to the Influence of School Training on Their Use of Leisure." MEd thesis, University of Manchester, 1937.

Harrison, Brian. "For Church, Queen and Family: The Girls' Friendly Society, 1874–1920." *Past and Present* 61, 1 (1973): 107–38.

–. *Prudent Revolutionaries: Portraits of British Feminists between the Wars.* Oxford: Clarendon Press, 1987.

Heathorn, Stephen. *For Home, Country, and Race: Constructing Gender, Class, and Englishness in the Elementary School, 1880–1914.* Toronto, Buffalo, and London: University of Toronto Press, 2000.

Heathorn, Stephen, and David Greenspoon. "Organizing Youth for Partisan Politics in Britain, 1918–c.1932." *Historian* 68, 1 (Spring 2006): 89–119.

Helgren, Jennifer. "Native American and White Camp Fire Girls Enact Modern Girlhood, 1910–39." *American Quarterly* 66, 2 (June 2014): 333–60.

—. "'Homemaker Can Include the World': Female Citizenship and Internationalism in the Camp Fire Girls." In *Girlhood: A Global History*, ed. Jennifer Helgren and Colleen A. Vasconcellos, 304–21. New Brunswick, NJ: Rutgers University Press, 2010.

Hellesund, Tone. "Queering the Spinsters: Single Middle-Class Women in Norway, 1880–1920." *Journal of Homosexuality* 54, 1–2 (April 2008): 21–48.

Hillcourt, William, and Olave Baden-Powell. *Baden-Powell: The Two Lives of a Hero*. New York: Putnam, 1964.

Hinther, Rhonda L. "Raised in the Spirit of Class Struggle: Children, Youth and the Interwar Ukrainian Left in Canada." *Labour/Le Travail* 60 (Fall 2007): 43–76.

Hoganson, Kristin L. *Consumers' Imperium: The Global Production of American Domesticity, 1865–1920*. Durham, NC: University of North Carolina Press, 2007.

Honeck, Mischa. "The Power of Innocence: Anglo-American Scouting and the Boyification of Empire." *Geschichte und Gesellschaft* 42 (2016): 441–66.

—. "An Empire of Youth: American Boy Scouts in the World, 1910–1960." *Bulletin of the German Historical Institute* 52 (Spring 2013): 95–112.

Honeck, Mischa, and Gabriel Rosenberg. "Transnational Generations: Organizing Youth in the Cold War." *Diplomatic History* 38, 2 (2014): 233–39.

Hopkins, A.G., ed. *Globalization in World History*. New York: Norton, 2002.

Howkins, Alun. "The Discovery of Rural England." In *Englishness: Politics and Culture*, ed. Robert Colls and Philip Dodd, 62–88. London: Routledge, 1986.

Humphries, Stephen. *Hooligans or Rebels?: An Oral History of Working-Class Childhood and Youth 1889–1939*. Oxford: Basil Blackwell, 1981.

Innes, Sue. "Constructing Women's Citizenship in the Interwar Period: The Edinburgh Women Citizens' Association." *Women's History Review* 13, 4 (2004): 621–48.

Inness, Sherrie A. "Introduction." In *Delinquents and Debutantes: Twentieth-Century American Girls' Cultures*, ed. Sherrie A. Inness, 1–15. New York and London: New York University Press, 1998.

—. "Girl Scouts, Camp Fire Girls, and Woodcraft Girls: The Ideology of Girls' Scouting Novels, 1910–1935." In *Continuities in Popular Culture: The Present in the Past and the Past in the Present and Future*, ed. Ray B. Browne and Ronald J. Ambrosetti, 229–40. Bowling Green, OH: Bowling Green State University Popular Press, 1993.

Iriye, Akira. *Cultural Internationalism and World Order*. Baltimore: Johns Hopkins University Press, 1997.

Irvine, A.M. *Nora, the Girl Guide, or, From Tenderfoot to Silver Fish: A Story for Girl Guides*. London: S.W. Partridge and Co. Ltd., 1913.

Jasen, Patricia. *Wild Things: Nature, Culture, and Tourism in Ontario, 1790–1914*. Toronto: University of Toronto Press, 1995.

Jeal, Tim. *Baden-Powell: Founder of the Boy Scouts*. New Haven and London: Yale University Press, 1989.

Jeffreys, Sheila. *The Spinster and Her Enemies: Feminism and Sexuality, 1880–1930*. London, Boston, and Henley: Pandora, 1985.

Jobs, Richard Ivan, and David M. Pomfret, "Introduction." In *Transnational Histories of Youth in the Twentieth Century*, ed. Richard Ivan Jobs and David Pomfret, 1–19. New York: Palgrave Macmillan, 2015.

Johnston, Scott. "Boy Scouts and the British World: Autonomy within an Imperial Institution, 1908–1936." *Canadian Journal of History* 51, 1 (2016): 33–57.

–. "Courting Public Favour: The Boy Scout Movement and the Accident of Internationalism, 1907–29." *Historical Research* 88, 241 (August 2015): 508–29.

Jolly, Margaret. "Introduction: Colonial and Postcolonial Plots in Histories of Maternities and Modernities." In *Maternities and Modernities: Colonial and Postcolonial Experiences in Asia and the Pacific*, ed. Kalpana Ram and Margaret Jolly, 1–25. Cambridge: Cambridge University Press, 1998.

Jones, Kenneth W. *Socio-Religious Reform Movements in British India*. Cambridge: Cambridge University Press, 1989.

Jordan, Benjamin Rene. *Modern Manhood and the Boy Scouts of America: Citizenship, Race, and the Environment, 1910–1930*. Chapel Hill: University of North Carolina Press, 2016.

Jordan, Ellen. "'Making Good Wives and Mothers'? The Transformation of Middle-Class Girls' Education in Nineteenth-Century Britain." *History of Education Quarterly* 31, 4 (Winter 1991): 439–62.

Kasturi, Malavika. "Law and Crime in India: British Policy and the Female Infanticide Act of 1870." *Indian Journal of Gender Studies* 1, 2 (1994): 169–93.

Kater, Michael H. *Hitler Youth*. Cambridge, MA: Harvard University Press, 2004.

Kaur, Ravinderjit. *Political Awakening in Kashmir*. Delhi: S.B. Nangia, 1996.

Kay, I.H. *The Girl Guide's Association Book of First Aid and Rescue Work*. London: The Girl Guides Association, 1946.

Kelcey, Barbara E. *Alone in Silence: European Women in the Canadian North before 1940*. Montreal and Kingston: McGill-Queen's University Press, 2001.

Kelm, Mary Ellen. *Colonizing Bodies: Aboriginal Health and Healing in British Columbia, 1900–1950*. Vancouver: UBC Press, 1998.

Kendle, John E. *The Round Table Movement and Imperial Union*. Toronto and Buffalo: University of Toronto Press, 1975.

Kennedy, Dane. *The Magic Mountains: Hill Stations and the British Raj*. Berkeley: University of California Press, 1996.

–. "The Perils of the Midday Sun: Climatic Anxieties in the Colonial Tropics." In *Imperialism and the Natural World*, ed. J.M. MacKenzie, 118–40. Manchester: Manchester University Press, 1990.

Kent, Susan Kingsley. *Making Peace: The Reconstruction of Gender in Interwar Britain*. Princeton: Princeton University Press, 1993.

Kerr, Rose. *The Story of a Million Girls: Guiding and Girl Scouting around the World*. London: The Girl Guides Association, 1936.

–. *The Story of the Girl Guides*. London: The Girl Guides Association, 1932.

–. *The Story of the Girl Guides*. London: The Girl Guides Association, 1937.

Kessler-Harris, Alice. *In Pursuit of Equity: Women, Men, and the Quest for Economic Citizenship in Twentieth-Century America*. Oxford and New York: Oxford University Press, 2001.

Kindersley, Ann, ed. *The Guiding Book*. London: Hodder and Stoughton Ltd, n.d.

Kipling, Rudyard. *Kim*. Oxford: Oxford World's Classics, 1998.

Kotchemidova, Christina. "From Good Cheer to 'Drive-By Smiling': A Social History of Cheerfulness." *Journal of Social History* 39, 1 (Fall 2005): 5–37.

Kracauer, Siegfried. *The Mass Ornament: Weimar Essays*. Edited and translated by Thomas Y. Levin. Cambridge, MA: Harvard University Press, 1995.

Kraftl, Peter. "Young People, Hope and Childhood-Hope." *Space and Culture* 11 (2008): 81–92.

Krebs, Paula. *Gender, Race, and the Writing of Empire: Public Discourse and the Boer War*. Cambridge: Cambridge University Press, 1999.

Kumar, Krishan. *Utopianism*. Minneapolis: University of Minnesota Press, 1991.

Kumar, Nita. "Mothers and Non-Mothers: Gendering the Discourse of Education in South Asia." *Gender and History* 17, 1 (2005): 154–82.

Lake, Marilyn. "Between Old Worlds and New: Feminist Citizenship, Nation and Race, the Destabilisation of Identity." In *Suffrage and Beyond: International Feminist Perspectives*, ed. Caroline Daley and Melanie Nolan, 277–94. Auckland: Auckland University Press and Pluto Press, 1994.

–. "'The Inviolable Woman: Feminist Conceptions of Citizenship, 1900–1940." In *Feminism: The Public and the Private*, ed. Joan Landes, 223–40. Oxford: Oxford University Press, 1998.

Lane, Margaret Stuart, ed. *More Camp-Fire Yarns*. London: Oxford University Press, 1925.

Langhamer, Claire. *Women's Leisure in England, 1920–60*. Manchester and New York: Manchester University Press, 2000.

Laqua, Daniel. *The Age of Internationalism and Belgium, 1880–1930: Peace, Progress and Prestige*. Manchester: Manchester University Press, 2015.

Laqua, Daniel, ed. *Internationalism Reconfigured: Transnational Ideas and Movements between the World Wars*. London and New York: I.B. Tauris, 2011.

Lawrence, Jon. "Paternalism, Class, and the British Path to Modernity." In *The Peculiarities of Liberal Modernity in Imperial Britain*, ed. Simon Gunn and James Vernon, 147–64. Berkeley and Los Angeles: University of California Press, 2011.

Lean, Mary. *Joan of Glen Garland: A Canadian Girl Guide Story*. London: The Girl's Own Paper Office, 1934.

Lears, T.J. Jackson. *No Place of Grace: Antimodernism and the Transformation of American Culture, 1880–1920*. New York: Pantheon Books, 1981.

Lee, Janet. "A Nurse and a Soldier: Gender, Class and National Identity in the First World War Adventures of Grace McDougall and Flora Sandes." *Women's History Review* 15, 1 (March 2006): 83–103.

Lester, Alan. "Imperial Circuits and Networks: Geographies of the British Empire." *History Compass* 4, 1 (2006): 124–41.

Levine, Philippa. *Prostitution, Race, and Politics: Policing Venereal Disease in the British Empire*. New York and London: Routledge, 2003.

Levitas, Ruth. "The Imaginary Reconstitution of Society, or, Why Sociologists and Others Should Take Utopia More Seriously." Lecture, University of Bristol, 24 October 2005. http://www.bristol.ac.uk/media-library/sites/spais/migrated/documents/inaugural.pdf.

Lewis, J.D., and S.J. Plaistowe. *Pages for Patrol Leaders*. London: The Girl Guides' Association, 1934.

Lewis, M.G. *What to Expect in Camp*. London: The Girl Guides Association, 1938.

Lewis, Su Lin. "Cosmopolitanism and the Modern Girl: A Cross-Cultural Discourse in 1930s Penang." *Modern Asian Studies* 43, 6 (2009): 1385–419.

Light, Alison. *Forever England: Femininity, Literature and Conservatism between the Wars.* London: Routledge, 1991.

Llewellyn Smith, Sir Hubert, ed. *The New Survey of London Life and Labour.* Vol. 9: *Life and Leisure.* London: P.S. King and Son, Ltd., 1935.

Lorimer, D.A. *Colour, Class and the Victorians: English Attitudes to the Negro in the Mid-Nineteenth Century.* Leicester: Leicester University Press, 1978.

MacDonald, Charlotte. "Body and Self: Learning to Be Modern in 1920s–1930s Britain." *Women's History Review* 22, 2 (2013): 267–79.

–. "Putting Bodies on the Line: Marching Spaces in Cold War Culture." In *Sites of Sport: Space, Place, Experience,* ed. Patricia Vertinsky and John Bale, 23–36. London and New York: Routledge, 2004.

MacDonald, Robert H. *Sons of the Empire: The Frontier and the Boy Scout Movement, 1890–1918.* Toronto: University of Toronto Press, 1993.

–. "The Wolf That Never Slept: The Heroic Lives of Baden-Powell." *Dalhousie Review* 61, 1 (1981): 5–26.

Mackay, Jane, and Pat Thane. "The Englishwoman." In *Englishness: Politics and Culture,* ed. Robert Colls and Phillip Dodd, 191–229. London: Routledge, 1986.

MacKenzie, John M, ed. *Imperialism and Popular Culture.* Manchester: Manchester University Press, 1986.

–. *Propaganda and Empire.* Manchester: Manchester University Press, 1984.

MacLeod, David I. *Building Character in the American Boy: The Boy Scouts, YMCA, and their Forerunners, 1870–1920.* Madison: University of Wisconsin Press, 1983.

MacQueen, Bonnie. "Domesticity and Discipline: The Girl Guides in British Columbia, 1910–1943." In *Not Just Pin Money: Selected Essays on the History of Women's Work in British Columbia,* ed. Barbara K. Latham and Roberta J. Pazdro, 221–36. Victoria: Camosun College, 1984.

Maloney, Alison. *Something for the Girls: The Official Guide to the First 100 Years of Guiding.* London: Constable, 2009.

Manela, Erez. *The Wilsonian Moment: Self-Determination and the International Origins of Anticolonial Nationalism.* Oxford: Oxford University Press, 2007.

Marcus, George E. "Ethnography in/of the World System: The Emergence of Multi-Sited Ethnography." *Annual Review of Anthropology* 24 (1995): 95–117.

Marr, M. Lucille. "Church Teen Clubs, Feminized Organizations? Tuxis Boys, Trail Rangers, and Canadian Girls in Training, 1919–1939." *Historical Studies in Education* 3, 2 (1991): 249–67.

Marshall, David. *Secularizing the Faith: Canadian Protestant Clergy and the Crisis of Belief, 1850–1940.* Toronto: University of Toronto Press, 1992.

Marshall, Dominique. "The Formation of Childhood as an Object of International Relations: The Child Welfare Committee and the Declaration of Children's Rights of the League of Nations." *International Journal of Children's Rights* 7, 2 (1999): 103–47.

–. "Peace, War and the Popularity of Children's Rights in Public Opinion, 1919–1959: The League of Nations, the United Nations and the Save the Children International Union." In *Children and War: An Anthology,* ed. James Marten. 184–99. New York: New York University Press, 2002.

Marshall, T.H. *Citizenship and Social Class.* London and Concord, MA: Pluto Press, 1992.

Matless, David. *Landscape and Englishness.* London: Reaktion Books, 1998.

Matthews, Jill Julius. "They Had Such a Lot of Fun: The Women's League of Health and Beauty between the Wars." *History Workshop* 30 (Autumn 1990): 22–54.

Mayhall, Laura E. Nym. "Creating the Suffrage Spirit": British Feminism and the Historical Imagination." In *Archive Stories: Facts, Fictions, and the Writing of History*, ed. Antoinette Burton, 232–50. Durham and London: Duke University Press, 2005.

–. *The Militant Suffrage Movement: Citizenship and Resistance in Britain, 1860–1930.* New York: Oxford University Press, 2003.

Maynard, A.M. *An A.B.C. of Guiding.* London: The Girl Guides Association, 1935.

–. *Hiking and Lightweight Camping.* London: The Girl Guides Association, 1933.

Maynes, Mary Jo. "Age as a Category of Historical Analysis: History, Agency, and Narratives of Childhood." *Journal of the History of Childhood and Youth* 1, 1 (Winter 2008): 114–24.

Maynes, Mary Jo, Birgitte Søland, and Christina Benninghaus, eds. *Secret Gardens, Satanic Mills: Placing Girls in European History, 1750–1960.* Bloomington and Indianapolis: Indiana University Press, 2005.

Mazumdar, Lakshmi, ed., *A Dream Came True.* New Delhi: The Bharat Scouts and Guides, 1997.

McCallum, Mary Jane. "'The Fundamental Things': Campfire Girls and Authenticity, 1910–20." *Canadian Journal of History* 40, 1 (April 2005): 46–78.

–. "To Make Good Canadians: Girl Guiding in Indian Residential Schools." MA thesis, Trent University, 2002.

McClelland, Keith, and Sonya Rose. "Citizenship and Empire, 1867–1928." In *At Home with the Empire: Metropolitan Culture and the Imperial World*, ed. Catherine Hall and Sonya Rose, 276–77. Cambridge: Cambridge University Press, 2006.

McClintock, Anne. *Imperial Leather: Race, Gender and Sexuality in the Colonial Contest.* New York and London: Routledge, 1995.

McLaglan, S.L. *Jiu-Jitsu for Girls: The Best Means of Self-Defence.* London: C. Arthur Pearson Ltd., 1922.

McNeill, William H. *Keeping Together in Time: Dance and Drill in Human History.* Cambridge, MA: Harvard University Press, 1995.

Mechling, Jay. "'Playing Indian' and the Search for Authenticity in Modern White America." *Prospects* 5, 17 (1980): 17–33.

Mein Smith, Philippa. *Mothers and King Baby: Infant Survival and Welfare in an Imperial World, Australia 1880–1950.* London: Macmillan, 1997.

Metcalf, Thomas R. *Ideologies of the Raj.* Cambridge: Cambridge University Press, 1994.

Miller, J.R. *Shingwauk's Vision: A History of Native Residential Schools.* Toronto: University of Toronto Press, 1997.

Miller, Susan A. *Growing Girls: The Natural Origins of Girls' Organizations.* New Brunswick, NJ: Rutgers University Press, 2007.

–. "Trademark: Scout." In *Scouting Frontiers: Youth and the Scout Movement's First Century*, ed. Nelson R. Block and Tammy M. Proctor, 28–41. Newcastle-Upon-Tyne: Cambridge Scholars' Press, 2009.

Middleton, Margaret. *The Health of Your Camp.* London: The Girl Guides Association, 1932.

Milloy, John. *A National Crime: The Canadian Government and the Residential School System, 1879–1986.* Winnipeg: University of Manitoba Press, 1999.

Mintz, Stephen. *Huck's Raft: A History of American Childhood*. Cambridge, MA: Harvard University Press, 2004.

Mitchell, Sally. *The New Girl: Girls' Culture in England, 1880–1915*. New York: Columbia University Press, 1995.

Morgan, Cecilia. "'A Wigwam to Westminster': Performing Mohawk Identity in Imperial Britain, 1890s–1990s." *Gender and History* 15, 2 (August 2003): 319–41.

Morris, Brian. "Ernest Thompson Seton and the Origins of the Woodcraft Movement." *Journal of Contemporary History* 5, 2 (1970): 183–94.

Moruzi, Kristine, and Michelle Smith, eds. *Colonial Girlhood in Literature, Culture and History, 1840–1950*. Basingstoke: Palgrave Macmillan, 2014.

–. *Constructing Girlhood through the Periodical Press, 1850–1915*. Farnham, Surrey: Ashgate, 2012.

Moss, Mark. *Manliness and Militarism: Educating Young Boys in Ontario for War*. Toronto: University Press, 2001.

Mukherjee, Sumita. "The All-Asian Women's Conference 1931: Indian Women and Their Leadership of a Pan-Asian Feminist Organization." *Women's History Review* 26, 3 (2016): 1–19.

Murdoch, Lydia. *Imagined Orphans: Poor Families, Child Welfare and Contested Citizenship in London*. New Brunswick, NJ: Rutgers University Press, 2006.

Myers, Tamara. *Caught: Montreal's Modern Girls and the Law, 1869–1945*. Toronto: University of Toronto Press, 2006.

Myers, Tamara, and Joan Sangster. "Retorts, Runaways and Riots: Patterns of Resistance in Canadian Reform Schools for Girls, 1930–6." *Journal of Social History* 34, 3 (Spring 2001): 669–97.

Nanni, Giordano. *The Colonisation of Time: Ritual, Routine and Resistance in the British Empire*. Manchester: Manchester University Press, 2012.

Nelles, H.V. *The Art of Nation Building: Pageantry and Spectacle at Quebec's Tercentenary*. Toronto: University of Toronto Press, 1998.

Nicholas, Jane. "Gendering the Jubilee: Gender and Modernity in the Diamond Jubilee of Confederation Celebrations, 1927." *Canadian Historical Review* 90, 2 (June 2009): 247–74.

–. *The Modern Girl: Feminine Modernities, Bodies, and Commodities in the 1920s*. Toronto: University of Toronto Press, 2014.

Nijhawan, Shobna. "Hindi Children's Journals and Nationalist Discourse, 1910–1930." *Economic and Political Weekly* 39, 33 (2004): 3723–29.

Norman, Alison. "Race, Gender, and Colonialism: Public Life among the Six Nations of Grand River, 1899–1939." PhD diss., Ontario Institute for Studies in Education, University of Toronto, 2010.

Norwood, Stephen Harlan. *Strike-Breaking and Intimidation: Mercenaries and Masculinity in Twentieth-Century America*. Durham, NC: University of North Carolina Press, 2002.

Oram, Alison. "Repressed and Thwarted, or Bearer of the New World? The Spinster in Inter-War Feminist Discourses." *Women's History Review* 1, 3 (September 1992): 413–33.

Osborne, Ken. "Public Schooling and Citizenship Education in Canada." *Canadian Ethnic Studies* 32, 1 (2000): 1–30.

—. "'Where Are the Ancient Pieties and Loyalties of the Race?' A 1923 Report on Teaching Civics." *Canadian Social Studies* 36, 1 (Fall 2001): https://sites.educ.ualberta.ca/css/Css_36_1/CLvoices_from_the_past.htm.

Paisley, Fiona. "Childhood and Race: Growing Up in the Empire." In *Gender and Empire*, ed. Philippa Levine, 240–59. Oxford: Oxford University Press, 2004.

—. "Citizens of Their World: Australian Feminism and Indigenous Rights in the International Context, 1920s and 1930s." *Feminist Review* 58 (1998): 66–84.

—. "Cultivating Modernity: Culture and Internationalism in Feminism's Pacific Age." *Journal of Women's History* 14, 3 (Autumn 2002): 105–32.

—. "From Nation of Islam to Goodwill Tourist: African-American Women at Pan-Pacific and South East Asia Women's Conferences, 1937 and 1955." *Women's Studies International Forum* 32 (2009): 21–28.

—. "Glamour in the Pacific: Cultural Internationalism and Maori Politics at Pan-Pacific Women's Conferences in the 1950s." *Pacific Studies* 29, 1/2 (December 2006): 54–81.

—. *Glamour in the Pacific: Cultural Internationalism and Race Politics in the Women's Pan-Pacific.* Honolulu: University of Hawaii Press, 2009.

—. "Performing 'New Zealand': Maori and Pakeha Delegates at the Pan-Pacific Women's Conference, Hawai'i, 1934." *New Zealand Journal of History* 38, 1 (2004): 22–38.

Pakenham, Thomas. *The Boer War.* New York: Random House, 1979.

Pande, Ishita. "Coming of Age: Law, Sex, and Childhood in Late Colonial India." *Gender and History* 24, 1 (April 2012): 205–30.

Paris, Leslie. "The Adventures of Peanut and Bo: Summer Camps and Early Twentieth-Century American Girlhood." *Journal of Women's History* 12, 4 (Winter 2001): 47–76.

—. *Children's Nature: The Rise of the American Summer Camp.* New York: New York University Press, 2008.

Parsons, Timothy H. "The Limits of Sisterhood: The Evolution of the Girl Guide Movement in Colonial Kenya." In *Scouting Frontiers: Youth and the Scout Movement's First Century*, ed. Nelson R. Block and Tammy M. Proctor, 143–56. Newcastle-Upon-Tyne: Cambridge Scholars Publishing, 2009.

—. "The Consequences of Uniformity: The Struggle for the Boy Scout Uniform in Colonial Kenya." *Journal of Social History* 40, 2 (Winter 2006): 361–83.

—. "Een-Gonyama Gonyama!: Zulu Origins of the Boy Scout Movement and the Africanisation of Imperial Britain." *Parliamentary History* 27, 1 (2008): 57–66.

—. "No More English Than the Postal System: The Kenya Boy Scout Movement and the Transfer of Power, 1956–1964." *Africa Today* 51, 3 (2005): 61–80.

—. *Race, Resistance, and the Boy Scout Movement in British Colonial Africa.* Athens: Ohio University Press, 2004.

Paul, Leslie. *Angry Young Man.* London: Faber and Faber Ltd., 1951.

—. *The Republic of Children: A Handbook for Teachers of Working-Class Children.* London: Allen and Unwin Ltd., 1938.

Pedersen, Diana. "'Keeping Our Good Girls Good': The YWCA and the 'Girl Problem,' 1870–1930." *Canadian Woman Studies* 7, 4 (Winter 1986): 20–24.

Pedersen, Susan. "Gender, Welfare and Citizenship in Britain during the Great War." *American Historical Review* 95, 4 (October 1990): 983–1006.

Peiss, Kathy. *Cheap Amusements: Working Women and Leisure in Turn-of-the-Century New York.* Philadelphia: Temple University Press, 1986.

Perry, Adele. "Metropolitan Knowledge, Colonial Practice, and Indigenous Womanhood: Missions in Nineteenth-Century British Columbia." In *Contact Zones: Aboriginal and Settler Women in Canada's Colonial Past*, ed. Katie Pickles and Myra Rutherdale, 115–22. Vancouver: UBC Press, 2005.

–. *On the Edge of Empire: Gender, Race, and the Making of British Columbia, 1849–1871.* Toronto: University of Toronto Press, 2001.

Pettipas, Katherine. *Severing the Ties That Bind: Government Repression of Indigenous Religious Ceremonies on the Prairies.* Winnipeg: University of Manitoba Press, 1994.

Pickles, Katie. *Female Imperialism and National Identity: Imperial Order Daughters of the Empire.* Manchester: Manchester University Press, 2002.

–. "The Old and New on Parade: Mimesis, Queen Victoria, and Carnival Queens on Victoria Day in Interwar Victoria." In *Contact Zones: Aboriginal and Settler Women in Canada's Colonial Past*, ed. Myra Rutherdale and Katharine Pickles, 272–92. Vancouver: UBC Press, 2005.

Pinkerton, Kathrene G. *Woodcraft for Women.* New York: Outing Publishing Company, 1916.

Pomfret, David M. *Youth and Empire: Trans-Colonial Childhoods in British and French Asia.* Stanford: Stanford University Press, 2016.

Porter, Bernard. *The Absent-Minded Imperialists: Empire, Society and Culture in Britain.* Oxford: Oxford University Press, 2004.

Potter, Simon J. "Webs, Networks, and Systems: Globalization and the Mass Media in the Nineteenth and Twentieth-Century British Empire." *Journal of British Studies* 46 (July 2007): 641–46.

–. "Who Listened When London Called? Reactions to the BBC Empire Service in Canada, Australia and New Zealand, 1932–1939." *Historical Journal of Film, Radio and Television* 28, 4 (October 2008): 475–87.

Potts, Mrs. Janson. *Hints on Girl Guide Tests: Tenderfoot, Second Class, First Class and Able Sea Guide.* Glasgow: Brown, Son and Ferguson Ltd., 1939.

Prang, Margaret. "'The Girl God Would Have Me Be': The Canadian Girls in Training, 1915–1939," *Canadian Historical Review* 66, 2 (1985): 154–84.

Pratt, Mary Louise. *Imperial Eyes: Travel Writing and Transculturation.* London and New York: Routledge, 1992.

Price, John. "'Heroism in Everyday Life': The Watts Memorial for Heroic Self Sacrifice." *History Workshop Journal* 63 (Spring 2007): 255–78.

Procida, Mary A. *Married to the Empire: Gender, Politics, and Imperialism in India, 1883–1947.* Manchester: Manchester University Press, 2002.

Proctor, Tammy. *Female Intelligence: Women and Espionage in the First World War.* New York: New York University Press, 2003.

–. *On My Honour: Scouts and Guides in Interwar Britain.* Philadelphia: American Philosophical Society, 2002.

–. *Scouting for Girls: A Century of Girl Guides and Girl Scouts.* Santa Barbara, CA: ABC-Clio, 2009.

–. "Scouts, Guides, and the Fashioning of Empire, 1919–1939." In *Fashioning the Body Politic: Gender, Dress, Citizenship*, ed. Wendy Parkins, 125–44. Oxford and New York: Berg Publishers, 2002.

—. "'A Separate Path': Scouting and Guiding in Interwar South Africa." *Comparative Studies in Society and History* 42, 3 (2000): 605–31.

—. "(Uni)forming Youth: Girl Guides and Boy Scouts in Britain, 1908–1939." *History Workshop Journal* 45 (1998): 103–34.

Prynn, David. "The Woodcraft Folk and the Labour Movement, 1925–1970." *Journal of Contemporary History* 18, 1 (1983): 79–95.

Pugh, Martin. *Women and the Women's Movement in Britain, 1914–1999.* 2nd ed. Houndmills and London: Macmillan, 2000.

Radhakrishna, Meena. *Dishonoured by History: "Criminal Tribes" and British Colonial Policy.* Hyderabad: Orient Longman, 2001.

Raibmon, Paige. "Living on Display: Colonial Visions of Aboriginal Domestic Space." *BC Studies* 140 (Winter 2003): 69–89.

Rappaport, Helen, ed. *Encyclopedia of Women Social Reformers.* Vol. 1. Santa Barbara, CA: ABC-Clio, 2001.

Readman, Paul. "The Place of the Past in English Culture, c.1890–1914." *Past and Present* 186, 1 (February 2005): 147–199.

Reese, Dagmar. *Growing Up Female in Nazi Germany.* Translated by William Templar. Ann Arbor: University of Michigan Press, 2006.

Reiter, Ester. "Camp Naivelt and the Daughters of the Jewish Left." In *Sisters or Strangers? Immigrant, Racialized and Ethnic Women in Canadian History,* ed. Marlene Epp, Franca Iacovetta, and Frances Swyripa, 365–80. Toronto: University of Toronto Press: 2004.

Roach Pierson, Ruth. "Experience, Difference, Dominance and Voice in the Writing of Canadian Women's History." In *Writing Women's History: International Perspectives,* ed. Karen Offen, Ruth Roach Pierson, and Jane Rendall, 79–106. Bloomington: Indiana University Press, 1991.

Rose, Sonya O. *Which People's War? National Identity and Citizenship in Britain, 1939–1945.* New York: Oxford University Press, 2003.

Rosenthal, Michael. *The Character Factory: Baden-Powell's Boy Scouts and the Imperative of Empire.* New York: Pantheon Books, 1986.

Rosselli, John. "The Self-Image of Effeteness: Physical Education and Nationalism in Nineteenth-Century Bengal." *Past and Present* 86 (February 1980): 121–48.

Rothschild, Mary Aickin. "To Scout or to Guide? The Girl Scout – Boy Scout Controversy, 1912–1941." *Frontiers* 6, 3 (1981): 115–21.

Rowbotham, Judith. *Good Girls Make Good Wives: Guidance for Girls in Victorian Fiction.* Oxford: Basil Blackwell, 1989.

Roy, Franzisca. "International Utopia and National Discipline: Youth and Volunteer Movements in Interwar South Asia." In *The Internationalist Moment: South Asia, Worlds, and World Views,* ed. Ali Raza, Franziska Roy, and Benjamin Zachariah, 150–87. Delhi: Sage, 2015.

Rupp, Leila J. "Challenging Imperialism in International Women's Organizations, 1888–1945." *NWSA Journal* 8 (Spring 1996): 8–27.

—. *Worlds of Women: The Making of an International Women's Movement.* Princeton: Princeton University Press, 1998.

Russell, Margaret M., ed. *The Mauve Games Book for Cripple, Hospital, Blind, Deaf and Post Guide Companies.* London: The Girl Guide Association, n.d.

Rutherdale, Myra. *Women and the White Man's God: Gender and Race in the Canadian Mission Field*. Vancouver: UBC Press, 2002.

Ryan, Deborah Sugg. "'Pageantitis': Frank Lascelles' 1907 Oxford Historical Pageant, Visual Spectacle and Popular Memory." *Visual Culture in Britain* 8, 2 (Winter 2007): 63–82.

Sandell, Marie. *The Rise of Women's Transnational Activism: Identity and Sisterhood between the World Wars*. London and New York: I.B. Tauris, 2015.

Sangari, Kumkum, and Sudesh Vaid, eds. *Recasting Women: Essays in Indian Colonial History*. New Brunswick, NJ: Rutgers University Press, 1995.

Savage, Jon. *Teenage: The Creation of Youth Culture, 1875–1945*. London: Viking Penguin, 2007.

Schmitt, Peter J. *Back to Nature: The Arcadian Myth in Urban America*. New York: Oxford University Press, 1969.

Selig, Diana. "World Friendship: Children, Parents, and Peace Education in America between the Wars." In *Children and War: A Historical Anthology*, ed. James Marten, 135–46. New York and London: New York University Press, 2002.

Sen, Samita. "Motherhood and Mothercraft: Gender and Nationalism in Bengal." *Gender and History* 5, 2 (Summer 1993): 231–43.

Sen, Satadru. *Colonial Childhoods: The Juvenile Periphery of India, 1850–1945*. London: Anthem Press, 2005.

—. "Schools, Athletes and Confrontation: The Student Body in Colonial India." In *Confronting the Body: The Politics of Physicality in Colonial and Post-Colonial India*, ed. James H. Mills and Satadru Sen, 58–79. London: Anthem Press, 2004.

Seth, Sanjay. *Subject Lessons: The Western Education of Colonial India*. Chapel Hill, NC: Duke University Press, 2007.

Shewell, Hugh. *"Enough to Keep them Alive": Indian Welfare in Canada, 1873–1965*. Toronto: University of Toronto Press, 2004.

Singh, Maina Chawla. *Gender, Religion, and "Heathen Lands": American Missionary Women in South Asia, 1860s–1940s*. New York and London: Garland, 2000.

Sinha, Mrinalini. *Colonial Masculinity: The "Manly Englishman" and the "Effeminate Bengali" in the Late Nineteenth Century*. Manchester: Manchester University Press, 1995.

—. *Specters of Mother India: The Global Restructuring of an Empire*. Durham and London: Duke University Press, 2006.

Sleight, Simon. *Young People and the Shaping of Public Space in Melbourne, 1870–1914*. Farnham, Surrey: Ashgate, 2013.

Søland, Birgitte. *Becoming Modern: Young Women and Reconstruction of Womanhood in the 1920s*. Princeton: Princeton University Press, 2000.

Smith, Michelle J. "Be(ing) Prepared: Girl Guides, Colonial Life, and National Strength." *Limina: A Journal of Historical and Cultural Studies* 12 (2006): 1–11.

—. *Empire in British Girls' Literature and Culture: Imperial Girls, 1880–1915*. New York: Palgrave Macmillan, 2011.

Springhall, John. "The Boy Scouts, Class, and Militarism in Relation to British Youth Movements, 1908–1930." *International Review of Social History* 16 (1971): 125–58.

—. *Youth, Empire, and Society*. London: Croom Helm, 1977.

Springhall, John, Anne Summers, and Allen Warren. "Baden-Powell and the Scout Movement before 1920: Citizen Training or Soldiers of the Future?" *English Historical Review* 102 (1987): 934–50.

Stanhope, Sally K. "'White, Black, and Dusky': Girl Guiding in Malaya, Nigeria, India, and Australia from 1909–1960." MA thesis, Georgia State University, 2012.

Stearns, Carol Z., and Peter N. Stearns, eds. *Emotion and Social Change: Toward a New Psychohistory.* New York: Holmes and Meier, 1988.

Steedman, Carolyn. *Dust: The Archive and Cultural History.* Manchester: Manchester University Press, 2001.

Stoler, Ann Laura. *Along the Archival Grain: Epistemic Anxieties and Colonial Common Sense.* Princeton: Princeton University Press, 2008.

—. "Tense and Tender Ties: The Politics of Comparison in North American History and (Post) Colonial Studies." *Journal of American History* 88, 3 (December 2001): 829–65.

Stoler, Ann Laura, and Frederick Cooper. "Between Metropole and Colony: Rethinking a Research Agenda." In *Tensions of Empire: Colonial Cultures in a Bourgeois World,* ed. Frederick Cooper and Ann Laura Stoler, 1–56. Berkeley: University of California Press, 1997.

Storrs, Monica. *God's Galloping Girl: The Peace River Diaries of Monica Storrs, 1929–1931,* ed. W.L. Morton. Vancouver: UBC Press, 1979.

Stovin, Harold. *Totem: The Exploitation of Youth.* London: Methuen and Co. Ltd., 1935.

Strange, Carolyn. *Toronto's Girl Problem: The Perils and Pleasures of the City, 1880–1930.* Toronto: University of Toronto Press, 1995.

Strong-Boag, Veronica. "'The Citizenship Debates': The 1885 Franchise Act." In *Contesting Canadian Citizenship: Historical Readings,* ed. Dorothy E. Chunn and Robert Menzies, 69–94. Peterborough, ON: Broadview Press, 2002.

—. "Intruders in the Nursery: Childcare Professionals Reshape the Years One to Five, 1920–1940." In *Childhood and Family in Canadian History,* ed. Joy Parr, 160–78. Toronto: McClelland and Stewart, 1982.

—. *The New Day Recalled: Lives of Girls and Women in English Canada, 1919–1939.* Toronto: Copp Clark Pitman, 1988.

Summers, Anne. *Angels and Citizens: British Women as Military Nurses, 1854–1914.* London: Routledge and Kegan Paul, 1988.

—. "Scouts, Guides, and VADs: A Note in Reply to Allan Warren." *English Historical Review* 102, 405 (October 1987): 943–47.

Sutherland, Neil. "Popular Media in the Culture of English-Canadian Children in the Twentieth Century." *Historical Studies in Education/Revue d'histoire de l'education* 14, 1 (2002): 1–34.

Tabili, Laura. *We Ask for British Justice: Workers and Racial Difference in Late Imperial Britain.* Ithaca: Cornell University Press, 1994.

Taylor, Verta, and Leila J. Rupp. "Loving Internationalism: The Emotion Culture of Transnational Women's Organizations, 1888–1945." *Mobilization: An International Journal* 7, 2 (2002): 141–58.

Tedesco, Laureen Ann. "The Lost Manhood of the American Girl: A Dilemma in Early Twentieth-Century Girl Scouting." *Children's Folklore Review* 27 (2004–05): 89–107.

—. "Progressive Era Girl Scouts and the Immigrant: *Scouting for Girls* as a Handbook for American Girlhood." *Children's Literature Association Quarterly* 31 (2006): 346–68.

Thompson, John Herd. "Canada and the 'Third British Empire,' 1901–1939." In *Canada and the British Empire*, ed. Phillip Buckner, 87–106. New York: Oxford University Press, 2008.

Tinkler, Penny. "English Girls and the International Dimensions of British Citizenship in the 1940s." *European Journal of Women's Studies* 8, 1 (2001): 77–94.

—. *Constructing Girlhood: Popular Magazines for Girls Growing Up in England 1920–1950.* London: Taylor and Francis, 1995.

Titley, E. Brian. *A Narrow Vision: Duncan Campbell Scott and the Administration of Indian Affairs in Canada.* Vancouver: UBC Press, 1986.

Todd, Selina. "Pleasure, Politics and Co-operative Youth: The Interwar Co-operative Comrades' Circles." *Journal of Co-operative Studies* 32, 2 (September 1999): 129–45.

—. *Young Women, Work and Family in England, 1918–1950.* Oxford and New York: Oxford University Press, 2005.

Topdar, Sudipa. "Knowledge and Governance: Political Socialization of the Indian Child within Colonial Schooling and Nationalist Contestations in India, 1870-1925." PhD diss., University of Michigan, 2010.

Tosh, John. "Imperial Masculinity and the Flight from Domesticity in Britain, 1880–1914." In *Gender and Colonialism*, ed. Timothy P. Foley, Lionel Pilkington, Sean Ryder, and Elizabeth Tilley, 72–85. Galway: Galway University Press, 1995.

Trentmann, Frank. "After the Nation-State: Citizenship, Empire and Global Coordination in the New Internationalism, 1914–1930." In *Beyond Sovereignty: Britain, Empire and Transnationalism, c. 1880–1950*, ed. Kevin Grant, Philippa Levine, and Frank Trentmann, 34–53. Houndmills, Basingstoke: Palgrave Macmillan, 2007.

Trepanier, James. "Building Boys, Building Canada: The Boy Scout Movement in Canada, 1908–1970." PhD diss., York University, 2015.

Trevithick, Alan. "Some Structural and Sequential Aspects of the British Imperial Assemblages at Delhi: 1877–1911." *Modern Asian Studies* 24, 3 (1990): 561–78.

Trotter, L.K., and O.I. Crosbie. *Team Games for Girl Guides.* Essex, UK: 1923.

Tusan, Michelle Elizabeth. "Writing *Stri Dharma*: International Feminism, Nationalist Politics, and Women's Press Advocacy in Late Colonial India." *Women's History Review* 12, 4 (December 2003): 623–49.

Tyacke, R. *Into a Wider World: Talks with Rangers and Cadets.* London: The Religious Tract Society, 1927.

Tyrrell, Ian. *Women's World, Woman's Empire: The Women's Christian Temperance Union in International Perspective, 1880–1930.* Chapel Hill and London: University of North Carolina Press, 1991.

Urwin, Cathy, and Elaine Sharland. "From Bodies to Minds in Childcare Literature: Advice to Parents in Interwar Britain." In *In the Name of the Child: Health and Welfare, 1880–1940*, ed. Roger Cooter, 174–99. London and New York: Routledge, 1992.

Vallory, Eduard. *World Scouting: Educating for Global Citizenship.* Basingstoke: Palgrave, 2012.

Valverde, Mariana. *The Age of Light, Soap, and Water: Moral Reform in English Canada, 1885–1925.* Toronto: McClelland and Stewart, 1991.

—. "When the Mother of the Race Is Free: Race, Reproduction and Sexuality in First-Wave Feminism." In *Gender Conflicts: New Essays in Women's History*, ed. Franca Iacovetta and Mariana Valverde, 3–26. Toronto: University of Toronto Press, 1992.

Vicinus, Martha. *Independent Women: Work and Community for Single Women, 1850–1920*. Chicago and London: University of Chicago Press, 1985.

Voeltz, Richard A. "'The Antidote to Khaki Fever?' The Expansion of the British Girl Guides During the First World War." *Journal of Contemporary History* 27, 4 (1992): 627–38.

Wall, Sharon. *The Nurture of Nature: Childhood, Antimodernism, and Ontario Summer Camps, 1920–55*. Vancouver: UBC Press, 2009.

—. "Totem Poles, Teepees and Token Traditions: 'Playing Indian' at Ontario Summer Camps, 1920–1955." *Canadian Historical Review* 86, 3 (September 2005): 513–44.

Walsh, Judith E. *Domesticity in Colonial India: What Women Learned When Men Gave Them Advice*. London: Rowman and Littlefield, 2004.

Warren, Allen. "Baden-Powell: Two Lives of a Hero, or Two Heroic Lives?" In *Heroic Reputations and Exemplary Lives*, ed. Geoffrey Cubitt and Allen Warren, 123–41. Manchester: Manchester University Press, 2000.

—. "Citizens and Empire: Baden-Powell, the Scouts and Guides, and an Imperial Ideal." In *Imperialism and Popular Culture*, ed. John M. MacKenzie, 232–56. Manchester: Manchester University Press, 1986.

—. "'Mothers of the Empire?' The Girl Guides Association in Britain, 1909–1939." In *Making Imperial Mentalities: Socialisation and British Imperialism*, ed. J.A. Mangan, 96–109. Manchester: Manchester University Press, 1990.

—. "Popular Manliness: Baden-Powell, Scouting and the Development of Manly Character." In *Manliness and Morality: Middle-Class Masculinity in Britain and America, 1800–1940*, ed. J.A. Mangan and James Walvin, 176–98. New York: St. Martin's Press, 1987.

—. "Sir Robert Baden-Powell, the Scout Movement, and Citizen Training in Great Britain." *English Historical Review* 101, 399 (1986): 376–98.

Watt, Carey A. "Education for National Efficiency: Constructive Nationalism in North India, 1909–1916." *Modern Asian Studies* 31, 2 (May 1997): 339–74.

—. "'No Showy Muscles': The Boy Scouts and the Global Dimensions of Physical Culture in Britain and Colonial India." In *Scouting Frontiers: Youth and the Scout Movement's First Century*, ed. Nelson R. Block and Tammy M. Proctor, 121–42. Cambridge: Cambridge Scholars' Press, 2009.

—. "The Promise of 'Character' and the Spectre of Sedition: The Boy Scout Movement and Colonial Consternation in India, 1908–1921." *South Asia* 29, 2 (1999): 37–62.

—. *Serving the Nation: Cultures of Service, Association, and Citizenship in Colonial India*. New Delhi: Oxford University Press, 2005.

Weber, Charlotte. "Unveiling Scheherazade: Feminist Orientalism in the International Alliance of Women, 1911–1950." *Feminist Studies* 27, 1 (2001): 125–27.

Weinbaum, Alys Eve, Lynn M. Thomas, Priti Ramamurthy, Uta G. Poiger, Madeleine Yue Dong, and Tani E. Barlow, eds. *The Modern Girl around the World: Consumption, Modernity, and Globalization*. Durham and London: Duke University Press, 2008.

Whelpton, Naomi, and Kitty Streatfeild. *Rangers*. London: C. Arthur Pearson Ltd., 1926.

Wiener, Martin J. *English Culture and the Decline of the Industrial Spirit, 1850–1980*. 2nd ed. Cambridge: Cambridge University Press, 2004.

Willinsky, John. *Learning to Divide the World: Education at Empire's End*. Minneapolis: University of Minnesota Press, 1998.

Winter, J.M. "The Impact of the First World War on Civilian Health in Britain." *Economic History Review* 30, 3 (1977): 487–507.

Woods, Michael. "Performing Power: Local Politics and the Taunton Pageant of 1928." *Journal of Historical Geography* 25, 1 (1999): 57–74.

Woodward, Marcus. *The Guide Nature Book: A Naturalist's Notebook for Girl Guides*. London: C. Arthur Pearson Ltd., 1923.

–. *How to Enjoy Wild Flowers*. London: Hodder and Stoughton, 1927.

–. *Nature's Merry-Go-Round*. London: C. Arthur Pearson Ltd., 1929.

Woolf, Virginia. *A Room of One's Own/Three Guineas*. London: Penguin Classics, 2000.

Woollacott, Angela. "Inventing Commonwealth and Pan-Pacific Feminisms: Australian Women's Internationalist Activism in the 1920s–30s." In *Feminisms and Internationalism*, ed. Mrinalini Sinha, Donna J. Guy, and Angela Woollacott, 81–104. Oxford: Blackwell, 1999.

–. *"To Try Her Fortune in London:" Australian Women, Colonialism, and Modernity*. New York: Oxford University Press, 2001.

Wu, Jialin Christina. "'A Life of Make-Believe': Being Boy Scouts and 'Playing Indian' in British Malaya, 1910–1942." *Gender and History* 26, 3 (November 2014): 589–619.

Wynne, May. *Girls of the Pansy Patrol*. London: The Aldine Publishing Company, 1931.

Zweiniger-Bargielowska, Ina. "The Making of a Modern Female Body: Beauty, Health and Fitness in Interwar Britain." *Women's History Review* 20, 2 (2011): 299–31.

INDEX

Note: "(i)" after a page number indicates an illustration. In entries and subentries below, Robert, Olave, and Agnes Baden-Powell are referred to as "RBP," "OBP," and "ABP," respectively, and the Baden-Powells are referred to as the "BPs." The biographical entries for Robert, Olave, and Agnes Baden-Powell are arranged chronologically rather than alphabetically.

Printed and bound in Canada by Friesens
Set in Caslon and Fournier by Artegraphica Design Co. Ltd.
Copy editor: Joanne Richardson
Proofreader: Carmen Tiempo
Indexer: Cheryl Lemmens

Guiding Modern Girls